THE KREMLIN CONSPIRACY

ABOUT ThE AUThOR

Douglas Boyd is probably the only British author who has confronted the KGB while enduring solitary confinement in a Stasi interrogation prison. He studied Russian language and history while training for signals interception at an RAF base in Berlin – snooping on Warsaw Pact fighter pilots over-flying East Germany and Poland. Back in civilian life, he spent several years at the height of the Cold War dealing with Soviet bloc film and TV officials, some of whom were undercover intelligence officers.

ALSO BY THE AUTHOR

April Queen, Eleanor of Aquitaine
Voices from the Dark Years
The French Foreign Legion
Normandy in the Time of Darkness
Blood in the Snow, Blood on the Grass
De Gaulle: the Man who Defied Six US Presidents
Lionheart
The *Other* First World War

THE KREMLIN CONSPIRACY

1,000 YEARS OF RUSSIAN EXPANSIONISM

DOUGLAS BOYD

The
History
Press

This book is dedicated to all the political prisoners detained in the Stasi's Lindenstrasse interrogation prison in Potsdam, and to our predecessors who suffered there under the KGB 1945–52 and under the Gestapo 1933–45

First published by Ian Allan Publishing, 2010
This edition published by The History Press, 2014

The History Press
The Mill, Brimscombe Port
Stroud, Gloucestershire, GL5 2QG
www.thehistorypress.co.uk

British Library Cataloguing in Publication Data.
A catalogue record for this book is available from the British Library.

ISBN 978 0 7509 6139 4

Typesetting and origination by The History Press
Printed in Great Britain

CONTENTS

PREFACE TO THE SECOND EDITION

In the early summer of 2011, during the run-up to the 2012 Russian presidential election, I was contacted by a very successful international businessman from one of the former Soviet satellite states. Highly intelligent and fluent in several languages, he might well have struck me as a top-rank KGB First Directorate officer, had this been in the Cold War period. For the sake of his anonymity, let's call him Dmitri.

From his first telephone call, it was apparent that he had done his homework: he knew a lot about me and my writing. This was borne out when he travelled from the Swiss frontier with his very beautiful Russian wife Sofia expressly to visit me at my home on the other side of France with a strange suggestion. It was that *The Kremlin Conspiracy* should be published in Russia. I replied that surely Russians knew their own history, so what would be the point?

Sofia had studied Russian history at Kazan University. According to her, the only history taught in Soviet schools and universities during the period of the USSR was what corroborated Marxist theory! Things, she said, had not greatly improved since and, although a history graduate, she had learned much from the first edition of my book. As to me finding a publisher in Russia, I explained that there were agents for that sort of thing, that not many books were translated into Russian, and …

Not having made all his money by letting problems get in the way of business, Dmitri said that he would help. The conversation was mostly in English, but in one of the Russian exchanges, I heard him mutter to Sofia, 'Lebedev'. The oligarch father and son Alexander and Yevgeny Lebedev were famous as British press barons, and Alexander had recently been seen live on a Russian television channel chat show punching another participant several times for disagreeing with him. There were rumours that Lebedev Sr intended to compete with Putin in the coming presidential elections – motive enough, Dmitri thought, for him either to publish my book in Russia, or arrange for a friend to do so. All that was necessary at that stage would be to supply a copy of the book with a synopsis and a specimen chapter in Russian. I explained that, although I could translate from Russian into English, I could no longer pretend to be competent in the other direction. No problem, said Sofia, who had been a journalist after leaving university. She would do it for me.

Which chapter? I asked. Both of them said, 'Oh, the last.'

Chapter 27 – the last in the first edition – entitled 'The Making of the President, Russian Style', explores the most likely origins of Vladimir Putin, which are not at all what his official biography would have us believe. I suggested that having it published in Russia would hardly amuse Mr P., so we might all end up drinking polonium cocktails, like Alexander Litvinenko in 2006.

Dmitri said he didn't think that was a real danger and shortly after their visit I received an email from Sofia which began:

27: Создание президента, русская версия
Столь скорополительными были все эти события (описанные в предыдущей главе), и лишь немногие на Западе были в курсе, что недавно назначенный директор ФСБ был человеком по имени Владимир Путин.
«Кто такой Владимир Путин?» спросил мир.

I went through her draft and asked for one or two points to be changed. Back came the fair copy. The next problem was getting it to Lebedev Sr because it is not easy to reach the super-rich. I asked a very persistent Russian friend living in what they call Londongrad for help. Within 24 hours she had dug up the address of Lebedev's private office. The book, synopsis and specimen chapter were despatched by registered post. I waited for a reply, which did not come. Rumours, which may or may not be true, had it that some sort of deal had meanwhile been cut and Lebedev had changed his political plans, presumably with some kind of quid pro quo. I never did find out whether Dmitri and Sofia had been actors in a scenario masterminded by him.

It's a very Russian story. As Winston Churchill said on the BBC in October 1930, 'Russia is a riddle wrapped in a mystery inside an enigma.' Nothing changes.

Douglas Boyd
South-west France
Autumn 2014

FOREWORD

Ex-prisoners never forget the first time the cell door slams shut and is bolted from the outside. The absence of a handle on the inside symbolises the loss of freedom. To that, the Judas-hole, through which the guard can see but the prisoner cannot, adds loss of dignity and privacy. Identity shrinks to a cell number. Cell No. 20 in the Stasi's Lindenstrasse interrogation prison in Potsdam measured just three paces by four, the floor space encumbered by a bed, a table and a chair. There was no running water. A smelly lidded bucket served as my toilet, emptied by a trusty during my brief exercise periods in a cobbled yard, where every step was watched by a guard with loaded sub machine-gun on a platform atop the 4m-high wall. To complete a tour of the yard took thirty normal paces.

Once a day during my solitary confinement, I was brought a tin jug of cold water and a chipped enamel basin in which to wash my face and try to clean my teeth. In the absence of any towel, I used my underwear, washing it every few days in the same bowl and drying it on the central heating radiator. Once a week, I was escorted to a warmish shower and given a small towel, already damp from previous users. Every two or three days I was given a mug of tepid water and a safety razor with much-used blade with which to shave. Three times a day a warder brought food: a slice of black bread and some unidentifiable brown jam with ersatz coffee for breakfast and noodles or potatoes with something like a meatball for lunch. Supper was even less exciting. When I stopped eating in protest at my detention, the prison governor was concerned enough to come and eat some of my lunch himself, explaining that it was the same food he and the guards ate. I started eating again to show that I was prepared to behave, if only someone would pay attention to me.

Always wearing a cheap civilian suit, my Stasi interrogator Lt Becker would arrive at any hour of the day or night and repeat the same questions to me about my duties at RAF Gatow, the names of my fellow servicemen and my German friends in Berlin. The questions were interspersed with his lectures on how good life was in the GDR, where I could apply for citizenship and be guaranteed a job as tractor driver on a collective farm in Saxon Switzerland, with a pretty blonde partner thrown in as part of the package. When I queried the automatic availability of the blonde, Becker assured me that she was there. An obedient party member was how he described her. The price for the job and the girl was to show that I was truly *vernünftig* (reasonable) and answer all his questions. I might not have been quite so courageous had I known that, under paragraph eight of the GDR law dated 11 November 1957, the penalty for my crime of entering the country illegally was a sentence of up to three years in a labour camp.

Some of my fellow prisoners had been caught trying to escape from the GDR, which was more rigorously punished. Other 'crimes' they had committed included telling a political joke or retailing news from Western radio or television. Their interrogations were much tougher than mine and frequently lasted all night, to be followed by a sleepless day in their cells, sitting bolt upright on the edge of the chair or standing without leaning against the wall. If Becker's visits in the small hours interrupted my sleep, they were not frequent enough to constitute maltreatment and nobody hammered on my door to wake me up if I dozed in the daytime because I was a Cold War pawn to be traded. Yet, in the Lindenstrasse, terror pervaded my cell like every other, as ubiquitous as the smell of the latrine buckets because it was inside every prisoner's mind, a product of the sheer impotence of being imprisoned without any idea for long it would last, in a totalitarian state where there was no right of trial or legal representation – in fact, no *rights* at all.

The guards were forbidden to talk to me. Between Lt Becker's irregular visits there were moments when I would, from utter loneliness, have told him anything he wanted to know for the sheer relief of exchanging words with a fellow human being. Fortunately, he lacked the interrogator's flair for gauging the state of a prisoner's morale, so none of his visits coincided with my moments of despair.

Although I had convinced him that my job in Gatow consisted of filling in forms for catering supplies and equipment, making tea and polishing floors, my real job as an RAF-trained linguist was to transcribe in Russian shorthand the intercepted transmissions from Soviet fighter pilots flying the latest MiG and Sukhoi jets over Eastern Germany and Poland. The real-time transcriptions were flown back to the Government Communications HQ in Cheltenham for analysis. For that reason, I have never been more frightened, before or since, than the morning when I was shown into the interrogation room and found, not Becker, but two men and a woman. As soon as the door was closed behind me, the woman said, '*My predstaviteli praviteltsva sovietskovo soyuza.*' 'We are representatives of the government of the Soviet Union ...'

It was difficult to keep the fear inspired by her words from showing on my face. While it was not hard to bluff Becker that I was a lowly clerk doing a boring administrative job, these KGB officers knew exactly what went on in the Signals Section of RAF Gatow. The two men fired questions at me in rapid succession, using the woman as translator. From time to time, she pretended to forget to translate a simple question. '*Zanimayetyes sportom?*' – 'Do you play sport?' '*U vas skolko lyet?*' – 'How old are you?' And so on. Each time, pulse racing at the narrow escape, I smiled as though it were all a joke while I waited for her to put the question into English. At the end of this real-life nightmare, I pretended to go along with their plan to 'spring' me from the prison and release me at the border of the British sector of Berlin, to make my own way back to Gatow. On one condition, they said: I must on no account tell Becker that they had been in the Stasi prison, in case he spoiled 'our' plan.

The last thing I wanted was to fall into the hands of the KGB. So, I kicked up such a fuss with the guards after being returned to my cell that Becker came to see what was wrong. He was visibly furious when I told him of the Russians' visit. His reaction was my first intimation that, even in the neo-Stalinist GDR, the half-million Russian troops stationed there were regarded as occupation forces, not brothers-in-arms. My Stasi file indicates that Becker's masters resented being pushed around by Big Brother: to spite the Russians for their intrusion, Department 3 of the Stasi's 7th Directorate recommended on the day after their visit that I be handed over through the East German Red Cross to the British Red Cross – a back-channel used by the two governments from time to time.

Not being informed of this, I became increasingly uneasy. At 6 a.m. on 12 May 1959 my breakfast was brought by a warder who wore a high-crowned cap with slashed peak, riding breeches and polished jackboots. He was always accompanied by a black Alsatian dog that used to sniff my crotch as though checking where to bite when given the command.

'*Mach's schnell*!' It was the first time he had spoken to me. He stood waiting while I ate, the dog watching. Then, '*Komm mit*!'

Expecting to be taken to the interrogation room, I was led instead to the small courtyard just inside the main gate of the prison. There stood Becker with two Stasi heavies in the front seats of an ancient Mercedes. Ushering me into the rear seat without saying where we were going, he handed me a packet of sandwiches as we erupted through the gate with a screech of tyres on the cobbles of the Lindenstrasse. I ate the sandwiches, which tasted delicious after all the bland prison food, as we speeded along the Autobahn to the Marienborn/Helmstedt checkpoint. A few hours later, after six weeks in solitary confinement, I was walking across the no man's land between East German territory and the British-occupied zone of Germany.

The sensation of unreality was unwittingly increased by the astute and charming lady in British Red Cross uniform to whom Becker handed me over. Without giving them a single quotable quote, she chatted to the Stasi officers for 20 minutes while the clock slowly ticked away the seconds to the agreed hand-over time. All their leading questions were parried with her innocent queries. One sticks in my mind: 'Do you drink tea in Eastern Germany? Really? How very interesting. I thought you drank coffee.' It was hard to contain the hysterical laughter that bubbled up inside me when I realised from her oh-so-English small talk that she had to be genuine.

On the British side of the crossing-point designated Checkpoint Alpha – Baker and Charlie were in Berlin – she handed me over to RAF Intelligence officers, after which came a long round of debriefing interrogations to ascertain how much I had given away. Opinions in the RAF hierarchy ranged understandably from wanting to sentence me to several years' imprisonment for getting caught on the territory of a Warsaw Pact state while engaged on classified intelligence work to patting me on the back for wriggling out of the KGB trap. Fortunately, the latter school of thought won, under the discerning judgement of Air Chief Marshal Sir Hubert Patch, who gave me a personal grilling in his office at Adastral House – and subsequently a reference for my first job on civvy street.

Apart from barber's rash, the only outward price I had to pay for my frightening six weeks in what inmates later ironically called *das Lindenhotel* in Potsdam was that Britain's recently introduced system of positive vetting of applicants for sensitive posts precluded any chance of continuing my linguistic intelligence career inside GCHQ at Cheltenham, as I had planned. Instead, I became an international sales executive for the Rank Organisation and went on to head the BBC's Eurovision office before becoming a staff television producer/director. In all these capacities, my knowledge of German, Russian and other European languages led to professional contacts with Soviet citizens and satellite officials who continued my education in the history of their countries' relationship with the bear next door. During the Cold War, they had to make detailed reports on everyone they met in the West, but we got along fine, especially after a few drinks, because my unsought learning curve in Potsdam gave me an understanding of their situation, spied on by the KGB clones imposed on their countries by Moscow. Thus, one way and another, I experienced the Cold War from both sides.

Whether it was really hot or cold depended, of course, on where you lived.

Douglas Boyd
Gironde, France
2014

***

A more ample account of this episode may be found in *Daughters of the KGB* (The History Press, 2015).

Sources used for dates and other details above are:
a MfS file 11626/62, released to the author by the Bundesbeauftragte für die Unterlagen des Staatssicherheitsministeriums der ehemaligen Deutschen Demokratischen Republik on 1 October 2008 in Berlin.
b *Das 'Lindenhotel' – Berichte aus dem Potsdamer Geheimdienstgefängnis* G. Schnell Berlin, ed. Links Verlag 2007.
c unpublished transcripts of her interviews with ex-prisoners loaned by Gabriele Schnell.
d the author's visit in autumn 2008 to the Normannenstrasse Stasi HQ and the former Lindenstrasse prison in Potsdam, which is now a memorial to the 4,000 people sentenced there to forcible sterilisation in the Nazi era and the thousands imprisoned there by the Gestapo prior to 1945, by the KGB 1945–52 and by the Stasi 1952–89.

INTRODUCTION

After the Gorbachev-Yeltsin restructuring of the economically stagnant USSR failed to prevent its collapse in 1989, optimists decided that the east–west confrontation which had dominated the second half of the twentieth century was over and the greatest danger left was the accidental launch of an ill-maintained Russian ICBM or an explosion in some ageing nuclear facility within the former Soviet Union. After Yeltsin resigned in favour of fast-track KGB officer Vladimir V. Putin, people in the west talked of Putin's power strategy as a 'new Cold War', with his most potent weapons being the huge reservoirs of oil and gas on which half of Europe now runs.

It is not a new war, but the same one. And it did not begin in 1945, as conventional histories assert, but can be traced very clearly all the way back to 1919, when Lenin founded the Communist International, or Comintern – an organisation specifically designed to foment worldwide revolution through Moscow's strict control of all the national Communist parties and the subversion of trade unions and other political parties in the democracies, with the aim of world domination.

But even that was not the beginning. The Comintern was Lenin's clever way of rebranding the expansionist imperative of his Tsarist predecessors, of whom Vladimir Putin and his clique of mega-rich ex-KGB officers and lawyers are worthy successors. Although many things about his parentage and career are deliberately concealed, Putin's first name – politely translated as 'noble prince' – contains two Russian roots: the stem of *vladet*, meaning 'to control or master', and *mir*, meaning 'world'. Revealingly, the traditional title for a Russian ruler was not *korolev*, meaning king of a nation, but *Tsar* – a corruption of 'Caesar', i.e. ruler of an empire – with Moscow and St Petersburg at different times claiming to be the third Rome.

In 2008 Putin swapped titles with Prime Minister Dmitri Medvedev, but this does not mean much in a country where Stalin used titles like General Secretary of the Party to conceal for three bloody decades his absolute control of the vast Soviet empire. Under whatever job titles they choose for themselves, Putin and his close associates command the largest armed forces in Europe, equipped with half the nuclear warheads in the world.

Admired by many Russians for his physical fitness and martial arts prowess – which put to shame the ailing gerontocracy that ruled the USSR for so long – from time to time Putin also flexes his military muscles. Aerial photographs in this book show a long-range Tupolev-95 bomber (NATO code name Bear) being intercepted in British airspace by fighter aircraft from RAF Leuchars in Scotland during August 2007. Capable of delivering a nuclear payload, the Tu-95 was on an electronic intelligence mission, analysing British radar defences and timing in-the-air reaction. These missions are regularly flown against targets in Europe and all the way round the globe to US bases on Guam in the mid-Pacific.

In the 1990s, the cost of the armed forces inherited from the USSR was crippling the budget of the Russian Federation and it seemed that a bankrupt Russia would have to sack the millions of men in its armed forces and neutralise its nuclear arsenal as a condition for obtaining the Western subsidies that appeared vitally necessary. Now, with massive oil and gas reserves already on-line and highly profitable, modernising Russia's still enormous military machine is a luxury the Putin clique can afford.

Increasing at 10 per cent per annum, the current defence budget is $190 billion for the period ending 2015,[1] until which time the most potent weapons in the Russian armoury are the enormous gas and oil reserves themselves, dependence on which gives Putin and his clique the power to plunge many European countries literally back to the dark ages. The three Baltic states – Latvia, Estonia and Lithuania – are totally dependent on Russian gas supplies that can be, and have been, turned off at will. So are Bulgaria, Slovakia and Finland. Romania, Poland, Austria, Hungary, Czech Republic and Greece are 60–80 per cent dependent on Russian gas and even Germany and Italy rely on Moscow for 40 and 32 per cent of their gas, respectively.

In a bizarre foretaste of future warfare, the re-siting by Estonians of a Soviet memorial in Tallinn to the Red Army's reconquest of their country in 1944 was punished in April 2007 by cyber attacks from Russian-controlled Transdniestria targeting the Estonian government, banks, media and communications facilities including internet servers. With no functioning computers or mobile phones, the country was brought to a standstill. The government's emergency radio bulletins asked all 900,000 Estonians to stay at home and not make any provocative moves. With 400,000 ethnic Russians implanted on their soil, there was no need to say against whom.

Was this attack just a warning shot for the recalcitrant Estonians who had dared to move a reminder of the Soviet 'liberation' of their country? Or was it a rehearsal for something else? Various Russian authorities have denied they had anything to do with the cyber attack, but the consensus among IT experts is that, while some of the techniques used, like ping floods and rentals of botnets, are within the capability of renegade hackers, the overall sophistication of the Estonian cyber attack required massive resources only available with state backing.

In Russian accounts, the Second World War is known as the Great Patriotic War, with official histories glossing over the awkward fact that Stalin chose to be Hitler's ally for the first twenty months of hostilities. After the German invasion of the Soviet Union in summer 1941, he swiftly begged help from the Western Allies he had been trying to undermine for two decades.

Yet, throughout the wartime alliance, his secret police spied on Western diplomats and harassed Westerners who risked their lives to help the Soviet war effort. In Britain and North America, the freedoms regarded as normal in democratic states were exploited by undercover Soviet agents working *against* the Western Allies. In Russia, the Comintern trained dissident nationals of many countries to exploit the inevitable post-war chaos by seizing power in their homelands as pro-Moscow puppet governments.

After 1945 Moscow confused the innocent by calling its spies and agents of influence 'peace-loving people'. The puppet states were 'democratic republics' or 'people's republics' and the United States was *glavny vrag* – the main enemy – with Britain in second place. The Communist Party of the Soviet Union (CPSU) sealed its captive millions off from the west, allowing only *apparatchiki* and intelligence agents to emerge. The only westerners allowed in were politicians and journalists of the left on 'fact-finding' tours, businessmen at risk of blackmail from honeytraps and the politically innocent and impressionable young.

Having grabbed Finnish Karelia, Besserabia, the Baltic states, Yugoslavia, Hungary, Romania, Poland, the Kurile Islands, South Sakhalin and half of Germany during the Second World War, Stalin continued to expand what US President Reagan called 'the evil empire' with Albania and Bulgaria (1946) and Czechoslovakia (1948). France, Greece and Italy just missed Communist take-overs because of civil war. In this, the Soviet dictator was a fitting proponent of the Kremlin complex that drove Ivan the Terrible and Peter the Great – as is his successor Vladimir Putin.

This book is not an attack on the Russian people or their rulers, although they may think it is. Its purpose? In the global village we now inhabit it is vital to understand our neighbours, and the best way to do that is to know their past, which has made them what they are.

Russian history can be summed up as a thousand years of conflict that expanded the realm of Muscovy from a wooden fort – the original meaning of *kremlin* – at a trading post deep in the forests of central Russia to a vast empire. Russians justify this expansionist tradition to themselves as 'the drive to the sea' of a landlocked people desperate to gain the freedom of the oceans. It was a long drive, ending in Tsar Nicholas II's nineteenth-century empire that spread across eleven time-zones from the Baltic to the Pacific – and to which, after the October Revolution, Canterbury's 'Red Dean' Hewlett Johnson gave his blessing as 'the Socialist sixth of the world'.

How does one begin to tackle so vast a subject?

PART 1:
HOT WARS

A strange superstition prevails among the Russians, that they are predestined to conquer the world, and the prayers of the priests in the church are mingled with requests to hasten and consummate this 'divine mission'.

Extract from a despatch dated St Petersburg, 28 January 1852, by Neill S. Brown, American Minister to Imperial Russia

1

GENGHIS KHAN, UNCLE JOE AND VLAD THE GASMAN

On 4 March 1936 William Bullitt, the American ambassador to the Soviet Union, sent an unusual cable to Secretary of State Cordell Hull in Washington. He listed what he called 'personal observations' about life in Russia: the climate was harsh; government officials were suspicious and secretive; accurate information was hard to obtain; the censorship was rigorous; the constant surveillance was oppressive; Russian diplomacy was adept at worrying a diplomat without even insulting him; and the overall conditions of life were disagreeable and tyrannical. Bullitt ended with the comment that the despatch presented 'an accurate picture of life in Russia in the year 1936'.

The observations, however, were those of his predecessor Neill S. Brown, who served as US Minister to Russia 1850–53.[1] In the intervening eighty years, bloodshed and famine had ravaged the country in the Russian revolution of 1905, the two revolutions in 1917, and the First World War. Although more than 100 million Russians had died violently and/or prematurely in these eight decades, the essentials of life in their country were unchanged. Political repression, perpetual surveillance by ubiquitous legions of spies and informers and the suspicion and hostility with which Western diplomats were treated even during the Second World War, when they were Russia's allies in its hour of great need, were not *Soviet* phenomena but *Russian*. They were not imposed on the Russian people by their Soviet masters with whom Bullitt had to deal, but on the Soviet system by its Russian creators.

Ambassador Bullitt had been given copies of Neill Brown's despatches by a secretary in the embassy named George Kennan after they were discovered among refuse in a building that had served as stables for the American legation in St Petersburg during the mid-nineteenth century. The United States then being the only major Western nation that did not have a professional diplomatic service, Brown had started life, in his own words, 'as poor as any man in Tennessee'. He worked as a farm labourer to finance his studies, qualified as a lawyer, fought as a sergeant major with the Tennessee Volunteers in the Seminole Indian Wars and was governor of his state before being made Minister to Russia as a reward for supporting the campaign of President Millard Fillmore. Speaking no language other than English, Brown communicated with the Russian authorities through his French-speaking secretary, French being the language of the Tsar's court and the educated classes.

In contrast, George Kennan was a career diplomat – a fluent Russian speaker who had studied in Berlin and served his country in Germany and the Baltic states before his first posting to Moscow. He was also perceptive enough to appreciate the historical value of Brown's despatches. The two diplomats shared not only similar experiences in the daily execution of their duties, but also a similar lack of appreciation by their masters in Washington. On one occasion Brown was driven to lament that he had not heard from his Secretary of State in over a year.[2] Similarly, while acting as *chargé d'affaires* in the absence of an ambassador during 1946, Kennan complained that President Truman's administration seemed not to care what its representatives in Russia were doing. Near despair drove him to compose what he called his 'long telegram' as a desperate plea for someone in Washington to pay attention to what was going on in post-war Moscow.

Since the establishment of diplomatic links between the US and Russia in 1808, the two countries based their relationship on a mutually profitable trading relationship, the avoidance of conflicts of interest and a common wariness of British sea power and French continental ambitions, which culminated in an Anglo-French fleet bombarding Petropavlovsk on the Kamchatka peninsula in 1855.[3] As Tsar Nicholas I said to a predecessor of Neill Brown, 'Not only are our interests alike, our enemies are the same.'[4] But there were also areas of conflicting interest when Brown arrived in St Petersburg on 23 July 1850. American whalers had bases on Siberia's Pacific coast; Russian fur-trappers worked out of Kodiak in Alaska, a Russian possession until 1867. America's Pacific seaboard had seen other incursions as far south as California, where the Russian colony at Fort Ross, just north of San Francisco, was only sold off in 1841.[5] Russia was suspicious of American designs on Sakhalin Island and had recently annexed from China the estuary of the Amur River; America was uneasy about Russia's designs on Japanese territory.

Presented three weeks after his arrival to the Tsar and royal family at the Peterhof Palace, built by Peter the Great, Neill Brown found Nicholas I friendly, praising Maj George Washington Whistler of the Baltimore and Ohio Railroad, who had just died of cholera in St Petersburg after constructing the railway between the capital and Moscow. While commending the Tsar's exceptional energy, Brown also deplored his inability to delegate – and his 'relentless hostility to democratic institutions'.[6]

All the problems Brown encountered in carrying out his duties in Russia can therefore be seen as normal parts of life there and not acts intended to make life difficult for the representative of a potential enemy state. Had he arrived before the Decembrist uprising of 1825 and the several European revolutions of 1848, after which Nicholas I introduced additional repressive measures, he would have found the atmosphere slightly less oppressive, but the pages of Russia's history are splattered with episodes of bloody repression by paranoid rulers and nothing Nicholas had done was new.

Neill Brown's assistant Edward H. Wright came from affluent New England stock. He frequented the *beau monde* of

St Petersburg society – an endless round of glittering balls, private receptions and elegant parties. He, too, commented on the soldiers and police everywhere, and wondered at the crowded streets where people moved about silently. 'There is,' he wrote, 'no noise, no busy hum of life – no laugh, no hearty salutation.' He also noted that the common people worshipped their autocratic ruler and blamed the cruelties of his rule not on Nicholas, but on his underlings.[7]

At the time of Brown's mission to the Imperial Court, the European colonial powers proudly proclaimed their destiny to civilise the world with a Bible in one hand and a gun in the other. Even in the anti-colonial United States there was a convenient belief that Protestant Europeans had what they called 'the Manifest Destiny' to expand the boundaries of their Christian civilisation westward to the Pacific and beyond. Implying a divine mandate and concomitant absolution for the genocidal violence and greed involved, the Manifest Destiny was used to justify extermination of Native American peoples and the acquisition of Texas, Oregon, New Mexico, Northern California, Hawaii and the Philippines.

Most people in the developed Western countries today like to believe that we have moved on from the philosophy of the colonial era. Yet in Russia, what Neill Brown called in his despatch of 28 January 1852 the 'strange superstition' still lives on. It has motivated Russia's rulers from the beginning, was the most important single cause of the Cold War, and flourishes still.

'A religious belief founded on fear or ignorance' is how the dictionary[8] defines superstition, its etymology indicating that such belief has the power to overcome rational thought and defy logical analysis. Yet, is it possible that fear and ignorance of the outside world are an intrinsic part of the mindset of Russia's past and present rulers? For most English speakers, whose countries were historically protected from hostile neighbours by sea or ocean until the advent of intercontinental ballistic missiles and ocean-going nuclear submarines, it is hard to appreciate the world-view of a people surrounded from time immemorial by enemies who may attack at any time, simply by marching or riding for a few days across the empty spaces that separate *them* from *us*. Yet for peoples dwelling on a continental landmass without any natural barriers like mountain ranges or great rivers to protect them from sudden attack, paranoid fear is both so natural and sensible that it becomes an ingrained characteristic.

But ignorance? Can ignorance of the outside world be an evolutionary advantage? The answer is yes, because it enables such peoples to demonise their neighbours, making retaliation and first-strike, allegedly pre-emptive, aggression against these neighbours a knee-jerk reaction to contact, executed swiftly, ruthlessly and without scruple time and again.

No modern ruler of the Russian people epitomises these characteristics better than Josef Vissarionovich Djugashvili. Under his revolutionary name of Stalin, meaning 'man of steel', he directed for three and a half decades a regime of state terror that held in thrall a population of 250-plus millions – a third of whom were not ethnic Russians. Like fellow dictators Hitler, who was not German, Napoleon, who was not French, and Herod, who was not a Hebrew, Stalin was not Russian. He was a Mingrelian-speaking Georgian from the Caucasus, who came to power *after* the 1917 October Revolution by sheer cunning, and held onto that power by ruthlessly eliminating any rival, killing *millions* of his innocent subjects and exiling millions of others to forced labour in sub-human conditions for no crime at all. Yet, because he was elevated by the professedly atheistic Communist Party to the status of living god, it used to be said by his long-suffering subjects that all the crimes committed against them were the work of his minions, acting without the personal knowledge of the man they called 'the little father of his people' or simply *vozhd*, meaning exactly the same as *der Führer*.

Nothing could be further from the truth. Among the women in his immediate entourage who hero-worshipped him, Stalin imprisoned and had tortured the wife of his faithful, long-serving personal secretary Alexander N. Poskrebyshev. Equally well known to Stalin was Polina Molotova, the wife of his foreign minister, who fell victim to his paranoia and went overnight from being the privileged head of the state perfume industry to the wretched status of a political prisoner, whose whereabouts were concealed by Stalin from her anxious husband.

The best-read ruler of Russia since Catherine the Great, Josef Stalin was a bibliophile with a personal library of 20,000 beloved books. When Shalva Nutsibidze was imprisoned simply because his wife had aristocratic connections, Stalin discovered that this famous Georgian poet spent the hours in his cell translating into Russian the medieval epic *Knight in a Panther's Skin*. Each day, the current pages were removed by guards, brought to the Kremlin and edited anonymously by Stalin. After being released, the incredulous Nutsibidze was invited to the Kremlin to meet his mysterious editor, who asked the poet's wife, 'Did we torture you too much?' as though there were a limit up to which torture was decent. Diplomatically, she replied, 'The past belongs to God.' On one day in 1940, Stalin personally signed 329 death warrants. Oh yes, he knew.

But few inhabitants of the USSR knew anything about the flesh-and-blood man who terrorised them all. For the last two decades of his life, Stalin lived almost entirely in the Kremlin fortress, emerging from time to time in a heavily armed convoy that sped through Moscow cleared of all other traffic to one of his two *dachi* outside the city boundaries, each guarded by several cordons of security troops. On his trips to the Crimean Riviera for winter sunshine, he travelled, as did the others of the Soviet elite, in a personal armoured train that sped non-stop for 1,200 miles along similarly cleared tracks, every mile of which was closely patrolled by armed security troops.

During much of the Second World War, for propaganda reasons the Western media dubbed the Red Army 'our gallant Russian allies'. Hailed as 'Man of the Year 1942' by *Time* magazine's edition of January 1943, Stalin was given the affectionate nickname of 'Uncle Joe' and pictured with suitably avuncular smile on the cover. He could afford to smile. In its March 1943 edition *Time* described the Soviet Russians as people 'who look like Americans, dress like Americans and think like Americans'. To Winston Churchill's horror, US President Franklin D. Roosevelt believed all his own propaganda and fell completely under Stalin's spell, which was all the more dangerous for the postwar world because the American president arrogantly declared that he could handle the Soviet leader 'better than (the British)

Foreign Office or my State Department'.[9] He also repeatedly tried to cut Churchill out of the decision-making circuit by meeting Stalin alone, expecting Churchill to take this in good part as the junior partner in the Atlantic Alliance. The British bulldog did not take it in good part, and said so, at which Roosevelt lied barefacedly by pretending that this was all Stalin's doing.[10]

Only a handful of other foreigners ever met Stalin, to make an assessment of the Soviet dictator undistorted by the continual terror in which he kept even his closest associates. One who did was George Kennan, whose US Foreign Service years included two long periods in Moscow. He described the *vozhd* for Washington's guidance when the Second World War neared its end in autumn 1944 as, 'courageous but wary; quick to anger and suspicion but patient in the execution of his purposes; capable of acting with great decision or waiting and dissembling as circumstances may require; outwardly modest and simple, but jealous of the prestige and dignity of the state he heads; not learned, but shrewd and pitilessly realistic; exacting in his demands for loyalty, respect and obedience.'[11]

Reading between the lines of Kennan's tempered diplomatic language, he could have been describing such despots as Ivan the Terrible or Peter the Great. Yet Kennan was far from being hostile to the Russian people. An astute observer of them and their leaders, he experienced both pre-revolutionary and Communist regimes at first hand and was later to make himself unpopular in Washington at the height of the Cold War by arguing that the tendency of Western political leaders and especially the Western military elite to demonise the whole Communist bloc was dangerous because it failed to take into account that decisions and actions taken in London, Paris, Bonn or Washington affected the other side's moves in the great confrontation of the twentieth century, which threatened to exterminate all human life.

Short, stocky, with one arm shorter than the other, Stalin walked with a curiously uneven gait from injuries to his legs sustained in two childhood street accidents. His face was heavily pockmarked by smallpox in infancy, the whites of his eyes yellowish, his teeth bad. He spoke Russian with a thick accent that betrayed his origins as the son of a Georgian washerwoman.

His father was either her illiterate alcoholic husband or, more likely, his unpriestly drinking companion, Father Charkviani. Young Josef grew up a *kinto*, or street-urchin, nearer in spirit and geographically to Teheran and Baghdad than Moscow or St Petersburg. His hometown Gori lay 50 miles from Tiflis, capital of the ancient Georgian people, finally subdued by Russian arms in 1879, the year of his birth.

In Father Charkviani's school at Gori, the street-urchin taught himself to read ahead of the other pupils and graduated early to the Tiflis Theological Seminary, where he was an exemplary student, attending services and singing enthusiastically in the choir. He then discovered the writings of Karl Marx, and took to the clandestine world of terrorists and revolutionaries of all political hues like a fish to water. Under the revolutionary name 'Koba' and a succession of false identities, by 1900 Stalin was fomenting industrial unrest all over the Caucasus with such callous disregard for the workers in the front line who were the targets of police bullets and the sabre slashes of mounted Cossacks that even his fellow conspirators were appalled. Arrested seven times and exiled to Siberia by the Okhrana[12] – the Tsarist secret police – Stalin escaped so easily each time that many Old Bolsheviks suspected he was a double agent, playing the situation both ways.

Intelligence officers, and especially those who defect, are all liars. With that caveat, an odd light was thrown by NKVD defector Alexander Orlov on this lingering suspicion among the Old Bolsheviks whom Stalin had executed on trumped-up charges. Orlov told the FBI in his debriefing that an NKVD researcher had found an Okhrana file dating from before the revolution, in which there were numerous denunciations of fellow Bolsheviks, written in Stalin's very distinctive handwriting. Of a small circle of trusted friends who saw this, only Orlov was still alive two years later – and that was because he was safely in the West. Among the others, Marshal Tukhachevsky was one of the first executed in Stalin's otherwise unexplained purge of the Red Army in June 1937. He was shot within 24 hours of being sentenced, in defiance of the Soviet law requiring a delay of 72 hours to permit an appeal.[13]

Orlov made this public in an article for an April 1956 edition of *Life* magazine. In the same issue, Russian-born journalist Isaac Don Levine wrote about a letter dated 12 July 1913 from Okhrana headquarters in Moscow to its Yeniseisk station that had allegedly been brought secretly to the US by a Russian émigré. The letter outlined Stalin's role as an informer beginning after his arrest in Tiflis in 1906, continuing through 1908 with his reports to the Okhrana in Baku and later in St Petersburg. Tests of the paper and the typewriter that had been used confirmed the authenticity of the letter, but Orlov thought it more probable that the letter had been forged by 'someone who knew the truth'.[14]

Of all this Kennan was unaware, or perhaps just being diplomatic, when he wrote:

Stalin's youth is shrouded in the mists of underworld revolutionary activity – largely in his native Caucasus. From that he graduated into the Dostoievskian atmosphere of revolutionary conspiracy in European Russia. His life has known only what Lenin called 'the incredibly swift transition from wild violence to the most delicate deceit'. The placid give and take of Anglo-Saxon life, in particular the tempering of all enmity and all intimacy, the balancing of personal self-respect, the free play of opposing interests – these things [are] incomprehensible, implausible to him.[15]

Despite his non-Russian origins, Stalin fits well into the long line of brutal Russian rulers that stretches from a Danish Viking named Rurik, who settled in Novgorod during the Dark Ages, to Yuri Long-Arm, Alexander Nevsky, Boris Godunov, Peter the Great, Vladimir Putin and Dmitri Medvedev – whose name, incidentally, means 'Mr Bear', an appropriate name for a Russian ruler.

The expansionist imperative noted by Neill Brown has been the driving force of Russia's rulers from the beginning, surviving many setbacks to rise phoenix-like from the ashes each time. The 1917 revolution killed the priests who prayed for the 'strange superstition' when Brown was *en mission* in St Petersburg, but during the seven godless decades that followed the October Revolution it throve again, served as never before by the apostles of Marx and Lenin, who invented a new religion that claimed to be scientific and infallible.

The promises of Communism seduced millions of discontented workers in the Western democracies and hundreds of thousands of liberal intellectuals who were unaware of, or closed their eyes to, the true conditions of life inside what they idealised as 'the workers' paradise'. Most of them had no idea that the Kremlin exercised iron control over the national Communist parties through the Comintern, and later the Cominform. Nor did they dream that Moscow regarded its best and brightest converts as dupes to spy on their own countries for military and commercial purposes, or that the mass of 'fellow-travellers' were intended as a fifth column to destabilise Western society, weakening its ability to resist Russian expansionism.

The casualties in the front line of this conflict were rarely Russian, which made them totally deniable. As a way of waging war, it was very cheap. It was also very effective in confusing uncommitted citizens in the democratic countries, who were often unable to see that the legitimate wage demands and industrial action of working people desirous of a fair share of the fruits of their labour were exploited by Communist activists taking orders directly from Moscow which had nothing to do with the welfare of the union members who had elected them. All the weak points of Western society were probed and exploited: poverty, racial tension, industrial disputes, and the women's movement. Like political smart bombs, this kind of subversion could be fine-tuned to divert the leverage of legitimate protest.

When the Berlin Wall was breached in 1989 and the USSR imploded with startling speed, the world relaxed after four and a half decades of living in fear of nuclear war. The architects of *glasnost* and *perestroika*, Mikhail S. Gorbachev and his politically savvy wife Raïssa, behaved and talked not unlike a Western president and his wife – which eventually cost them the presidency. If Gorbachev's successor Boris Yeltsin seemed a thoroughly Russian character – a boisterous, bottom-pinching boozer – he did not frighten us by threatening annihilation. It truly seemed that the Russian Bear was hibernating and might not wake up with a sore head.

Yet, a century before the Cold War began, British Foreign Minister and Prime Minister Lord Palmerston commented, 'It has always been the policy and practice of the Russian Government to expand its frontiers as rapidly as the apathy or timidity of neighbouring states would permit, but usually to halt and frequently to recoil when confronted by determined opposition; then to await the next favourable opportunity to spring upon its intended victim.'[16]

Palmerston would not have been surprised that, a couple of years after apparently accepting the loss of its satellites in Europe and Asia, Russia was using new weapons to bully its neighbours again. Weapons in the current Russian armoury include oil and gas, but there is nothing new about the strategy. With hindsight, it can be seen that the collapse of the USSR was just another Palmerstonian setback, after which the new generation of men in the Kremlin, with the Putin-Medvedev clique at the helm of the Russian ship of state, are obsessed with that 'strange superstition' identified by Neill Brown a century and a half ago. Like the Romanovs before the revolution and the Communists after 1917, today's oligarchs are in thrall to what one might call in modern usage 'the Kremlin Complex'.

HOW AND WHY DID IT ALL BEGIN?

Many modern Russian faces indicate a mingling of Tartar or other Asiatic blood in the past. So some people say it can all be traced back to the Mongol conquest of Russia when Genghis Khan's shaman Kokochu told the Great Khan that it was the will of Heaven for him and his family to rule the whole earth.

In fact, it goes back even further than that.

2

SLAVES, AMBER, FURS AND TERROR

hili byli, dyed i baba ....'Way back in Granddad's and Grandma's time,' is how Russian fairy tales begin.

The origins of the Russians are as vague as a fairy tale, lost in prehistory not because they predate Greece and Rome, but because the people living in the heartland of modern Russia at the end of the Dark Ages were still illiterate herdsmen and foresters many centuries after numeracy and literacy had spread around the Mediterranean basin. Like all illiterate people, they took pleasure in telling, listening to, and singing sagas of great deeds – as Russians still do.

Slavery was not restricted to the Africans shipped across the Atlantic or the million white slaves of Islam. The buying and selling of people is so general in primitive societies that it comes as no surprise to learn that these remote forest- and plain-dwellers were the natural prey of human traffickers from the slave-owning countries south of the Black Sea. The very word *Slav* is derived from the words for 'slave' in Greek and Latin. Invading the USSR in 1941, Hitler played on this with his slogan *Slaven sind Sklaven* – Slavs are slaves – to justify treating as sub-human the millions of inhabitants at the mercy of the Wehrmacht, the

Waffen-SS and the Einsatzgruppen death squads in the vast territory conquered during the first months of Operation Barbarossa
– his surprise attack on the USSR in summer 1941.

Although traders in furs and amber travelled through the area
along primitive trade routes at least as far back as 1500 BC, they
left no written records. Between the fourth and ninth centuries AD, various migrating nomadic peoples including the Huns,
Avars, Goths and Magyars passed through what is now Russia,
leaving little archaeological evidence of their passage. Nor do
we know where the first Russians came from, although the language contains clues suggesting that the people who originally
evolved it were pastoral nomads living with their herds in the
grasslands of the steppes. For example, the Russian verb to find
is *na'idti* or *nakhodit'* – meaning literally to step on something
otherwise invisible in long grass.

That there was some trading contact with Mediterranean
visitors during the prehistoric period is shown by early coins
and artefacts unearthed by archaeologists. However, since history is made of written records, it is true that there is no Russian
history before 988, when Grand Prince Svyatoslav of Kiev welcomed Greek Orthodox missionaries sent by the patriarch of
Constantinople and had all his male subjects baptised. These
missionaries translated religious texts into a form of Russian
for their eastern Slav converts, using their own uncial script
with extra characters for sounds that did not exist in Greek –
like *ch, sh, shch* and *ts*. With St Cyril being the best known
of these missionaries, the modified Greek alphabet used by
Russians, Ukrainians, Bulgarians, Belorussians and Serbs is still
called Cyrillic. The downside of this gift of literacy was that the
Greek alphabet isolated them from the Renaissance and the
Enlightenment, whereas the western Slavs – Poles, Czechs and
Slovaks – given a modified Latin script by their missionaries,
merged naturally into the mainstream of European evolution.

If Russians are understandably sensitive about the idea of
being descendants of primitives regarded as slaves by the civilised world, Slavophile Russian historians also tend to reject the
otherwise generally accepted etymology of *russkiy* and *Rossiya* –
meaning 'Russian' and 'Russia' respectively – being derived from

rus, a Viking word for oar. Island dwellers like the British envisage the Vikings leaping ashore from their *drakkar* long ships powered by single square-rigged sails, yet it was more often by oar-power that the Norsemen penetrated the interior of the continent along the great rivers, against current and wind.

The first permanent settlements in what is now the Russian heartland were established by Scandinavian trader-raiders who settled in the Ryazan area, south-east of Moscow, early in the ninth century. At this time Moscow was just a *kreml* or stockaded trading post in the forests. Intermarriage with local women, after the native males had been disposed of, produced the *varyagi* or Varangians, a mixed stock whose loose federation was ruled by a single leader or *khagan*, replacing the previous tribal chiefs. The first Russian dynasty, which lasted in parts of the area from 1157 to 1598, owes its name to a Varangian *knyaz* or princeling called Rurik who originated in Danish Jutland. From his base at Novgorod – literally, 'the new town' – the Varangians raided and traded in amber, furs and slaves far down the Volga River to the Black Sea, reaching Constantinople in 860 and roaming onwards to Baghdad, as testified by hoards of coins dug up in Russia and dated to this period.

The earliest extant Russian history text is dated 1377. It is a copy of *Povest vremennykh let* – the account of bygone years – originally compiled in Kiev about 1113. Based on Byzantine sources and orally transmitted sagas, it tells of an earlier ruler named Svyatoslav (936–72). Possibly a grandson of the legendary Rurik, he spent most of his adult life conquering one neighbouring tribe after another while his redoubtable mother Olga directed affairs of state back home.

Svyatoslav's usual technique was to send messengers to his neighbours one after another, announcing his intention to attack them. The ultimatum to submit or die was remarkably successful. He defeated the Khazars on the lower reaches of the Don River and the Ossetians and Circassians in the north Caucasus. After he conquered both the Volga Bulgars and their Balkan cousins, the end of the story has a familiar ring: Svyatoslav had embarked on this military expedition at the request of the Byzantines, with whom he was at the time allied, but afterwards he refused to hand over the territory and spoils of war because he wished to establish a Russo-Bulgarian empire of his own. Having bitten off more than he could chew, he was defeated by a larger Byzantine army in 971, to be killed the following year when ambushed by the nomadic Turkic Pechenegs.

It fell to his son and successor Vladimir (960–1015) to weld together the conquered peoples into a cohesive state based on Kiev in modern-day Ukraine. At its apogee, Kievan Rus stretched from the open steppe in the south-east northwards to Lake Ladoga and the upper Volga basin and owed its prosperity to trading and raiding via the great riverine routes from the Baltic to the Black Sea. The benefits of contact with Byzantium

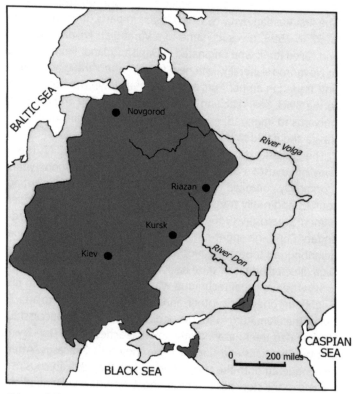

Extent of Kievan Rus (c.1050).

were many: with the new Orthodox Christian religion came the first code of laws, architecture, art, music and a faint whisper of literature. Although Vladimir's twelve sons and numerous grandsons inherited considerable territory, none of them was powerful enough to take overall control of a society where ninety other princelings had retinues of up to 2,000 warriors. Like the knightly vassals of Western European kings, these men did no productive work and their requisitioning of horses, food, clothing and weapons must have placed a great strain on the primitive economy. Unlike their Western counterparts, they had no long-term loyalty based on fixed fiefs, and thus honed the paranoia of their leaders by frequently changing allegiance.

Exploiting the internecine struggles between these Kievan princelings and their supporters, Turkic nomads from Central Asia fought first on one side, then another. The settled towns were natural targets for the Pechenegs and Kipchaks, whose pastures on the steppe lay only a day's ride from Kiev, and whose repeated savage incursions led a sizeable part of the population of Kievan Rus to emigrate northwards, where the rigours of a savage winter were a small price to pay for the comparative safety of forests in which their mounted enemies, travelling with families and herds, could not easily pursue them. The inevitable end came after a Byzantine princess named Helena Komnene was given as wife to Yuri Long Arm, Grand Prince of Kiev (1099–1157). Their son Andrei Bogolyubsky, Prince of Rostov and Suzdal, stormed Kiev and sacked the city in 1169, his followers burning monasteries and churches, raping women, slaughtering men and enslaving the survivors.

The earliest well-documented Russian hero was Grand Prince Alexander of Vladimir (1220–63), still revered as Alexander Nevsky in memory of his victory at the Neva River in 1240 over a Swedish army blocking Russian access to the Baltic. Triumph going to his head, Alexander took his courtesy title of prince somewhat too seriously and was exiled from Novgorod. Shortly afterwards, Pope Gregory IX had the idea of converting the whole Baltic hinterland to the Roman church and despatched the Teutonic Knights to 'pacify' the area. In panic, Novgorod invited Alexander back. After a series of skirmishes, in April 1242 he defeated the invaders in a famous battle on frozen lakes near Pskov, and continued fending off Swedish, German, Lithuanian and Finnish advances from the west.

Already, the precondition of 'healthy' paranoia was in place, for the Russians were constantly surrounded by enemies. To the south and east, the Kipchaks had moderated their raids and now sought an alliance against 'terrible strangers from the east', who turned out to be the Mongol hordes from Central Asia. Reasoning that, if the buffer zone where the Kipchaks pastured their herds fell to the Mongols, they would be next in line, two Kievan princes called Mstislav joined forces with their former enemies to confront the new common foe, only to be roundly defeated at the battle of the Kalka River in 1223.

For whatever reason, the Mongols withdrew, reappearing thirteen years later in greater force: 35,000 mounted archers led by Batu Khan. Learning from Sun Tzu's *Art of War*, Khan first despatched undercover agents to spy out the land and sow discord: the rich were promised that trade would be safer under Mongol suzerainty; the poor were promised prosperity; ethnic and religious minorities were promised greater freedom. Having subjugated the Bulgars and Kipchaks, in November 1237 Batu Khan demanded the submission of the city of Vladimir. One month later, his horde besieged and sacked Ryazan, then Moscow. Too late, Yuri II of Vladimir sent his sons to confront the enemy, seriously underestimating them. In February 1238, Batu laid siege to Vladimir and burned it to the ground. Another bloody defeat for the Rus followed at the Sit River on 4 March. Dividing the horde, Batu sent smaller armies to completely destroy fourteen other important cities. Sun Tzu wrote, 'Kill one, frighten a thousand.' Batu Khan killed every man, woman and child in the conquered towns, so that their neighbours would surrender without resisting him.

Modern demographers estimate that the Mongols slaughtered around half the population. By the summer of 1238 the Crimea was devastated, with Kiev burned to the ground again in December. In the north, Moscow was at first subordinate to Vladimir, but made a deal with the Mongols to collect the annual tribute from other Russian principalities, including Novgorod and Tver. Called the Tartar-Mongol Yoke, the tribute was levied for the next three centuries. Although taxing the Russians, the Mongols and Tartars did not interfere in domestic affairs, tolerating the Orthodox Church even after their own conversion from shamanism to Islam. Occasional resistance peaked in 1380 when the army of Grand Prince Dmitri of Moscow (1350–89) held off a mixed force of Tartars and Mongols at the Battle of Kulikovo, south of Moscow on the Don River. Adding the epithet 'Donskoi' to his name, the prince became another Russian hero, but by 1450 one in five princely families of the Rus had Tartar or Mongol blood and Tartar was the court language in the Grand Duchy of Muscovy.

After Ivan III refused to continue paying tax to the Golden Horde in 1480, Khan Akhmet encamped his army on the banks of the Ugra River about 150 miles southwest of Moscow, awaiting the arrival of Lithuanian allies before advancing further into Russian territory. When they did not appear and he received news that his base near Ryazan was under attack by Ivan's allies, Akhmet withdrew. Ivan claimed a great victory and proceeded to subjugate Novgorod and Tver, making Moscow the capital in every sense. By a combination of treaties, marriages and conquest, the Grand Duchy rapidly tripled in size under Ivan's rule.

Following the Byzantine example, the various rulers of the Rus protected the Orthodox Church in return for the priests' endorsement of their divine right to rule. With the end of the Byzantine Empire in 1453 and the Ottoman Turks' conquest of the Balkans, the grand dukes of Muscovy were lauded by the priests as the only remaining defenders of Orthodox Christianity. In 1472 Ivan III married Sofia Palaeologos, niece of the last Byzantine emperor. More important than her dowry was the Byzantine concept of absolute monarchy that she brought with her. Moscow was now hailed as the third Rome – after Constantinople and Rome itself – with its rulers styling themselves 'Caesar,' pronounced *Tsar*.

Grand Prince Ivan IV of Moscow, better known as Ivan the Terrible, was proclaimed Tsar on his father's death when he was only 3 years old. His mother ruled as regent until her death, allegedly by poison, in 1538. In the power vacuum, *boyary* – or noble warriors – launched another period of internecine strife, which left young Ivan with a lifelong mistrust of them. Officially crowned 'Tsar of all Russia' at the age of 17 in 1547, Ivan married Anastasia Romanova to get onside the most powerful of the families that might have opposed him. He also instituted some reforms, setting up the *zemsky sobor*, a feudal council of nobles. However, after 1560, when increasing paranoia convinced him that his family and closest counsellors had all betrayed him, he created the *oprichnina* – a vast territory

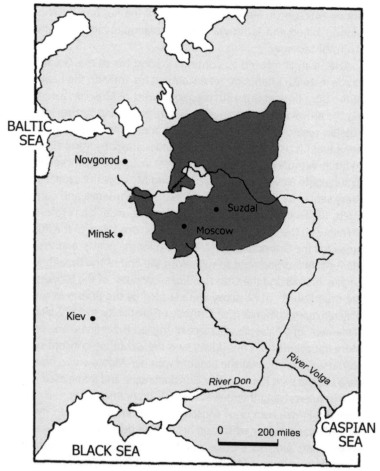

Principality of Moscow in 1482.

administered as crown lands to finance his personal house-hold. Like Stalin living cut off from his people in the Kremlin, Ivan withdrew from society behind the screen of *oprichniki* – a bodyguard of 6,000 men, whose duty it was to detect and eliminate internal enemies.

No one was safe. Priests, princes and peasants alike were tor-tured and executed on suspicion. In 1570 an entire city fell victim to his wrath: Novgorod was attacked and pillaged, its priests publicly flogged to death, while their tormentor perversely drew up his own complicated rules for monastic life, devised intricate religious ceremonies and paid monks to pray for the souls of his victims – numbered by his own modest account at 4,000.

As a warlord, Ivan expanded the duchy by conquering the khanates of Kazan in 1552 and Astrakhan in 1556. This east-ward expansion would eventually reach the Pacific Ocean. More immediately, he felt that trade with Europe required access to the Baltic and invaded Livonia (modern Latvia and Estonia) in 1558. When Sweden and Poland joined forces to frustrate him, the Crimean Tartars seized their chance to attack Astrakhan; in 1571 they burned Moscow to the ground, leaving only the Kremlin standing.

Eastward expansion continued as a private initiative of the powerful Stroganov family. Exploiting estates and mineral resources in the Urals, they protected themselves with a private army led by a condemned Cossack named Yermak, whose men penetrated deep into Siberia along the Obi and Irtysh rivers during 1581–2, subsequently handing over their conquests to the Tsar in return for pardons.

By then Ivan had killed his eldest son in a fit of rage while the prince was trying to shield his pregnant wife from his father's violence. So, when Ivan died in 1584, the succession passed to his dim-witted son Fyodor I, whose main interest lay in bell-ringing. What saved him from instant assassination was his brother-in-law, a very astute *boyar* named Boris Godunov, who had married Ivan's daughter Maria. Eventually immor-talised by Pushkin and by Moussorgsky's eponymous opera, Boris was appointed regent for Fyodor by the dying Ivan, after which Boris Godunov switched off the charm that had formerly characterised him at court and used his new power to banish any fellow *boyary* who might oppose him. These included the influential Romanov family, whose doyen was forced to take holy orders in a remote monastery that became his prison.

On Fyodor's death, a *zemsky sobor* elected Boris to the throne in 1598 after fourteen years as regent. He proved a far-sighted ruler, strengthening the state, reforming the judicial system and even sending favoured students to be educated in Western Europe. However, his personal paranoia also led him to expand the *oprichniki*, and ever since, a vast network of informers to spy on the whole population has been an intrinsic part of the Russian state apparatus. A famine in 1601–03 and resultant epidemics were the undoing of Boris: a pretender claiming to be Fyodor's dead half-brother Dmitri led an army of Cossacks and Polish mercenaries into southern Russia the following year. Initially successful at holding off the interlopers, Boris died, leaving the country torn by a series of conflicts known euphemistically as *smutnoye vremya* – the time of troubles – in which other pretenders rose and fell, with a Polish prince briefly on the throne of Muscovy. When the Muscovites rebelled, their city was again burned to the ground.

Thus, ignominiously, ended the Rurik dynasty.

3

A TIME OF GIANTS: PETER AND CATHERINE: ALEXIS AND NAPOLEON

In February 1613 an assembly of freemen from fifty Russian cities elected a 16-year-old boy from the Romanov family to be their new Tsar. Among Mikhail Romanov's first priorities was the recovery of territory lost during the Troubles. Thanks to a rift between the Polish-Lithuanian Commonwealth and the Swedes, he was able to make a truce with his Western enemies by 1619 and secure a protectorate over the formerly Polish part of Ukraine, together with Kiev and Smolensk. In 1649 he formalised the institution of serfdom, whereby the tied peasants were the property of the landowners on whose estates they lived, thus setting the stage for another rebellion, led by a third hero whose exploits are still sung today.

In 1667, with Mikhail's son Alexis I on the throne, the son of a prosperous Cossack family named Stenka Razin gathered together on the upper reaches of the Don a band of escaped serfs who literally had nothing to lose but their lives. For three years they carried out daring raids on Russian and Persian towns around the Caspian Sea. A popular folk song tells of Stenka falling in love with a captured Persian princess. When taunted by his men, *tolko noch' s'nei provozilsya, sam nautro baboi stal* – after one night with her he had become as soft as a woman himself – Stenka proved his manhood by drowning her in the Volga. A legend, perhaps, but the campaign he unleashed in 1670 on the fortified cities along the Volga's banks is fact.

His undisciplined army of 7,000 ragged rebels were mainly motivated by the prospect of loot, rape, and torturing captured officers and nobles. In their bloody progression up the Volga, their numbers were tripled by serfs and urban workers rebelling against the nobility and bureaucracy, but not their quasi-divine ruler. However, alarmed at the insurrection's spread into some central provinces of the Russian state, Tsar Alexis sent an army to put down the rebellion. Trained by European instructors, the army easily defeated Stenka's rabble in October 1670. Betrayed by Cossacks, Stenka was brought to Moscow and tortured, then executed by quartering in Red Square. Alexis' forces then savagely reduced the rebel strongholds and executed their leaders. By December 1671, it was all over.

Even without marauding serfs, life in Russia was hard, and every foreigner an object of suspicion. Tudor and Stuart embassies from Britain were 'beaten in with clots and such things as lay in the streets', i.e. excrement, when they dared to set foot outside. Sent as ambassador by Charles II in the 1660s, Guy de Miège complained that his 'freedom was so regulated and constrained that for the first few days we were shut up close in our House and not permitted to stir abroad'. He was relatively lucky; a later diplomat complained that his entourage was not permitted to enter Moscow but, like many other foreigners, was kept waiting for weeks outside the city in filthy hovels, whose owners were 'more like beasts than men'.[1]

By contemporary European standards, Russia was primitive, filthy and corrupt – which is why the first modernising Romanov went down in history as Peter the Great. Born in 1672 as Alexis' fourteenth child, he succeeded his half-brother Fyodor III as Tsar jointly with his half-brother Ivan before his eleventh birthday, their 25-year-old half-sister Sophia acting as regent. Even as a child, Peter stood out from the litter of siblings by virtue of his size, physical strength and a native intelligence without formal schooling. Sidelined by Sophia and literally at risk of his life from her supporters – the *streltsy* or archers – Peter was saved by his mother fleeing with him to the village of Preobrazhenskoye, near Moscow. There, he became fascinated by the technology of the Westerners living in the *nemetskaya sloboda*, or German concession, and adopted their Western-style clothes. Assembling a gang of equally wild youths, he grew up a domineering, paranoid, vicious drunkard – characteristics that flowered in his Most Drunken Assembly of Fools and Jesters, whose bisexual orgies he orchestrated down to the least detail.

In August 1689 the *streltsy* rebelled. Although Sophia attempted to exploit this in her own interest, she was outmanoeuvred by the family of Peter's mother and banished to a convent. Still nominally joint Tsar with his half-brother until Ivan's death in 1696, Peter left the boring business of state administration to his relatives. More interested in drunken brawls and the latest shipbuilding techniques, he left Russia in 1697 to study the latter first-hand in Holland and Britain, taking with him the 'Great Embassy' of 250 men of all classes, who were to study naval construction techniques, the general sciences and the art of war. In addition, Peter recruited 750 European specialists in these areas to work in Russia.[2]

In his absence, the *streltsy* and Cossacks revolted to bring back Sophia. The rebellion was put down before Peter's return, but gave his unfocused violence a target. In a reign of terror that recalled the time of Ivan the Terrible, he personally supervised the torture of nearly 2,000 suspects. Hundreds of people were killed, their corpses left on public display. Forcing Sophia to become a nun, he had 197 of her supporters hanged in her convent as a lesson to her.

His interest in ships triggering the same 'drive to the sea' that had obsessed previous rulers of the landlocked Grand Duchy, Peter declared war on Ottoman Turkey with the aim of securing the Bosphorus and thus access to the Mediterranean. The campaign succeeded only in capturing Azov, which did not stay Russian for long, but he also established a naval base at Taganrog on the Don estuary and founded a Black Sea fleet. Turning to the west, where access to the Baltic was still blocked by Sweden, he made an alliance with its former ally, Poland-Lithuania. With

Denmark also onside, the Great Northern War against Sweden from 1700 dragged on for two decades, but won Russia four provinces on the Gulf of Finland. In the east, Peter also consolidated the frontier with China.

The Grand Duchy having grown to the size of an empire, in 1721 Peter re-titled himself *imperator,* or emperor of all Russia – a vast swathe of conquered territory stretching from the Baltic to the Pacific, three times the size of continental Europe. But what's in a name? He and his successors continued to be called *Tsar* in popular usage – right down to the last Romanov autocrat, assassinated in 1918.

Peter imposed modernising reforms on the European model, personally hacking off his courtiers' traditional beards and ordering them to adopt Western dress like him. To break the power of the *boyar* assembly, he replaced it with a nine-man Council of State, turned the Orthodox Church into a government department and reorganised the administration to triple tax revenue. His most enduring monument is the new capital he had constructed in the swampy lower reaches of the River Neva, at the cost of hundreds of thousands of labourers' lives. Named after him, St Petersburg and its naval base on the island of Kronstadt was his access to the Baltic, but also Russia's window into Western Europe, where the industrial revolution was evolving the technology needed to modernise his backward country. Slowly, during his lifetime and afterwards, Western technology crept into Russia, usually introduced by foreign speculators who used their own capital to set up factories and processing plants for raw materials.

Peter had swiftly put away his first wife, who did not suit his erratic lifestyle, and later took the mistress of his closest drinking companion to his own bed. Marfa Skronowska was a Lutheran Latvian who had been taken prisoner during the Great Northern War. A serving wench, re-christened Yekaterina or Catherine when converted to the Orthodox religion, after producing four children by Peter out of wedlock, she scandalised the court by becoming his wife, and was crowned empress-consort in May 1724. Less than a year later, Peter was dead, having typically neglected to appoint an heir, so the Latvian serving wench was proclaimed empress.

Her neurotic, alcoholic grandson Peter III, who hero-worshipped Russia's great enemy Frederick II (the Great) of Prussia, was the unlikely catalyst in the continuing westernisation of Russia. While awaiting the call to the throne, he married 16-year-old German princess Sophie Friederike Auguste of Anhalt-Zerbst in 1745. She, in contrast, was intelligent, highly ambitious and a Russophile. Bored with her reputedly impotent husband and humiliated at court as 'that German woman', Sophie produced children by three different fathers while laying plans to depose her husband as soon as he came to power and so grab the throne for herself.

One of Peter's first acts on taking power in 1762 was to abandon Russia's allies and make peace with Frederick the Great. It was the opening for which Sophie had been waiting. Her current lover Grigori Orlov, father of one of her children, had a brother named Alexei who commanded Russia's naval forces. Together with Sophie, the two brothers masterminded a coup d'état which deposed Peter III in June 1762 and put her on the throne. No great beauty, but respected for her erudition by liberal elements in the upper classes, Sophie was proclaimed empress and autocrat in St Petersburg's Kazan Cathedral. Within the week, she became a widow when Peter was conveniently assassinated, probably by Alexei Orlov, and commenced her thirty-four-year reign as Empress Catherine II, who became known as Catherine the Great.

From the outset, Catherine wanted to make Russia prosperous and powerful, to establish a new, more liberal society and create a glittering court to rival Versailles. To replenish the state treasury exhausted by the war, she seized the one-third of productive land and serfs belonging to the Church, reducing the clergy to salaried civil servants. As a diplomat, she kept on good terms with Prussia and France, and Austria. Her solution to the problem of the ill-defined kingdom of Poland was to place a devoted former lover on its throne.

Reforming Russian society was less easy, since the ideas of European political philosophers were inappropriate to her backward realm. Rather naïvely, in 1767 she convened a congress of delegates from all social classes except the serfs to ascertain their aspirations and frame a constitution. The endless debates produced no agreement, so although the resultant *nakaz Kateriny Velikei* – or Instruction of Catherine the Great – envisaged a free society in which all men were equal with a code of laws devoid of capital punishment, torture or serfdom, it also upheld the principle of absolute power for the autocrat, who was above the law.

The Instruction was a pipe dream. Seeing that emancipation of the serfs would never be tolerated by the landowners, Catherine legitimised the very system she had condemned as inhuman – even imposing serfdom on the Ukrainians, who had been free. By the end of her reign, there was scarcely a free peasant left in her empire, and the condition of serfs was worse than it had been before: they could be sold as slaves, couples separated and their children disposed of at their owners' whim.

Frustrated as a reformer, Catherine used a war with Russia's traditional enemy Ottoman Turkey to stake all on national grandeur. By 1773 the hardships of the war and repeated epidemics made the country ripe for rebellion. The man of the moment was an invalid Don Cossack officer named Yemelyan Pugachoff, who claimed to be the assassinated emperor Peter III and led the greatest uprising Russia was to see before 1917, culminating in the capture of the city of Kazan. By June 1774 Pugachoff's troops were ready to march on Moscow, when the current war with Turkey ended in a Russian victory and Catherine was able to divert troops to crush the rebels by savage reprisals. On 14 September 1774, betrayed by his own Cossacks as Stenka Razin had been, Pugachoff was confined in a metal cage for transport to Moscow and public execution there by beheading and quartering.

Previously, Catherine had kept her activities in the bedchamber separate from those in the council chamber, but when Guards officer Grigori Potemkin became her lover, she found in him a highly intelligent partner with whom to share her power. Their physical relationship lasted only two years, but he continued to be treated as an equal by his empress for the rest of his life. A shrewd politician and diplomat, he strengthened Russia's southern flank as governor of 'New Russia', i.e. southern

Ukraine, and annexed Crimea from the Turks in 1783, building up the Black Sea fleet in its new home port at Sevastopol. Russia now held the north shore of the Black Sea as far as the Caucasus, which Potemkin saw as a position of strength from which to subjugate Turkey and gain access to the Mediterranean. The second Russo-Turkish war, in which he served as commander-in-chief, did not achieve this aim, although it did expand Russian possessions southwards.

Catherine avoided a European war throughout her reign by prudently respecting Russia's treaties with its Western neighbours, but added 200,000 square miles to the empire, with the number of her subjects nearly doubling from 19 million in 1762 to 36 million on her death in 1796. On one occasion, she remarked, 'If I could live for 200 years, the whole of Europe would be brought under Russian rule.'[3] The apogee of her glory came in 1787 when Potemkin personally escorted her across the newly acquired southern expanses of her empire to the Crimea – a long journey for which he ordered everything she might see to be smartened up in advance, although the fake villages constructed for her approval appear to be apocryphal.

The problem with Peter the Great opening a window to look out was that other people could see in. One of them was Napoleon Bonaparte.

Catherine the Great's grandson Alexander I was a complicated, paranoid character who came to the throne by arranging his father's assassination. Once crowned, he continued the expansion of the empire, grabbing Finland from the Swedes and Bessarabia from the Turks in 1812, as well as much Polish-speaking territory. Although initially seduced by Napoleon's flattery that they were two giants who could together rule the world, in 1812 he realised that the French emperor had simply been keeping him onside while consolidating his European victories. In June, led by Napoleon, the Grande Armée of 600,000 men crossed the Neman River[4] separating Polish territory from Russia..

Alexander's forces retreated, adopting a scorched-earth policy. The consequent logistics problems slowed the French advance and it was early September before Napoleon's army reached the western approaches to Moscow, where Gen Mikhail I.

Kutuzov confronted 130,000 foot soldiers, 28,000 cavalry and 500 cannon of the Grande Armée at Borodino with his own forces of 135,000 infantry, 25,000 cavalry and 600 cannon. On 7 September Napoleon ordered his infantry to advance in close order on a 3-mile front, presenting an unmissable target to the Russian guns. In *War and Peace*, Tolstoy summed up the carnage as 'a continuous slaughter that could be of no avail to either the French or the Russians'. Six hours' combat saw thousands of corpses strewn along the front. Around midday, the French artillery got the advantage but bad visibility due to smoke from the hundreds of cannonades made Napoleon hesitate to commit 30,000 troops held in reserve, thus forfeiting a decisive victory. In the night, Kutuzov disengaged, leaving 15,000 Russian dead on the field of battle with another 35,000 wounded, against 10,000 dead and 20,000 wounded on the French side.

Napoleon entered Moscow a week later to find the old capital a ghost town, abandoned by its inhabitants. Whether an accident or started deliberately, fire spread rapidly throughout the city of wooden houses. Still today, Russian children learn the folk song *Pozhar moskovskii* that tells of the Great Fire of Moscow, which 'roared and blazed' to deny the invader any shelter. At the first approach of winter, with his army starving, Napoleon wrote to Alexander with a plea for help, appealing to the memory of their former friendship.

With Alexander turning a deaf ear, Napoleon's only way out of the trap he had dug himself was to retreat. Bolstered by a rumour that he had died in Russia, a nearly successful coup d'état in Paris on 23 October brought him hurrying homeward. The French withdrawal was turned from retreat to rout by the onset of wintry weather, as his abandoned army followed through the blizzards and swamps, harried all the way by Cossack cavalry. Starving and wounded stragglers were murdered for a pair of boots or less by gangs of marauding peasantry. After a bloody battle at the Berezina River in November, Napoleon's no-longer-grand army numbered fewer than 10,000 men fit for combat. In recent years, archeological excavations of mass graves in the Baltic states and elsewhere along the route of the retreat tell the story of what happened to the half-million men who never came home, their only certain memorial the regimental buttons of their long-rotted uniforms found among the bones in mass graves.

Among the coalition forces in the victory parade in Paris on 31 March 1814 were Cossack cavalrymen who did leave one enduring memento in the French language. Booted feet on the tables of Parisian cafes, they yelled, *'Bystro, bystro!'* at the waiters, meaning faster, faster! Two centuries later, French cafés are still called bistros. Alexander was hailed as the saviour of Europe and invited to preside over the Congress of Vienna in 1815 that re-drew the political map of the continent, granting him the Polish crown. In his poem *Dva Velikana*, the text of which provided the Russian rock band Piknik with an eponymous hit in 1997, the author Lermontov likened Alexander and Napoleon to two giants confronting each other, victory going to the greater. General Kutuzov, however, modestly remarked that the victory over Napoleon was really owed to Russia's best soldiers, General January and General February, who arrived early in 1812.

In December 1825 one indirect result of Napoleon's invasion was an abortive revolution led by officers returning from France convinced that their medieval society must change. When the Decembrist rising failed, the ringleaders were shot or imprisoned by the newly crowned Tsar Nicholas I, and the others exiled to Siberia, taking their wives and families with them. All the Decembrists achieved was the creation of a Ministry of State Domains that operated an administration down to the level of each group of villages, or *volost,* governed by a mayor elected by male householders. The laudable intentions were to introduce medical services and stockpiling of food in case of crop failure, to build schools and improve traditional methods of agriculture, but the programme foundered because the ministry's central and provincial staffs were as corrupt and inefficient as the rest of Russian bureaucracy.

The opposition to serfdom grew slowly, not so much from liberal thought as because it was apparent to the middle classes that this medieval institution was an obstacle to progress in a world where industrial development required a free labour force to operate the machines in factories if Russia was to catch up with its European neighbours. The serfs remained worse off than their remote ancestors, unable to marry or leave their estate without permission from their owners long after serfdom had ended in most European countries. For minor offences both men and women were viciously flogged with the *knout*. Nicholas I attempted a radical overhaul of the civil service, but since the provincial governors exercised authority through *ispravniki*, or magistrates who were elected by the local landowners, the abolition of serfdom was abandoned because it would have meant them losing a self-renewing unpaid labour force.

4

COLLISION IN
THE CRIMEA

The thirty-year reign of Nicholas I ended as Western ideas were penetrating Russian heads in the form of improved musket balls.

Why? In the Ottoman province of Palestine, the Church of the Nativity in Judean Bethlehem marked the site where the Roman Emperor Constantine's formidable mother St Helena had been persuaded that Christ was born. Russian Orthodox monks wanting to place a star on the roof of the church were opposed by Roman Catholic monks in a brawl that caused several deaths. As 'protector of Orthodox believers in the Ottoman Empire', Nicholas I alleged that the provincial Turkish authorities had deliberately incited the killings in Bethlehem. He therefore declared war on Turkey 'to protect the Orthodox monks from further violence'.

This was just his excuse for another round in the long struggle on the interface between the Russian and Ottoman empires. With Russia now an acknowledged European power, Nicholas wanted a suitably powerful navy. However, the White Sea Fleet based in Archangel could only put to sea when the Arctic ice permitted. The small Far Eastern Fleet, tasked with guarding the

Asiatic seaboard against Japanese and American incursions, was too remote from Europe to be of any use there. Deployment of the Baltic Fleet was dependent on whoever controlled the Danish straits, and the Black Sea Fleet could only emerge into the Mediterranean by permission of the Ottoman Empire, which controlled the Bosphorus Strait and Dardanelles.

That right was guaranteed by treaty, but Nicholas saw unfettered control of the straits as the first step to Russia becoming a world power with an ocean-going navy. Invoking his responsibility to the monks killed in Bethlehem, he moved troops into the Ottoman provinces of what is now Romania. France and Britain owed the Sublime Porte no favours but neither power wished to see the Russian Black Sea Fleet freely coming and going into the Mediterranean. In a volte-face worthy of George Orwell's *1984*, France's on-again, off-again hostilities with Turkey over Greek independence were called off and the new French monarch Napoleon III was granted by the Sublime Porte the status of 'protector of the holy places of Jerusalem'. England's motive was simpler: an abiding wariness of Russia's covetous eye on the Indian sub-continent.

Napoleon III having spent happy years of exile north of the English Channel while waiting to be called to the French throne, a military alliance against Russia seemed to the governments in Paris and London a good chance of impressing Austria – the great power of Europe – with the potential of a Franco-British alliance. Accordingly, on 23 September 1853, the Royal Navy was ordered to Constantinople. Its morale thus bolstered, the Turkish army under Omar Pasha attacked the Russian invaders on 4 October and won a victory at Oltenitza, the effect of which was more than cancelled out when Nicholas I's Black Sea Fleet destroyed a Turkish fleet shortly afterwards off Cape Sinop, 200 miles northeast of Ankara. On 3 January 1854 the tide of war swung the other way when French and British warships protecting Turkish transports in the Black Sea drove off attacking Russian vessels in an engagement which was the first occasion since the crusades when French and British forces fought on the same side.

Undeterred, on 20 March Russian troops marched south into what is modern Bulgaria. Seven days later, Britain and France formally declared war on Russia. The first Anglo-French troops reached Varna in Bulgaria on 30 May, landing in the middle of a cholera epidemic. Austria had massed 50,000 men under arms in Galicia and Transylvania to counter the Russian threat in the Danubian principalities. That the war did not escalate and set all Europe ablaze was largely due to a Prussian cavalry officer with an extraordinary talent for diplomacy. Edwin von Manteuffel was sent by King Frederik Wilhelm IV of Prussia to St Petersburg, where he persuaded Nicholas I to withdraw his troops from the Danubian principalities. Travelling immediately from there to Vienna, he next dissuaded Austria from joining the war against Russia. Instead of showing gratitude, Tsar Nicholas rejected the settlements proposed by France, England, Austria and Prussia at the peace conference in Vienna on 8 August 1854, but von Manteuffel at least had the satisfaction of knowing he had averted a major European war.

Despite the impossibility of *conquering* the country that had destroyed Napoleon's Grande Armée in 1812, Paris and London decided to bloody the nose of the Russian bear by using land forces to destroy Russia's Black Sea naval base at Sevastopol on the Crimean peninsula. Regrettably, the joint Anglo-French command was shared between a French general dying of tuberculosis and 67-year-old Lord Raglan, who had served as the Duke of Wellington's military secretary in the Peninsular War forty years before and absent-mindedly referred to the current enemy as 'those Frenchies'. The Turkish contingent in the coalition forces included levies from Egypt, Serbia, the Danubian principalities, Tunis and Tripoli. Gen Ismail Pasha's infamous *bashi-bazouks* were regarded as the least reliable of all the troops, more prone to pillage and rape than standing firm and obeying orders. Coalition cavalry included Polish mercenaries and Cossacks who lived in Ottoman territory.

On the battlefield as in the factory, there were lessons in technology the Russians had to learn. In 1849 Capt Claude-Etienne Minié made spherical musket balls obsolete by inventing smaller-calibre bullets with a conical tip, which had greater range and were more accurate. William Russell, the London *Times* correspondent in the Crimea, described how volleys of Minié balls clove 'like the hand of the Destroying Angel' through the disciplined ranks of Russian soldiery armed with outdated muskets and ammunition.

The pointless Charge of the Light Brigade at Balaclava was just one example of the confusion on both sides, witnessing which caused General Pierre Bosquet to comment, '*C'est magnifique, mais ce n'est pas la guerre. C'est de la folie.*' It's magnificent, yet it's not war, but madness.

Shortly before that battle, on 20 September 1854, the Russian commander of Sevastopol, Prince A.S. Menshikov, had 37,000 men in prepared positions at the River Alma to block the Allied advance. He also brought along thirty young ladies of the garrison for an alfresco lunch, at which they were hoping to view through telescopes the sight of the invaders being mown down by volleys of Russian musketry as they climbed out of the river valley beneath.

The ladies were hastily bundled off home when things got serious. After a series of skirmishes lasting all day, Menshikov decided to hasten after them. Suspecting a trap, the mutually distrustful Allied commanders did not pursue the enemy, which could have ended the campaign within days. Thus given time to strengthen Sevastopol's defences and scuttle a squadron of warships to block the harbour entrance, on 5 November Menchikov took the initiative, launching 40,000 men through dawn mists against the weaker end of the Allied siege line, held by 8,000 English troops, many of whom died in their tents before they were fully awake. As reported in the *Times*, for two hours the balance of advantage in the battle of Inkerman swung to and fro until in mid-morning a French corps of 3,000 men including cavalry attacked the Russians on the flank at the same time as a further 8,000 Russians attacked the main French positions. Not until after midday were the Russians driven off with casualties totalling 15,000 – against 2,600 English and 900 French dead and wounded.

French being the second language of the Russian officers, they mingled freely with their opponents during the numerous truces to recover the wounded and bury the dead, exchanging cigars and champagne while learning of another technical breakthrough: news of the war was reaching Paris and London within hours by telegraph via a submarine cable laid under the Black Sea especially for the purpose. The downside of the submarine telegraph cable was that it also placed the French commander at the mercy of his monarch, who had grown a military moustache to prove that he was a better strategist than any mere general.

The sheltered south-east coast of the Crimea is the Russians' winter Riviera, but the Allied soldiers were mostly encamped on the bleak heights above Sevastopol, where Menshikov's ally General Winter moved to the attack soon after Balaklava. On 14 November a violent storm flooded the shallow Allied trenches, blowing away many of the twelve-man bell tents and leaving thousands of men with no shelter at all. All firewood for miles around being requisitioned for earthworks, men wearing summer uniforms died from exposure long before winter great-coats were issued in December.

Food shortages were made worse by private contractors supplying bad meat and short measures. Ammunition was also scarce, with many transports driven aground after being refused permission to enter harbour because Raglan gave priority to moorings for his richer officers' private yachts. Ships arrived at Cossack Bay without prior notice and lacking manifests; others docked at Constantinople and were sent back to Europe without being unloaded. In Cossack Bay the quayside was covered with rotting food, soaked boxes of ammunition and powder barrels, with the water of the harbour between the steam- and sail-powered transport ships covered by a carpet of refuse and excrement. There was a lack of forage for the pack animals that might have moved supplies up to the plateau, where starving cavalry remounts ate each other's manes and tails in desperation. Only late in January 1855 was the situation rectified after British civilian navvies constructed a narrow-gauge railway up to the gale-swept plateau.

News of this chaos eventually reached London in the highly critical despatches of William Russell. By February the ground-swell of public criticism toppled the government, with Lord Palmerston becoming Prime Minister and Lord Panmure the new secretary for war. This resulted in some improvement in the organization and administration of the British Army, and as spring approached the chaos slowly cleared. At Üsküdar on the Bosphorus the death rate before Florence Nightingale's arrival had been 44 per cent; in six months, she reduced it to 2.2 per cent by imposing elementary nursing practices. On the Crimean peninsula, a new-style medical corps was set up to provide hospital services before the long sea-crossing, but only after hundreds of thousands had died unnecessarily. On the Russian side, the wounded continued to die as before.

Another casualty of the winter was Nicholas I, who died of pneumonia on 3 February and was succeeded by his son Alexander II. Aged 36 and educated by a Swiss republican tutor, the new Tsar was known to be liberal and pro-European in comparison with his overbearing father.

Although the siege lines were not continuous and fast-riding couriers passed in and out of Sevastopol, Alexander did not sue for peace. In February and March violent sorties from the garrison dented but did not destroy the Allied siege lines, strengthened by the arrival of 13,500 Swiss, Germans and Poles and a contingent from Piedmont-Sardinia. On 9 April the Allies began their second great bombardment of Sevastopol: 520 guns poured 165,000 rounds into the complex of defences and were answered by 998 Russian guns firing 90,000 rounds in reply. The bombardments thundered on for ten days, directly causing 6,131 casualties to the defenders, 1,587 to the French and 263 in the much-reduced British line. Except to the dead and wounded, it made little difference because each night the Russians repaired that day's damage to the defences, mainly of wicker baskets filled with earth.

By the spring, Lord Raglan had only 11,000 men fit to man the trenches. The French were down to 90,000, plus 50,000 Turks – all facing 100,000 Russians. Having anticipated that the campaign would be 'over by Christmas', Raglan now had to reduce rations so close to starvation level that the French took over responsibility for supplying their British allies.

Hoping that an Allied success would force Alexander to sue for peace, Napoleon III ordered a major French attack for 1 May, targeting an important Russian bastion from which heavy mortar fire was damaging the French lines. Repeated onslaughts had little effect. On 3 May another truce was called to bury the dead, decomposing in the hot sunshine, after which the Russians began to build a new fortification on high ground overlooking the French lines. Resenting Napoleon III's continual interference by telegraph, the French commander resigned, leaving his successor to take the obvious step of 'accidentally' cutting the telegraph cable. The siege dragged on, with burying the dead made more even repugnant as bodies swollen by the heat came apart at the joints.

At the end of July, Alexander sacked Menshikov and replaced him with Prince Gorchakov, whose first act was to launch an attack on 16 August with four infantry divisions and two artillery brigades across the Chornaya River. When this failed to achieve a breakthrough, Gorchakov wisely sent a despatch to St Petersburg stating that he saw no point in prolonging the defence. On 8 September, after a three-day Allied barrage by 800 cannon, a critical strongpoint was taken and held by the French, after which Gorchakov had the remaining forts blown up, scuttled every ship in harbour to render them useless to the Allies, and evacuated Sevastopol.

The peace treaty was not ratified until 2 March 1856, after a second winter spent by the surviving Allied soldiers rebuilding some of the destroyed fortifications as shelter against the weather. With more casualties from cholera, dysentery, typhus and frostbite than from cold steel, shrapnel and bullets, the Crimean War cost 256,000 Russian lives – half of them from disease and exposure – and 252,600 Allied soldiers' lives, of which only 70,000 were in combat.

5

LIES, SPIES AND BLOOD IN THE STREETS

nly eight years after the world's first steam-hauled passenger rail service opened between Manchester and Liverpool, a Russian railway track was laid in 1838. Running just 18 miles between St Petersburg and the royal 'palace-village' of Tsarskoye Selo, it was a toy for Tsar Nicholas I, intended for the conveyance from the city of noble guests invited to banquets and balls when he was in residence there. In fairness to Nicholas, he did also set up the Department of Railways, under which the cities of St Petersburg and Moscow were linked by rail four years later, thanks to the ill-starred Major Whistler. However, by 1850 Britain had an impressive 5,000 miles of line owned by a dozen major companies and ninety smaller ones, while the vast Russian empire had less than 660 miles of permanent way, due to three impediments: the need to entice foreign engineers and raise foreign capital, and the long distances involved, compared with the relatively short runs between British cities.

In 1848 Karl Marx and Friedrich Engels – two of a number of revolutionary philosophers criticising capitalism at the time – joined forces to publish a pamphlet entitled *Manifest der Kommunistischen Partei*. This manifesto purported to present a scientific interpretation of European history from feudalism to capitalism in terms of the class struggle, and prophesied that capitalism would metamorphose into socialism and then communism via the abolition of private property and such modern ideas as graduated income tax, universal free education and the abolition of child labour. Opening dramatically with the words, 'A spectre is haunting Europe – the spectre of communism,' it ended with two of the slogans that would be heard a million times in Russia post-1917. One was, *The workers have nothing to lose but their chains.* If 'workers' were replaced by 'serfs,' that was true enough in Russia. The other slogan was, *Workers of all countries, unite.*

With memories of the Decembrist rebellion still fresh, this slim pamphlet would have sent shivers down the spines of Russia's rulers – except for one thing. Marx had worked out 'scientifically' that the Communist Revolution would take place in a capitalist society, like the Germany with which he was familiar, or in France, Italy or Austria, all simmering with revolutionary movements at the time.

Although many Russians realised that continuing industrialisation on the Western model would destroy the very structure of their society, Nicholas I was more concerned that repeated serf rebellions would eventually destroy Russia from within. Yet when his son Alexander II issued the Edict of Emancipation in 1861, most of the 19 million serfs on state estates and 22 million on private estates exchanged one kind of misery for another. While a few borrowed money and became self-made men and women, many were turned away from the only homes they had to scratch a living in the urban slums. The compensation paid to their former owners for loss of free labour was funded by an emancipation tax on the ex-serfs, payable over forty-nine years, but many had no means of paying it, and the allotments they were given on which to grow their food were often smaller than the land of which they had had the use before.

Anton Chekhov's play *Vishnyovy Sad – The Cherry Orchard –* although not premiered until 1904 at the Moscow Arts Theatre, seizes well the issues of nineteenth-century Russia in which its author grew up. In short, the Ranevskii family forfeits its estate because Madame Ranevskaya cannot bring herself to sell off her famous cherry orchard, which would enable the mortgage on the rest of the estate to be repaid and life to continue. Like many other masterpieces, the play interweaves the author's personal experiences with the Zeitgeist: the landowning classes frozen in a self-destructive wallow of regret that their traditional way of life is no longer possible after the Emancipation. The indecisive family, the bewildered ex-serf, the ex-peasant turned self-made entrepreneur – they are all there. The play ends to the sound of Madame Ranevskaya's beloved trees being chopped down anyway, but the off-stage sound effect might as well have been the distant whistle of a train, for nothing better epitomised the changing world depicted by Chekhov.

One thing that did not change in Russia was the expansion-ist imperative: conquests included the khanates of Bokhara, Kokand and Khiva in Central Asia. In the spring of 1876 the Bulgarians rebelled against their Ottoman masters. Sent to repress the rebellion, 10,000 *bashi-bazouks* did so with rape and massacre – after which, in a gesture of Pan-Slav solidarity, Serbia and Montenegro declared war on Turkey and Alexander seized the excuse to attack the Ottoman Empire on 21 April 1877. Russian troops and their Romanian allies pushed deep into Turkish territory, taking Batumi, Kars and Trebizond on the south-eastern corner of the Black Sea. They also captured Edirne, just over 100 miles from Constantinople, thus dangerously close to the Bosphorus and Dardanelles in London's view. However, the Treaty of San Stefano, which recognised these gains, was overturned by the Congress of Berlin in June-July 1878, at which Russia was compelled to give up much of the conquered terri-tory while Austro-Hungary grabbed Bosnia and Herzegovina in the Balkans and Britain propped up the ailing Ottoman Empire to ensure that the Russian fleet based in Sevastopol could not freely access the Adriatic and Mediterranean.

One effect of prosperous Russian bourgeois families sending sons and daughters to study in Europe was the growth of a layer of society for which was invented the neologism 'intelligentsia' – one of the few Russian words to achieve universal currency. These young people returned with such dangerous ideas that the government banned the teaching of philosophy in Moscow

University. Too late. It seemed that every intellectual already had his or her pet ideology. The Nihilists – a term popularised by Ivan Turgenev in his novel *Otsy i Dyeti* – fathers and sons – switched from anarchy to a mystical belief that the peasants who tilled the soil possessed some earthy wisdom which could solve all Russia's problems. Most Nihilists thus re-oriented themselves as Narodniki from *narod*, meaning 'people'.

The 'strange superstition' acquired a new potency through a movement called Slavophilism, whose adherents wished to free Orthodox Slavs from Muslim-Turkish domination, yet regarded as traitors the Catholic Poles, Czechs, Slovaks and Croats – as well as the Orthodox Ukrainians, who openly yearned for independence from their Russian masters. The cult of Slavophilism in turn developed after the humiliation of the Crimean defeat into Pan-Slavism, whose followers held that all the 150 million Slavs in Europe and Asia were bound by some mystical racial bond which transcended all their differences and would, once they were united under the guidance of Mother Russia, lead them to their true destiny among the nations of the world. The idea fell flat among most non-Russian Slavs, who decided that they preferred Austrian, Hungarian and even Turkish overlords, compared with conditions in Russian-occupied Poland and Ukraine.

There were in the last quarters of the nineteenth century many political philosophies in Russia, whose adherents split into schisms and squabbled endlessly with each other. The most extreme included the Populists, who endorsed terror as an instrument of change. In 1879 their attempted assassination of Alexander II failed, as did the following five attempts. To deal with the mushrooming anti-government movements, interior minister Loris Melkov set up a secret police force of undercover operators and agents provocateurs who joined revolutionary groups to betray them from within – which did not prevent Alexander II being murdered in 1881 after a bomb thrown at his armoured carriage wounded several members of his mounted bodyguard. Courageously but imprudently, the Tsar stepped down to offer sympathy to the wounded, permitting a suicide bomber to blow up both himself and the Tsar with a back-up bomb.

The succession passed to the 36-year-old crown prince, whose glittering coronation ceremony at St Petersburg on 14 March 1881 hailed him as 'Alexander III, Emperor of all the Russias, King of Poland and Grand Duke of Finland.'

Continuing internal unrest saw the secret police legitimised as *Otdeleniye po Okhraneniyu Obshchestvennoi Bezopasnosti i Poryadka,* or the Department for Defence of Public Security and Order. Under the acronym of Okhranka or Okhrana, this forerunner of the KGB was tasked with infiltrating and subverting trade unions, political parties and discussion groups – and generally spying on the whole population, for Alexander III was intent on restoring the old order. Schools and universities excluded the lower classes; the judiciary was brought back under central control; Russian was imposed as the sole official language throughout the Empire; and the Catholic religion was disadvantaged vis-à-vis the Orthodox Church. Jews, discriminated against since Catherine the Great, found themselves confined under the 'Temporary Laws' to the Pale of Settlement, with some exceptions: certain merchants and artisans, those with higher education, and those who had completed their military service could settle anywhere except in Finland; and unmarried Jewesses might live in St Petersburg, providing they were teachers or registered prostitutes.

Alexander's finance minister was the man of the moment. Employing the brightest and best Russians, Poles, Ukrainians and Jews, Count Sergei Witte pushed through a programme of modernisation that included a State Bank to facilitate capital loans to industry, savings banks, joint-stock company law, convertibility of the rouble and promotion of technical education. He also astutely floated huge loans in Western Europe to finance Russian industrialization and railway construction. His predecessor Count Kankrin had declared that a line to connect the Baltic Sea with the Pacific Ocean would be technically and financially impossible for several centuries to come,[1] but Witte saw a trans-Siberian line as the best means to stimulate the economy of the eastern provinces, make Russia the interface between Europe and the Far East, and unite the otherwise unmanageably vast Empire, spread across eleven time zones and covering a sixth of the planet's land-mass.

Starting in 1891, in the teeth of yet another famine that swept across the empire, construction of the line began. As Hitler was to find half a century later in 1941, the railway gauge chosen in Russia was not Robert Stephenson's standard 4ft 8½in gauge adopted in most European countries.[2] American railways not being standardised at the time, Witte agreed that Major Whistler should employ a non-European 5ft gauge, offering marginally improved passenger- and freight-carrying potential in wider carriages and also complicating the logistics of any invader.

In 1891, Alexander III also made a move that had never been attempted by any predecessor: alliance with a Western European power. After losing the war with Prussia 1870–1, France was increasingly nervous of German unification under Bismarck and keen to have a powerful ally on the other side of Germany who would force the Germans to fight on two fronts, should they invade again. The Franco-Russian Entente for mutual assistance in case of aggression by the common enemy was signed in 1894.[3]

France was also the biggest single source of foreign capital needed by Witte. With this secured, the construction of *Transsibirskaya Magistral'* – the Trans-Siberian Mainline – was by any standards both technically and administratively a huge challenge, with numerous stretches being tackled simultaneously under Witte's overall control. In March 1894, shortly before personally opening the Far East segment of the Trans-Siberian in Vladivostok, Alexander III's ill-fated son, the future Tsar Nicholas II, became indirectly one of the Trans-Siberian's first casualties. While visiting Japan on a round-the-world goodwill tour, he narrowly missed death at the hands of a Japanese policeman who hated the idea of the new railway transporting thousands of Russian troops to the Pacific seaboard to threaten his homeland. After recuperating aboard one of the Russian ships in Kobe harbour from a sabre cut to his face, the crown prince travelled on towards his ghastly destiny, succeeding his father as emperor later that year.

The year 1894 also saw the start of the Sino-Japanese war, which ended in 1895 with Japan the clear victor. Under the Treaty of Shimonoseki, China recognised the independence of Korea – coveted by Japan for its mineral resources and strategic location

– and gave away Taiwan, the Pescadores Islands and the Liaotung Peninsula in southern Manchuria, plus a huge indemnity and certain trading privileges on Chinese territory. Russian fears of this Japanese expansion on the Asian mainland had support from both France and Germany, who joined forces in what was called the 'triple intervention', which obliged Japan to hand back the Liaotung Peninsula in return for an additional indemnity from China.

The expansionist imperative now prompted Nicholas II to push into the power vacuum thus created by concluding treaties with China that included Russian occupation of the peninsula and the right to build a branch line connecting the port of Lu-shün on its southern tip, to Harbin and the Trans-Siberian Mainline. The deep-water harbour of Lu-shün, ice-free throughout the year, was swiftly converted into the heavily fortified naval base of Port Arthur, and a civilian port established nearby at Darien (now Ta-lien).

News of this did not go down well in Tokyo – or London. At the height of the 'Great Game' touched on by Rudyard Kipling in his novel *Kim,* Russian agents were inciting unrest among the tribes on the North-West Frontier as a way of weakening the British Raj in the Indian sub-continent. Queen Victoria's government thus had no intention of helping Russia anywhere – never mind that the Tsarina was one of her many granddaughters. In 1902, therefore, Britain signed a treaty with Japan, under which each side agreed to respect the other's interests in China and Korea. Since the crumbling Manchu dynasty in China was no threat to anyone, this was a warning shot against Russian expansionism in the Far East.[4]

After ten years' construction work, by 1901 only the difficult topography around Lake Baikal was holding back completion of the Trans-Siberian. There, interim services were provided by train ferries across the lake in summer and a temporary track laid on the ice in winter. On 18 September 1904 the circum-Baikal section of permanent way was also in normal service, making it possible for the first time to travel from the Baltic to the Pacific in a week, which Nicholas II's government hailed as a great advance for the development of the northern Asian landmass with its immense untapped mineral resources.

Ever since 1860, when a military/administrative base was founded on the Pacific coast and dubbed Vladivostok –

The Russian Empire of Nicholas II.

meaning Lord of the East – Tokyo had feared this eventuality and decided in February 1904 that it was time for a pre-emptive attack before the Tsar's Far Eastern forces could rapidly be reinforced from European Russia over the new railway link. The Russo-Japanese War began on 8 February with a surprise torpedo attack by the Japanese battle fleet on the Russian naval squadron at Port Arthur. This was followed up by the sinking of blockships loaded with cement on 27 March to prevent use of the harbour, plus a naval blockade. In the same month, a Japanese army landed in Korea and quickly overran the peninsula. In May, a second Japanese army landed on the Liaotung Peninsula, cutting off the Port Arthur garrison from reinforcement by the main body of Russian forces in Manchuria and then pushing northward to win pitched battles at Fu-hsien and Liao-yang before the Russians finally fell back on Mukden (now Shen-yang).

In October 1904, strengthened by reinforcements brought in along the Trans-Siberian, the Russians went over to the offensive. On the other side of the world, Admiral Zinovi Rozhdestvensky set out with the Russian Baltic Fleet from the Latvian port of Liepaja to relieve the blockade of Port Arthur. On the way, he nearly provoked war with Great Britain by attacking British trawlers fishing on the Dogger Bank in the North Sea after mistaking them for Japanese torpedo boats! Compensation was paid to the families and a memorial to the British civilian casualties can still be seen in their home port of Hull.

On the Liaotung Peninsula, the Japanese siege of Port Arthur continued, although several assaults on the base had failed at a cost of 58,000 Japanese lives, including both sons of the commanding general. On 2 January 1905, after the last sea-worthy ship in harbour was scuttled, Port Arthur's commander surrendered in an act of gross incompetence or corruption despite having 10,000 combat-worthy men and three months' food and ammunition still in hand.

Official Western observers were present with both belligerents. Major Marcel Cheminon, who spent the whole war as one of the French observers with the Russian army, returned to Paris with maps and detailed accounts of all the major battles.[5] We also have the observations of the official British Mission to the Japanese armies and of General Sir Ian Hamilton, who went out at his own expense and left an interesting 'scrapbook' of personal experiences during the war. The Westerners present observed that, while both the Japanese and Russian soldiery were largely conscripted peasants, the Japanese, trained by German instructors, were more courageous, better drilled and more disciplined than their opponents. General Hamilton, for one, was shocked by Commanding General A.N. Kuropatkin's profligate waste of his soldiers' lives, and by the way his officers exposed themselves from bravado, thus revealing their men's positions to Japanese artillery observers.

War reporting had moved on since the submarine telegraph bringing updates on the Crimean War back to London and Paris. To cover the Russo-Japanese War, the London *Times* had several correspondents in the theatre, one of whom chartered a merchant ship to cruise the Yellow Sea transmitting despatches from an onboard transmitter to a relay station in the British treaty territory of Weihawei on the Chinese mainland for onward transmission to London. By this roundabout route, news of the colossal loss of life and the disastrous generalship on the Russian side fuelled protests in St Petersburg, where troops fired on demonstrating workers on Bloody Sunday, 22 January, heralding the start of the 1905 Revolution.

Commenting on the event, British Ambassador Charles Hardinge confirmed that the victims were harmless unarmed peasants and workers marching to the Winter Palace to present a petition to the Tsar. Like a powder train, demonstrations spread throughout Russian-occupied Poland, Finland, the Baltic states and Georgia, where national independence movements took advantage of the disorder. In retaliation, the ultra-reactionary Black Hundreds attacked socialists and Jews, but support for the revolt included military units along the Trans-Siberian. In Tokyo, too, there was a growing anti-war movement, with the chief of staff proposing that the conflict, which had nearly bankrupted Japan, be brought to a speedy end, after which the cabinet debated peace terms – and funded the purchase of weapons for the revolutionaries in Russia. Revolution, however, was for export only: when the editor of *Heimin Shimbun* newspaper published the Communist Manifesto, he was thrown into jail.

The final land battle of the Russo-Japanese War was fought at Mukden at the end of February between Russian armies totalling 330,000 men and Japanese forces totalling 270,000. The Russians lost 89,000 men against 71,000 Japanese dead, which indicates that the Japanese generals were more careful of human life than their European opposite numbers. Russian care for the wounded not having improved since the Crimean War, the chief medical officer of the Second Russian Army committed suicide in despair. After several days of conflict, Kuropatkin disengaged and withdrew northward in a blinding dust storm, leaving Mukden to the Japanese. The focus of attention now moved to the naval confrontation that could not be long in coming.

On 14 April Rozhdestvensky's Baltic Fleet anchored in Vietnam's Cam Ranh Bay to regroup. On 14 May he belatedly set course for the surviving Russian naval base at Vladivostok, Port Arthur having already surrendered. Admiral Togo Heihachiro's more modern, better-armed warships were waiting in ambush in the Tsushima Strait between Japan and Korea. In the long and bloody battle of Tsushima 27–29 May the Russian fleet lost over 200,000 tons of shipping, against Heihachiro's losses of 300 tons. Casualties were similarly disparate, with 4,830 Russian sailors killed and 6,000 taken prisoner, including the admiral, while Japanese casualties totalled less than 200. When the news reached St Petersburg, there was a public outcry and bitter criticism of the government, followed by numerous mutinies among returning survivors of the Far East campaign – most famously when the crew of a battleship in Odessa harbour protested about their maggot-infested food. Ordered to shoot the mutineers, the firing squad refused, later providing Soviet filmmaker Sergei Eisenstein with inspiration for the best scene in his 1925 epic *Battleship Potemkin.*

The Japanese victories at Mukden and Tsushima forced the Russian government to the peace table in the ignominious position of being the first major European power to be vanquished by an Asiatic enemy.[6] The war was also the first modern one, with railway communications crucial, cavalry entirely irrelevant and decisive naval battles fought between steam-driven steel warships. The huge casualty figures for no gain in the war against Japan were a significant factor in weakening the Russian forces' will to fight in the First World War that culminated in the collapse of the eastern front in 1917.

The torpedo attack on the Russian warships in harbour at Port Arthur before any declaration of war should also have been a clear warning to the US Navy twenty-four years later. Among the junior officers wounded at Tsushima was Ensign Isoroku Takano who, under his adopted name of Yamamoto, was commander-in-chief of the combined Japanese fleet in 1941 and the architect of the surprise attack on Pearl Harbor.

At the peace conference held in Portsmouth, New Hampshire, between 9 August and 5 September 1905, US President Theodore Roosevelt acted as mediator. Despite Count Witte's negotiating skills, the Treaty of Portsmouth gave Japan everything it wanted: control of the Liaotung Peninsula and Port Arthur, the South Manchurian railroad leading to the port – and also half of Sakhalin Island. Russia agreed to evacuate southern Manchuria, to be handed back to China, and Japan's right to occupy Korea was recognized.

Humiliated, the Tsar and his ministers turned their attention to the internal problems that threatened to shake the structure of Russian society to the core. In the streets of Moscow and other cities, red flags were everywhere and uniformed police nowhere to be seen. Six weeks after the treaty, industrial action by railway workers turned into a general strike that rapidly spread to most major cities. In Ivanovo, north-east of Moscow, the first *soviet* or workers' council was formed, followed by others in St Petersburg, Moscow, Odessa, and other cities. Originally set up to direct the strike, these committees swiftly took on the character of an alternative administration. On 30 October Nicholas II issued the October Manifesto, which appeared to end the absolute powers of the monarchy and promised the establishment of a *Gosudarstvennaya Duma*, or elected state parliament.

These concessions did not meet the demands of the radical revolutionaries, nor would the liberal opposition consent to participate in a hastily formed new government. The more moderate, or hungry, workers saw the October Manifesto as a victory and returned to work. Feeling its way, the government arrested the leaders of the St Petersburg *soviet*, including Leon Trotsky. In Moscow a new general strike was called, with barricades and fighting in the streets. Military units were despatched to Poland and Georgia, where nationalist revolts were suppressed with bloodshed, but in the east the Tsarist government did not regain complete control of the Trans-Siberian and of rebellious army units until the beginning of 1906.

In Estonia and Latvia a wave of unrest under the banner of independence from Russia brought looting and burning of country properties that was eventually stamped out by the occupation troops, who executed ringleaders and exiled thousands of rank-and-file independence fighters to Siberia. The Lithuanians' resistance to their Russian overlords was more measured, with a congress of 2,000 from all political factions in Vilnius passing a resolution demanding the establishment of an autonomous state.

On 23 April 1906 the Fundamental Laws were promulgated, making the Duma the lower of two houses of parliament, the other being the Council of Ministers. The Tsar remained supreme commander of the armed forces, alone responsible for declaring war and able to dismiss any minister he chose. He – or she in the event of female succession – retained the right to rule by decree when the Duma was not in session.[7] Even when it was, the Duma had only limited control over the budget and none at all over the executive branch of government. In addition, the civil rights and suffrage granted by the Fundamental Laws were far more limited than those promised by the October Manifesto.

Nicholas II can have had no knowledge of physics. His empire was a powder keg that needed only a spark – *iskra* in Russian – to explode. *Iskra* already existed in the form of the Marxist schism uneasily headed by 47-year-old Vladimir I. Ulyanov, better known as Lenin, and was the title of its small-circulation revolutionary newspaper. Instead of lessening the pressure on the turmoil of volatile social elements to dissipate the force of the eventual explosion, Tsar Nicholas applied more repression, tamping the unrest down, so that when the explosion came, it would shatter the entire infrastructure of Russian society.

6

DEATH IN SARAJEVO, MONEY IN THE BANK

The date is 28 June 1914. The scene is familiar from television documentaries and cinema reconstructions: Archduke Franz Ferdinand, heir presumptive to the throne of the immense and powerful Austro-Hungarian Empire, is riding in all the finery of his comic opera uniform with his consort, Sophie von Hohenberg, in an open car through the streets of Sarajevo – the administrative capital of the Austro-Hungarian province of Bosnia-Herzegovina. A young Serb terrorist named Nedjelko Čabrinović throws a bomb at the cortège. It explodes beneath the vehicle following Franz Ferdinand's, but 19-year-old Gavrilo Princip launches a second attack as Franz Ferdinand and Sophie are being driven to hospital to visit an officer wounded by the bomb. At 11.15 a.m. they are both shot dead by Princip.[1]

Behind the grainy, flickering, black-and-white images of two deaths that led to millions more lay the 'strange superstition' in the guise of the Pan-Slav liberation movement. Col Dragutin Dimitrijević, head of military intelligence in neighbouring Serbia, was also the undercover head of the terrorist organisation *Ujedinjenje ili Smrt* – meaning Union or Death[2] – to which Čabrinović and Princip belonged. Dimitrijević despatched his youthful assassination team to kill Franz Ferdinand during the royal visit to Sarajevo in the belief that terror was the instrument to 'liberate' the Slav subjects of the Austro-Hungarian Empire. In fairness to Serbia, when its prime minister heard of Dimitrijević's plot, he did try to warn the Austrian government, but in language so diplomatic that his message was unclear in Vienna.

Never has ambiguity caused greater loss of life. Knowing that the assassination had been planned in Belgrade, the Austro-Hungarian foreign minister drafted an ultimatum to Serbia, relying on German Foreign Ministry assurances that it would prevent Russia from stepping in to protect 'poor little Serbia'. The possibility of international escalation was clearly considered because, although the terms of Vienna's ultimatum were approved internally on 19 July, it was not delivered in Belgrade until the evening of 23 July when the French president and prime minister were travelling home from a state visit to Russia and thus in no position to concert any immediate reaction with the Tsar's government in St Petersburg under the Triple Entente between Britain, France and Russia.[3]

On 24 July, Russia announced its support for Serbia, which replied to the ultimatum the following day, accepting most of the conditions but protesting against demands for the dismissal of the guilty officials and for Austro-Hungarian representatives to investigate hostile organisations in Serbia. Although Serbia did offer to submit these two issues to international arbitration, in the absence of unconditional acceptance Austro-Hungary promptly severed diplomatic relations and ordered a partial mobilisation.

Returning from a Baltic cruise on his royal yacht, Queen Victoria's grandson Kaiser Wilhelm II learned of the situation with no great alarm. There was a treaty of mutual support between Germany and Austro-Hungary dating from 1879, under which each partner would come to the other's aid in the event it was attacked by Russia. However, since Austro-Hungary had not been attacked, the Kaiser instructed his foreign office to inform Vienna that the assassination merited temporary occupation of the Serbian capital Belgrade, but not a full-blown war. Unfortunately, his Acting Foreign Secretary Arthur Zimmermann had already encouraged Emperor Franz Joseph in Vienna to avenge the death of his son and heir by declaring war on Serbia – which was done on 28 July, with Austro-Hungarian artillery bombarding Belgrade the very next day.

In a gesture of Pan-Slav solidarity, Nicholas II then ordered partial mobilization against Austro-Hungary. On 30 July, the order was changed to a general mobilisation after Austro-Hungary mobilised forces on its frontier with Russia. Throughout the Balkan wars of 1912 and 1913, Britain and France had restrained Russia from getting involved and Germany had similarly restrained Austro-Hungary. The Kaiser had been hoping to keep this new dispute on the level of a local Balkan conflict, but now found himself trapped by the mutual defence treaty with Vienna into issuing a 24-hour ultimatum on 31 July requiring the Russians to halt their mobilisation. He also sent an 18-hour ultimatum to the Quai d'Orsay in Paris, requiring an undertaking that France would remain neutral in the event of war between Russia and Germany.

Neither ultimatum evoking any reply within the time limits, on 1 August Germany ordered general mobilization and declared war against Russia, prompting France to also order a general mobilisation. On the following day, German troops entered Luxembourg and Berlin demanded the right for its troops to cross neutral Belgium in order to attack France. On 3 August Germany declared war against France. That night German forces entered Belgium, to whose defence Britain was committed. There was a flurry of diplomatic moves attempting to prevent the escalation but by12 August – less than seven weeks after the assassination in Sarajevo – Europe was divided into two camps. Eventually the Entente, consisting of Britain, Belgium, France, Italy, Japan, Russia, Serbia and Montenegro, was at war with the Central Powers bloc composed of the German and Austro-Hungarian empires, plus Russia's old enemy, the Ottoman Empire.

Inside Russia, considerable privation was caused by the German navy blockading the Baltic Sea and German and Turkish warships preventing imports of war materiel and food via the Black Sea. On both sides of the battle lines, socialist parties supported their governments' war efforts despite having agreed at pre-war international meetings to exploit the opportunity of an imperialist war to overthrow those governments. From his safe exile in Switzerland, Lenin called for socialists to transform the imperialist war into civil wars in their countries, arguing that the true enemy of the worker was not the worker in the opposite trench but the capitalist at home. Workers and soldiers alike, he proclaimed, should turn their weapons on their officers and rulers, to seize the chance of destroying the system that was plunging them into the greatest carnage the world had seen.

British Consul Robert Bruce Lockhart met Lenin several times in Moscow and described him:

> There was nothing in his personal appearance to suggest the super-man. Short of stature, rather plump, with short thick neck, broad shoulders, round red face, high intellectual fore-head, nose slightly turned up, brownish moustache and short stubbly beard, he looked at the first glance more like a provincial grocer than a leader of men.[4]

Lenin's rival Lev Davidovich Bronshtein[5] concealed his Jewish origins beneath the Russian-sounding name Leon Trotsky. He too had grown up in middle-class comfort. When commissar for foreign affairs after the revolution, it was he who signed Bruce Lockhart's travel passes.

Bruce Lockhart described Trotsky as having:

> … a wonderfully quick mind and a rich, deep voice. With his broad chest, his huge forehead, surmounted by great masses of black waving hair, his strong, fierce eyes and his heavy pro-truding lips, he is the very incarnation of the revolutionary. He strikes me as a man who would willingly die for Russia, provided there was a big enough audience to see him do it. He is neat about his dress. He wore a clean soft collar and his nails were carefully manicured.[6]

In step with many Russian social democrats, Trotsky refused to support the war effort of the Tsarist regime. With incontrovertible logic, he added, 'A bayonet is a weapon with a worker at both ends.'

СОВѢТЪ НАРОДНЫХЪ
Комиссаровъ.

Петроградъ.
27 - еревремя 1918 г.
№ 564.

Прошу всѣ Организаціи, Совѣты и Комиссаров

вокзалов оказывать всяческое содѣйствіе членам

Англійской Миссіи госп. Р.Б. ЛОКАРТУ, В.Л.ГИК-

СУ и Д. ГАРСТИНУ.

Комиссар по иностранным Дѣлам

За Секретаря

Lockhart's travel pass signed 'L Trotsky'. The handwritten note orders officials not to steal Lockhart's food!

For two and a half years the static killing match in the trenches of the western front consumed men and spewed out corpses. The German general staff originally intended rapidly crushing France with the famous Schlieffen Plan[7] and then rushing battle-hardened divisions eastwards across Germany's excellent internal rail network to invade the vulnerable tongue of Russian-occupied Poland, while Austro-Hungary launched an offensive into Russian-occupied Poland from the south-west.

The Russian general staff wanted to concentrate all imme-diately available forces against Austria, merely containing the German forces facing it until its own comparatively lethargic mobilisation was complete. However, the French government desperately needed to divert German divisions from the drive on Paris and persuaded the Russians to launch a diversionary pincer movement against East Prussia with the Vilna Army attacking in the east and the Warsaw Army from the south. The Russian com-manders ought to have learned some lessons from their defeat in the Russo-Japanese War, but made the same mistakes. Although all sides were intercepting and/or jamming each other's diplo-matic radio traffic, Russian military radio communications were transmitted uncoded, and were easily intercepted by front-line German wireless intelligence units, which were so efficient that Marshal Joffre's order of the day for the Battle of the Marne in September 1914 was intercepted and read by the German high command before it had reached the French front line.[8]

Worse, between the two prongs of the Russian attack, there was no radio link and no coordination, because the two army commanders detested each other. The result was a resounding defeat for Russia at the Battle of Tannenberg 26-30 August, where Russian losses were 92,000 men taken prisoner and 30,000 casualties. Two weeks later, their losses totalled 250,000 men. The terrible casualty rate continued for the next two and a half years until 1.3 million Russians had died in combat or from wounds, with 3.9 million taken prisoner.

In the hope of swiftly bringing the war in the east to an end, so that all their forces could be concentrated on the western front, the Central Powers were exploring the possibilities of a deniable 'dirty trick' operation to foment industrial unrest in Russia and mutinies in the Russian armies. On 7 August 1914 Lenin had been arrested in Cracow by the Austro-Hungarian authorities as a suspected spy, but was released two weeks later when they realised that his anti-Tsarist activities could provide the Central Powers with what was later called a fifth column, *if they could get him back to Russia.*

There were at the time a bewildering number of secret agents rushing across Europe on trains under various names and alibis, claiming to represent every faction in the political spectrum. Most have disappeared from history, but one who has not was a Russian expatriate theatrical impresario and arms dealer using the names of 'Dr Helphand' and 'Alexander Parvus,' who had made a fortune in the Balkan wars.[9] At the beginning of March 1915, Zimmermann was requesting from the Imperial Treasury a subsidy to the Bolsheviks of 2 million marks, as negotiated by Helphand-Parvus. In July, Zimmermann's boss Gottlieb von Jagow upped this budget to 5 million marks.

On 30 September a murky Estonian secret agent called Kesküla, aka A. Stein, revealed the conditions under which Lenin would be prepared to sign a peace treaty with the Central Powers in the event of a revolution in Russia bringing the Bolsheviks to power. Two points merit consideration here. Point 4 proposed full autonomy for all nationalities. Point 7 was a plan for Russian troops to be moved after the ceasefire from the eastern front into British India,[10] which would oblige Britain to withdraw troops from the western front for the defence of the Raj. Whether that was intended as a replay of the Great Game Tsarist agents had been playing for decades, or was simply included in the programme as bait to loosen the German purse-strings, is unclear. Lenin was reported as saying at this time that he had no idea what to do after taking power because the important thing was to seize power and work out what to do with it later. If true, it was a rather disingenuous statement for a man who had spent his entire adult life scheming for this moment.

A number of financially important German individuals like millionaire industrialist Hugo Stinnes and banker Max Warburg also held talks with Russian agents and intermediaries. Stinnes reportedly offered 2 million roubles to subsidise anti-war propaganda in Russia while Warburg also allocated substantial funds for 'publishing activities' there.'[11] The Bolsheviks needed generous subsidies because, although their name was a *claim* to be the majority party – *bol'she* meaning 'bigger' – they were a minority even in the revolutionary councils and needed to bombard the uncommitted 99 per cent of the population with propaganda if they were to have anything like sufficient support to stage a coup d'état. Despite the difficulty of obtaining, and the high cost of, newsprint in cash-strapped Russia, their covert financial backing enabled them to produce no less than forty-one daily and periodical publications that promised peace, food and land to the dispossessed, the hungry and those yearning for an end to the killing. In a massive PR campaign to make themselves respectable and popular, they hammered away at public opinion with the simplest of slogans – none of them overtly Marxist.[12]

Inside Russian conditions deteriorated as the infrastructure of Tsarist society crumbled. Lenin was still in Switzerland and Trotsky was in Canada when soldiers sent to restore order joined forces with the rioters and occupied the Duma on 26 February 1917. Riots over the scarcity of food culminated on 8 March with starving women textile workers marking International Women's Day[13] by walking out of their factory in St Petersburg, which had changed its German-sounding name at the start of the war to the Russian form Petrograd, meaning 'Peter's town'. Their protest was one with which the hungry Russian millions sympathised. After violent demonstrations in the streets with widespread looting of bread shops and grain stores, Nicholas II ordered the strikers back to work. When they did not obey, troops were ordered to fire on the demonstrators, triggering the February Revolution (March not having begun under the old Russian calendar).

Meriel Buchanan, daughter of the British ambassador at the time, returned from a trip to Finland on 12 March and found the streets of Petrograd blocked by overturned cars and trams. Soldiers from the Guards regiments refused to fire on the strikers, to the total incomprehension of the Tsar at military headquarters in Pskov. The arsenal in the Peter and Paul fortress was captured by the rebels, who distributed firearms to all and sundry. Tsar Nicholas had just discovered dominoes and was currently devoting more time to mastering the intricacies of the various games than to affairs of state. His diary of appalling banality makes clear how a coach ride, or kissing an icon, were the high points of his days. Letters from Tsarina Alexandra in Tsarskoye Selo were hardly calculated to bring him up to date. Born Princess Alix of Hesse-Darmstadt, her sympathies were ambiguous, although a contemporary joke had her young son looking unhappy in a corridor of the Winter Palace. When asked, 'What's the matter?' the Tsarevich replied, 'When the Russians are beaten, Papa cries. When the Germans are beaten, Mama cries. When am I to cry?'

Alexandra blamed all the social unrest on the Duma and advised her husband that the workers would go quietly back into the factories if threatened with being sent to the front. When strikers were being gunned down in the streets of Petrograd, she devoted her daily letter to Nicholas to a visit to Rasputin's grave: 'It seems to me that everything will be all right. The sun is shining so brightly and I feel such peace and comfort at his dear grave. He died to save us.'[14]

The truth was that the gun smoke from the fusillades in the streets had swept away the incense-perfumed mystical-religious bond between the Russian ruler and his long-suffering people. Governmental corruption and inefficiency were rampant. The Duma was the best thing to come out of the 1905 revolution, but Nicholas' successive dissolutions of it had spread dissatisfaction even among moderate elements. By now, peasants were illegally seizing land and the empire's ethnic minorities were clamouring for self-determination. After the Provisional Committee of the Duma called on him to abdicate so that it could form a provisional government, Russia's last Tsar formally renounced his throne and titles at Pskov on 15 March, abdicating in favour of his brother, Grand Duke Michael, who sensibly refused the honour the following day. Thus, three centuries of Romanov rule came to a sordid end with the royal family under house arrest at Tsarskoye Selo.

The provisional government continued to support the war effort. Challenging its authority was a body calling itself the Soviet of Workers' and Soldiers' Deputies, consisting of 2,500 delegates claiming to represent the workforce and military units in the Petrograd area. On 1 March its Order No. 1 directed soldiers to obey only the *soviet* and not the provisional government. By then, Meriel Buchanan was working as a volunteer nurse in a Red Cross hospital for wounded soldiers. They too caught the political fever of the times and were so insubordinate to doctors and nurses that the hospital had to be closed, with no alternative care for the injured. 'An atmosphere of dread seemed to brood over the town', she wrote in her memoirs, describing how 'ruffians with unshaven faces took control of the streets'.[15]

Since all that prevented the Soviet of Workers' and Soldiers' Deputies from declaring itself the real government of Russia was fear of provoking a conservative counter-coup in favour of the Tsar, it ordered the royal family to be transported by train nearly 2,000 miles eastward to Tobolsk in Western Siberia, there to await its fate.

For some time Lenin and the other expatriate revolutionaries in Switzerland had been negotiating with German Foreign Office officials for safe transport back to Russia. Since their reappearance on the political scene there was certain to raise the political temperature and foment mutinies throughout the Russian armies on the eastern front, forcing the provisional government to sue for peace, the German Foreign Ministry agreed on 25 March to make available clandestine transport facilities to take them to the Baltic coast and then via neutral Sweden and Finland to Russia.[16] Proving that there is nothing new about deniable clandestine operations, the mission had been approved by German Chancellor Theobald von Bethmann-Hollweg, conducting negotiations with Lenin through a chain of intermediaries, though the Kaiser had not been initially informed of this ungentlemanly ploy.[17]

The German Foreign Ministry now hit a last-minute snag when the émigrés realised that returning to Russia in this way would see them accused in Petrograd of being German agents – which they effectively were. Paranoia being a characteristic of revolutionaries, Lenin and Zinoviev feared that a greater danger was that staying any longer in Switzerland risked them being sidelined by their fellow revolutionaries already active in Russia. To feed the pretence that they were acting on their own unassisted initiative[18] it was agreed that they would pay their own third-class fares and the train would be granted extra-territorial rights while crossing Germany. To great relief among the small circle privy to the plan in the German High Command and Foreign Ministry, on 4 April the Russians indicated their readiness for a party of 'twenty to thirty' to leave for Russia.[19]

On 16 April 1917, thirty-plus revolutionaries, including Lenin's bourgeois mistress Inessa Armand, boarded what became known as 'the sealed train' in Berne. It was actually a single, green-painted carriage of eight second- and third-class compartments, single men roughing it in third while families travelled in second, with one second-class compartment reserved for Lenin, his wife Nadezhda Krupskaya and Inessa Armand. All the doors were locked, with the exception of one, in the compartment of the two German escorting officers on board. So well kept was the secret of these arrangements that they missed a connection and had to spend one night locked up incommunicado in a small provincial hotel. Never has there been more 'smoke and mirrors'. Almost unknown inside Russia, Lenin owed his influence in social democratic émigré circles partly to covert support from the Okhrana's European offices, which supported him because he was unable to work with anyone for long before precipitating yet another schism in the ranks of the revolutionaries.[20] Now he was travelling to his appointment with destiny thanks to a German plot to foment mutiny in the Russian armies.

Idealists like to believe otherwise, but clandestine operations officers know that revolutions cost money – with which Lenin and his comrades were richly provided through a chain of bankers moving funds covertly from Germany through special accounts. Cut-outs and front companies were used so that the money would not be traceable to the German government. Some estimates put the funds paid through the Swedish Nya Banken, whose director Olof Aschberg admitted to being the Bolsheviks' banker, as high as 60 million gold marks, equivalent to $1,000 million today.[21] One bagman alone, N.M. Weinberg, Petrograd agent for Berlin bankers Mendelssohn & Co., paid out 12 million roubles to the Bolsheviks.

As head of the Cheka – the Bolshevik secret police formed on 20 December 1917 – Felix Dzerzhinsky[22] was ordered to recover the incriminating receipts. A minor Polish aristocrat, Dzerzhinsky was a dysfunctional sociopath devoted to death and destruction. He lived night and day in his office, eating only snacks, and was so devoid of normal emotion that he forced his wife to have their son adopted into a working-class family, to ensure that he grew up 'socially correct'. Dzerzhinsky arrested Weinberg, stripped and tortured him in the Butirky prison. The receipts having been forwarded to Berlin, Weinberg could not save himself, so Dzerzhinsky ordered him shot.[23]

The amounts handed over to a group of dissidents who *might* stage a coup d'état were colossal for the time, and similar amounts were being paid by Britain to anti-Soviet forces. Given the escalating costs of the war, German financing of the Soviets seemed a worthwhile gamble in Berlin. As so often, fixation on the short-term target completely blinded the planners to the long-term danger. The Kaiser's eastern front commander General Max Hoffman afterwards wrote, 'We neither knew nor foresaw the danger to humanity from the consequences of this journey of the Bolsheviks to Russia.'[24]

7

THE RAINBOW
OF DEATH

Despite all the cut-outs, back-channels and front companies, when Lenin and his companions returned to Petrograd in mid-April, the means of their arrival and the new-found affluence of the Bolsheviks understandably resulted in accusations by the provisional government and others that they were paid German agents sent to undermine the Russian war effort. In May 1917 two official investigations were launched, as a result of which in July the minister of justice publicly accused the Bolsheviks of treason. Some of the leaders were arrested with Trotsky; others went underground or fled abroad again, like Lenin, who took refuge in Finland.

Soviety, representing all shades of anti-war feeling, sprang up in major towns and in the army, increasingly defiant of the provisional government. Clamouring for an end to the war on any terms, the First All-Russian Congress of Soviets began on 16 June, with the socialist revolutionaries in a majority, followed by the Mensheviks, and the Bolsheviks least represented. After an army coup nearly toppled the discredited provisional government, unable to halt Russia's slide into economic chaos, the *soviety* gained public support as a viable alternative.

The German-subsidised PR campaign of the Bolsheviks included a daily printing of 300,000 copies of *Pravda*[1] under editorial control of Lenin in Finland, using Krupskaya as courier. Thanks largely to this, by September both the Petrograd and Moscow *soviety* were under Bolshevik control.

At the end of October, Lenin emerged from hiding in Finland. Hundreds of thousands of copies of the iconic painting of his arrival at Petrograd's Finland station used to occupy a place of honour in the communist pantheon. They show him waving heroically from the footplate of Finnish locomotive No. 293 – which is now the centrepiece of a Bolshevik shrine in the modernised station. His timing was impeccable, for Petrograd was already largely in Bolshevik hands. On 6-7 November (25-26 October in the old calendar), they and far-Left Socialist Revolutionaries occupied government buildings, telegraph offices, power stations and other strategic points. The October Revolution, as it was called, was the death-knell of the provisional government, whose leaders sought asylum abroad, leaving the Second All-Russian Congress of Soviets to form a new government, in which power lay with the Bolsheviks, who formed a central committee, itself subordinated to an elite policy office, or Politburo, consisting of seven members. Strangely in such a xenophobic country, the Politburo was headed by three non-Russians: Ulyanov the Tartar, Bronshtein the Jew, and Djugashvili, the Georgian street urchin tasting real power for the first time – otherwise Lenin, Trotsky and Stalin. Among their first acts was the revelation of secret treaties between the Tsarist regime and the Western Allies, including Russian plans to grab Constantinople and the Bosphorus immediately after victory.[2]

Among the foreign writers attracted by the extraordinary events in Russia were authors Hugh Walpole and Somerset Maugham. Ardent sympathisers with the Bolsheviks included American journalists Louise Bryant and her lover John Silas Reed. Bryant had been raised by a stepfather who was an engine driver, but Reed came from a prosperous middle-class family, attending Harvard University before taking up journalism, writing for the far-Left magazine, *The Masses*. She was an anarchist and feminist; he a Communist. Pursuing their on-again, off-again relationship in which involvement of playwright Eugene O'Neill gave him the plot for his play *Strange Interlude*, Bryant and Reed arrived in Russia together in 1917 to write up the October Revolution in glowing terms for American left-wing publications. The romance, the poems and letters they left, the tragedy of Reed's death from typhus in 1922 and the overall situation of Russia at the time made *Reds*, the 1981 film about them, starring Diane Keaton and Warren Beatty, with Jack Nicolson playing O'Neill, a box office draw in many countries.

The Bolsheviks needed friends like that. With the party's financial stability assured by a further 15 million German marks in November,[3] the new Soviet government of Russia opened negotiations at Brest-Litovsk to end the war on the eastern front. In January 1918 Trotsky, as People's Commissar for Foreign Affairs, personally took charge of the Russian delegation and amazed the Central Powers' representatives by haranguing them like a mob in the street, calling for 'a democratic peace without annexations, reparations, respecting the right to national self-determination'. His blatant stalling tactics were based on an obsession that widespread strikes in Germany must rapidly spark a revolution there and render the negotiations pointless. General Hoffmann finally ran out of patience, brushed aside all the rhetoric, and made Trotsky a take-it-or-leave-it offer: if the Soviet government really wanted peace, it would have to renounce all claims to the formerly Russian-occupied areas of Poland, plus the Baltic states and Ukraine.

Given the urgent need to resolve the internal chaos in Russia and Stalin's proclamation at the Third Congress of Soviets that same month of the right of 'all peoples to self-determination through to complete secession from Russia',[4] one might think that Trotsky would have agreed to any terms that left Russia itself intact. After all, the *soviety* that he claimed to represent wanted 'peace at any price'. Yet he was, even at this critical moment, unwilling to give away as much as a square centimetre of the former Tsarist empire. Meaningless slogans were being chanted in the streets, so he invented a new one on his return to Petrograd: 'Neither war nor peace,' i.e. a ceasefire without a formal treaty.

Despite the fine talk of national self-determination for ethnic minorities, and although still in a state of unresolved hostilities with the Central Powers, the Bolsheviks invaded Ukraine in January 1918 to stamp out the fires of independence there. The Ukrainian government proclaimed independence from Russia on 22 January but immediately had to evacuate Kiev, which was occupied by Soviet troops. In Brest-Litovsk, the Central Powers signed a separate peace treaty with the Ukrainian delegation on 9 February and launched a new offensive against Russia one week later, forcing Trotsky back to the conference table. On 23 February General Hoffmann gave him two days to get serious and three more to conclude a treaty. Realising that the Soviet government could be brought down by public anger at home if the war continued, Lenin threatened to resign if the German terms were not agreed to. So, on 3 March the deal was done, with Russia accepting the loss of Ukraine, the Polish and Baltic territories and Finland. Those territories have been estimated as representing 'half the human, industrial and agricultural resources' of the Russian Empire. Lenin called it 'an obscene peace'[5] but, as with France in 1940, most of the Russian population heaved a sigh of relief that their surviving menfolk could return home.

Dirt sticks, and Lenin had no wish to be known as an agent of the German monarchist regime. So, early in 1918, Edgar Sisson, a former employee of the US Committee on Public Information, was contacted by pro-Bolshevik foreigners including Colonel Raymond Robins, a Red Cross administrator working in Russia. They offered Sisson fifty-three – some say sixty-eight – documents apparently proving that huge injections of German money both before and after the October Revolution had made possible the Bolshevik takeover, and that Lenin's quid pro quo had been to force through the signature of the second Brest-Litovsk treaty against the wishes of party colleagues.

After Sisson's return to Washington, some of the documents were declared genuine, some doubtful and others forgeries or copies of missing originals. They were nonetheless published that autumn amid a furore of disagreement over their authenticity. However, when the documents were closely scrutinised by, among others, George Kennan in 1956, they were nearly all pronounced forgeries on the grounds of spelling and other gross errors that were childishly obvious to anyone who could read German and Russian. And yet, German Foreign Office files discovered in the immediate aftermath of the Allied victory in 1945 confirm the story of the Sisson papers.[6]

The explanation is not hard to find. The Bolshevik secret police – at first called Vecheka and later Cheka, an acronym of *Chrezvychaynaya Kommissiya* – or Special Commission (for Combating Counter-revolution and Sabotage) – had inherited the penchant for forgery from the Okhrana, whose officers produced the famous 1903 hoax *The Protocols of the Elders of Zion*. So what better way was there for the Bolsheviks to disprove the allegations of taking German bribes than by having Sisson publish the 'proof' of those accusations, but in a form that would be proven false by, of all people, the capitalist enemy?

Lenin's other great embarrassment at the time was that his party could no longer be called Marxist. Among other reasons why, the manner in which it came to power in the October Revolution *contradicted* Marxist teaching. The way round this was to re-invent the Bolshevik party by claiming that its historical justification was a new political philosophy called Marxism-Leninism. Once that essential contradiction in terms had been accepted, his followers' gullet of credibility was stretched so wide that all subsequent contradictions were swallowed whole. In the resultant jargon-infested ideological confusion, there was only one determinant of orthodoxy: the Communist Party itself. Indeed, the party shortly became the sole arbiter of truth, while truth in Russia became whatever the party decreed it to be. It was the Inquisition clothed in red, before which dissenters purged their heresies, if at all, by long periods of forced labour in Siberia.

George Kennan put it well in a despatch of 1944:

A daring tour de force which the American mind must make, if it is to try to find Russian life comprehensible, (is) to understand that for Russia, at any rate, there are no objective criteria of right and wrong. There are not even any objective criteria of reality and unreality. What do we mean by this? We mean that right and wrong, reality and unreality, are determined in Russia not by any God, not by any innate nature of things, but simply by men themselves. Here men determine what is true and what is false. The reader should not smile. This is a serious fact.[7]

Significantly, the two major organs of the Bolshevik or Communist Party from 1917 to the implosion of the USSR in 1991 were entitled *Pravda* and *Izvestiya*. *Pravda* means 'truth', *Izvestiya* means 'information'. For seventy-four years, it was an article of communist faith that what was in *Pravda* was the official truth and what was not there was untrue. Russian émigrés inevitably punned on the titles: *Nyet pravdy v'Izvestiakh, net izvestiyakh v'Pravde* – there's no truth in *Izvestiya* and no information in *Pravda*. Westerners, like the author, who had to read the turgid reports of committees and verbatim accounts of Politburo speeches that filled both papers, found they made excellent bedtime reading, guaranteed to induce sleep rapidly.

In destroying the infrastructure of the Tsarist regime, including its secret police, the October Revolution produced a brief interlude of personal freedom such as Russia had never known. Uncounted thousands, then hundreds of thousands, and eventually 3 million Russians took the chance to flee abroad, leaving their homes, property and businesses as Lenin initiated a programme of 'war communism', which meant the nationalisation of banks, shipping, railways, grain supplies, mining, oil, all businesses employing more than ten people – and, to the peasants' horror, all land. This was now to be farmed collectively on strict instructions from commissars following directives 'from above,' i.e. from people whose credentials were political and who knew nothing about growing crops or raising animals.

Coming on top of the depredations of war, this finally shattered the economy. With factories closed for lack of raw materials, workers and their families starved to death. The problems of the Bolshevik government, composed of theoreticians with scant hands-on experience of anything useful, were compounded by the exodus of the middle classes, including most of those with managerial experience. They were right to leave, for many who did not were arrested, imprisoned for years or executed. The more provident refugees headed for wherever their money had been stashed away; others ended up in Shanghai, Singapore, India, Latin America, Australia – wherever local regulations permitted them to settle, however precariously, and live on a pittance. Because so many had fluent French, in Paris and Marseilles princes, dukes and generals drove taxis, waited on tables and carried bags; their wives cleaned floors and took in washing and ironing.

The Russian Empire was temporarily dead. In its place, four socialist republics were established: the Russian and Transcaucasian soviet federated socialist republics and the Belorussian and Ukrainian soviet socialist republics. In Ukraine, despite the installation of a soviet regime that ousted a provisional government after the break-up of the Tsarist empire, there was no wish to be 'south Russia' any longer. Ukrainians looked to Austro-Hungary for protection, which was forthcoming because of the importance to the Central Powers of the fertile black soil *chernozem* grain-growing area – to regain which the Red Army twice invaded to re-impose Russian rule.

The situation became even more complicated after the second Treaty of Brest-Litovsk, which caused a rift between the Bolsheviks and other revolutionary socialists who opposed Lenin's autocratic dissolution of the Duma. Lenin re-baptised his party the All-Russian Communist Party[8] to mark its opposition not only to capitalists and Tsarists but also the foreign socialist parties who had supported their capitalist governments during the war and all the Russian left-wing parties. These former allies who had helped bring down the Tsarist regime were henceforth to be treated as dangerous enemies.

With the Baltic states and Finland no longer Russian territory, Lenin considered Petrograd too exposed as the seat of government and moved it 400 miles eastwards, back to Moscow. Dated 30 April, extracts from Report No. 9 of the German minister in Moscow to his chancellor in Berlin give a chilling picture of life in the city:

> Anyone who knew the capital in the days of its glory would hardly be able to recognise it now. In every part of the city, and especially in the central commercial quarter, countless

bullet-holes in walls and windows are evidence of the bitter battles that were fought for its possession. Even the Kremlin has suffered terribly. Various of its gates are badly damaged; the Iberian Gate has been partly destroyed and is now only boarded up. Hardly any better-dressed people are to be seen – as if the whole of the previously governing class and the bourgeoisie had disappeared off the face of the earth. Hardly anything can be bought in the shops except dusty remnants of past splendour, and these only at fantastic prices. It is unwise to go out towards evening, and at that time of day one often hears rifle fire and more or less serious skirmishes seem to take place continually. The factories are at a standstill and the land is still, to all intents and purposes not being cultivated.[9]

Now commissar for war, Trotsky employed Tsarist officers closely supervised by political commissars to turn the Red Army into a professional force. Of the several hostile armies it faced, Admiral Alexander Kolchak's Rightists based at Omsk in Western Siberia were being trained with assistance from British and US military advisers. In the Kuban steppes, the so-called White Army commanded by General Anton Denikin was preparing to march on Moscow.

Under pressure from the German offensive in northern France in the spring of 1918, Britain attempted to reactivate the eastern front by landing a small expeditionary force at Murmansk in March, where the local *soviet* hoped it would repulse approaching Finnish White troops. In the Far East, Japanese forces landed at Vladivostok against local protests and were steadily reinforced. Czech and Slovak deserters from the Austro-Hungarian army had been permitted for linguistic reasons to serve in their own units of the Tsarist armies. Now authorised to leave Russia via the Far East after laying down all heavy equipment, they rightly suspected the consequences of disarming totally. Increasingly violent confrontations between them and Trotsky's Red Army ended with the Czechs taking control of a critical stretch of the Trans-Siberian, along much of which armoured trains belonging to both sides thundered eastwards and westwards laying waste towns and villages suspected of harbouring the enemy.

Ex-Tsar Nicholas and his family were being held at Ekaterinburg in the villa belonging to a rich industrialist, who had sensibly emigrated. When White forces approached in July 1918, the local *soviet* was ordered to prevent their rescue at all costs. On the night of 16-17 July, the Tsar, Tsarina, their four daughters and invalid son Alexei were all herded into the cellar of the villa and messily shot to death, together with their doctor, servants and dog. The bodies were burned, cast into an abandoned mine shaft, and then re-buried elsewhere.[10]

Proving that no one was safe from an assassin's bullet in Russia, on 30 August 1918, after Lenin had spoken at a meeting in a Moscow munitions factory and was walking back to his car, a 30-year-old Ukrainian member of the Socialist Revolutionary Party called Fanya Kaplan accused him of betraying the revolution. For attempted assassination of a Tsarist official, she had already served eleven years' hard labour in Siberia before being released after the February Revolution. When Lenin turned to answer her, Kaplan fired three shots from her revolver. Two bullets hit him. Wounded in the neck and arm, Lenin collapsed and was driven to his apartment inside the Kremlin, refusing to be taken to a hospital for removal of the bullets in case more assassins were waiting there. Several conspiracy theories were based on the alleged poor eyesight of Kaplan and her refusal to say who had given her the revolver. Conveniently, she was executed three days later.

The assassination attempt triggered a Red Terror at the beginning of September. Dzerzhinsky now ordered the Cheka rank-and-file to arrest and summarily execute anyone remotely suspected of anti-Bolshevik feelings. The victims, many killed after torture, ran into uncounted thousands. To be condemned, it was not necessary to be guilty of anything; the problem for the innocent was to prove their innocence. A joke of the time tells of a kangaroo arriving at the Polish frontier and asking for asylum on the grounds that the rabbits in Russia are being killed. 'But you're not a rabbit', says the frontier guard. 'How do I prove that?' retorts the kangaroo.

The Red Army was now fighting a multi-front civil war against the White armies and 200,000 men in interventionist contingents from Britain, the United States, Japan and France, plus the Ukrainian Independence Army. After war in the west ended with the Central Powers' surrender to the Entente on 11 November 1918, the original purpose of the foreign interventions was overtaken by events. The French forces in the Ukraine withdrew during March and April 1919, followed by other interventionist forces, with the British contingent in the far north leaving last. Further support from the West for the White armies commanded by General Denikin in the south and Admiral Kolchak in Siberia consisted of materiel only. In the Far East, the Japanese hung on, eventually withdrawing under pressure from the US in 1922.

As late as 1920 there was still a small but viable White army in the Crimea under Denikin's successor General Pyotr Wrangel.[11] The Red Army eventually drove this army into a pocket in the Crimea, where Wrangel held out long enough to evacuate 150,000 soldiers and civilians by sea. Several hundred officers and NCOs who found themselves stranded and starving in Constantinople accepted free passage on French ships taking them directly to North Africa, where Cossack, Polish and Russian cavalrymen were recruited wholesale to form the 1st Cavalry Regiment of the French Foreign Legion. So many of these émigrés were of the nobility that the regiment was dubbed 'Le Royal Étranger'.

Inside Russia, perhaps the most important rebellion came in the Tambov region, 300 miles south-east of Moscow, where the *prodrazverstka* programme of forcible requisitions by Bolshevik commissars meant death by starvation for the peasants who had produced the grain. Calling themselves the Blue Army – as distinct from the Red and White armies, the Polish Blue Army, the Green Army of Ukrainian nationalists and the Black Army of Russian and Ukrainian anarchists that made a rainbow of death hovering over their blighted land – the Tambov rebels elected their own constituent assembly that returned all land to the peasants. This had been one of the original, but long since discarded, vote-catchers of the Bolsheviks. In October 1920 the Tambov army numbered over 50,000 peasants plus deserters from the Red Army. Other peasant revolts in Samara, Saratov, Tsaritsyn, Astrakhan and Siberia suffered the same sad fate as the Tambov rebels: crushed by 30,000 Red Army soldiers and Dzerzhinsky's Cheka detachments using poison gas. In that area alone, at least 50,000 people were interned in seven concentration camps, but total losses among the civil population of the region 1920–2 were estimated to be four or five times higher.

More alarming to Lenin was a rebellion by soldiers and sailors who had been among the Bolsheviks' most faithful supporters during the October Revolution. In sympathy with widespread strikes and demonstrations against the famine and epidemics caused by the government's failure to provide basic food for the civilian population, for restricting political freedom and for placing all workers under military law, the garrison of the island fortress of Kronstadt in the Gulf of Finland formed a Provisional Revolutionary Committee in March 1921.

The 10,000 sailors and 4,000 soldiers on the island demanded an end to the Bolsheviks' monopoly of power, the release of other socialists from prison, and the establishment of political freedom and civil rights. The Bolsheviks responded by accusing the rebels of being in foreign pay. Had this been true, the revolt would have taken place a few weeks later after the thaw when Kronstadt was a defensible island that could have been re-supplied from abroad by sea. With the island joined to the mainland by thick ice, Trotsky despatched 60,000 Red troops to put down the rebellion, with party commissars manning machine guns in the rear to force them onto the ice swept by the garrison's machine guns. On 17 March, when the Bolshevik forces finally entered Kronstadt citadel, a few rebels managed to escape across the ice to Finland, causing a major problem for the newly independent Finnish state. Casualties were heavy on both sides, with captured rebels summarily executed or sent to prison camps set up by Dzerzhinsky.[12]

As the Tambov rebels and the Kronstadt garrison learned too late, the Bolsheviks occupying all seats in the Soviet of People's Commissars and key posts at every level of government made the Russian Soviet Federated Socialist Republic a dictatorship. Trotsky's eventual victory over all the other elements in the Civil War had nothing to do with popular support and was mainly due to the Red Army's brutally established control of European

Russia, in which it could be deployed and coordinated far more easily than forces of the several enemies on the periphery of the old empire, separated from each another by vast distances. It was nevertheless an amazing military achievement for a civilian – and ultimately the cause of Trotsky's assassination.

The uprising at Kronstadt made Lenin realise that his rigid adherence to the doctrine of war communism had not only brought the national economy to the brink of meltdown, but also provoked a real danger of counter-revolution. Accordingly, at the Tenth Party Congress in March 1921 he unveiled the New Economic Policy (NEP), involving the return of most agriculture, retail trade, and small-scale light industry to private hands, with the state retaining control of heavy industry, transport, banking, and foreign trade. Entrepreneurs who took advantage of this to start up small businesses and farms were known as *nepmen*. Money, which had been abolished under war communism, was also re-introduced the following year. The peasants were again allowed to own and cultivate land – and pay taxes for the privilege. What the public was not told was that Lenin only intended it as a temporary expedient to reboot the economy and give the party time to consolidate its power.

Lenin and Trotsky had assumed that the success of their revolution would light a powder train, igniting fires of rebellion worldwide. On the night of 7-8 November 1918, King Louis (or Ludwig) III of Bavaria was deposed by a Red coup. Its leader, Kurt Eisner, was assassinated three months later, after which the Bavarian revolutionary committees carried out a Red Terror purge of enemies and imposed a short-lived Soviet republic, which was repressed by federal German troops in May 1919, after which a backlash White Terror was unleashed against the defeated communists.

Just five days after the Bavarian coup, Hungary proclaimed itself a republic, independent of Austria. Serbian, Czech and Romanian troops occupied two-thirds of the country. On 21 March 1919, the rump was declared a soviet republic, whose government was led by Béla Kun. A POW captured in 1916, he had stayed in Russia after the revolution and become an agent of the Cheka, sharing with his sadistic mistress Razalia Zemlyachka the distinction of assassinating 50,000 White officers, many burned alive or drowned in barges deliberately sunk with them battened down below decks.[13]

Kun created a Hungarian Red Army that reconquered much of the territory lost to the foreign invaders, at the same time eliminating all political opposition in his own Red Terror. He alienated the peasantry by confiscating private estates for the state instead of distributing the land to those who lived and worked on it. That same month of March, Lenin inaugurated the Communist International or Comintern to assist and control Communist revolutions outside Russia.[14] When Soviet reinforcements Kun had been promised for a revenge invasion of Czechoslovakia failed to arrive, the economy came to a standstill and food distribution ceased. Having lost any vestige of popular support, Kun's brief but bloody regime ended on the second day of August. To save his life, he fled to Vienna and led other unsuccessful coups in Germany and Austria during the 1920s, but was eventually accused of Trotskyist deviation and eliminated in Stalin's purges.

Although in Ukraine guerrilla bands continued for years to harass Bolshevik occupation forces, once Russia itself was secured, Trotsky cast his net wider. After the Turkish surrender to the Entente in 1918, the three Transcaucasian republics of Azerbaijan, Armenia and Georgia enjoyed temporary freedom, but this did not suit Moscow. In April 1920 the Azerbaijan government surrendered to the Red Army. In December 1920 the former Russian province of Armenia was incorporated into Soviet Russia, and the rest of the country handed over to Turkey. During February to April 1921 the Red Army invaded and reconquered Georgia, Stalin's homeland.

In Central Asia, the October Revolution had prompted Uzbekistani Muslim nationalists to declare autonomy, terminated by the Red Army in February 1918. This sparked a prolonged anti-Russian resistance movement, despite which the Emir of Bukhara and the Khan of Khiva were deposed in 1920, so that by the end of 1921 communist puppets controlled the region under Moscow's firm hand. Neighbouring Turkmenistan was laid waste by war between invading Bolshevik troops and those of the Social Revolutionary Transcaspian Provincial Government supported by a British force of 1,200 men based in Persia but, after the withdrawal of this in April 1919, Soviet rule was imposed by force. In Kazakhstan, the Red Army drove out White forces and easily overcame a weak provisional government established after the demise of the Tsarist regime. Here also, a communist puppet government was imposed in August 1920 – after which, as in the other Central Asian republics, an influx of Russian settlers changed the demography for ever.

A mere five years after the October Revolution, the Russian Empire existed again – at the cost of millions of lives and the loss of ethnic and political identity for millions more that would last three generations. On 30 December 1922, the four Soviet republics united in the Union of Soviet Socialist Republics. The carefully chosen word 'union', which implied equality and voluntary association of equals, stopped three generations of Western liberals seeing that the USSR ruled from Moscow was the old Tsarist empire re-created in five bloody years. Looked at another way, it was the only empire to be amassed in the twentieth century.

PART 2:

WAR BY
OTHER MEANS

A single death is a tragedy. A million deaths is a statistic.

Josef Stalin

8

THE COMINTERN: WAR ON THE CHEAP

In March 1919, with a political sleight of hand that confused many foreign observers unaccustomed to Soviet double-talk, the 8th Congress of the CPSU followed orders from the top to 'instruct' the Central Committee – usually referred to as 'Tseka' from the initials of its title *tsentralny komityet* – to elect from its ranks a new Politburo of five members. Lenin and Trotsky were jockeying uneasily for pole position. Stalin was quietly gathering the reins of power into his hands. The other two members were Lev Kamenev, married to Trotsky's sister, and Nikolai Krestinsky. After Lenin died, Trotsky, Kamenev and Krestinsky would be murdered by Stalin because they knew too much about him.

The justification for the new arrangement was that questions of state too urgent to await the next meeting of the Central Committee needed to be resolved by a small permanent executive, which could rapidly make all urgent policy decisions on a day-to-day basis. Effectively, the Central Committee thus became a rubber stamp for Politburo decisions. It was a far cry from the slogan that had resounded through the bloodstained streets of Petrograd. Nobody now chanted, 'All power to the soviets!' for the role of the *soviety* was reduced to knee-jerk endorsement and enforcement of orders from above on pain of imprisonment or worse.

Because the party secretariat planned the agenda of all meetings, vetted all documentation and also transmitted Politburo decisions to the party's rank-and-file, a critical post in this concentration of power was that of *otvetsvenny sekretar* – or responsible secretary. In 1922, when this post was translated into that of General Secretary of the CPSU, abbreviated to *Gensek,* its first holder was to become the Politburo's most influential member. He was, of course, Josef Stalin, who left the dirty work in 1919 to Trotsky's Red Army and Dzerzhinsky's Cheka – suppressing with prison bars, poison gas and bullets a whole range of 'internal enemies' and 'counter-revolutionary elements' ranging from non-Bolshevik socialists to strikers, 'saboteurs' and non-Russian independence fighters.

It is estimated that at least 10 million people died violently or prematurely during the October Revolution, the civil war and the devastation and dislocation that ensued. Millions more were starving to death across the length and breadth of the Soviet empire, many of them, later called 'displaced persons', desperately seeking parents, children and friends who had been torn from them hundreds or thousands of miles away, years before. Hundreds of thousands of homeless children with no surviving adult relatives wandered across the land, begging and stealing. It was a time of despair, desolation and deprivation so well captured in Boris Pasternak's *Doctor Zhivago* that the book won him both a Nobel Prize for Literature and expulsion from the Union of Soviet Writers – muzzling him professionally within the Soviet Union while millions read his work outside it.

There is no question that the vastness of the conquered territory prevented the Bolshevik leadership from learning the conditions it had brought about, because on 19 March 1922 Lenin called on the Politburo for stronger measures, citing the famine that left thousands of corpses along the roads and starving people driven to cannibalism.[1] Yet, instead of listening to the voice of his suffering people, Lenin was heeding the ghostly whisper of Genghis Khan's shaman Kokochu. He was actually listening to the prompting of his own dreams of world domination but, since he had much Tartar blood in his veins, Kokochu may have had something to do with it. Indeed, with trademark goatee beard shaved off – as he had done when on the run – and with his moustache grown longer and drooping, Ulyanov/Lenin could easily have passed for one of the Great Khan's mounted warriors.

Warfare had now escalated from eighteenth-century pitched battles to the far more costly total war exemplified by four years of attrition on the western front. The financial and social stresses of the enormous effort required to mobilise, train and transport halfway across the world millions of citizen-soldiers and to equip them with the sophisticated weapons invented by the armaments industry, had breached the formerly watertight bulkheads of societies in which everyone knew his or her place and most people stayed there. As a result, the Western belligerents had suffered strikes, demonstrations, and mutinies at the front and even some full-blown, if short-lived, revolutions. In his less monomaniacal moments, Lenin may possibly have acknowledged to himself and Krupskaya that even the October Revolution might not have taken place but for the catalyst of the Great War.

From there, a quantum leap of theoretical politics enabled him to convince himself that the Tsarist dream of world conquest was at last within the grasp of the man in the Kremlin – i.e. himself – because there was a far more cost-effective way of inducing that unrest and using it to conquer the capitalist democracies than by going to war against them with guns and gore. The personal liberties enjoyed by their citizens – such as free speech, secret elections, trade unions and unrestricted travel – did not exist in the Soviet Union for good reason. With trained agitators exploiting them in the West, it would be possible to bring down the democracies from within. There was enough social injustice and poverty in every country to inspire socialists wanting to 'make a better world'. If left alone, however, some might find socialist, national-socialist or other non-Communist ways of working out their own salvation. Even followers of Marx might have their own ideas about applying his theories – or they might, like Eisner and Kun, choose the wrong moment or lack the political sense or ruthlessness to mount a successful revolution and consolidate power afterwards.

To ensure that none of these things happened, Lenin decreed that it was imperative to inculcate into revolutionary socialists an unswerving discipline to the Soviet party line, so they could be trained in Russia and financed on return to their own countries to influence public opinion through propaganda, to infiltrate and/or subvert other political parties, and to manipulate the trade unions. By controlling a country's workforce through these, Lenin was certain that a small number of dedicated activists could paralyse free-market economies as thoroughly as if a virus had been injected into the arteries of capitalism.

If simultaneously all the fault lines based on class, sex, colour, religion and ethnic tensions that reached deep into every democratic society were being ripped open by propaganda and political action, a disciplined pro-Soviet Communist party would have the ruthlessness, the techniques and the guidance from Moscow to grab power in the subsequent power vacuum and civil chaos, and hang on to it by eliminating both rivals and allies. So long as all the foreign activists had it dinned into them that 'Moscow knows best', each post-revolutionary society would be based on the Soviet model and become a satellite of the USSR.

To completely document his strategy for a communist world centred on Moscow would fill a library of books, but the Soviet fostering of communism in Britain is a fair example. First, a selection was made of the socialist parties that had done their best to undermine the British government's war effort. Three hard-line parties were selected and the leadership of the British Socialist Party, the Socialist Labour Party and Sylvia Pankhurst's Workers' Socialist Federation were welded into a new party: the Communist Party of Great Britain (CPGB). That required money, so veteran communist activist Theodore Rothstein, who had been welcomed to Britain in 1891 as a 19-year-old refugee from Tsarist Russia, became one of the early bagmen, bringing to Britain money, as well as gold and jewels[2] confiscated from Russians and foreigners who had fled after the revolution or been murdered. The proceeds were used to get the CPGB off to a flying start: the initial subsidy exceeded £50,000 – in modern terms, about £1 million[3] – this at a time when money was desperately needed to stave off famine in many parts of Russia.

CPGB founder member Bob Stewart wore a bulging money belt around his ample waist on his return from trips to Moscow. His comrade Jack Murphy shuttled back and forth from Russia to Britain, carrying thousands of pounds in a money belt and accounting for every penny to his Soviet paymasters. On one documented trip, he brought in £12,600 – roughly £250,000 in modern value.[4] The job was not without its risks: Comintern courier Michael Borodin was arrested while briefing Scottish CPGB members and spent six months eating porridge in Glasgow's Barlinnie prison before deportation back to the land where his sentence for such activities would have been a miserable death.

The bickering Socialist International was riven into two opposing groups: parties which had supported their governments' war efforts versus those who had not. On 4 March 1919, Lenin made the organisation irrelevant by summoning the First Communist International, abbreviated with the Soviet penchant for acronyms and neologisms to 'Comintern'. Only nineteen foreign parties had representatives in Moscow at this dangerous time to accept or reject his ground rules, which suited him well. At the second Comintern congress in 1920, attended by delegates from thirty-seven countries, Lenin imposed his doctrine of 'democratic centralism'. Like most of the dialectic, the term meant the opposite of what it appeared to mean.

'Democratic' meant that each Moscow-approved party could send delegates to the Comintern meetings, *provided they conformed to twenty-one conditions laid down by Lenin*, which required them to model their structure on disciplined lines in conformity with the Soviet pattern and to expel all moderate socialists and pacifists, especially those who rejected violent tactics and Lenin's dictatorship. Whatever the believers wanted or pretended to believe, the Comintern was thus a weapon of Soviet foreign policy and not a vehicle of socialist internationalism. The catch, in any case, was that the approved foreign parties would have voting rights 'democratically' in proportion to the size of their membership. Since the Russian party was by far the largest, it could always out-vote the others, who were bound to accept the 'democratic' majority vote.

'Centralism' actually meant from the top: Comintern headquarters were in Moscow, its executive was selected by the Politburo, meetings were called when the executive decided, and all power between the meetings lay with the permanent staff, controlled directly by the Kremlin.

With the Comintern acting as headquarters and tradecraft school of a fifth column working throughout the non-Communist world by subversion and the infiltration of trade unions and other political parties, Lenin was effectively declaring a covert war on the same democratic governments with whom he claimed to desire normal diplomatic relations, to get Russia back on its feet.

In April 1920 the League of Nations appointed Norwegian philanthropist Fridtjof Nansen high commissioner for the repatriation from Russia of a half-million German and Austro-Hungarian POWs. Lenin refused to recognise the league, but was prepared to deal with Nansen on a personal basis. The operation was successful, with no one suspecting that the returnees included a number, like Hungary's Béla Kun, who had been indoctrinated in captivity and came home hard-line Communists.

Nansen was also appointed by the International Committee of the Red Cross to head an urgent famine relief operation in Russia. Although the Soviet government allowed him to open an office in Moscow, Lenin rejected aid from the American Relief Administration (ARA), which provided food and other essentials for war-ravaged European countries, because that implied Western superiority. Not until 1921 would the ARA be allowed to begin famine relief operations and open medical clinics in areas devoid of hospitals or even doctors, to save uncounted thousands of Russians from starvation and sickness. Had it been allowed to commence operations earlier, it could have saved many more.

In a time when few working-class people had travelled abroad, except under mobilisation during the First World War, one of the perks for the foreign activists was expenses-paid travel to Moscow. Jack Murphy described after his first visit there how the foreign comrades from each country were schooled late into the night, every night, by Comintern staff specialising in that target country. No mean talker himself, Murphy commented, 'The Russians seemed incapable of exhaustion by discussion. We had got to learn that a Communist Party ... had to be disciplined, a party organised on military lines.' To teach him what that meant, Murphy was arrested in Moscow on suspicion of being a spy for the British police. Although he was investigated and cleared, it was a narrow escape. As he admitted dryly afterwards, 'The Russians have a method of dealing with police spies that does not leave any room for continued activity.' Obedient to the party line, Murphy and the other British communists accepted the premise 'Moscow knows best'. As historian Francis Beckett commented in his well-documented history of the CPGB, 'it was an illusion that was to cost them much misery in the next seven decades'.[5]

The ultimate privilege accorded to important foreign visitors was a personal interview with Lenin himself, regarded with quasi-religious awe as the genius of the revolution. That hard-headed Scot, Willie Gallagher, who had been convicted in 1916 under the Defence of the Realm Act for anti-war activities in the Clydeside dockyards, fell completely under Lenin's spell. The uncompromising feminist Sylvia Pankhurst did not, and argued with the great man over a number of issues, which explains why she never achieved within the Moscow-controlled CPGB the position her previous political record merited.

Neither of these revolutionary socialists fulfilled Lenin's criteria for a boss of the CPGB because they were too independent to accept Comintern orders unquestioningly. Instead, Moscow selected 31-year-old boilermaker Harry Pollitt, a member of Pankhurst's Workers' Socialist Federation who had grown up in the grinding poverty of a northern mill town near Manchester. He was a genial and charismatic public speaker, whose main achievement so far as Lenin was concerned had been using cash brought from Moscow by Sylvia Pankhurst for the 'Hands Off Russia' campaign to bribe London dockers not to coal up the SS *Jolly George*, whose cargo of munitions was intended for Poland's war of independence from Russia.[6]

To ride herd on Pollitt, Moscow appointed his complete opposite: the brilliant, humourless and embittered 35-year-old academic Rajani Palme Dutt. Son of a Swedish mother and an

Indian father, Dutt hated everything about Britain, the British and their way of life. That it was flawed and exploitative of the working classes, no one would now disagree. That it was nowhere near as flawed and exploitative as the regime he worshipped, was something to which Dutt shut his eyes resolutely. Whether Moscow was exploiting his anglophobia or he was using Moscow's authority with the aim of destroying a country he hated, is a moot point.

The third member of CPGB's governing trio was Harry Inkpin, who seems to have been chosen as a rubber stamp for the decisions of Dutt and Pollitt, under whom the CPGB pursued its grimly pro-Moscow course throughout its existence.[7] Inkpin's brother Albert was general secretary and one of the first 'martyrs', imprisoned for six months in 1920 for publishing pro-Soviet propaganda and again in 1921 after police raided the party's premises in King Street, Covent Garden – a property that had been purchased with Soviet money, and the sale of which was to save the discredited CPGB from insolvency half a century later.

To finance the CPGB, whose low membership came nowhere near justifying its expenses, the Comintern initially sent £65,000 per year – equivalent to around £1.3 million today. After Norwegian CP organiser Jacob Friis was sent to impose economies on the spendthrift British comrades, the flow of cash lessened, being augmented whenever there was special need. Subsidies continued until the mid-1930s – and much later for the CPGB newspaper the *Daily Worker*. It must have seemed good value for money that the party managed to have three candidates elected to Parliament in the 1930s.

When such a loveless and unlikeable man as Dutt falls in love, he falls hard. He met his soulmate in an equally hard-line Estonian woman Comintern agent named Salme Murrik, an illegal immigrant who slipped into Britain in 1920. They made a grim pair, whose Soviet ruthlessness frequently antagonised their British comrades until Lenin summoned the Central Committee of the CPGB to Moscow to give them a lesson in socialist reality. A few years later, the more recalcitrant would not have returned, but they all did, after being convinced by Lenin's brainwashing – as Willie Gallagher had been – that 'Moscow knows best'. Discipline inside the CPGB improved, apart from internecine sniping among the leadership, often triggered by Dutt's paranoid suspicion of all his colleagues.

So powerful was their subsequent belief in Moscow-style Communism that it withstood the evidence of their own eyes and ears that the USSR was a tyranny, where their own friends and trusted mentors could be imprisoned, tortured and executed without trial, and where those whom they had been taught to revere as gods in the communist pantheon could be denounced with fatal results as capitalist spies, paid saboteurs and 'counter-revolutionary elements'.

Perhaps one day some psychologist will explain why such dyed-in-the-wool atheists found in their contacts with the leadership of the CPSU what other believers would call a religious experience.

9

SECRET AGENTS IN SKIRTS

iven the relatively primitive international communications at the time, a critical role in imposing Moscow's
instructions on the foreign communist parties and providing the funds to carry them out was played by couriers who
could travel on genuine or false passports safely in the West.
They were thus mostly not Soviet citizens and, because women
drew less suspicion in those days, many were female.

These mysterious agents of the Comintern took very real risks
of arrest – and worse – in many countries. They came from rich
homes and poor ones, but all wanted to 'make a better world'
and believed devoutly that Marxism-Leninism was the best way.
One of the poor ones was Frieda Truhar, a young woman born
in 1911 to Croatian immigrants who had crossed the Atlantic in
steerage to settle in a grim Pennsylvania steel town, where she
grew up witnessing her father and other men doing dangerous
and underpaid work in steel mills and mines, with hired thugs
breaking strikes and armed police putting men and women in
jail for demanding improved working conditions or payment.

Frieda took her first political steps at the time of the October
Revolution when she was 7 years old, distributing leaflets during

the 'Hands Off Russia' campaign and collecting pennies for 'the starving children in Russia'. In 1919 the United Steelworkers of America, to which her father belonged, closed down every steel plant in western Pennsylvania. Reprisal came swiftly: on 2 January 1920 US Attorney-General Mitchell Palmer had 6,000 union activists jailed, among them many friends of the Truhars. The Palmer Raids, as they were called, saw twenty-two workers killed and all union activists arrested unless they went underground, many staying in the Truhar home, used as a safe house for comrades on the run.

Ten years later, at the time of the Wall Street crash of 1929, Frieda was not yet 18 but had graduated early to read economics at the University of Pittsburgh, where she earned a reputation as an outspoken socialist and feminist. Organising collections for the wives and families of striking textile workers in North Carolina imprisoned on charges of murdering strike-breakers sworn in as deputy sheriffs, she was arrested for the first of many times at a protest meeting and spent the night in jail, singing The Red Flag to keep her spirits up.

Like millions of others, her father was unemployed, so she had to leave college and take a poorly paid job in an engineering factory to contribute to the family budget. Frieda's independent feminist outlook changed overnight when she met a Scottish activist. Pat Devine was a born demagogue who took advantage of her youthful admiration of his front-line political record, as recorded in her memoirs:

One morning, Pat asked me out to coffee. As we sat opposite each other in the café, he said, 'Why don't we get married?'

Speechless, I was dazzled by this handsome, assured man with his strong personality. Still in a daze, I went home, proudly announced to mama, 'I'm going to marry Pat. He asked me today and he wants it to be soon because he's so busy.' Defiantly, I added, 'He's wonderful. You've heard him speak. He's brave too, tells the cops where to get off.'

She said, 'He's a fine revolutionary, but you know nothing of the private man, what he'd be like as a husband. He's too old for you, Frieda: thirty-one to your eighteen.'

> I retorted, 'But you don't understand. Everyone likes him, but he picked me.'
>
> As my mother commented much later, I was in love with the political hero, not the man – and Pat wanted a Communist virgin, who would hero-worship him. Despite all the talk of sexual equality between socialist comrades, reality turned out to be making his meals, providing clean shirts and being available in bed when he wanted.[1]

The one-way marriage was interrupted by Pat Devine's arrest for illegal entry into the United States. While he served his sentence, Frieda continued manning picket lines and organising welfare for families of the unemployed in the West Virginia coalfields in the depths of the Depression, but felt unable to cut loose from her husband whose imprisonment made him a martyr for the cause. It was his eventual deportation back to Britain that set Frieda on the path to becoming a Comintern courier at the age of 20.

Marriage had been a deep disappointment, its lowest point coming when she had an abortion because Pat did not want a child. However, when she announced that she did not intend to follow him to Britain, Frieda's mother, who had brought her up a feminist, argued that a communist woman's place was with her husband. To prove the point, she was going, against her better judgement, to accompany Frieda's father to Russia, where he had signed on 'to build socialism' as a bricklayer in a new steel town near Nizhny Tagil on the eastern slopes of the Urals.

Frieda bowed to bourgeois-communist morality, skipping bail to rejoin Pat in Britain early in 1932. Apart from brief conjugal visits, Pat Devine lived his own life as a full-time activist, leaving Frieda to sublimate her yearnings in the same political activities she had in America. He was in jail yet again when she was taken under the wing of Willie Gallacher and met Harry Pollitt, who gave her a typing job in the CPGB King Street HQ.

Having barely adjusted to life in Britain, Frieda was soon told by Pat to join him in Moscow, where he had been promoted to work at Comintern headquarters:

> My emotions as I disembarked in Leningrad [as St Petersburg/
> Petrograd had been re-named] might be compared with those
> of pilgrim to Mecca or Rome. The briefest glimpse of the city
> as I drove to the station, drab streets, unpainted buildings,
> gold-domed churches glistening in the late afternoon sun, a
> sparkling river spanned by a beautiful bridge. Then the over-
> night train to Moscow.[2]

Lodged in the shabby Hotel Lux with workers from many countries equally ardent for worldwide revolution, who included
her cousin Sophie, Frieda worked in the Comintern typing pool
near the Kremlin and had little contact with ordinary Russians.
Walking to work, she saw malnourished men and women begging in the streets and the starving *besprizorny* – homeless
orphans with distended bellies and desperate eyes – and the
endless queues of patient people outside empty stores hoping
to buy whatever was delivered that day, which could then be
bartered for something more useful. The privileged Comintern
workers had permission to use the *valyuta* stores of the *nomenklatura*[3] to buy things never seen in the shops. But many things
– coffee, chocolate and feminine hygiene articles – were unobtainable even there and were brought in by comrades returning
from the West, to be shared around.

The Comintern staff took their meals in the Lux restaurant, run
on the basis of Orwell's *Animal Farm* – 'All animals are equal, but
some are more equal than others'. Frieda discovered that Sophie
and Pat were graded Class 1 employees of the Comintern and
had chicken plus extra food parcels, while a Class II typist like herself received one meatball for supper. Defying Pat's unthinking
acceptance of this privilege, she divided their food equally, even
sharing it with other girls in the typing pool. Occasionally, when
a comrade returned from a dangerous illegal assignment abroad,
there was a party with plenty to drink, but never much to eat.[4]

To those who have grown up accepting that contraception is
the responsibility of both partners, her next dilemma is unfamiliar.
Pat had no place in his totally committed lifestyle for paternity.
When Frieda became pregnant again because he refused to use
condoms, he was furious, accusing her of being responsible for

the problem. Abortions were legal in Russia – in fact, frequent because most Russian men would not use contraceptives.

Pat procured Frieda a rail ticket to visit her parents, more than 1,000 miles to the east of Moscow, so that she could have the abortion in Nizhny Tagil where her mother could look after her. There, Frieda decided to have the child, which was still-born. No consolation came from the busy father; instead, her post-natal depression lifted when she was invited to the Bolshoi Theatre by Jimmie Shields, editor of the London *Daily Worker.* In the box permanently reserved for the Comintern – formerly the Tsar's box – she met Georgi Dimitrov, the famous Bulgarian Comintern agent who had turned the tables on Goering at the trial in Berlin when he was accused of setting fire to the Reichstag,

> The door opened and my excitement was great as Jimmie introduced himself and me. All that evening I looked more at Dimitrov than at the performance of *Othello*. It was the most memorable moment of my young life and I was the envy of all my friends in the Lux.[5]

That meeting at the Bolshoi began Frieda's lonely and danger-ous life as an illegal courier, using her British passport as Pat's wife: international train journeys carrying secret documents and considerable sums of money in her clothes and secret compart-ments of her luggage and furtive meetings in Paris, Amsterdam, Prague, Zurich, Basel and Hitler's swastika-bedecked Berlin with strangers who exchanged passwords and vanished into the shadows. Occasionally, she took a plane – a rare event in those days – to avoid passing through hostile countries. Then she would go back to the sordid Hotel Lux, to find that Pat was sleeping in her absence with other women there, all captivated by his political record.

With all the foreigners cooped up in the Lux, that was common enough, and Frieda had fallen in love for the first time in her life with her contact in Vienna. Although it was against all the rules, she could not wait to be sent back there. However, her successful European missions earned her an unwanted promotion. She was 23 years old in the autumn of 1934 when ordered to take funds to China, a country torn apart by the civil war between Chiang Kai-Shek's Kuomintang army and Mao Tse-Tung's Red Army, fighting its way across several thousand miles in the Long March.

At this point, Stalin was still thinking he would be able to control a China emerging from the chaos of the warlords and the civil war. With the Kuomintang preventing commercial bank transfers to their enemies, Frieda's mission was to smuggle in American banknotes worth $100,000 – equivalent to more than $1.5 million today – to purchase arms for the Reds. She travelled to London to obtain a new passport without all the give-away European visas and was told by her contact to wear a full body corset to conceal the money belt. As the weather got hotter on shipboard in the Indian Ocean, it was an uncomfortable assignment.

Shanghai was an eye-opener: the squalid Chinese quarters where few Europeans ventured; the luxury of the French concession and international settlement where Chinese were admitted only as servants. Told to stay in a cheap hotel, Frieda waited with increasing unease for her contact, who did not turn up for days. Relieved at last to hand over the money and take off the sweaty corset, Frieda was dismayed when ordered to stay in Shanghai and give respectability to a safe apartment where an illegal transmitter was hidden. Fortunately, at the time she had no idea that the two Chinese radio operators of the Shanghai cell's link with Comintern Centre had been arrested and tortured into giving away the whereabouts of their transmitter shortly before. There was only one problem with Frieda's new job: the American replacement radio operator expected her to do her comradely duty and relieve his sexual frustration on demand. After several months of locking him out of her room each night, Frieda had to leave Shanghai hurriedly when her name was placed on a British arrest list.

This was a closer call than it might seem. Since the savagely repressed 1927 communist uprising in Shanghai, the Chinese, French and international settlement police forces collaborated on one thing only: eliminating communists. Of Frieda's foreign comrades, at least one American had been murdered by the Municipal Police Special Branch in collusion with British military intelligence.[6]

Smuggled aboard a Soviet cargo ship with a suitcase in which were concealed highly incriminating documents, Frieda endured a typhoon in which other ships were sunk, and entered Vladivostok harbour behind an ice-breaker. After a week aboard the Trans-Siberian, she was back in Moscow, handing over the documents and being debriefed. Expecting high praise for the risks she had run in China and the initiative she had shown, she was allocated a dirty bedroom at the Lux and awoke covered in lice, with the house doctor mocking her fears of typhus, from which a friend had died in Russia.

Commuting again to European capitals with money and hidden documents, Frieda returned to Vienna, made more dangerous since the 1934 Austrian Nazis' attempted coup d'état. There, her dreams were shattered on finding that her lover had been arrested and was probably dead.

Frieda's faith in the cause was still intact, but her mother's socialist dreams had melted like snow on the water in remote Nizhny Tagil. Having prudently kept her American passport, she left the USSR after advising her daughter to do the same by applying to rejoin Pat, who had been sent to stoke the fires of revolution in Eamonn de Valera's Ireland, now independent of Britain. It was as well that she did, for very soon Comintern agents with Frieda's tradecraft and knowledge were not allowed to leave the USSR, but were shot or sent to the Gulag to keep their mouths permanently shut. As a pre-echo of this, Frieda's father, who had taken Russian citizenship, was refused an exit visa like thousands of other foreign volunteers. Fortunately, Cousin Sophie's close relationship with Dimitrov procured an impressive-looking document covered in Comintern seals that frightened the frontier guards into letting him leave the USSR.

Dutiful comrade and loyal wife, Frieda endured another twenty years of marriage to Pat – at first in Ireland, where the enemy was not the local fascists, but priests who inveighed against Communism as the Antichrist and granted absolution to their communicants wanting to throw Pat Devine into the Liffey. From Dublin, the daredevil girl Comintern agent now travelled to Britain and settled down to life as wife, mother and party worker.[7]

By comparison with other female Comintern agents, Frieda Truhar was extremely fortunate. One who came from a very different background was Margarete Buber-Neumann, whose father was a prosperous brewer in Potsdam, Germany. Both of his daughters espoused socialism because it promised a better future than German women's traditional lot: *Kuche, Kirche und Kinder* – kitchen, church and children. In an unhappy divorce, Margarete's first husband gained custody of their two daughters and emigrated with them to Palestine. Margarete was 25 when she joined the German Communist Party (KPD) in 1926. After falling in love with Heinz Neumann, communist MP, member of the KPD Politburo and Comintern delegate, she discovered that two of the 'guests' they were hiding in their Potsdam-Babelsburg apartment were Georgi Dimitrov and his wife.

Margarete first visited Moscow in 1931, starry-eyed like Frieda until she saw a crowd of ragged children outside a bakery in Gorky Street begging for bread. Told that there would be no more scenes like this at the end of the first Five-Year Plan, she could not forget the starving children, but, as she later wrote, 'The faithful Communist is unbelievably good at excusing negative aspects of Communism as temporary problems on the way to an all-justifying end.'[8]

When in 1932 the Comintern ordered the KPD to support the Nazis in overthrowing the Social-Democratic government of Prussia, Heinz Neumann rebelled, correctly forecasting that this would accelerate the rise to power of Hitler's avowedly anti-communist party. For maintaining that the party must fight fascism at every turn, he was expelled from the KPD Politburo and given dangerous assignments in Spain and Switzerland, while Frieda undertook courier missions that occasionally allowed her to see him. When both eventually returned to Moscow, most of their old friends in the Hotel Lux avoided them in a climate of fear and tension quite unlike the euphoria of 1931–2. Fortunately, Dimitrov was now Gensek of the Comintern and employed multi-lingual Heinz Neumann as a translator. Margarete and he were then sent to Brazil for purposes unknown, but retribution for Neumann's rebellion followed on his return to Moscow. In April 1937 he was arrested by the NKVD, never to be seen again.

It was usual in the USSR for relatives to take food parcels to one prison after another, knowing that the guards would accept them only if the addressee was there. Margarete did this without success until July 1938, when she too was arrested. From Moscow's Butirki prison she was transferred to a work camp in Kazakhstan under appalling conditions.

Among Stalin's most hypocritical betrayals was the delivering of imprisoned German Communists to Hitler under the Ribbentrop-Molotov Pact. From the Kazakhstan Gulag, Margarete was transported to the women's concentration camp at Ravensbrück, where she survived five years of seeing fellow-prisoners used for medical experiments, shot or killed by lethal injections or gassing. In early April 1945, the camp was evacuated and 24,500 prisoners began a death march. As Allied troops approached, the guards released German prisoners, including Margarete. Fortunately, this happened four days before the Red Army arrived, so that she narrowly escaped being returned to the Gulag, or worse. Instead, she began a new life at the age of 44, writing of her experiences and vilified by the Left for her uncompromising hatred of *all* totalitarian dictatorships.[9]

10

FAMINE, PURGES AND BUNDLES OF USED NOTES

I n the spring of 1922 Lenin fell seriously ill and underwent surgery to remove a bullet from Fanya Kaplan's gun still lodged in his neck. A month later he was semi-paralysed, unable to speak. He never completely recovered, dying from a cerebral haemorrhage in January 1924. Towards the end, he attempted to persuade Trotsky to undermine Stalin and prevent the sly Georgian from seizing power after his death. Trotsky refused, so Lenin left behind a political time-bomb entitled *pismo k syezdu* – a letter to the Congress. Among its recommendations was his wish that Stalin be divested of all the powers he had accumulated as Gensek of the Central Committee.

Four months after Lenin's death, his widow Krupskaya sent a copy of the testament to the Central Committee for it to be read out to the Thirteenth Party Congress as he had wished. The Tseka, however, was already dominated by Stalin, who banned its publication, or any mention of it. Leaked abroad, probably by Krupskaya, it remained unknown inside the USSR for three decades until Nikita Khrushchev used it as a *pièce de conviction* in his 1956 denunciation of Stalin's crimes.

Thus, when the General Strike brought Britain to a standstill in 1926, Stalin's heavy hand was on the helm of the Comintern. The British Trades Union Congress (TUC) called the strike in support of the coal miners, who were locked in bitter dispute with the mine owners. Three million union members answered the TUC call, but the government's use of servicemen and volunteer strike-breakers ended the main strike after only nine days. Pollitt was already in jail at the time with eleven other CPGB members under the Incitement to Mutiny Act of 1797. Dutt, meanwhile, had moved to Brussels because in Britain Murrik could not go out in the daytime without risking arrest as an illegal immigrant. In Belgium she was free to move about and travel abroad – essential for her work as a Comintern courier.

Distance, however, did not weaken the iron control that Dutt exercised over the CPGB. From Moscow, acting through him, the Comintern imposed on the British comrades a new party line entitled Class against Class, under which they were to terminate all friendships outside the CPGB and treat all former allies in other left-wing parties as enemies. Friendless in any case, Dutt went along with this; Pollitt and others did not.

The settlement of the miners' dispute – the original cause of the General Strike – after seven long months was a sordid series of deceit and lies by the mine owners, who reneged on every promise, banking on the miners' families being ill and hungry to drive the men back to work and keep them there. After the Foreign Office broke off diplomatic relations with Moscow over Soviet support for the General Strike, Comintern money to the tune of £270,000 continued to arrive and was distributed in the coalfields to buy food, clothes and medicine, understandably winning widespread support for the CPGB, which held the purse-strings. Party membership shot up to 10,000, but was down to just over 3,000 two years later largely because, in slavish adherence to the doctrine of Class against Class, Dutt ordered an ill-advised campaign to smear the character of the miners' independent leader Arthur Cook.[1] This attempt at a Soviet-style character assassination nauseated the British public – which did not stop the Comintern making similar errors many times, because its Achilles heel was perpetual deafness to what the foreign comrades said. CPGB representative Jack Murphy spent most of his time in the Soviet capital nervously toeing the shifting party line, as when he cravenly proposed the expulsion from the Comintern executive of Trotsky.

While couriers brought Comintern funds to fill the CPGB's coffers, a flood of instructions also reached the King Street headquarters by clandestine radio transmissions. The Illicit Wireless Interception Unit of No. 4 Company Royal Corps of Signals was working with Scotland Yard's radio station at Denmark Hill, tasked with intercepting diplomatic and other coded traffic. In 1930 it detected a considerable volume of unlicensed transmissions from Britain on the international amateur radio wavebands. Direction finding on these transmissions prompted a police raid on a house in the London suburbs, which was the British base in a worldwide Comintern network, receiving instructions from Moscow[2] and relaying the replies to and from foreign parties and undercover agents, who included the staff of Russian banks and the Arcos trading company. A Special Branch raid on Arcos headquarters in London on 12 May 1927 revealed evidence that the company was a front for espionage and Soviet propaganda. Several Soviet citizens and diplomats were expelled two weeks later. In the tit-for-tat diplomatic game, Moscow replied in kind and for two years there were no diplomatic relations between Britain and the USSR.

Most transmissions to and from Comintern Centre were in cipher, except for what is called 'operators' chat'. Some messages were addressed to code names, while others were signed indiscreetly by Pollitt himself, regularly begging for money after the Comintern reduced and eventually stopped subsidising the CPGB, except through bulk orders for CPGB publications and copies of the *Daily Worker*. In addition, party members had free holidays and health care in the USSR – the author's headmaster and his friend Dean Hewlett Johnson of Canterbury Cathedral were among those who benefited. Promising activists were sent to the Lenin School for training in undercover work in their own countries or as Comintern couriers.[3]

Not until 1997 did declassified decryptions of coded messages to Pollitt and other CPGB leaders reveal the extent to which they followed Moscow's every order – for example to refute leaks about Stalin's purges in the Soviet Union and the inhuman treatment of millions of peasant families during his forced collectivisation programme under the first Five-Year Plan, that placed all economic activity under state control. On 1 July 1929 all the concentration camps in the USSR were integrated into the economy as sources of unpaid labour called *ispravitelno-trudovye lageri* – corrective labour camps. Marx had written, '(The) one and only means of correcting offenders (is) productive labour.'[4] However, the acronym for the camps' administration, *Glavnoye Upravlenie ispravitelno-trudovykh Lagerei,* became a five-letter synonym for a living death: Gulag.

While the priority afforded Stalin's ruthless drive for industrial modernisation achieved some startling results, by the end of 1932 collectivisation had resulted in the deportation of 1.2 million *kulaki* – the peasants who had been successfully farming their own land under NEP – to remote regions of Siberia and Central Asia, where hundreds of thousands died.

The *Manchester Guardian* Moscow correspondent Malcolm Muggeridge wrote of meeting some of them at the railway station of Rostov-on-Don in the Caucasus:

> A group of peasants were standing in military formation, five soldiers armed with rifles guarding them. There were men and women, each carrying a bundle. Somehow, lining them up in military formation made the thing grotesque – wretched looking peasants, half-starved, tattered clothes, frightened faces, standing to attention. These may be kulaks, I thought, but if so they have made a mighty poor thing of exploiting their fellows. I hung about, looking on curiously, wanting to ask where they were to be sent – to the north to cut timber (or) somewhere else to dig canals – until one of the guards told me sharply to take myself off.[5]

That evening, he joined a crowd in a street:

> It was drifting up and down while a policeman blew his whistle; dispersing just where he was, then re-forming again

behind him. Some of the people in the crowd were holding fragments of food – inconsiderable fragments that in the ordinary way a housewife would throw away or give to the cat. Others were examining these fragments of food. Every now and then an exchange took place. Often, what was bought was at once consumed. There is not 5 per cent of the population [here] whose standard of life is equal to, or nearly equal to, that of the unemployed in England on the lowest scale of relief.[6]

Muggeridge again:

At a railway station early one morning, I saw a line of people with their hands tied behind them, being herded into cattle trucks at gunpoint – all so silent and mysterious and horrible in the half light, like some macabre ballet.[7]

When he described peasants starving to death within sight of full granaries guarded by armed men, few people believed him. His later despatches were not used and he was sacked by the *Manchester Guardian*, editorially in sympathy with 'the great Soviet experiment', as it was called.

Another correspondent in Russia was Arthur Ransome, writing for the *Daily News* and the *Manchester Guardian* – later to become a best-selling author of children's stories with his *Swallows and Amazons* series. He did toe the pro-Soviet editorial line, and apparently never went looking for the truth about the famines. After meeting Lenin and Trotsky, he fell in love with the latter's secretary, Yegenia Petrovna Shelepina, who became his second wife. Bruce Lockhart, writing of his time as a consular official in Moscow, reported giving her a false passport to enable her to leave Russia and come to Britain with Ransome. This must have been a bluff to fool the British Home Office by implying that Shelepina had had to be smuggled out of Russia, because KGB files released after the end of the USSR indicate that she brought with her jewellery worth 2 million roubles, which was sold in Paris for the Comintern, before becoming the respectable wife of a successful author living in the Lake District.

Muggeridge, who stayed in Russia for eight months, suffered the fate of those who bravely swim against the tide – a tide, in this case, of fellow-travellers who came for a few days and saw what they were taken to see. Who dared contradict Dean Hewlett Johnson of Canterbury Cathedral when he applauded Stalin's 'steady purpose and kindly generosity'? Socialist opinion-former George Bernard Shaw made a lightning-conducted tour and pronounced himself fully satisfied that there was ample food for all in the workers' paradise – thus earning himself the hatred of the starving peasants when this was repeated in *Izvestia*.

Another Russian-speaking British journalist who dared to tell the truth about collectivisation was Gareth Jones, sometime personal secretary to Lloyd George, Britain's Prime Minister during the First World War. Jones' most bizarre visit to the USSR was in 1931, as interpreter for Jack Heinz II, heir to the canned soup fortune. Heinz was carrying sample cans of the 57 Varieties food range in the naïve hope of persuading the Narcomsnab Soviet Food Commissariat to buy enormous quantities of the company's products. Jones also visited Lenin's widow Krupskaya, who told him that after an argument with Stalin he had threatened her in these terms: 'Look here, old woman, if you don't behave yourself, I'll appoint another widow to Lenin!'[8] Since Lenin's mistress Inessa had died in 1920, whom Stalin had in mind to replace Krupskaya is a mystery.

'Joneski', as his Russian friends called him, was a reporter of conscience, who returned to Russia in 1932 and wrote articles for the Western press exposing the shortcomings and failure of Stalin's first Five-Year Plan – the ultimate lunacy of centralised planning. He wrote in one article, 'I walked through the country visiting villages and investigating twelve collective farms. Everywhere I heard the cry, "There is no bread. We are dying."'[9]

In January 1935 Joneski accepted a commission from American press baron Randolph Hearst to write another series of articles on the USSR. With journalists forbidden to visit the areas worst afflicted by the collectivisation famine, he bought a ticket from Moscow to Kharkiv in Ukraine, and alighted without permission at a small wayside station. Proceeding on foot, he was again greeted in every village with *'Khleba nyetu'* – there is no bread. In the most fertile grain-growing area of the USSR, all the peasants were emaciated with swollen bellies. Further south, in the region of Poltava, he learned, there were villages in which everyone had already starved to death.

For exposing in the Hearst newspapers what he called the Soviets' 'man-made famine' and taking photographs of emaciated, ill-clad orphans begging for food, Joneski was declared *persona non grata* and barred from re-entering the Soviet Union. Stalin's chubby foreign minister Maxim Litvinov instructed the Soviet ambassador in London to protest strongly to Lloyd George about Jones' behaviour. Undaunted, in July 1935 Joneski accepted another Hearst invitation to investigate Japanese-occupied Manchuria. There he met some of the tens of thousands of desperate refugees from Soviet Outer Mongolia, pastoral nomads whose herds – their only wealth and sustenance – had been confiscated by the commissars, who allowed the herdsmen to escape into Japanese-occupied territory with their lives but little more.[10]

Joneski wrote to his parents on 23 July when setting out into the interior of the country with a journalist accredited to the Deutsches Nachrichtenbüro press agency, Dr Herbert Müller, in a car put at their disposal by Wostwag, a Soviet-front trading company: 'We are going through bandit country to Dolonor. I am told they are very pleasant bandits and do not attack foreigners. Dr Müller knows the bandit leader quite well and we may call to see him.'[11]

Unbeknown to Joneski, the Wostwag manager Adam Purpiss was an undercover NKUD officer and Müller, married to a Chinese wife, was a Comintern agent who trafficked in antiques. After the car was hijacked by bandits, Müller was released unharmed with a ransom demand for the release of Joneski. On 1 August the Jones family in Barry, Glamorgan, received a cable from Changkiakow: Well treated. Expect release soon. Love, Gareth. It was not to be. On 16 August the London *Evening News* reported, 'Gareth Jones found murdered.' The *Evening Standard* carried the text of the Deutsches Nachrichtenbüro cable from Müller, beginning, 'Gareth Jones is no more. His body, pierced by three bullets, is lying in Pao Ch'ang.'

Like many later investigative reporters, Jones died in circumstances that make it difficult to know who was responsible. Were Müller and Purpiss ordered to get rid of a journalist who had already embarrassed Moscow more than enough? Or had he asked too many questions of the Japanese occupiers of Manchukuo? It is impossible to say.

A number of Western journalists were persuaded one way or another to toe the party line. Lincoln Steffens, the widely-syndicated American muckraker, famously announced on his return from the USSR, 'I have seen the future and it works.' For two decades, the doyen of the Moscow foreign press corps was Walter Duranty of the *New York Times*, described by Muggeridge as 'a plain little crook'. Duranty was an unpleasant man whose pro-Soviet reporting was a critical factor in President Roosevelt's 1933 decision to recognise the Soviet Union, despite all Duranty's colleagues knowing that his reporting was false. Having turned a blind eye to the Ukrainian millions killed by Stalin, when news of the famine and epidemics became known in the West, Duranty shrugged, 'You can't make an omelette without breaking eggs.'

Some people will say anything for a price. Other Moscow correspondents believed that Duranty was a necrophiliac who was allowed the privilege of unsupervised nocturnal visits to the city morgues in return for his favourable reporting. Writing of the 'unprecedented, fantastically successful experiment of re-educating socially dangerous people in conditions of free socially useful work,'[12] the most famous living Russian author, Maxim Gorky, was the highly privileged pasha of a harem organised on Stalin's instructions by OGPU on Gorky's return to Russia in 1929 from self-imposed exile on Capri.

As the *vozhd* and other Politburo members travelled in their personal luxury trains through the famine areas of Ukraine while en route to their holiday villas in the Crimea, they saw plenty of signs of the 10 million people dying of starvation and the empty villages from which millions more had been deported. Engineered by rigidly doctrinaire town-dwellers with no understanding of agriculture, the great 1930s Ukrainian famine, known as *holodomor*, was, in Joneski's words, an entirely man-made catastrophe unprecedented in peacetime.

Of the millions starving to death in the Soviet Union, it is not by chance that 5 million were Ukrainian. In Ukraine, the grain harvest of 1932 resulted in below-average yields, largely because of the disruption caused by the collectivisation campaign, but this was just sufficient to sustain the population until Moscow set requisition quotas at an impossibly high level. Brigades of security police and party officials toured the Ukraine confiscating not only the reserve for planting in the following spring but also the grain needed as food to survive the winter. A law passed in August 1932 made the theft of state property a capital crime. Since grain was decreed the property of the state, uncounted peasants died in front of firing squads for stealing for their starving children a few kilograms of their own grain from state granaries.

By the spring of 1933 starvation was general in Ukraine. Far from sending relief supplies, Moscow ordered the exportation of over 5 *million* tons of grain to the West during this period in payment for machine tools, tractor assembly lines, turbines, mining and other machinery required for Stalin's crash programme to modernise Soviet industry.[13] By the time the famine subsided after the 1933 harvest, so depopulated were large areas of Ukraine that Russian settlers were brought in to repopulate the empty villages, where women were harnessed to ploughs because all the horses had been slaughtered for food. Effectively, vast areas of Ukraine had been Russified without a war. Russian-speaking acquaintances of the author who lived in Ukrainian cities at this time never heard Ukrainian spoken. As far as they were concerned, they lived in 'south Russia'.

With Stalin suppressing publication of the 1937 census, for half a century Soviet officialdom refused to acknowledge the scale of the genocide, which modern demographic analysis estimates to have killed off more than 7 million country-dwellers.[14] However, although obediently denied by the Western parties, including the CPGB, the news leaked out. Fred Beal was an organiser of the US National Textile Workers Union who travelled through Ukraine during this time. He had left the US on a false passport while appealing against a twenty-year sentence for the murder of a police officer during a raid on union offices in North

Carolina. Previously a convinced Marxist, he was so disillusioned by the evidence of his own eyes in villages with no single living inhabitant, swarming with rats feasting on corpses, that he preferred to go back and face years in prison in America rather than stay in the Soviet Union. 'The union officials ate well', he said after his return. 'But the workers were starving. I never saw the equal of that misery in this country.'[15]

The next test of the CPGB came in 1932 when Sir Oswald Mosley left the Labour Party to found the British Union of Fascists, having been 'outed' as a fascist in the pages of the *Daily Worker*. As historian Francis Beckett commented, this was not an amazing achievement, because if you call everyone else a fascist, you are bound to be right sooner or later! Unwittingly, Mosley did the CPGB a great favour with his attacks on Jews, especially in London's East End, after which many Jews joined the party and others gave money to the CPGB, which they considered the only bulwark against growing European anti-Semitism. One of those who joined was a quiet, discreet hairdresser named Reuben Falber. Son of Polish-Jewish immigrants, he rose steadily through the ranks to become CPGB assistant general secretary in 1957, taking over as the party's bagman when Moscow again subsidised it after the Soviet invasion of Hungary drove so many British communists to tear up their membership cards that the party would otherwise have collapsed. Hidden in the loft of Falber's modest bungalow in Golders Green in north London were sacks of used sterling notes handed to him by KGB officers in the London embassy. Only a few select comrades knew where the money that kept the party machine going had originated. Falber quietly juggled the illicit cash and laundered it through various front companies.[16]

The growth of the British party during the 1930s was monitored by MI5 through mail interception, telephone taps and police raids. There was also a check on people of suspect political affiliation who worked in sensitive positions. One was Percy Glading, an ex-member of the CPGB Central Committee who had spent time in India trying unsuccessfully to recruit anti-British activists to the communist cause. Immediately after this, in June 1925, he was given back his old job at Woolwich Arsenal.

Vetting was so slack that in 1926 Harry Pollitt was almost employed there, which precipitated a tightening up of security that led to Glading's dismissal as unsuitable for employment in such an establishment.

In 1937, he began working directly for Soviet military intelligence,[17] using friends inside the arsenal to obtain blueprints and other classified documents, which he photographed and passed on to his Soviet contacts. In 1938 he and fellow CPGB members George Whomack and Albert Williams were arrested while in possession of secret documents. At their subsequent trial, they were sentenced to imprisonment for terms ranging from two to six years, after which party members employed in defence establishments handed in their membership cards and went undercover.

In July 1936 General Francisco Franco led his North African troops into Spain to unseat the Republican Socialist-Communist coalition government – the first move in what became the Spanish Civil War. The British government immediately embargoed arms supplies to the Republican government, after which Britain's official policy of non-intervention was denounced by the *Daily Worker*, whose circulation soared. Stalin saw a successful Soviet intervention as the perfect way to gain a foothold in Western Europe, and despatched the 1st Soviet Tank Brigade, plus aircraft repainted in Republican colours, flown by Soviet pilots until some Republican volunteers could be trained as pilots.[18]

After the Comintern was ordered to beat the recruiting drum by fanning the fires of anti-fascism, Pollitt defied Britain's 1870 Foreign Enlistment Act on 5 December by appealing in the paper for volunteers to fight Franco. Clandestine enlistment saw 2,200 Britons of both sexes, all social classes and a wide spread of socialist hues being surreptitiously handed rail tickets for Paris at London's Victoria Station on the first leg of a journey that included crossing the Pyrenees on foot in midwinter blizzards. Sometimes, their contact at Victoria, keeping one eye on the prowling MI5 officers, was Frieda Truhar, now a mother but still putting the cause first.

On Comintern instructions, the CPGB and the other foreign parties sent political commissars to keep up morale among their volunteers – and to spy on them, with sometimes fatal consequences among the volunteers. On arrival, as each volunteer was formally enlisted in the ranks of the International Brigades, his or her passport was taken away. Those who protested were told, 'In the International Brigades, such documents are unnecessary. You are a fighter against Fascism.' Those who survived and asked for the return of their passports were told that they had been lost. In this way Soviet espionage officers collected a pool of genuine Western passports into which new photographs were later inserted.[19]

At the same time, political commissars were weeding out free-thinking comrades. Ernest Hemingway, in his classic account of the war *For Whom the Bell Tolls* painted the portrait of senior commissar André Marty as a man who would kill deviants from the party line without compunction. The commissars also liked to give military orders, causing Fred Copeman, commander of the British brigade, to comment bitterly, 'There were too many bastards running around giving orders and not enough of them fighting … useless, silly orders and irresponsible to (sic) human life.'[20] British volunteer Eric Blair, better known under his pen-name of George Orwell, enlisted in the Republican militia, but fled Spain in May 1937, disgusted at the way communists murdered their allies of different political persuasions.

He wrote of 19-year-old-Bob Smillie, who died, not in battle, nor taken prisoner by Franco's fascists, but on his own side of the lines in a Republican prison, 'Here was this brave and gifted boy, who had thrown up his career at Glasgow University to come and fight against fascism … and all they could find to do with him was fling him in jail and let him die like a neglected animal.'[21]

NKVD Col Alexander Orlov[22] confessed to the FBI after his defection in 1938 that he was despatched to Republican Spain to organise guerrilla training for volunteer saboteurs and spies who were to work behind the fascist lines, one of whom was young Ramón Mercader, later famous as Trotsky's assassin. What he did not tell them was that he was also responsible for the assassination of alleged Trotkyist POUM Communists and anarchists fighting on the Republican side. His most important single coup in Spain was to persuade the Republicans in October 1936 to let him embark three-quarters of Spain's gold reserves on Soviet ships commandeered in the port of Cartagena, so that the gold could be taken to safety in Britain or the US where Franco could not seize them. In secure and heavily guarded caves near Cartagena where the Republicans kept their main ammunition store, there were 10,000 crates, each containing 145lb of gold ingots. Prices of gold bullion fluctuate considerably, but in today's values, this would represent around $1.5 million per crate. Of this treasure cache, Orlov spirited on board the Soviet vessels some 7,900 crates of ingots.

The timing of Orlov's operation was critical: on 20 April 1937 the Non-Intervention Committee based in London put into effect the Non-Intervention Committee Sea Observation Scheme, under which the British and French blockaded Nationalist ports and German and Italian navies blockaded Republican ports. By then, most of the Spanish gold had been unloaded, not in Britain or the US but in Odessa. Since he had successfully bluffed his Spanish contacts into letting him remove the gold without giving a receipt for the number of crates, Moscow afterwards claimed that its market value less than covered supplies delivered to the Republicans during the war. Until then, the Spanish comrades had thought that Soviet support was a gesture of socialist solidarity. Rarely has a victim been so neatly conned out of his money.[23]

In an attempt to draw Germany further into the conflict on a full war footing, Orlov was ordered to send Soviet aircraft in Republican colours to bomb the German pocket battleship *Deutschland* lying off the island of Ibiza, killing twenty-three and injuring eighty-three Kriegsmarine personnel. For once, moderation prevailed in Nazi Berlin and revenge was limited to a naval bombardment of the port of Almeria and withdrawal of German and Italian warships from the blockade.[24]

Senior British commissar and Comintern representative Bill Rust was using his cover as official correspondent with the Republicans for the *Daily Worker*. Its circulation was growing and CPGB membership was burgeoning, thanks to the anti-fascist image – which was just as well, with direct subsidy from Moscow now going to the foreign parties driven underground in countries under fascist rule. A number of communists also worked in deep cover on the other side of the lines. Among them, Kim Philby, a Soviet agent since 1933, was writing for the conservative London *Times* in order to repair his establishment image after marrying Austrian Communist Litzi Kohlman.

This was the time of Stalin's purges, to which comrades in the West resolutely shut their eyes. Determined to kill off all the Old Bolsheviks who knew too much about him, in December 1934 Stalin ordered Genrikh Yagoda, then boss of the NKVD, to arrest former Politburo members Grigori Zinovyev and Lev Kamenev for 'moral complicity' in the murder of Sergei Kirov, party boss in Leningrad. Tried in secret, they were re-tried in public in August 1936 at the first show trial of the Great Purge. Accused of con- spiring to assassinate Stalin and other leaders, Zinovyev and Kamenev confessed, in the vain hope of saving their families. Shot within two days of each other, they were declared innocent by the Soviet Supreme Court in 1988.

With Yagoda himself becoming a purge victim, the second show trial was staged by his successor, the sadistic 5ft-tall baby- faced Nikolai Yezhov, who adored being photographed beside Stalin, apparently never thinking that he too would be air- brushed out of the photographs after his own execution made him a non-person. In the second trial, twenty-one important members of the CPSU were accused of Trotskyist conspiracy and espionage for Germany and Japan; four were jailed, the others executed. And so it went on until ninety-eight of the 139 people elected to the Central Committee of the CPSU in 1934 were executed during the following three years, while 5 million Soviet citizens were being worked to death in the Gulag. And how did the leaders of the CPGB greet news of the sentences? They con- gratulated Soviet justice for meting out 'well-merited sentences of death'.[25]

However, NKVD officers in Spain and elsewhere in the West, including Orlov who had trained as a lawyer, knew the truth about the trials based on confessions under torture and were getting nervous. Not only had increasing numbers of their friends and colleagues been recalled to Moscow and never heard of again, but Yezhov had also instituted a 'special duties' unit that would later be known as *Shmersh*,[26] to track down and assassinate those who refused to return, although knowing that the Soviet law of 8 June 1934 decreed that their relatives in the USSR were equally guilty traitors under the principle of *krugo-vaya poruka* – collective responsibility.[27]

Inside the USSR, purges continued. Between 1936 and 1938 Stalin executed or sent to the Gulag three of his five marshals, thirteen of fifteen senior army generals, sixty-two of eighty-five corps commanders, 110 of 195 divisional commanders and 220 of 406 brigade commanders. More than half the officers ranked colonel or higher disappeared, leaving the Red Army a headless beast, with all remaining ranks terrified of making decisions lest they attract attention.[28] Hitler's speeches and his book *Mein Kampf* had made it crystal-clear that he intended a *Drang nach Osten* – a drive to the east to gain *Lebensraum*, or living space for the German-speaking peoples at the expense of the 'inferior races' living there. Yet, instead of strengthening the command of the Soviet armed forces, Stalin's paranoia emasculated it.

The foreign comrades who had come to the USSR as political refugees were also easy targets for Stalin's paranoia, especially those whose governments would not protect them because their national parties had been banned. They 'disappeared' by the score. In one case, after the arrest of his long-term sweet-heart, veteran Polish-born communist Rose Cohen, whose son was taken away and placed in a state orphanage, Harry Pollitt took courage in both hands and went to Comintern boss Georgi Dimitrov to ask for his help in getting her released. Cohen was tried on trumped-up charges and shot. Pollitt was warned off, as was Willie Gallagher, elected as the solitary communist MP in the 1935 General Election, more on his own merits than the public image of the CPGB. He later confessed that Dimitrov took his time before answering, 'Comrade Gallagher, it is best you do not pursue these matters.' So, Gallagher didn't.[29]

With Stalin's paranoia at its height, there were many matters *not to be pursued*. On 2 July 1937 the Politburo ordered local party secretaries to arrest all anti-Soviet elements in their areas. After trial by a *troika* of the secretary, procurator and local NKVD chief, they were to be executed if placed in Category 1; if in Category 2, they were to be deported to Siberia. The procedure under Politburo Order 00447 of 30 July was like a Five-Year Plan to increase productivity of death. Names and details of supposed guilt were unimportant. Each region was given a target figure for arrests. Initially, these totalled 72,950 to be shot and 259,450 to be deported – together with all their family members. Such was the momentum of this madness that regional party secretaries eagerly exceeded their quota and asked for new targets, to prove their own loyalty. Between 28 August and 15 December, the Politburo sanctioned a further 70,500 executions. Local party bosses used this carte blanche to settle old feuds and remove rivals.

When Nikita Khrushchev denounced Stalin's purges at the Twentieth Congress of the CPSU in 1956, he omitted mention of his own energetic participation by personally signing death warrants for thousands over and above the quota for the Moscow region, and then asking permission to shoot more. When even Stalin questioned the number of 'enemies' thus to be eliminated, Khrushchev enthusiastically replied, 'You can't imagine how many there are. The city of Stalinabad was given a quota of 6,277 to shoot, but actually executed 13,259.'[30] A simultaneous genocide was unleashed by Yezhov under Order 000485, directed against 'Polish diversionists and espionage groups', which saw 110,000 Poles shot and a further 34,000 deported. In the insane bloodletting, some historians estimate that 1.5 million innocent people were arrested and a high percentage of them executed.[31] As reward for his bloody record in Moscow, Khrushchev was appointed first secretary of the Ukrainian Party, and arrived in Kiev to find that most of the Ukrainian Politburo had already been purged. Given approval to purge a further 2,140 Ukrainians, he unleashed a new Terror in which 106,119 people were arrested.

Yezhov the Dwarf personally attended many night-long killing sessions, anaesthetising himself with alcohol, but he began to worry when Stalin ordered him to purge many of his own protégés[32] and Georgian secret police chief Lavrenti Beria was appointed as Yezhov's first deputy. The writing was on the wall for the Dwarf, who was unwise enough to denounce Stalin's favourite Malenkov, in whose office he was arrested by Beria.

Taken in December 1938 to the Sukhanovka prison, whence 21,000 of his victims had been driven after torture to the NKVD firing range at Butovo, outside Moscow, Yezhov broke down repeatedly, begging not to be hurt. To ensure complete secrecy, he was taken to a small out-station in Varsonovskii Pereulok, where he had to be carried into the execution chamber, weeping hysterically. His ashes were thrown into a common grave.

Stepping up to head the NKVD, Beria had an uncanny physical resemblance to Hitler's great murderer Heinrich Himmler: both looked like inoffensive bank clerks. In Beria's case, his mild appearance and warm family life apparently concealed a lust for personally beating and torturing victims of both sexes and kerb-crawling in his official black Zil limousine along Moscow streets at night, picking up women and girls, the younger the better. A Western visitor to his office suite after Beria's demise found one large room completely tiled and equipped with a gynaecological examination table. Stalin turned a blind eye to this, enjoying family singsongs of Georgian folk music with the new master of the NKVD.

Whether the British comrades gathered the full extent of the purges on their free trips to Moscow, is anyone's guess. Knowing what had happened to Rose Cohen did not stop Harry Pollitt going there sixty times. He also went clandestinely to Spain on several occasions, acting as postman, taking letters to and from the volunteers who had friends and family back in Britain. In the very last weeks of the fighting, he was near the Republican front lines, looking out of place in his three-piece suit and trilby hat among the ragged, exhausted survivors of the British Brigade. One week after the German occupation of Austria, Stalin ordered the International Brigades to remain in Spain to the bitter end to give him bargaining chip with Hitler, who wanted them out. Pollitt's mission was to stiffen the wilting resolve of men who could see all too clearly that their cause was lost. Many of their friends were dead and they were likely to die too, if they stayed. But they trusted Pollitt, and they did stay. The survivors returned home after months languishing in filthy, overcrowded *Falangista* prison cells, listening to the screams of the tortured and the shots of the firing squads in the prison yards.

11

ONE MAN, ONE PISTOL, ONE MONTH = 6,287 MEN DEAD

fter its defeat by Japan in 1905, Russia temporarily renounced its interests in southern Manchuria. Ten
years later the Japanese compelled the local warlords to
grant trading rights and a ninety-nine-year lease on a large part
of the country, subdued by its Kwantung army, which in 1931
took advantage of the Chinese civil war to occupy the rest of
Manchuria. The puppet state of Manchukuo thus created was
nominally ruled by the last Chinese emperor Pu Yi and recognised only by El Salvador, Costa Rica and the Vatican. The League
of Nations ruling that Manchuria remained an integral part of
China led Japan to quit the League in 1934. Disturbed by a million Japanese settlers in Manchukuo plus reinforcements for the
Kwantung army, Stalin signed a non-aggression pact with China
in 1937, so that in theory the two countries could take joint
action to dislodge the Japanese foothold on the Asian mainland.

After Hitler's annexation of Austria in March 1938, the French
and British governments forced Czechoslovakia to cede the
Sudetenland to Germany at the end of September, supposedly
in the interests of world peace. While the world watched and
waited for Hitler's next move in Europe, a war was being waged

in the Far East, where the Kwangtung army fought and lost two important battles against Soviet forces.

Contradicting all the Comintern PR against fascism, there had for some years been clandestine military collaboration between the USSR and Nazi Germany. Prohibited under the Versailles Treaty from modernising its armed forces, Germany had acquired naval facilities in Russia and three bases on land: at Lipetsk for training Luftwaffe pilots, at Kazan for testing tanks and at Tomka for chemical weapons research.[1] On 10 March 1939 at the Eighteenth Party Congress, Stalin hinted at an imminent non-aggression pact with Hitler. On 19 August, after a delicate dance by British and French diplomats had failed to conclude any alliance with the Soviet Union against Hitler's Germany, he informed the Politburo that Nazi Foreign Minister Joachim von Ribbentrop was coming to Moscow to agree a pact clarifying Russian and German spheres of influence in Eastern Europe. Hitler was making an offer that Stalin could not refuse, for what Russian ruler had ever spurned an offer of more territory? The fact that it was not Hitler's to give bothered neither side in this deal.

Stalin also told the Politburo that there was going to be a long war, which was a wonderful thing because no communist party could come to power in Western Europe during peacetime, whereas the economic stresses of a major war would provide the ideal economic conditions – as the First World War had in Russia.[2] So much for Lenin's strategy of 'attack from within' through the Comintern.

The German-Soviet Non-Aggression Pact was signed in Moscow on the night of 23-24 August 1939, with a secret protocol carving up Eastern Europe. Hitler's troops invaded Poland on 1 September. When Neville Chamberlain issued the famous ultimatum and received no reply from Berlin, Britain declared war against Germany on 3 September. A clue to what Pollitt felt, slavishly following Moscow's instructions and betraying those young believers in Spain, lies in his first action after Britain declared war. As a lifelong anti-fascist, he assumed it was his duty to international communism to publish an anti-German pamphlet entitled *How to Win the War.* On 7 September Stalin ordered Dimitrov to instruct the foreign parties, in the spirit of the Non-Aggression Pact, to cease all anti-fascist or anti-German propaganda and to denounce *and hinder* their governments' war efforts against Germany.

Pollitt, Dutt and two other CPGB nominees were on the Comintern executive, which had not met for four years. During this time, all decisions were made by the secretariat in Moscow, which had no British member. On the very the day that Pollitt's pamphlet was published, Dimitrov's cable arrived at CPGB headquarters in King Street. It read: 'The Communist parties, particularly of France, Britain, Belgium and the USA, which have taken up positions at variance with this standpoint, must immediately correct their political line.'[3]

In the US, party boss Earl Browder obeyed immediately; in Brussels, the Belgian Communist Party did likewise; in Paris, the PCF reversed its initial support for the war effort, getting itself outlawed as a result, with half its parliamentary *députés* arrested and the others on the run. In London, Pollitt was incredulous that the CPGB was being ordered to support a fascist enemy whose actions in Spain he had personally witnessed. Frieda Truhar was in the audience at the noisy meeting when party cards were torn up, with Pollitt and *Daily Worker* editor Johnnie Campbell made to eat crow. She wrote, 'Depressed by it all, I sat still, my son quiet in my arms … I felt unable to grasp this, let alone get up and challenge it. Again, that phrase, which had been dinned into us, surfaced, *Moscow knows best*.'[4]

Most young people are naturally idealistic. After the CPGB was told by Moscow to exploit this by organising a youth section in 1921, the British Young Communist League (YCL) was born. The man chosen to lead it was Bill Rust, who handed over to equally hard-line Dave Springhall, dismissed from the Royal Navy for attempting to convert his shipmates to Bolshevism. Swiftly building a record of enforcing every directive from Moscow, at the time the Pact was signed, Springhall was in Moscow. When he returned to London on 24 September, Pollitt was forced to inform the Central Committee of the new policy. Springhall, Dutt and Rust did an immediate about-turn 'to correct the British party line', but this time Pollitt listened to his own conscience, as did

Gallagher and three others. With Dutt lambasting them for *their* insincerity, Pollitt's pamphlet was withdrawn and replaced by a complete contradiction written by Dutt, entitled 'Why this War?'

A few days later, Pollitt and Campbell were punished by being expelled from the CPGB Politburo. Sacked as general secretary, Pollitt returned to his trade as a boilermaker. Having had her suspicions all along about his party comrades, his mother had kept his tools oiled and ready for use. The party's sole sitting MP, Willie Gallagher could hardly be expelled, but Dutt continued mercilessly haranguing him and the other heretics who refused to recognise that Stalin was, like the Pope, infallible – and to be obeyed at all times without question.

The Russian invasion of eastern Poland by 600,000 troops under marshals Kovalov and Timoshenko on 17 September – ostensibly to protect non-Polish ethnic minorities – was accomplished by the Red Army at little cost because the Blitzkrieg by Wehrmacht and Luftwaffe forces had eliminated all organised Polish resistance. Given the history of Poland, it is extraordinary that its high command had apparently made no provisions for such a stab in the back.

With no prior declaration of war, the Red Army took full advantage of the confusion resulting from the German invasion and the Polish army's unpreparedness for this second attack. In the town of Ostróg on the Polish-Russian border, the mayor was wrong-footed when he heard Soviet forces approach behind a band playing the best known *Polish* marching song. In Kopyczyńce a municipal official informed the bewildered citizens that they would beat back the Germans now that their brother Slavs had come to help. Jews ran out to kiss the soldiers who, they thought, would save them from the Gestapo. After a few local skirmishes, small adjustments of territory were made between Soviet and German forces. The Jews fled with the Soviet troops. Ukrainians grabbed a few possessions and headed the other way on the withdrawal of their German protectors. Those who felt they had made the wrong choice desperately attempted to reverse it. In his memoirs, Khrushchev admitted being amazed, seeing long lines of people applying for transfer to German-occupied Poland because 'most of (them) were members of the Jewish population. They were bribing the Gestapo agents to let them – return to their original homes' after a brief taste of Soviet occupation.[5]

Red Army soldiers had been indoctrinated by their commissars to tell Poles that Russia was a land of plenty. Unfortunately, they were supposed to say of everything, 'We make it in factories.' So when Poles asked whether they had unrationed meat or fresh fruit back home, they replied mechanically, 'We make it in factories.' The Soviet soldiery, for its part, was stunned to find that anyone could buy as much food as he could pay for in Polish shops, and freely purchase clothes or watches – although those who flashed around their purchases found themselves arrested and sentenced to up to twenty years in the camps for 'counter-revolutionary praise of capitalism'.[6] A few young soldiers warned Polish acquaintances, 'Kharasho ne buyet!' – meaning, things will get worse. Some repeated the Soviet joke that there were only three categories of people in the USSR: those who have been in prison, those who are in prison and those who will be in prison. Soon the suffering Poles jested sadly that NKVD was an acronym of Nie wiadomo kiedy wrócę do domu – impossible to say when I shall return home.

As First Secretary of the Ukrainian CP, Nikita Khrushchev donned military uniform and 'led his troops' with Timoshenko and the evil genius of NKVD mass deportations Ivan Serov, who was to share with Khrushchev the work of eliminating all Polish priests, officers, aristocrats and intellectuals, the aim being to leave only a peasant rump alive to grow food. The suffering in eastern Poland swiftly matched that in the west, only with different victims. Contradicting the Soviet government's 'justification' of its invasion of Poland by the need to protect the Ukrainian and Belorussian minorities there, between 309,000 and 320,000 people were deported eastwards from the formerly Polish provinces of western Ukraine and western Belorussia. From mid-February to the end of June 1940 long trains of cattle trucks wended their way eastwards transporting these poor people. With inadequate food and no medical attention, over 30 per cent of deportees were dead within the year, many dying in transit, their bodies abandoned unburied en route.

Meanwhile, an additional half-million people, mostly men, had been imprisoned in Poland under conditions of insanitary squalor, gross overcrowding and sporadic torture for periods averaging six to eight months, during which 50,000 of them were executed.[7] Even members of the Polish, western Ukraine and western Belorussia communist parties were arrested because their parties had been unilaterally 'disbanded' by the Comintern with no reasons given.

This was Soviet colonisation at its most ruthless – and cost-effective. According to Foreign Minister Vyacheslav M. Molotov, the campaign cost the Red Army only 737 deaths and 1,862 wounded. During the twenty-one months of Soviet occupation before Hitler invaded the USSR in Operation Barbarossa on 22 June 1941, seven waves of arrests resulted in 1.25 million Polish citizens – or 9 per cent of the population – being deported to labour camps, prisons and forced settlements in remote regions of the Soviet Union.[8] Particularly targeted were those Poles who had fought in the war against Russia in 1920. Known as *osadniki* – or settlers – they had been rewarded by small properties near the eastern frontier with Belarus and Ukraine, and were thus easy to identify and conveniently placed for deportation. Those Beria considered most anti-Soviet were arrested for 'special treatment'; all the others were deported en masse to remote parts of the Soviet Union.[9]

Some idea of the atmosphere of these deportations comes from one victim, Wiesława Saternus. In the early hours of 11 February 1940 her father was awoken by three NKVD men who, like modern hijackers, used excessive violence to gain the family's terrified obedience. With the children crying at the sight of their father being beaten up, their mother was given thirty minutes to bundle up a few things that might be useful. One of the NKVD men picked up a doll and gave it to Wiesława, telling her that where they were going, there were no dolls. Thirty minutes after the knock on the door, the whole family, including the elderly grandmother, who just happened to be visiting, were roughly loaded onto a truck. Other witnesses described children too young to climb up being thrown aboard like sacks of potatoes. At the local station, families were immediately locked inside freight cars still filthy and vermin-infested from transporting animals to slaughter. In the middle of a Polish winter, they began a journey of weeks that ended at a remote forestry settlement in Siberia. On the way, as it would be for the next years, hunger was the main enemy. Old people and children died, their bodies thrown out of the trucks at the next halt. 'The hunger was horrible', Wiesława still recalls today. 'It can't be understood by anyone who hasn't experienced it. Real hunger damages a human being. A person becomes an animal.'[10]

But what did the perpetrators of these deportations feel? NKVD man Nikolai Dyukarev was one of them. 'I don't know what happened to (the people we rounded up like that),' he says now. 'But it was very hard work. It wasn't very pleasant. When I was young, it was different, there were orders that had to be obeyed. But now I think about it, it's hard to take the children away when they're really small. I would rather not talk about it.'[11] Some of his comrades did show compassion, advising their victims to take warm clothing and food and even helping them to pack; others told the bewildered families to take nothing because they would be back by supper-time – so that they left all their possessions behind to be plundered by the men who arrested them.

And what about those singled out for 'special treatment'? Galina Stavarskaya was 19 when arrested by the NKVD near Lviv and accused of belonging to a Ukrainian nationalist organisation. If true, the allegation made her one of the people the Red Army had invaded ostensibly to protect. Beaten with fists and rubber truncheons by three men, who tore her curly hair out by the roots, she was thrown into a cell so packed with bodies that she had to get what sleep she could on the floor soaked in urine overflowing from the communal latrine bucket. And she was one of the 'lucky' ones who were not shot.[12]

The dismemberment of Poland accomplished without serious clashes between German and Soviet forces, Ribbentrop flew back to Moscow on 27 September to tidy up the map of Eastern Europe and avoid conflicts of interest. So nakedly imperialistic were the Russian demands at the negotiating table that Molotov was still denying the details thirty years later. He had abandoned his family name Scriabin in favour of the revolutionary name meaning 'hammer' because he saw himself as the hammer of counter-revolution, of the party itself, and certainly of fascism. Yet, Ribbentrop felt so much at home with Stalin, Molotov and Co at the Kremlin banquet that he remarked to an aide, 'It's just like being with our own (Nazi) old comrades.' It must have been the vodka talking: for all his vices, Hitler never terrorised his close associates as Stalin did.

Counsellor Gustav Hilger from the German Embassy in Moscow acted as Ribbentrop's interpreter, and was also completely taken in by the ambiance.[13] Stalin was playing the same cards he would later use with President Roosevelt, acting the part of a good-humoured host while outmanoeuvring his visitors, elated by their apparent success in dealing with him. Just before Ribbentrop's first visit, he had told the Politburo that 'the Soviet Union (had to) do everything possible to prolong the war and exhaust the Western Powers'.[14]

With Hitler's agreement to his host clawing back the Baltic republics that had belonged to Imperial Russia, by 3 October Latvia, Lithuania and Estonia had all 'agreed' to accept Soviet occupation forces and Serov issued to the NKVD units involved a long directive entitled, Instructions regarding the Manner of Conducting the Deportation of anti-Soviet Elements from Lithuania, Latvia and Estonia.[15]

Emboldened by this easy expansion, Stalin next demanded that Finland accept border revisions permitting construction of a Soviet naval base west of Helsinki. At the time, the Finns had 200,000 men in arms to face seventy divisions of the Red Army, totalling 1 million men. When the Finns refused, Stalin unleashed five Soviet armies with 1,000 tanks against them on 30 November. This time, there was no pretence of saving ethnic minorities. Finland was protected on its eastern flank by the Mannerheim Line of concrete fortifications and by the terrain of lakes and forests impassable for wheeled vehicles and even tanks. The Winter War, as it became known, was a saga of heroism, in which the heavily outnumbered Finnish forces lost around 50,000 men against Soviet losses of more than 200,000. The true figures were never revealed by the Kremlin because they were too embarrassing.

One weapon invented by the Finns was afterwards re-invented and named after Molotov. Lacking anti-tank guns, the Finns stuffed rags into bottles of gasoline and hurled them into the driving slits of Soviet tanks at close quarters. Despite numerical superiority of about five to one, the Russian advances stalled, with the main drive from Leningrad halted by the bunkers of the Mannerheim Line and the difficult terrain, in which the Finns fought with unrivalled tenacity, aided by the sudden onset of winter.

After the 9th Soviet Army was smashed in December at the battle of Suomussalmi, Stalin concealed his own responsibility by ordering General Lev Mekhlis of the NKVD to purge the army's command. Following open-air mock trials in front of their men, the officers were shot on the spot. Despite them taking the blame, Stalin's reaction to the Finns' stubborn resistance was a nervous breakdown and psychosomatic illness. Khrushchev found him in the Kuntsevo dacha, wallowing in self-pity and incapable of taking decisions. It was a syndrome to be repeated when Hitler invaded Russia the following year.

On 1 February 1940, fourteen fresh Soviet divisions were hurled against a 10-mile sector of the line near Summa, where relentless artillery bombardment finally broke through. In midwinter conditions far below zero, armour and infantry advanced as the Soviet Air Force broke up Finnish counter-attacks, making Finland's eventual collapse certain. France and Britain had both promised military assistance, but the too-little-too-late British-French-Polish expeditionary force never reached Finland, and was diverted to Norway instead, leaving the government in Helsinki obliged to sue for peace on 6 March 1940 after taking losses of 70,000 against Soviet losses many times higher. On 12 March Stalin's envoy Andrei Zhdanov imposed a treaty by which Finland ceded to Russia 9 per cent of its territory and 20 per cent of its industry: the entire Karelian isthmus, the port/city of Viipuri, part of the Rybachy Peninsula and land for the construction of a naval base on the Hanko Peninsula 60 miles to the west of Helsinki.

Stalin could now face the Kremlin portraits of Tsars like Ivan the Terrible and Peter the Great as an equal, which Leo Tolstoy's son Alexei told him he was, exhorting him to follow in the same Russian tradition.[16] In the seven months since signing the pact, at the cost of a mere quarter-million soldiers' lives, Stalin had gained a vast buffer space on his western borders, and could now turn his energy on the last of the territories handed to him by Hitler.

On 22 March 1940, one of the many thousands of purged Red Army officers was released from the Gulag. Immediately sent to the Romanian border to participate in the occupation of Besserabia, General Konstantin Rokossovski was minus nine teeth, with three broken ribs and his toes smashed with a hammer during captivity. After thirty months of torture and imprisonment, he went on to command six Soviet divisions that trapped and captured the German 6th Army at Stalingrad.

Although of Polish origin, Rokossovski was useful, but Stalin was mulling over what to do with the thousands of his compatriots arrested or captured as POWs in September 1939. Grigory Kulik, now commanding the Polish 'front', was elevated to marshal rank just after his beautiful wife had been arrested and thrown into Beria's Moscow prison, the Sukhanovka. There she was murdered by Stalin's favourite executioner Vasili M. Blokhin, for whom it was a busy year. Beria was recommending that 14,700 Polish officers and intellectuals were 'anti-Soviet elements' who should be eliminated. Kulik, flushed with his new rank, and perhaps unaware that his wife had been killed, recommended that the officers among them should all be exterminated. Some were released, but 26,000 – the cream of the Polish officer corps – were held in three special camps. Under an order personally approved by Stalin on 5 March, every one of the 4,443 prisoners at the Kozielsk camp on the Polish-Russian border was shot between 3 April and 13 May 1940 in Katyn Forest near Smolensk after being herded to the edge of mass graves, where they were machine-gunned by NKVD executioners using German ammunition to confuse possible investigators. The killers were liberally plied with alcohol as a reward for this arduous work and for the shooting of a further 3,896 Poles held in the Starobielsk POW camp near Kharkov.

For the men in the execution squads it was so much part of normal life that 11-year-old Nina Voevodskaya was taken by her uncle, who was an NKVD officer, to see the Poles waiting their turn in railway wagons inside the forbidden area. From behind barred windows, she recalls, 'the Poles were waving hallo to us ... They were young, dressed in uniform. I can even now remember how handsome they were.' Why were they so cheerful? In a variation of the Nazi 'showers' at the concentration camps, they had been inoculated and given food on the trains, which they assumed meant they were being sent to a work camp.[17]

The administrative problem of killing so many men in secret – as distinct from simply machine-gunning them on the edge of mass graves, in which case there would have been numerous witnesses and local people who heard the shooting – was overcome by Blokhin, who went to the camp at Ostrakhov with two assistants and set up a special killing chamber, lined with sandbags to absorb stray bullets and deaden the sound. There, after careful checking of their names, Blokhin's target was to shoot 250 Poles in the back of the head *on each of twenty-eight consecutive nights.* Clad in a leather slaughterhouse apron, boots and leather gauntlets, he used a German Walther 9mm pistol, achieving the incredible target of 6,287 victims for his month's work. A further 7,800 Poles considered guilty of 'resistance' were also executed at this time. For this Stakhanovite labour, Blokhin was awarded the Order of the Red Banner and a small cash bonus.

The only possible rationalisation for this eradication of Poland's officer corps and intellectuals was the age-old expansionist imperative, which dictated killing all adult males in conquered territory to prevent rebellion.

Much later, when Stalin discussed with the Polish émigré government from London the formation of a Polish army to fight the Germans, he was asked to release the Polish officer POWs, and said they had all escaped to Manchuria. In private, he admitted, 'We made a mistake.'

In June 1940, Zhdanov was sent as proconsul to Estonia, where he promised that everything would be done 'democratically'. With roughly 60,000 Estonians, as well as 75,000 Lithuanians and 34,250 Latvians executed or deported by Zhdanov and Serov, Stalin joked that Beria would 'take care of the accommodation of any Baltic guests'.[18]

Meanwhile, the West had for the first time been learning of the extent of espionage by Soviet diplomats. In Washington during October 1939 the House Un-American Activities Committee heard evidence from Walter G. Krivitsky, who had been Soviet *rezident* in The Hague, with wide-ranging responsibility for Comintern espionage in Europe. Alarmed at the likelihood of becoming a victim of the purges taking place in Russia, Krivitsky and fellow spy Ignace Poretsky decided to defect. Poretsky's assassination by Shmersh in Switzerland prompted Krivitsky to leave Europe for America, where he published *In Stalin's Secret Service* – the first detailed account of Soviet anti-Western espionage to be made public. He also travelled to Britain and was debriefed by MI6, but died back in the US during February 1941 in mysterious circumstances that bore the hallmarks of a Shmersh elimination.

Before then, one other murder planned in Moscow attracted worldwide interest. Of the members of the 1920 Soviet Politburo, all except one had by August 1940 been killed by Stalin. The only man he truly feared as a rival, Leon Trotsky had been expelled from the Politburo and the Central Committee. Exiled in 1928 to Central Asia, he was banished from the USSR in January 1929. Since then, he had been in hiding in several countries, narrowly escaping a number of Soviet assassination attempts.

Under the principle of *krugovaya poruka* – collective responsibility – Trotsky's daughter Nina was refused medical treatment and died of tuberculosis in 1928. His son Sergei was brought back to Moscow from a labour camp in 1937 and shot, being declared innocent of any crime by the Russian Supreme Court after the fall of the USSR. Trotsky's other son Lev died in mysterious circumstances in Paris in 1938. Stalin's paranoia finally caught up with him in a suburb of Mexico City called Coyoacán shortly after he signed a contract to write about Soviet world strategy for the right-wing Hearst Corporation – an unlikely partner for an Old Bolshevik. If the contract was intended as an insurance policy, it failed miserably.

Trotsky's murderer Ramón Mercader was a 26-year-old Comintern agent whose mother Maria Caridad was a fanatical commissar personally responsible for murdering twenty or more

POUM volunteers during the Spanish Civil War – a bloody activity in which her son had also shown such promise that he was selected for special training in Russia. The chain of command controlling Mercader ran from Stalin to NKVD boss Laventi Beria and Pavel Sudoplatov, deputy director of the NKVD's Foreign Department, who admits in his book *Special Tasks*, that he was responsible for 'sabotage, kidnapping and assassination of our country's enemies beyond the country's borders'.[19]

As his man on the spot, Sudoplatov chose Nahum Eitingon, who had set up several networks of émigré Russians in the US to spy for the USSR. Eitingon suggested the code name for the operation, dubbed *utca*, or duck, which in NKVD slang meant disinformation.

The first attempt to kill Trotsky was a failure. A dozen Spanish communists broke into their intended victim's fortified villa on 21 May 1940 with automatic weapons and hand grenades. Incredibly, Trotsky and his wife survived by hiding under a bed when the room was sprayed with bullets through the locked door.

Eitingon briefed Mercader on a more subtle approach. Trotsky's loyal secretary Sylvia Agelof was the ideal target for a NKVD seduction. Sexually inexperienced, in Paris she had fallen for the calculated advances of Mercader, posing as a sympathiser of the Trotsky faction. Using the identity of a Canadian citizen named Frank Jacson [sic], Mercader now used Ageloff to ingratiate himself with Trotsky's friends. On 20 August, he arrived at the villa with an ice pick hidden inside his jacket. Within minutes, the point of the ice pick was buried deep in the skull of Trotsky, who died the following day, still an ardent believer in the imminent worldwide Communist revolution.

Narrowly escaping death at the hands of Trotsky's bodyguards, Mercader received the maximum sentence of twenty years for the crime, Mexico having no death penalty. Moscow denied responsibility for the murder and Mercader refused to divulge his true identity or motives. However, Kremlin-watchers noted that Eitingon was rewarded for the successful assassination by promotion to deputy director of Glavnoe Razvedyvatel'noe Upravlenie (GRU) – Soviet Military Intelligence. Later decryption of extensive intercepted radio traffic after the murder between

NKVD Centre and Mexico City included plans to spring Mercader from prison. If any doubt remained, the USSR blew its cover completely after his release in 1960 by making him a Hero of the Soviet Union with the Order of Lenin. He was buried in Kuntsevo cemetery under a false name, Ramón Ivanovich Lopes.

Emboldened by winning so much territory under the Non-Aggression Pact, Stalin despatched Molotov to Berlin in November 1940 with further territorial demands for Soviet annexation of the rest of Finland and Romania, plus Bulgaria and parts of Turkey, Hungary and Iran. The banquet given by Molotov in the Soviet Embassy for Ribbentrop, Goering and other Nazi luminaries was interrupted by RAF bombers – a foretaste of Berlin's future. With Operation Barbarossa now far advanced in planning, Hitler ordered Molotov to be cold-shouldered. He returned to Moscow empty-handed.

In Britain, complying with Stalin's pro-German party line caused the banning of the *Daily Worker* on 21 January 1941 – but not before Dutt had it print a rabid accusation that Sir Walter Citrine, General Secretary of the TUC, was plotting with his French counterparts 'to bring millions of trade unionists behind the Anglo-French imperialist war machine'. This new attempt at a Moscow-style character assassination not only failed but also exposed the CPGB's true allegiance when Citrine sued and evidence was presented in court that demonstrated beyond any doubt how completely supine was the *Daily Worker's* editorial staff vis-à-vis its Comintern masters. Coming, as this did, after Krivitsky's revelations, Dutt had done great harm to the party's cause in Britain.

12

THE POLITBURO
TAKES A SHORT RIDE

fter a coup d'état in Belgrade overthrew Yugoslavia's pro-German government on 26 March 1941, Hitler ordered a ten-day Blitzkrieg to re-install a government friendly to Berlin. The move was a costly error, diverting forces required for Operation Barbarossa – the invasion of the Soviet Union – and caused a fatal one-month delay in its launch.

The Red Army High Command was dangerously inexperienced after all the purges. Compounding the problem, Stalin lived in the closed world of the Kremlin, surrounded by a chorus of sycophants orchestrated by Molotov and Zhdanov, who were constantly telling the man they called *khozyaïn*, or boss, of his genius at everything from literary criticism to economics and music. Each day, *Pravda* and *Izvestia* sang his praises. From Leningrad to Vladivostok any mention of his name was prefaced by 'the great'. This constant adulation caused Stalin to think himself a master of grand strategy, although in fact he was unable to read a map correctly. As the winter of 1941 gave way reluctantly to spring in Russia, he convinced himself that Hitler's war in the west, culminating in a long struggle with Britain, would weaken the armed forces of the Reich to the point where the Red Army could easily annihilate them and win the whole European continent previously subjugated by German force of arms.

All Soviet armament factories and training schedules were geared to this pipe dream being realised at a time of Stalin's choosing *after mid-1942*. Because Stalin was gambling everything on a first-strike against a weakened enemy, he refused to plan for defence. To give Hitler no reason to turn on him before he was ready, he therefore ordered the shaven-headed defence commissar Semyon Timoshenko and thickset chief of the general staff Georgi Zhukov not to make any move on Russia's western borders that could be construed in Berlin as provocation. Accordingly, regular shipments of vital metals like copper, molybdenum and nickel continued to be delivered to Germany, together with 232,000 tons of petroleum products and 632,000 tons of grain in the first four months of 1941.[1] Red Army commanders had regularly to tolerate German officers making 'friendly' tours of inspection. Local air commanders watched impotently as Luftwaffe pilots flew low-level photo-reconnaissance missions over the western defences, which were in chaos because the acquisition of eastern Poland under the Pact required construction of a new defence line 150–200 miles to the west of the pre-1939 Stalin Line. The new line was still under construction, undermanned and with gaps of up to 40 miles between strongpoints. Much of the heavy armament had been removed from the Stalin Line, but was not yet installed in the new line and was therefore useless in either place. If this was the reason why Hitler had given Stalin half of Poland, it was a very successful ploy.

Red Army commanders on the ground were aware of the German build-up taking place opposite them, but their reports to Moscow were blocked by Timoshenko and Zhukov, terrified of giving Stalin any news that contradicted his world-view after the former chief of staff was shot for prudently proposing a fallback command post on the western front. Information did not flow in the other direction either: reports from Comintern and other agents abroad indicating an imminent German offensive did not reach Timoshenko and Zhukov.

As summer succeeded spring of 1941 a number of these reports had been proven wrong. When Churchill sent a personal warning through the British ambassador in Moscow, Stalin's paranoia convinced him it was a capitalist plot, and that Hitler would never repeat Germany's error of 1914–18 by fighting a war on two fronts. No one dared point out that the ground war in the West was over, with Britain unable to invade the Continent in the foreseeable future. This was, in fact, exactly the time when Hitler *had* to attack in the East.

The Comintern's two most valuable agents at the time were in Tokyo. With American writer Agnes Smedley, Richard Sorge set up a network of highly placed informants while employed as political adviser to the German ambassador. On 12 May 1941 he sent to Moscow a shattering report: 170 German divisions will attack on 20 June! Still Stalin forbade any preparations, arguing that 149 Soviet divisions on the western frontiers were more than enough to hold any attack. He refused to listen when told by Zhukov that a German division was roughly twice as large as a Soviet one, as well as being far better equipped and combat-experienced.

On paper, Stalin had 9,200 combat aircraft against Germany's 2,000-odd, but few Russian aircraft had two-way radios and very few pilots had more than twelve hours' flying time since the beginning of the year. Hardly any had combat experience. Soviet tanks outnumbered Hitler's by 14,200 to 3,350 but were so badly maintained that it was impossible to say how many were combat-ready at any one time. On the western borders there were fewer than 1,500 with armour and guns that gave them a chance against the latest Wehrmacht and Waffen-SS Panzers.

Even these were still split up among other formations, preventing deployment in fast-moving armoured columns, which was exactly the same error that had caused France's defeat by the Wehrmacht in May and June 1940. If anyone in the Red Army had read Guderian's or De Gaulle's writings on modern armoured warfare, Stalin's purges, which made the expression of new ideas a fast track to a firing squad, kept their mouths firmly shut.

Red Army radio communications systems were rudimentary, orders being transmitted on vulnerable above-ground cables.

Bridges in the crucial frontier areas had never been strengthened to carry tanks or heavy artillery, nor were they mined to permit rapid demolition in a retreat. Yet, despite repeated confirmation from German deserters of a massive build-up on the eastern front, no preparations were made to repulse the imminent invasion.[2]

Yet, the fight against 'internal enemies' was proceeding apace. In the Baltic republics Beria's NKVD teams were hard at work arresting politicians, army officers, landowners, business-men and even police officers. Sentenced to labour camps for five to eight years, they and their deported families totalling 170,000 men, women and children, afterwards faced twenty years' exile in Siberia.[3]

Thus far, Stalin had controlled the government as first sec-retary of the CPSU, forcing others to put their names to his policies, so that he was not responsible in the public mind for the famines or purges that killed so many. On 5 May 1941 he appointed himself prime minister in place of Molotov.[4] It thus became vital for Zhukov and Timoshenko to have daily access to him, but he refused to see them once between 11 and 18 June. Finally unable to ignore them, he belatedly agreed that Soviet aircraft and runways of forward airfields should be camouflaged. Molotov was ordered to instruct the ambassador in Berlin to obtain reassurances of Hitler's good faith, but no reply could be obtained. German vessels were hastily clearing Soviet territorial waters. German Embassy staff in Moscow were openly burning documents. The Wehrmacht was removing anti-tank barriers all along the front. On the Russian side, only the Soviet navy was on a war footing – and this because it was historically so unimpor-tant that Stalin had omitted to place it under his personal control with the army and air force.

At 3 a.m. on 22 June, cities on a 1,500-mile front from Sevastopol in the Crimea to Estonia's capital Tallinn were being bombed by aircraft bearing Maltese crosses. Communications between Moscow and the front were non-existent. With Soviet units annihilated where they stood or falling back in disorder, orders arrived, if at all, long after any possibility of executing them. When summoned back to Moscow to give a situation report, the best idea Zhukov could come up with was to use the 3 million men between the Germans and Moscow as sand-bags to absorb the German momentum and thus gain time to set up two defensive arcs to protect the western approaches to the capital.

After the first week of hostilities, Hitler's troops occupied all pre-1939 Poland. While the Red Army fought sporadically or retreated, the NKVD was pursuing its own agenda, moving some 150,000 prisoners from Poland to the east, or killing them before the Germans could liberate them – as the Nazis would do with concentration camp inmates in 1945. After the Soviet retreat from Lviv in Ukraine, prisoners' relatives found in the prisons only heaps of bodies, many so mutilated they were unidentifiable.[5]

Stalin spent much of his time unavailable for consultation in his dacha at Kuntsevo, with no one else making decisions in case they led to a bullet from Blokhin in the back of the neck. More than a week after the invasion began, on the afternoon of 30 June, the half-dozen next most powerful men in the USSR met in the office of Molotov, trying to solve the problem and not lose their lives. At one point Nikolai Voznesensky, the econo-mist responsible for getting Soviet industry back on its feet after being transported thousands of miles to the east, took his life in his hands by saying to Molotov, 'Vyacheslav Mikhailovich, we'll follow you!' The other members of the Politburo pretended they had not heard.[6]

Instead, Beria proposed forming a State Defence Committee, chaired by Stalin. Molotov was hesitant but Malenkov, Mikoyan, Voroshilov and Voznesensky agreed. They drove out to the dacha in two cars, to find Stalin sitting in the dining room with curtains drawn. From his reaction to their arrival, it was appar-ent he feared they had come to arrest him. This would have been a fair reward for his inactivity and hindrance of Zhukov and Timoshenko – let alone for killing off thousands of the Red Army's best officers. Relieved to find that his visitors were terri-fied to take any initiative without his approval, he immediately endorsed Beria's plan.[7]

Hitler's Operation Barbarossa mobilised 3 million men in a three-pronged offensive aimed at the Ukraine in the south,

Minsk and Moscow in the centre and the Baltic states with Leningrad in the north. The first three weeks of fighting cost 600,000 casualties out of Zhukov's written-off 3 million men. German spearheads advanced up to 350 miles in places during the first ten days, during which territory inhabited by 20 million Soviet citizens was captured. Stalin's failure to plan the defence of his country meant that this ground would not be regained until the end of 1944 – at a cost of further millions of lives.[8] However, as he remarked on another occasion, 'One death is a tragedy, a million deaths is a statistic.'

On 28 August 1941, Stalin dissolved the Volga German Autonomous Soviet Republic, ordering the forcible deportation of 367,000 ethnic Germans from there and another million or so other ethnic Germans who had been living elsewhere in Russia for generations, some since they had been invited to settle in Russia by their compatriot Catherine the Great. Uncounted thousands perished after being shipped in cattle cars to Siberia and Kazakhstan – largely depopulated of its pastoral nomads, who had fled into Chinese territory to avoid a similar fate.

While Churchill's adviser Lord Beaverbrook and Roosevelt's special envoy Averell Harriman were discussing Soviet military aid requirements in Moscow on 1 October, a mere 250 miles away General Guderian's Panzers broke through the Russian lines near Briansk. Immediately, the priority of Hitler's offensive changed: Moscow became the main objective. As the foreign VIPs were repeatedly toasted in an extravagant feast that was overwhelming to a visitor accustomed to rationing in wartime Britain, Stalin was visibly nervous, and for good reason. So was Hitler, Oberkommando der Wehrmacht war games having repeatedly shown that the Russian campaign had to achieve victory in three months, or fail. The race was on between the over-stretched German supply lines and the advent of winter – with a further 665,000 Russian soldiers surrounded.

By 5 October, Russian reconnaissance aircraft reported long lines of German tanks driving through a 12-mile gap in the front only 60 miles from the Kremlin. On 7 October, Stalin asked Beria whether he had any go-betweens in Berlin who could initiate peace negotiations. Zhukov mustered another 90,000 men as cannon fodder by press-ganging untrained civilians and Gulag prisoners. With enormous loss of lives, the German advance was slowed. On 18 October the twin defenders of Russia that General Kutuzov had dubbed General January and General February came to the rescue, with the first snowfall impeding the German advance. With the thaw, even tracked vehicles became bogged down.[9]

Astoundingly, at this juncture when every man and woman in Russia was an asset, if only to die for the fatherland, Stalin's individual murders included Dr Bronka Poskrebysheva, wife of his faithful *chef de cabinet*, whose body was thrown into a mass grave with some of the 157,000 servicemen who were shot for 'cowardice'; 837,000 others were condemned to different punishments. Industrial plant workers were still being shipped eastwards, one step ahead of the German advance. In Moscow, Stalin's treasured collection of books was moved by special train to safety while terrified thousands waited in the stations for trains that did not come. Food shops were looted, officials burned records – and important prisoners were murdered before the Germans could liberate them. Beria's special tasks expert Sudoplatov was ordered to blow up the Politburo's dachas so they could not fall into German hands, and to place demolition charges on the main buildings and bridges of the capital.

When the slush re-froze, the German advance resumed, but in the meantime a report from Richard Sorge in Tokyo that the Japanese High Command was planning to advance southward against Pacific targets rather than against the USSR enabled Lazar Kaganovich, a deputy premier and member of the Defence Committee, to move 400,000 men along the Trans-Siberian railway from the Far East to Moscow, with 1,000 tanks and 1,000 aircraft. Sorge's feed of priceless information now dried up completely after he was arrested, being garrotted by a Kempei Tai executioner in October 1943.

On 15 October the diplomatic corps was ordered to leave Moscow for Kuibyshev, 600 miles to the east, whither the Soviet government was relocating. American reporter Quentin Reynolds was attached to Harriman. He described the scene, waiting for the evacuation train in the Kazan station:

Snow was swirling down in large dry flakes, turning to slush as it hit the pavements. For a while I stood near the main door watching the ambassadors trudge in. The smoke from hundreds of cigarettes grayed the air and, as the hours of waiting for the train passed, the individuals became part of a mass of humanity. At last, word came that the train was ready. In the classless society of Russia, you travelled on trains either 'soft' or 'hard'. The diplomats got the 'soft' coaches. The rest of us travelled 'hard'. Once we sat on a siding for seven hours, not at all cheered by the spectacle of a bomb- and machine-gun-scarred train on the next track. At other times we went onto sidings while trains laden with troops and guns passed en route for Moscow.[10]

Kuibyshev's population had swollen from 200,000 to nearly a million. On a visit to a munitions factory he was supposed to write up, Reynolds was driven past:

… a cluster of bleak wooden buildings surrounded by a wire fence. [Knowing that the censors would not allow us to write about it], our guide readily identified it as a concentration camp for political offenders. A mile or so beyond the camp, we came to a large group of prisoners working on the road with picks and shovels. A few soldiers with rifles were guarding the group quite carelessly. It was obvious that there was no place for the prisoners to run and hide. Dressed in their shapeless gray clothing, they stood just off the road and watched us pass, their faces expressionless. All of them were women.[11]

There were bomb craters inside the Kremlin, where Stalin was working in a bunker. On 16 October his personal switchboard was loaded aboard a train just before Kaganovich's reserves halted the German advance at cost of another 155,000 Russian lives after the Panzer spearheads had briefly been within sight of the Kremlin towers. Russian losses would have been lower, had the newcomers been even half-trained. Aged 18, conscript Nikolai Brandt had no idea how to reload his rifle. Nor had his NCOs. Brandt remembers, 'I turned to the platoon commander, who said the same: "You have to warm it up. The breech has frozen."' Not until he reached the battalion commander, could anyone show Brandt how to reload. Wounded by fragments of a mortar shell, his life was saved because he was hurled into deep snow by the explosion, allowing him to crawl after nightfall back to the Soviet lines.[12]

With winter now firmly in charge, the Wehrmacht's motor vehicles had to be kept running all night if they were not to be frozen solid by dawn. Many German soldiers were still wearing summer uniforms. In the bleak scorched-earth landscape now disappearing under the snow all around them, there was nothing to eat, save what came along their overstretched supply lines. Like Napoleon's Grande Armée, the hitherto invincible Wehrmacht had been defeated by the Russian winter.

To add to Hitler's problems, on 7 December 1941 Admiral Isoroku Yamamoto's successful aerial attack on the US Pacific Fleet at Pearl Harbor was all the justification President Franklin Roosevelt needed. By 11 December America was at war with all the Axis powers. From that moment, given the industrial might and untapped manpower of the United States, an Allied victory was virtually certain, but the wartime photographs of Stalin beaming beside Western guests conceal the clandestine offensive he was conducting against his new allies.

In 1941, responsibility for internal state security and external espionage passed from the NKVD to the NKGB. The head of its first chief directorate, Lieutenant Colonel P.M. Fitin, activated a network of illegal undercover agents in Britain and America. As early as 31 July 1941, a coded message from Moscow Centre to the NKGB *rezident* in London mentions one of them – illegal agent-runner Ursula Buerton, code-named 'Sonja'. As in the US, much use was made of pre-war CP members to provide low-grade intelligence and as a recruiting pool. The famous Cambridge spies including Blunt, Burgess, Maclean and Philby were all in place, providing high-quality material, as were their counterparts in the US. Espionage was also carried out by accredited Soviet diplomats in both countries, such as the Soviet consul-general in New York – code-named *zavod* – who figures frequently in the traffic. GRU and Naval GRU officers, employees of the Soviet AMTORG purchasing agency – codenamed *fabrika* – and employees of the TASS news agency, were both sources and agent-runners, as were Comintern agents. In addition, there were illegals – people under deep cover in the target country, whose case officers were often based in neighbouring countries.

Allies frequently spy on each other, but the espionage onslaught against Russia's allies conducted by Fitin was unprecedented in its scale and in the high risk of embarrassing discovery – and therefore only justifiable as forward planning for a war against the Western Allies after Germany had been defeated with their help.

13

MY ENEMY'S ENEMY IS ALSO MY ENEMY

O n 8 May 1942 Molotov was despatched to London to urge Churchill to speed up a cross-Channel invasion of the German-occupied Continent that would provide some respite for the exhausted Soviet forces by forcing Hitler to transfer whole armies back to Western Europe. Roosevelt had sent Army Chief of Staff George C. Marshall to London to set this up for April 1943, but the British general staff was certain that this would be logistically impossible – as the disaster of the Dieppe raid in August 1942 confirmed. Molotov's second task was to accelerate delivery of much-needed war materiel via British-occupied Iran and by sea to the White Sea ports of Murmansk and Archangel.

In Russia's second city Leningrad, where the German-Finnish siege was in its eighth month, a million people were dead or dying from starvation. Even at this time of national emergency, however, Stalin gave Molotov a third task: to obtain agreement from the Western Allies that Russia could retain after the war all the territory it had acquired under the German-Soviet Pact.[1] In London, Foreign Secretary Anthony Eden refused to agree to this, but with his customary urbanity reassured Molotov on

26 May to some extent by concluding a 20-year Anglo-Soviet treaty. Molotov travelled on to Washington, where he failed again to obtain agreement on the occupied territories, but clinched a Lend-Lease deal with Roosevelt, under which thousands of Harley-Davidson motorbikes, Studebaker trucks, C-47 aircraft and other materiel was shipped into the USSR through Iran.

On 19 June a German aircraft crashed behind the Russian lines carrying the plans for Hitler's summer offensive. Stalin refused to believe them genuine. Sure enough, in the first week of August, the Germans were again racing eastwards, this time towards Stalingrad – the major industrial centre on the Volga and a vital communications link with southern Russia and the crucial Caucasus oilfields. On 12 August, Churchill arrived in Moscow to inform the *vozhd* that there could be no large-scale Allied invasion of Europe in 1942, although Allied landings in French North Africa were planned for that autumn. To Stalin, Britain's prime minister was still an advocate of the foreign intervention twenty-five years earlier, so he accused Churchill of deliberately postponing the second front to bleed Russia dry and of wilfully suspending the Arctic convoys. These were exposed to Luftwaffe planes patrolling from bases in Norway and wolf packs of U-boats, making each trip extremely costly in sailors' lives and tonnage sunk. The two equally stubborn men fell out. General Sir Alan Brooke confided to his diary that at one Kremlin banquet there were nineteen courses, with toasts of vodka to be swallowed after each one. Generals from both sides fell unconscious to the floor, but Churchill, who was a hardened alcoholic, ended the night on his feet in an atmosphere of truce, if not friendship.

Stalin's most pressing problem was the battle for Stalingrad – the city on the Volga to which he had given his name, in recognition of having organised its defence against the White forces during the civil war. German artillery and air support under General Friedrich von Paulus were pounding the city flat. Panic instructions were given in the Kremlin to Nikolai Baibakov, Deputy Commissar for Oil Production, to keep production flowing until the very last moment as German troops approached, then blow up the oil wells just before they arrived. Should he fail in either duty, Stalin told him that he would be shot.[2]

Brought up a Mingrelian-speaker among Abkhazians, Beria was despatched to the Caucasus like a pince-nez'd angel of death to ensure that was done. He also had another mission at this strategically crucial time, which had nothing to do with the war against Germany and everything to do with stamping out secessionist dreams among the Caucasian peoples. After millions of Ukrainians had welcomed the German invasion, seen as a blessed release from Russian oppression, Beria's army of NKGB troops was tasked with snuffing out anti-Soviet aspirations among the Chechen, Ingush, Ossetian, Georgian and other Caucasian peoples.

On 19 November the weakly-held flanks of the German forces in the Stalingrad salient were attacked by large Soviet formations that materialised out of the snow and fog. Within eight days, the two Soviet pincers joined up and von Paulus' 6th Army was trapped. British radio intercept operators and linguists of No. 3 Field Unit of Y Service in Iran and Iraq listened in to the radio traffic between 6th Army and Field Marshal Von Manstein's Army Group Don, which was tasked to break through and relieve the encircled men.[3] It became plain that no breakthrough could be expected. By New Year's Eve, Army Group Don was in turn trying desperately to extricate itself from the rapid Soviet advance. A month later, on 31 January 1943, Station Z, a British monitoring station in North Africa, intercepted the brief final transmission from von Paulus' headquarters at Stalingrad. Promoting him to field marshal, Hitler had ordered the 6th Army to fight on until every man was dead. Yet, the transcribed message read: *Besprechungen mit dem Feind angefangen.* We have begun talks with the enemy.[4]

Reichsmarschall Hermann Goering, who had promised that his Luftwaffe would supply 6th Army with rations, ammunition and armament when it was cut off, had failed once again. The last German pilots braving the ring of anti-aircraft batteries and patrolling Soviet fighters dropped small packets of Iron Crosses instead of pallets of food, medical supplies and ammunition to the starving, frostbitten men dying in the snow below them. With the capitulation of von Paulus began the great Soviet drive to push the Germans back, annihilating as many as possible in the process.

On 22 May 1943, Moscow radio announced that the Comintern had been dissolved. While it is true that all the economic crises of the West in the 1920s and '30s had failed to produce a single communist revolution, or even to win enough members for any national party to become a serious political force, the move was Stalin's ploy to enable him to claim that the Soviet government had no further intention of interfering in the internal affairs of allies without whom it could not win the war against Germany.

In the clandestine world nothing changed, and the lines of communication from Moscow to its agents remained in place. The following month, one of these thousands of spies in the West commenced his duties in the Soviet Embassy at 285 Charlotte Street in Ottawa. Igor Gouzenko would become world-famous two years later, but was then an unknown 24-year-old. Equipped with the false identity of 'civilian employee' by GRU, he was an experienced cipher clerk with rank of lieutenant in the Red Army and the high security clearance required for encoding and decoding messages between GRU Centre in Moscow and the military attaché in Ottawa, Colonel Zabotin. Two mistakes that Moscow rectified soon afterwards were to let Gouzenko rent an apartment among Canadians instead of living with other Soviet staff under strict surveillance – and to bring his pregnant wife with him.

There was also a discrete NKGB espionage operation in Ottawa, about which Gouzenko was supposed to know nothing. However, with Zabotin running several networks of spies in North America, the new cipher clerk realised that these allies of Russia among whom he was now living – and who were convoying much needed war material to his homeland at the cost of many hundreds of Canadian lives – were being targeted by his colleagues in the embassy as enemies. An important factor in his awakening was the contrast between what he had been taught about the Western democracies and the lifestyle he saw around him. Where were the starving workers exploited by ruthless bosses, he wondered, observing that the poorest of his Canadian neighbours lived far better than any Soviet citizens he had ever met. In Canadian elections, he was amazed to find a choice, not just of candidates, but also of parties with radically differing programmes. The fact that his neighbours in Somerset Street, Ottawa, could freely disapprove of them in public, made him suspect a deep-laid trap, until he came to understand what free speech means in a democracy.

The abundance of coded radio transmissions between Moscow and Soviet missions in Allied and neutral countries was running into four figures per month each way for each out-post, as recorded by the Signals Intelligence Service of the US Army. On 1 February 1943 at its headquarters in Arlington Hall, Virginia, a top secret code-breaking programme, later dubbed 'Venona',[5] began recording for later cryptanalysis the spate of double-coded messages from Moscow to legal and illegal Soviet agents in the Western democracies. In November 1943 Signals Corps reservist Lt Richard Hallack made the first breakthroughs, revealing that five different codes were being used. If messages to and from AMTORG Purchasing Commission employees and diplomatic staff might have been legitimate traffic, it became clear that the NKGB, GRU and naval GRU each had its own code, for what could only be espionage purposes. With a paral-lel signals intercept programme in Britain codenamed ISCOT, it was soon apparent that the radio traffic covered only urgent or simple messages, while the volume of secret material supplied by Soviet spies in the West was so colossal that it had to be sent back to Moscow by diplomatic courier.

Stalin's obsession with dispossessing whole nations on the periphery of Russia continued unabated during the war. In mid-October 1943 the Karachai autonomous region was simply removed from maps, half being added to Russia and half to the Georgian SSR, the entire population being rounded up like cattle for the slaughterhouse by 53,000 of Beria's NKGB troops. They almost outnumbered their victims: all men of military age being conscripted into the Soviet forces, only 69,267 old men, women and children had to be herded into the cattle trucks. To save space and economise on rolling stock, they were allowed to take no possessions with them – not even warm clothing. On the long journey in freezing weather, 40 per cent died before reaching their destination, including 22,000 children.[6]

On 27 December 1943, in bitter midwinter weather, Beria and Serov turned their baleful eyes on the Kalmyks, a people of Mongolian origin living north of the Caspian Sea. Accused of voluntarily handing over their herds of cattle to the Wehrmacht – what choice had they had? – more than 90,000 Kalmyk women and children were crammed into American Lend-Lease trucks and driven to the nearest railheads, to be despatched to destinations so far separated in Central Asia and Siberia that they ceased to exist as a cohesive people. Reduced to eating grass and roots in some places, only one in fifteen families survived the typhus epidemic that broke out among them. On eventual demobilisation at the end of the war, 20,000 of their menfolk, including wounded soldiers dragged out of military hospitals, were to suffer the same fate, working as forced labourers in forestry, mining and construction on starvation rations. According to the 1939 census, the pre-war Kalmyk population was 134,000; twenty years later this was reduced to 106,000 including all the births in exile.[7]

On 28 November 1943, Churchill and Roosevelt arrived for the Big Three Conference in Teheran tired and in ill-health. After a far shorter journey, Stalin arrived fighting-fit, boasting of the Red Army's triumphs at Stalingrad and in the Kursk salient, where the largest tank battle in history had involved 6,000 tanks, 2 million men and 4,000 aircraft, and where the German defeat marked the true end of Hitler's offensive capability on the Eastern Front. The *vozhd* was delighted that he had obliged the two Western statesmen to travel so far for his convenience. His instinctive talent for splitting alliances against him paid dividends when Roosevelt agreed to stay in the 'safety' of the Soviet Embassy, leaving Churchill in the British Embassy physically and metaphorically the odd man out.

Stalin held secret talks with Roosevelt, from which Churchill was excluded and in which Roosevelt's success as an American politician led him to overestimate disastrously his influence on the Soviet leader. With no knowledge of Russian history, the US President was so much in thrall to Stalin's charm offensive that the *vozhd* could hardly believe his ears when his guest opined that India – the jewel in Britain's crown for which the Tsars had unsuccessfully played Kipling's Great Game – was ripe for revolution and independence. Roosevelt also ignored Churchill's warnings of Stalin's plans for expansion into southeastern Europe after the war through subversion and installation of puppet regimes.

An unusually close account of this power-play comes from a non-political source, the British prime minister's Scotland Yard bodyguard, Walter Thompson. He noted how easily Stalin talked Roosevelt round on a number of issues in their private tête-à-tête conversations, and how Churchill was roundly snubbed when trying to catch up on the private talks by inviting the American president, whom he had thought his friend, to lunch in the British Embassy. Thompson also commented on the way Roosevelt looked up to Stalin both literally from his wheelchair and figuratively with admiration – and how he curried favour with Stalin by making jokes at Churchill's expense, which left Thompson's master 'very distressed'. A shrewd, although usually silent observer of the world leaders in whose company he spent so much time, Thompson wrote:

> [Roosevelt's] view of Stalin was emphasised on the occasion he remarked to Mr Bullitt, the American ambassador in Moscow, 'Stalin doesn't want anything but security for his country, and I think that if I give him everything I possibly can and ask for nothing in return, *noblesse oblige*, he won't try to annex anything and will work for a world of democracy and peace.'

With a policeman's instinct for telling truth from lies, Inspector Thompson commented, 'What a tragedy!'[8]

One of the subjects on which Roosevelt acquiesced completely with the Soviet dictator was the future of France, agreeing with Stalin that no Frenchman aged 40 or over who had participated in the government of occupied France should be eligible for office after the Liberation, and that it would be necessary 'to sort out the ruling classes' and make all levels of French society 'honest'.[9] More alarmingly, he rejected Churchill's advice that a strong France was important for the stability of postwar Europe.

Apart from being confined to a wheelchair, into which and out of which he had to be lifted, Roosevelt was a very sick man with little time to live – as was obvious to everybody at the Teheran Conference. He tired easily and Stalin made the most of this weakness by frequently leading the conversation round to the president's favourite hobby-horse of destroying the French and British empires after the war. Despite warnings by the US chiefs of staff that American forces would almost certainly find themselves in armed confrontation with Soviet forces at the end of the war with Germany, Roosevelt was on record as believing that Russia was now going to evolve 'following ... constitutional lines'.[10]

Reversing his thinking of two years earlier, he told Stalin off the record that he agreed with the Soviets keeping those parts of Poland occupied in 1939, but did not wish that to be made public for fear of losing the Polish-American vote in the upcoming US elections. Thus the postwar fate of the country in whose defence Britain and France had declared war was subordinated to American domestic politics. With remarkable casualness, at a late-night meeting the borders of Poland were moved westwards, giving Stalin the eastern provinces of the country and compensating the Poles with German territory in the west at the cost of displacing 12 million people.

Whenever Churchill tried to bring the exiled Polish government in London into the conversation, Stalin alleged that they were traitors, dealing with the Germans behind everyone's back. With no support from Roosevelt, Churchill had to let this blatant falsehood pass uncorrected, and agreed to tell the London Poles to be thankful the Red Army was saving their country from complete oblivion.[11]

When the conference broke up on 2 December, Stalin was back on home ground within hours, cock-a-hoop at the wedge he had driven between the two Western Allies and convinced that it was his personal strategic genius that now had the Germans on the run westwards. The bit between his teeth, he re-imposed all-night, alcohol-fuelled meetings that kept his fellow Politburo members exhausted. Mikoyan wrote privately, 'When victory became obvious, Stalin got too big for his boots and became capricious.'[12]

The roll-back of German troops was called 'liberation' in Moscow and the fiction was given currency in the Western media. For those living in the 'liberated' territory, the end of German occupation began a new time of terror. By the end of the year, when the siege of Leningrad was finally broken, Beria's hard work there caused the arrest of 931,544 alleged collaborators during the siege.[13] In Ukraine, where Stalin's favourite Nikita Khrushchev was the uncrowned king, he and Beria were masterminding a war not only against the Germans, but also against three separatist armies using German weapons to fight the returning Soviet troops – not for Hitler but for their own independence.

For centuries, Russian mothers had crooned a lullaby, *Spi, mladenetz, moi prekrasny* – Sleep, my little one, while the moon looks down on your cradle. Harmless stuff, one might think, but the second verse is a giveaway: *Zloi Chechen polzyot na bereg, tochit svoi kinzhal* – the evil Chechen is climbing up the river bank, sharpening his dagger, with which to slit your throat … With an image like that ingrained in the mind, no Russian eyes shed tears when Stalin erased the Chechen-Ingush autonomous region from all the maps in the USSR on 23 February 1944. Commanded by Beria's deportations expert Ivan Serov, an army of 19,000 Chekists and 100,000 security troops, who could all have been fighting the Germans, arrived in Grozny three days earlier. In the depths of a bitter winter, some 387,229 Chechens and 981,250 Ingush old men, women and children were brutally rounded up and transported in Studebaker trucks to the railheads, where long trains of unheated carriages and cattle trucks assembled by Kaganovich waited to take them into exile in Central Asia. Due to the appalling weather, some Chechen villages could not be evacuated in time for the railway schedules; to complete the task, their inhabitants were shot or burned alive in their homes.[14]

Much of the inadequate food supplies allocated for the transit was stolen by the guards. At least one in five deportees died en route and starvation continued to stalk them after their arrival, as they lived in caves and dugouts among a hostile population forbidden to have any contact with these imagined traitors, and with only the harshest work in mines available to them, women included. The natives' hostility is understandable because famine stalked the whole expanse of the USSR and nobody wanted to share with newcomers what little food could be had.

To complete the Orwellian nightmare in which his individual victims became un-persons, air-brushed out of photographs and all mention of them removed from books, of which millions had subsequently to be re-printed, Stalin ordered every reference to the Chechens and Ingush to be expunged from maps, encyclopaedias and other works of reference. Conquered under the Tsars, repressed and deported under the Soviet regime, the survivors of the deportation were not allowed to return until 1957, when they were treated as unwanted incomers by the Russians who now lived in their former homes. The hatred and despair that Stalin sowed in February 1944 were still costing lives fifteen years later in western Ukraine and Lithuania, where anti-Soviet partisans continued the fight. In Chechnya his innocent victims continued to die until 2009, after the tragic hostage-taking in a Moscow theatre during October 2002 and the Beslan school massacre two years later.

14

POOR POLAND!

Forgetting the cruelty that caused the misery of millions and the deaths of hundreds of thousands, Beria's deportations would have qualified as madness in time of peace. That such a vicious land-grab and genocide took place during desperate fighting, wasting the potential of hundreds of thousands of able-bodied armed men and using hundreds of trucks and scores of trains that should have been transporting men and munitions to the front, shows how genocide targeting women and children whose men were fighting for the USSR had equal priority in the Kremlin with the war against Hitler.

After the Chechen deportation, Beria turned his evil eyes on other racial minorities whose land could be expropriated on the grounds that they might see the Germans as possible liberators from Russian domination by reasoning that my enemy's enemy is my friend. The Crimean Tartars and the Balkars now suffered deportation and dispossession of their lands, afterwards re-settled by ethnic Russians. The Serov-Beria team proudly claimed 1.5 million victims in southeastern USSR alone, for which Stalin approved 413 medals and cash awards for loyal service. By the end of the war, 3.5 million old men, women and children had been deported to Siberia and Central Asia.

Behind the dry statistics lie a universe of misery masterminded in the warm and well-stocked Kremlin: families herded on bleak winter nights at a few minutes' notice into freezing trucks or freight wagons with only the few possessions they could carry to last them for the years of exile ahead, deprived of comfort, medical care and basic hygiene; children and adults soiling themselves for weeks on end without toilet facilities; old people and babies dying of starvation and thirst in locked freight cars on the weeks-long journeys into exile among strangers who hated them. Roughly half the deportees of all ages starved to death or died of untreated illness and overwork in exile. Mere words cannot convey the suffering, grief and incomprehension. With the nearest Germans now far away and incapable of counter-attack on such a wide front, these people represented no danger, because the true collaborators in German-occupied areas had already headed westwards with their retreating protectors. And when the surviving menfolk returned wearing the medals they had earned at the front, they too were arrested and deported – 9,000 of them, plus 700 party members, whose only 'crime' was to be ethnic Tartars.[1]

Without any protest from the Western Allies, who were concentrating on the war against the Axis powers, Stalin was thus able to Russify millions of square miles of territory that had been the homelands of fifty-six distinct nationalities with their own cultures and languages. Discovering in 1946 that the Turkic Meskhetians were by oversight still living in southern Georgia, he exiled them too. For each of these peoples, the disaster was at least on the same scale as the Holocaust of the European Jews and the Turkish genocide of the Armenian people, yet no one outside the USSR protested. Inside the USSR, prudent people said nothing. Indeed, in the seven decades of Soviet rule, it became the norm for Russians to speak in a low mumble with little facial movement, so that only the person to whom they were talking could fully understand what they were saying.

Then a whistle was blown. In April 1944 a senior official working for the Soviet trade mission in Washington requested political asylum. Viktor A. Kravchenko had joined the Communist Party as a good career move when aged 24 in 1929, but whatever faith he may have had in the party was shattered by the widespread starvation in his native Ukraine caused by Stalin's enforced collectivisation.

Immediately his absence was noted, the Soviet authorities demanded his return, but Kravchenko was debriefed by the FBI and given a new identity to protect him from assassination by Shmersh. His best-selling account *I Chose Freedom* opened millions of people's eyes to the realities of forced labour and lack of liberty under Stalin's rule. Among the Moscow-orchestrated smear attacks, that of the French communist weekly *Les Lettres Françaises* enabled Kravchenko to sue the publishers in 1949 for alleging that his book was a fake, ghost-written by American intelligence officers. For the trial in Paris, Stalin had Kravchenko's former colleagues and his ex-wife flown in to testify that he was a pervert, mentally sub-normal and a liar. Fortunately, Kravchenko's lawyers were able to trace and bring to court Margarete Buber-Neumann. Her faithful communist husband having been shot during the purges, and having herself been imprisoned both in the Gulag and in Nazi concentration camps thanks to Stalin's betrayal, she testified before the court that there was no difference between Hitler's and Stalin's dictatorships. Kravchenko won the case.

On 6 June 1944, the long-awaited second front opened with the Allied invasion of Normandy, cueing Stalin's major attack on 23 June that sent spearheads racing westwards to re-take Minsk in Russia and Lviv in Ukraine.[2] Close behind followed a puppet Polish government under Bolesław Bierut, so that the areas of eastern Poland 'liberated' by the Red Army could immediately be handed over to the Polish Committee of National Liberation, comprising Bierut and a team of Polish communists who had spent the war years in Moscow being trained for this moment. One of their first acts was to sign an agreement accepting all Russian territorial demands on Polish territory while, alongside them, the NKGB was arresting anyone who might have collaborated with the Germans and anyone suspected of 'anti-Soviet thoughts' – a net so widely spread that it encompassed nearly everyone in Poland when their country was invaded for the second time in five years by Soviet troops.

Coming after Stalin's murder of the thousands of officers, politicians and other Poles, this was a second warning for the Polish government-in-exile in London and for the Armija Krajowa – or Home Army living undercover inside Poland – of the fate awaiting their country when occupied by Soviet forces in the wake of the retreating Germans. In a desperate attempt to forestall that, General Tadeusz Bór-Komorowski ordered the men and women of Armija Krajowa to attack the weak German garrison in Warsaw with small arms on 1 August. Within three days, they had gained control of most of the city. Enraged, Hitler sent reinforcements, backed up by heavy air and artillery attacks that lasted for two whole months.

The Red Army took the suburb of Praga, just across the Vistula River from Warsaw, on 15 August. General Rokossovski, himself the son of a Polish officer, ordered no serious attempt to cross the river or give artillery support while his men watched the Germans reduce Warsaw to rubble, in which more than 200,000 civilians and 10,000 combatants died. It is true that Rokossovski's forces were exhausted; it is also true that the Germans mounted a powerful counter-attack east of Warsaw on 2 August, but such circumstances had never stopped Stalin giving his generals an impossible order and shooting them for failing to deliver. Nor, with the exception of one flight of American aircraft that was permitted to refuel behind the Russian lines en route to Warsaw, would Stalin allow Western pilots to land on Soviet airfields after airlifting supplies to the beleaguered fighters dying daily in Warsaw.

On 18 August the official reply to the American ambassador from the commissariat for foreign affairs read in part:

> The Soviet government cannot, of course, object to English [sic] or American aircraft dropping arms in the region of Warsaw, since this is an American and British affair. But it decidedly objects to British or American Aircraft, after dropping arms in the Warsaw region, landing on Soviet territory, since the Soviet government does not wish to associate itself either directly or indirectly with the adventure in Warsaw.[3]

To give Churchill his due, he persisted in trying to gain Roosevelt's support in this harrowing situation, but the American president thought Stalin's 'friendship' too important to risk upsetting him. This left Churchill in an extremely awkward situation, having put in writing to Foreign Secretary Eden in 1942 that permanent Soviet occupation of eastern Poland was contrary to the

Exhorting Home Army fighters not to waste ammunition, the poster reads, 'Each bullet, one German'.

principles of freedom and democracy set forth in the Atlantic Charter. Abandoned now by Roosevelt, he was reduced to telling the exiled Polish leader Gen Władysław Anders in Italy that Britain could no longer defend the territorial integrity of the country for which it had gone to war.

Anders had been Stalin's prisoner in the Lubyanka, and warned the British prime minister that the Soviets advancing into his homeland were emasculating the nation by arresting everyone who had resisted the Germans. 'We have our wives and children in Warsaw,' he said, 'but we would rather they perish than have to live under the Bolsheviks.' As for himself and his men, 'All of us prefer to perish fighting than live on our knees.' Churchill assured him that Britain would not abandon them[4] – a promise that was not kept by Britain's post-war government.

One of Anders' unsung heroes who survived the severe fighting in Italy at Monte Cassino, piercing the Germans' Gustav Line and costing over 7,000 Polish lives, was Alex Poznansky. Like most of his comrades in II Polish Corps, he never took the risk of returning in 1945 to what had been his home. He told the author twenty years afterwards, 'When we learned the news, we thought, "What the hell are we doing here, fighting in British uniforms? They don't care about our country, so why should we fight their war?" But we carried on, because at least that way we were killing one lot of enemies.'[5]

So ill-defined were the shifting battle-lines within Warsaw that the few courageous Allied aircrew who risked the long round trip from airfields in southern Italy, which placed them at the limit of fuel capacity even without full loads, unwittingly dropped most of their supplies into the hands of the Germans. Some eighty Polish aircrew and around 100 others in RAF uniform paid with their lives for this gallantry. Allied aircrew who had to make emergency landings on Soviet-held territory found themselves locked up in POW camps and robbed of all personal possessions by their guards, with their aircraft impounded, instead of being re-fuelled and repatriated immediately. Andrew Wiseman, a Russian-speaker in RAF uniform, protested to the Soviet camp commander, who shrugged and said, 'It's war. What do you expect?'

In contrast with the hyping of Uncle Joe and 'our gallant Russian allies' in the Western media, state-controlled Soviet media never mentioned the sacrifices and achievements of the millions of Allied soldiers, sailors and airmen, so the guards did not know that the USSR had any allies. When Wiseman taught his fellow-prisoners to say to robber-guards who demanded their wrist-watches at gunpoint, *'Ya soyuznik'* – meaning, I am an ally – the guards replied, *'Kharasho, soyuznik, davaite chasy'* – okay, ally, hand over your watch.[6]

Heroism is not enough in modern war. When the Home Army was nearing the end of its resources, on 14 September some 3,000 men of Stalin's '1st Polish Army' crossed the Vistula and linked up with the Home Army for a few days, but the slender bridgehead was not held. Thinking ahead to a totally manipulable Polish communist state, he had also created a Soviet 'Polish Air Force', in which all the pilots were Russians who had taken a crash Polish-language course. In the last two weeks of September, some Soviet aircraft appeared over Warsaw and dropped about 50 tons of supplies – but without parachutes, so that much of what did land in Polish-held areas was destroyed on hitting the ground.

By 2 October, Bór-Komarowski's forces had to surrender from lack of ammunition and food. With Rokossovski and his troops listening across the Vistula, German firing squads saved Stalin the trouble of eliminating the only armed resistance that could have opposed Bierut's puppet government in Lublin. When the '1st Polish Army' did cross into Warsaw early in 1945, they found the city unrecognisable: buildings not destroyed in the fighting had been systematically dynamited by the departing Germans, leaving most house walls no higher than tombstones to mark the graves of the quarter-million Poles who had died there. Roughly one in ten had been combatants, but non-combatant status had not saved the others because this was genocide.

Stalin could justifiably feel pleased that his masterly inaction throughout the five critical months of Warsaw's struggle had killed so many politically dangerous Poles, while the Home Army caused the diversion of German troops who could have been fighting the Red Army. As a bonus, the *vozhd* could pretend to London and Washington that his hands were clean.

Behind the statistics are, once again, not just the dead but also all the living whose lives have been irrevocably damaged. Alex Poznansky's younger brother was one of the 20,000 Home Army fighters who died in Warsaw; one who survived was Halina Szopińska. Interviewed for the 2009 BBC TV series *Behind Closed Doors*, she recounted her interrogation by the NKGB. Insulted, beaten and sexually humiliated, she was accused of conspiring with the British and the Germans to fight the Russians. Her daily exercise was taken in a prison yard whose walls were splattered with the brains of those shot in the night. After ten years in various Soviet prisons in Poland, she was released to find that her husband had taken another wife, by whom he had fathered two children. Her health broken partly by tuberculosis endemic in the prisons, she was, in the words of historian Laurence Rees, 'just one human casualty of the Soviet occupation of Poland'.[7]

By the end of January 1945, Zhukov's troops had crossed the River Oder, the natural boundary between Poland and Germany. On 3 February Churchill and Roosevelt flew to another Big Three Conference at a place of Stalin's choosing. Landing at Saki, near the west coast of the Crimean peninsula, they and their staff of several hundred advisers had to face an uncomfortable 100-mile road journey through mountainous terrain down to Yalta on the sheltered south-eastern coast of the peninsula, where the conference was to be held in the Livadia Palace, formerly the Tsar's holiday home. Neither Western leader was in good health. Waxen-faced Roosevelt sat for much of the time staring vacantly into space, having only weeks to live. In contrast, Stalin arrived full of energy, resplendent in a specially designed military uniform for the first time as though the recent victories were all of his own making. He was also pleased that he had again exhausted the other two Allied leaders by making them undertake long and tiring journeys before the horse-trading at the conference began.

The war in Europe was near its end, although many thousands of civilians and soldiers were yet to die, and high on Stalin's agenda was the post-war expansion of the Soviet Union. While confirming the agreement reached at Teheran that Russia should annex eastern Poland, the two Western leaders were less happy

with Stalin's idea of compensating Poland with the German territory that lay east of the Oder-Neisse Line. The harsh punishment
of Germany under the Versailles Treaty in 1919 having been
used by Hitler as an alibi for revenge, they considered Stalin's
plan would leave Germany determined to recover its lost territory and provide the motive for a third European war.

Churchill still championed the Polish government-in-exile in
London, and Roosevelt talked of free elections in Poland. The
vozhd once again outmanoeuvred them both by changing the
subject to a discussion of Roosevelt's planned post-war United
Nations Organisation (UNO). Having previously insisted on a vote
for each of the sixteen Soviet republics, on the reasonable argument that the British Empire would claim several votes, Molotov
reduced his demands to two or three votes. Churchill and
Roosevelt took the bait and the question of Poland was shelved,
with Stalin claiming that all Poland was rejoicing at its liberation
by the Red Army.

In return for a promise to join belatedly in the war against
Japan, Stalin also won Roosevelt's agreement to him grabbing
the Kurile Islands and southern Sakhalin, which had been ceded
to Japan after Russia's defeat in the 1904–5 Russo-Japanese War.
Here again, the native populations were to be forcibly deported
and replaced with ethnic Russian settlers.

Stalin's other triumph at Yalta was to have British foreign minister Anthony Eden agree with Molotov that *all* ethnic Russians
taken prisoner by, or surrendering to, the Western Allies after
serving in the German armed forces should be repatriated to the
Soviet Union at the end of hostilities. No one could have been
unaware by then that this was tantamount to a death sentence,
even for those who had left Russia before or at the revolution
and who had therefore never been *Soviet* citizens.

When Churchill got back to London, he stated in the House of
Commons that the Soviet leadership wished to live 'in honour-
able friendship and equality with the Western democracies' and
that Stalin's word was to be trusted.[8] Politicians have to convince
themselves that they are right in order to convince others, but
he chose a strange way of presenting the news from Yalta to the
War Cabinet, contrasting his own allegedly successful handling

of Stalin with the way his predecessor Neville Chamberlain had been duped by Hitler. Was this a give-away that he was secretly ashamed of having betrayed the Poles? Cutting through all the hype in London and Washington, General Anders called the Big Three's carve-up of his country a calamity, to which Churchill retorted, 'We have enough troops today. We do not need your help. You can take away your divisions. We shall do without them.'[9]

In the same month of February 1945, another round of arrests of just about everybody who might have resisted the Russian takeover of Poland gave the lie to Stalin's promise that there would be free elections there. In one incident alone, more than 240 freight wagons of prisoners, whose only crime was being Polish, were despatched eastwards from Białystok.[10]

On 5 July, the US recognised Bierut's puppet government as the legitimate government of Poland, and Britain did so the following day. As Lord Palmerston had said a century before, 'Nations do not have friends. They have interests.' Churchill had decided, as the odd man out at Teheran and Yalta, that Britain's interests would now be served by abandoning the countries of Eastern Europe – and some even closer home, as when, travelling back from Yalta, he told the commander-in-chief of the Allied forces in Italy, Field Marshal Alexander, that Britain had no interest in what happened to Italy after the cessation of hostilities.[11]

15

A VERY DIFFERENT KIND OF WARFARE

In May 1945, US military intelligence officers examining German Foreign Office archives in Saxony, on territory about to be handed over to the Red Army, discovered a partly burned codebook that the Germans had recovered in June 1941 from the Soviet consulate in Petsamo, Finland. This was now put to use in the Venona Project, as was a second Soviet codebook, recovered in Schleswig by an officer from Arlington Hall. Over the following thirty-five years, until the programme ended on 1 October 1980, Venona decrypts were instrumental in identifying many Soviet spies including Klaus Fuchs, Harry Gold, David Greenglass, Theodore Hall, William Perl, Guy Burgess, Donald Maclean, Kim Philby, Harry D. White and Julius and Ethel Rosenberg – the husband and wife executed for espionage on 19 June 1953.

By the time of the next Big Three conference at Potsdam, south-west of Berlin, between 17 July and 2 August 1945, Roosevelt was dead and 60-year-old President Harry Truman represented US interests. Roosevelt's motto had been always 'Let not your right hand know what the left hand doeth'. Even his closest associates were often shut out of decision-making

circuits that concerned them.[1] Thus Truman had not been prepared for the burdens of presidential office by briefings on the
international situation or the relationship between the wartime
Allies. It was left to Churchill to attack Stalin for literally walling
off from the West all the areas conquered by Soviet forces.

The declaration issued at the conference stated, 'It is the
intention of the Allies that the German people be given the
opportunity to prepare for the eventual reconstruction of their
life on a democratic and peaceful basis.' This 'peaceful basis'
was agreed as the division of the country into four zones administered by Soviet, British, US and French armies of occupation.
Austria was likewise divided into four occupation zones with
Berlin and Vienna being similarly split into four sectors.

The results of the British General Election were announced
during the conference. Humiliated by his defeat at the polls,
Churchill was replaced in Potsdam by his wartime deputy
Clement Atlee, leader of the Labour Party. From being the
youngest of the Big Three, Stalin was now the eldest, the most
experienced and the most cunning by far. Although unwell and
showing his age, he was also the best poker player at the table.
Soviet spies working inside the vast Manhattan Project had fed
intelligence back to Moscow regarding their secret work, so
the poker-faced *vozhd* knew exactly what Truman meant when
he whispered outside the main meeting that America had just
tested a bomb of unprecedented magnitude after the first
atomic bomb was detonated at the Alamagordo test site in the
New Mexico desert on 16 July.

Throughout the conference, in Berlin Red Army troops were
loading onto horse-drawn carts loot ranging from carpets
and coats to cast-iron stoves. The city had been substantially
destroyed in the fighting and the remaining inhabitants were
trying to come to terms with their situation, a few miles from
the Western sectors, where relatives were picking up the
pieces of their shattered lives under hostile French garrison
troops, the standoffish British forces and the more friendly
Americans. But on the Potsdam side of the Glienicke Bridge
desolation was the rule, with chronic food shortages, people
living in bomb- and shell-shattered houses and round-ups of

anyone remotely connected with the Nazi Party, but also those who had been active before 1933 in *any* political party.

A strange insight into conditions in the Soviet zone comes from American father and son Charles and John Noble, who owned and managed a factory producing Praktica precision cameras in Dresden. After the US entered the war, the Nobles were not harassed as enemy aliens because their factory was *kriegswichtig* – important for the Nazi war effort. Although their movements were naturally restricted, they were allowed to continue production. With the arrival of the Red Army, the Nobles were accused of espionage to justify the seizure of their factory and its stock of expensive cameras and lenses. They found themselves in late 1945 incarcerated in the infamous concentration camp at Buchenwald, where some fellow prisoners had been liberated by the Red Army, then re-arrested by the NKVD and sent back to the same horrors. Renamed Special Camp No. 2, nothing had changed in Buchenwald: prisoners continued dying from starvation and disease as they had since the camp was set up in 1937.

In 1945, a Nazi canteen and welfare facility in a disused factory at Berlin-Hohenschönhausen was designated by the NKVD 'Special camp No. 3' where Soviet occupation directive 00315 of 18 April 1945 required 'spies, subversive elements, terrorists, Nazi Party activists, police and secret service personnel, administrative officials and other hostile elements' to be incarcerated without trial. Internees included many Poles, Russians and other non-Germans, of both sexes and all ages. Here up to 4,200 prisoners were – in the words of the official guide – 'penned in like animals', in many cases for years. Scant food, no hygiene and insufficient bedding saw prisoners dying of exposure in the camp surrounded by bilingual warnings: *Betreten verboten – vkhod postoronnim vospreshchon* – Entrance forbidden.

Between the Soviet takeover in July 1945 and October 1946, the official statistics show that 886 people died, but it is known that more than 3,000 perished in the camp. The unidentified bodies were dumped in bomb craters and on rubbish dumps nearby. The camp was then closed and forced labour used to construct *das U-Boot* – the submarine – a warren of underground corridors and cells where the NKVD continued interrogations with little food, sleep deprivation, physical and mental violence and confinement in cells half-filled with water. The only way out was via the verdict of a Soviet military tribunal, which awarded long sentences to German politicians, including communists, and to Red Army personnel suspected of deviant thinking. Almost all of these prisoners who filed a class action for rehabilitation at the collapse of the German Democratic Republic (GDR) in 1990 were declared innocent by the Russian authorities.

When the Stasi took the prison over in March 1951, conditions changed little. In the expanded terror-city of Hohenschönhausen, prisoners included Jehovah's Witnesses, the leaders of the 1953 uprising, non-communist and communist politicians, publishers, authors, broadcasters, teachers and lawyers,[2] including some kidnapped in the West, drugged and driven into the GDR. On one peaceful afternoon in the autumn of 1958, when the author was sailing on the Havel Lake, a distant commotion near the south shore saw a Stasi motor launch hi-jacking a West Berlin lawyer, who had sailed his yacht near to, but not across, the line of buoys marking the border.

Herbert Paulmann was a police detective in Berlin-Mahlow, arrested by the Russians in July 1946 for arresting a Red Army soldier caught literally red-handed after stabbing a German civilian to death. Accused of anti-Soviet sentiment, he was taken to the Lindenstrasse prison in Postdam and held for interrogation by the NKVD, at times in a four-man cell containing forty prisoners, where sleep was impossible. On top of this, beatings and semi-starvation reduced his weight in ten months to that of a 10-year-old, so weak that he signed a confession to crimes he had not committed as the only way of staying alive.

He described being called from his cell for transfer:

I had lost my sense of time. The prison doctor wrapped my swollen legs in paper bandages and I had to crawl on all fours, not to the interrogation room but to a large room where four women and three men stood waiting. Each had a bundle of clothing. Clothes were hurled at me too: a woman's hat, a silk coat and a pair of knickers. Because I had to crawl, I was last into the truck, followed by two guards with Alsatisan dogs. They drove us to Sachsenhausen [the Nazi concentration camp, redesignated Special Camp No. 7], where we had to line up at the entrance, but I was too weak to stand. The camp interpreter then said, 'You must each have a sheet, a mattress cover and pillow slip. Anyone who hasn't, goes back to Potsdam!'

I had nothing but the women's clothing chucked at me before getting into the truck. I thought, Oh God, now they will send me back to that terrible place. Then the four women said, 'What haven't you got?' And one tore her pillow slip in half for me, another gave me half her sheet and another half her mattress cover. I still wonder today at the unselfish bravery of those women.[3]

In Sachsenhausen, Paulmann found some Jewish and political prisoners who had been there under the Nazis. Nothing had changed, they said. Cared for by a prisoner-doctor, he survived long enough to catch jaundice, brain fever and tuberculosis, endemic in the camp. At the end of 1949, a Russian guard handed him a postcard. On one side could be written only two words: *Ich lebe* – I am alive. On the other, he was to write the address of his home:

And then it happened. My address was no longer in my damaged brain! I stood there, not knowing where I had lived. It was terrible – a terrible shock. The first time in three and a half years' imprisonment that I could tell my wife I was still alive, and I no longer knew her address.[4]

Sachsenhausen was closed down in 1950. Transferred from Russian custody to the Stasi's infamous Torgau prison, Paulmann was released in January 1954, still suffering from tuberculosis, to find that his wife was living with another man. As he said, 'It was a great let-down, but I could understand her. Three and a half years without any sign of life from me and two children to look after … I was thankful to have survived, but before me now there was nothing.'[5]

Like uncounted millions of prisoners emerging from years of Stalinist political imprisonment, Herbert Paulmann, the honest detective, had lost everything.

Charles Noble was fortunate enough to be released in 1952, but his son was sentenced to a further fifteen years in 1950 and deported to the Gulag, set to work in a coal mine near Vorkuta, less than 150 miles from the Barents Sea, where accidents, overwork and the Arctic climate killed half of the inadequately clothed and fed prisoners. After smuggling out an SOS message to the West, he was released in response to a specific request from President Eisenhower in 1955 and wrote two books about his experiences, which are a rare testimony.

After Truman's brief word to Stalin about the A-bomb at the Potsdam Conference, Beria was relieved of his day-to-day NKGB functions and given carte blanche to catch up on the American lead. Between 330,000 and 460,000 workers and 10,000 scientists and technicians were conscripted – many working in forced labour camps – to overhaul the West.[6] Just how far they had to go was apparent over Japan on 6 August, when a B-29 bomber dropped an atomic bomb on Hiroshima that levelled four square miles of the city centre, killing 70–80,000 people and injuring a further 70,000-plus. The death toll had been higher in conventional fire-storm raids in both Germany and Japan, but since this was the effect of one bomb, and not a thousand bomb-loads, the psychological effect was immense. When the die-hard element in Emperor Hirohito's councils refused to surrender, a second A-bomb was dropped on Nagasaki on 9 August. Even this repeat performance did not completely convince the Japanese government that continued fighting was pointless.

To fulfil his undertaking at Yalta to support the war against Japan, Stalin had three months after the end of hostilities in Europe, during which Soviet troops were transferred en masse by the Trans-Siberian to the Far East, with a declaration of war on Japan on 8 August – by which time Soviet participation in the Pacific theatre was irrelevant to the Allied war effort. Delaying his attack until the last minute reflected Stalin's obsession that the West had deliberately delayed opening the second front to bleed the USSR of its manpower. To economise on Russian lives in this campaign, as many as half of the men in Red Army uniform were ethnic Poles from the eastern provinces that had been absorbed into the Ukraine after 'liberation'. Not surprisingly, they made unenthusiastic soldiers and were subjected to 'political re-education' by their commissars. For the few Soviet lives lost in the fighting before the Japanese surrender, clawing back the Kuriles and southern Sakhalin was a territorial bargain in Stalin's eyes. The native inhabitants, once again, were expelled and replaced by settlers from European Russia.

At the Yalta Conference Stalin had also demanded the restoration of Tsarist Russia's 'rights' over Manchuria. With US president Roosevelt mesmerised by his host, no objections were made. So, on 9 August, Soviet troops also moved into Japanese-occupied Manchuria. By 15 August all resistance had been crushed and the Red Army was plundering the conquered territory, requisitioning food supplies, gold bullion and industrial machinery – Manchuria having become the most highly industrialised area of China under the Japanese occupation. The many thousand Japanese servicemen who surrendered were transported by forced marches and ships to mining camps in the far north of Siberia, whence a handful of survivors made it home twenty years later. With Japan divested of any diplomatic rights, complicated negotiations were required between Washington and Moscow to allow the 1.5 million Japanese civilians in Manchuria to return to their homeland.

Rather than risk the lives of hundreds of thousands more Allied soldiers in an invasion of the Japanese home islands, where every member of the population had been ordered by Emperor Hirohito to die fighting – and which could have meant millions of civilian deaths also – the US meanwhile prepared a third atomic bomb, which was rendered unnecessary by the formal surrender signed on 2 September aboard the USS *Missouri* in Tokyo Bay.

Afterwards, enjoying the mild autumn at Sochi, Stalin called for maps after a dinner with Molotov present. Gloating over the enormous expansion of territory acquired during the war, he used the stem of his favourite Dunhill pipe as a pointer, and said:

In the North, everything's in order. Finland wronged us, so we've moved the frontier further back from Leningrad. The Baltic states, which were Russian territory from ancient times, are ours again. All the Belorussians are ours now, Ukrainians too – and the Moldavians [by which he meant Romania] are back with us. So, to the west, everything's okay. [In the East] the Kurile Islands are ours and all of Sakhalin. In China and Mongolia, all is as it should be.

He prodded the Dardanelles at the bottom of the map with his pipe. 'Now, this frontier I don't like at all.' When he also mentioned Russian 'claims' on Turkish territory and Libya, Molotov, who knew how dangerous making a joke with Stalin could be, was unable to resist quipping, 'And I wouldn't mind getting Alaska back.'[7]

Underlying the superficially good-humoured exchange about the southern buffer zone was the clandestine war that no peace treaty was going to halt. Albania was ruled by Enver Hoxha in his capacity as secretary-general of the Albanian Communist Party. In Greece the communist partisans of EAM-ELAS had overrun the whole country, gone underground after British intervention and were set for a lengthy civil war that they looked certain to win. In Bulgaria, which had not declared war on the USSR but been invaded by Soviet forces anyway, Comintern boss Georgi Dimitrov had carefully timed his return after twenty-two years of exile to be appointed prime minister of a communist-dominated coalition government, and was already assuming dictatorial control of the country, with the ruthless purging of *all* political opponents.

In Romania, the national communist party was not popular, but Soviet intervention had brought it to power under Gheorghe Gheorghiu-Dej and Anna Pauker, who had spent the war in Moscow being trained for this moment. A measure of the subservience of all these Moscow puppets was a contemporary cartoon in a Romanian newspaper, for which the cartoonist paid dearly. It showed Pauker on a sunny day in Bucharest, huddled beneath an umbrella. A passer-by says, 'But Anna, it's not raining.' She replies, 'It is in Moscow.'

Stalin's greatest coup 'at the bottom of the map' was affected by one of the Cambridge University circle to which Philby, Maclean, Burgess and Blunt belonged. Despite having been an active communist pre-war, James Klugman was commissioned as a major in the British Army and managed to get himself parachuted into occupied Yugoslavia as deputy head of SOE there. He used this position to discredit the numerically strong anti-communist Četnik partisans with the British Political Warfare Executive, MI6 and the Foreign Office. As a result, Allied arms and supply drops went exclusively to their bitter enemies, the communist bands led by Moscow-trained Josip Broz, who had taken the *nom de guerre* Tito. Thanks in large part to Klugman, after the German retreat from Yugoslavia Russia had what it had wanted for centuries: an apparently secure foothold in the Balkans, ruled by a man Stalin thought his puppet.

Tito, however, had learned all the tricks during his time in Moscow. Proclaiming the Federal People's Republic of Yugoslavia in November 1945, he rigged elections, intimidating, imprisoning and killing non-communist politicians and executing collaborators, Catholic priests and even wartime comrades whom he now distrusted. After Tito broke with Moscow, flying his true colours as a Yugoslav dictator and not a Russian pawn, several attempts were made to assassinate him. Klugman was hardly the type to point a gun at someone but, true to form, he obeyed Moscow's instructions to denounce the wartime leader he had praised and admired by writing a deplorable little book *From Trotsky to Tito* justifying Stalin's attacks on the fellow-tyrant who would not knuckle under. Tito did achieve two impossible things: he kept Moscow at bay and united for thirty-five years the seven republics that made up Yugoslavia, each of whom hated all the others. After Khrushchev's denunciation of Stalin in 1956 and Tito's subsequent rehabilitation by the CPSU, the CPGB withdrew Klugman's embarrassing pamphlet.

Turkey had not been a belligerent in the war, so there were no grounds for repeating the Tsarist-era attempts to gain control of the passage from the Black Sea to the Adriatic and Mediterranean. Stalin wanted not only this, but also a piece of Africa, and was hoping to keep his occupation forces in northern

Iran. Molotov, who was given the task of wheedling these concessions out of the West, played it safe by saying, 'It's good that the Tsars conquered so much land for us in war. This makes our struggle with capitalism easier.'[8] In one sentence, he summed up the Politburo's employment of international communism as a tool to expand the Russian empire.

On the map in his Crimean villa that so pleased Stalin, the vassal states controlled by this handful of obedient puppets stretched in places as far as 400 miles beyond the expanded, internationally agreed western frontiers of the USSR.

'In the west, everything's okay', he had said. He now required his Moscow-trained protégés ruling the Eastern European vassal states to dance attendance at any hour of the day or night that suited his erratic body-clock. From Prague came Klement Gottwald, who had spent the war in Russia and was soon to be made prime minister of Czechoslovakia with the support of Soviet occupation troops. Mátyás Rákosi came from Budapest, where he imposed the AVO secret police – modelled on the NKGB – on his suffering countrymen after returning from wartime exile in the USSR. From Tirana came Stalin's lifelong admirer, Enver Hoxha, who was busily eliminating opponents, abolishing private property, collectivising Albania's agriculture and closing churches and mosques. Georgi Dimitrov came too, from Sofia. From Berlin came ex-Comintern agent and wartime exile Walter Ulbricht, now heading the ultra-Stalinist puppet administration of the Russian-occupied zone of Germany. Bierut and Berman came from Warsaw. Just once, Bierut stepped out of line, asking Stalin in 1950 about the fate of Polish leaders who had 'disappeared' in the USSR. Stalin pretended that he had asked Beria to investigate their whereabouts but, as Bierut was leaving, Beria hissed at him the advice, 'Fuck off – or you'll regret it.'[9] Thus did the denizens of the Kremlin treat the leaders of the puppet republics.

Of the three Western Allies, Britain was bankrupted by the war, grappling internally with unemployment and austerity and externally with independence movements throughout the Empire. In France, the first post-liberation head of government Charles De Gaulle had similar domestic and colonial problems in addition to battling the pro-Moscow Parti Communiste Français

(PCF) which had worked throughout the four years of German occupation to Moscow's directives in preparation for a coup d'état at exactly this moment.

The United States had doubled its gross domestic product during the war and alone had the military-industrial potential to intervene in Europe, but no American politician was going to lose votes by contradicting the slogan, 'Bring the boys home'. The lesson of President Woodrow Wilson's attempt to impose a collective security organisation after the First World War and to intervene in the Russian civil war was all too clear to Truman and his Secretary of State James F. Byrnes. The United Nations Organisation that now succeeded Wilson's discredited League of Nations was a compromise. At the Yalta Conference, a basic charter had been hammered out with a number of important disagreements. So, when the organisation was formally established on 24 October 1945 as an international watchdog, it was a toothless hound.

In the enormous buffer area between the USSR and the Western democracies, millions of Europeans were now Stalin's prisoners – and they had no allies to protest for them until a courageous young man blew the whistle on the other side of the Atlantic.

Cypher clerk Igor Gouzenko left the Soviet Embassy in Ottawa on 5 September 1945, having learned that he was shortly to be posted back to Moscow with his wife and son. The doubts that had been building up during his stay in Canada had grown into certainty that he did not want his young son, born there, to grow up in Russia. This was the last day on which he would have access to the secret traffic in the GRU *rezidentura* before his replacement took over, so when Gouzenko left the embassy at 8 p.m. he was carrying carefully selected files that gave details of Major Zabotin's network of spies.

Gouzenko went first to the office of the *Ottawa Times*, hoping to do a deal similar to that which Kravchenko had made with the *New York Times*, but so agitated was he and so ill able to express himself in English, that no one took him and his collection of indecipherable Russian documents seriously. Terrified at what he had done, he went home for the night, but left the apartment at 511 Somerset Street early next morning. His son Andrei safely deposited with an English neighbour, Gouzenko took his wife Anna, now heavily pregnant again, to the office of the Crown Attorney, where a Royal Canadian Mounted Police (RCMP) officer interviewed the two distraught Russians and promised that a senior colleague would see them next morning. By now, Gouzenko knew time was running out. If the embassy staff caught up with him, his family would be kidnapped and shipped back to Russia where the doctrine of *krugovaya poruka* would ensure that he and his wife were shot after torture and their son placed in a party orphanage.

Back at the apartment, the Gouzenkos cowered in the bedroom while a Russian accredited as an embassy driver hammered on the door until told by neighbours to go away. They included Sergeant Harold Main of the Royal Canadian Air Force, who did not altogether believe Gouzenko's story, but cycled to the nearest police station to get help. Another neighbour agreed to take in the distraught parents and little Andrei 'in case anything should happen in the night'. Two RCMP constables, summoned by Main, arrived at 511 Somerset Street in a patrol car. They listened to the desperate Russian's story and agreed to keep the building under observation.

At 11.30 p.m. Sergeant Main heard Gouzenko's apartment door being forced and signalled the waiting policemen, who found four Russians ransacking the apartment, searching for the missing documents. Their spokesman was Vitali Pavlov, accredited as second secretary at the embassy but actually the NKGB *rezident*. When the two constables accused the Russians of breaking and entering, Pavlov insisted on diplomatic privilege. They were allowed to return to the embassy, while the Gouzenkos spent the night under police guard in the neighbour's apartment.

On the morning of 6 September Gouzenko was escorted by police to the Canadian Minister of Justice. William Mackenzie King, who was prime minister and foreign minister, did not want this embarrassing walk-in to spoil what he considered the excellent diplomatic relationship between Canada and the USSR. A bizarre character, who regularly asked political advice of his deceased mother through a medium, Mackenzie King thought that a quiet chat with the Soviet ambassador would be the best way to stop Soviet espionage in his country – if indeed there was any.

A senior British intelligence officer passing through Ottawa thought otherwise, yet FBI Director J. Edgar Hoover infuriated the British by ordering the Canadians to put Gouzenko on ice for two weeks while the Bureau was busy following up leads from ex-Soviet spy Elizabeth Bentley, who had been acting as intermediary between an NKGB agent code-named 'Golos' in Washington and his network of highly placed informants and agents in US Government employ.

The Soviet Note received by the Canadian Department of External Affairs on 8 September accused Gouzenko of stealing money and protested at the 'rudeness' of the Ottawa police towards accredited diplomats. The Canadian authorities were requested to arrest Gouzenko and his family and hand them over for deportation back to Russia. A further note was received on 14 September but, by that time, Russian-speaking officials had examined Gouzenko's papers and realised that in them lay the full details of Zabotin's extensive GRU spy rings, together with copies of Moscow's instructions to Zabotin to secure classified information on the Canadian order of battle, troop movements, weapons and munitions, technology – and also for controlling existing spies and recruiting new ones in the armed forces, universities and government.

So successful had Zabotin been in Canada, particularly in extending the Soviet spy network, that he had been awarded the Order of the Red Banner and the Order of the Red Star just one month previously. Recalled to the USSR shortly after the defection, he left with other compromised Soviet diplomats aboard SS *Aleksandr Suvorov*, a Russian ship that departed from the port of New York in a hurry, failing to comply with harbour regulations. Surprisingly, he was not shot, but sent with his wife and hitherto privileged teenage son to a labour camp in the Gulag, eventually being released after Stalin's death in 1953.

His successes in Canada had been largely due to talent-spotting by two Canadian Communist Party members, Ukrainian-born Sam Carr and Polish-born Member of Parliament Fred Rose. Both had been Comintern agents for twenty years, sent to Canada for the specific purpose of espionage, subversion and infiltration of trade unions.

Among the other fish landed in Gouzenko's net was British scientist Dr Alan Nunn May. Working on the development of the atomic bomb, he had passed to Zabotin both secret data and a sample of uranium 235 from the separation plant at Oak Ridge, Tennessee – for which he was later sentenced to ten years' imprisonment. Of the network wrapped up by Gouzenko's defection, Fred Rose was sentenced to six years' imprisonment and others received sentences totalling twenty-seven years.[10] Sam Carr, like all the best Comintern agents, disappeared before trial, slipped across the open border with the US and continued working there for Moscow until 27 January 1949, when he was arrested in Manhattan. Refusing to cooperate with the FBI, he was extradited to Canada and also served six years' imprisonment.

As with all defections, the cruellest price was paid by innocent relatives of the defectors left behind in Russia. Gouzenko's elderly mother died under interrogation in the Lubyanka and Anna's mother, father and sister Alia were imprisoned for five years, Alia's daughter being taken away and placed in an orphanage.[11]

Subsequent investigation revealed that there were at least four other Soviet spy networks in Canada at the time, but the scales were not lifted from Mackenzie King's eyes. After reading the report of the Royal Commission on the Gouzenko case, he wrote in his diary, 'I am sorry about this. I am afraid it will be made use of by Russia as an effort on the part of Canada to destroy Communism and may hinder rather than further the object we have in mind.'[12]

Naïveté like this made Soviet espionage easy. MI5, for example, never thought of vetting Nunn May's contemporaries at Trinity College in Cambridge, including Burgess, Maclean, Cairncross, Blunt and Philby. However, Gouzenko's defection and the material he had so courageously brought with him did open eyes and minds in Western intelligence agencies to the extent of Soviet espionage before, during and after the Second World War. From that moment on, politicians more worldly than Mackenzie King were aware of the very different kind of war being waged from Moscow against *all* the Western democracies.

The author as a 19-year-old RAF Russian linguist with Soviet soldiers in Berlin (above, right) and at the door of the cell where he was kept in solitary confinement (above, left) in the Stasi prison in Potsdam. Only the barred ground-floor windows of its street frontage (below) betrayed the misery within.

The hard men (and women) who ruled Russia: Alexander Nevsky (above, left) defeated the Swedes; Ivan the Terrible (above, right) killed his eldest son; Peter the Great (below, left) built St Petersburg; German-born Catherine the Great (below, right) wanted 'the whole of Europe to be Russian'.

At Port Arthur in the war against Japan (1904–05) Russian soldiers gloated over piles of Japanese corpses (above) before their humiliating defeat and retreat (below) triggered the 1905 Revolution.

In the October Revolution, Lenin promised Russia's starving jobless millions that he was building an earthly paradise (above). Trotsky used the Red Army (below) to crush all opposition to the Bolsheviks with bayonets, bullets and poison gas.

During the civil war soldiers had to march vast distances to the front, like these White troops in 1920 (above). There were frequent atrocities on both sides. The Czech interventionist forces hanged every Red activist they found in Ukraine (below).

Vladimir Ulyanov, aka
Lenin (above, right),
and Lev Bronstein, aka
Trotsky (above, left),
fought for control of the
Bolshevik movement.
Dysfunctional psychopath
Felix Dzerzhinsky (below)
headed the Cheka secret
police, personally torturing
his prisoners.

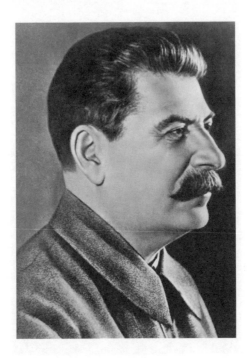

Trotsky ignored Lenin's warning that Josef Djugashvili, aka Stalin (above), was ruthlessly power-hungry, and died when Stalin sent Smersh assassins to kill him in Mexico (centre, below).

Later to become a famous children's author, Arthur Ransome (above) was a reporter in Russia for the *Manchester Guardian*. He failed to report the millions of deaths from starvation caused by the forced collectivisation. In Kharkiv (below) dead bodies littered the streets.

Ignoring all the deaths, American muckraker Lincoln Steffens (left) visited Russia briefly and said, 'I have seen the future and it works.' Also from the US came left-wing reporters Louise Bryant (below, right) and her lover John Silas Reed (below, left), who praised the 'socialist experiment' in Russia.

In August 1939 Molotov signed the Nazi–Soviet Pact (above), which allied the USSR with Hitler for the first twenty months of the Second World War. By November 1940, the relationship had soured and Molotov got the cold shoulder from Hitler's foreign minister, Ribbentrop, (below) in Berlin.

At the Teheran Conference in 1943 (above), Stalin captivated US President Roosevelt, and British Prime Minister Winston Churchill was not happy. When the Polish Home Army rose up against the German occupation of their country, Stalin let Hitler destroy Warsaw. On 5 October 1944 the Poles surrendered and were marched off to their deaths (below).

In summer 1945, hundreds of thousands of women raped by the Red Army fled to the West (above). In 1948 Stalin tried to drive the Western Allies out of Berlin. A third world war was avoided by Allied aircraft flying 24/7 into Berlin for eleven months, carrying everything from coal and concrete to candy for the kids (below).

When the author told his Stasi interrogator he had heard bands playing in the May Day parade, Lieutenant Becker replied, 'What you heard was the spontaneous demonstration of the workers.' This (left) is what it looked like.

The first truly spontaneous demonstrations in the GDR came on 17 June 1953, when workers rebelled. The government crushed them with Soviet tanks (right). Hundreds died and thousands were sent to hard-labour camps.

Winston Churchill and financier Bernard Baruch (above) introduced 'Iron Curtain' and 'Cold War' into every language when Stalin launched his espionage offensive against his allies after the Second World War. Thousands of spies stealing British and US nuclear secrets included Colonel Rudolf Abel (below, left) and Colonel Konon Molody, aka Gordon Lonsdale (below, right).

These agents used traitors like Kim Philby (right), who spied for the USSR for three decades inside MI6.

Great-grandmother Melita Norwood (below, left) said she had 'no regrets' when KGB archives published in 1999 revealed she had passed classified material to Moscow for forty years. British communist Len Beurton gave cover to Soviet agent Ursula Kuscinski (below, right) by marrying her. Code-named Sonja, she transmitted several thousand messages from British traitors and Soviet agents to Moscow from their home near Oxford.

Vladimir Putin (right) rarely smiles, but the Kremlin is laughing when Russian long-range Tupolev 95 bombers intrude into British airspace to analyse the radar system. In this incident in August 2007 (below), one of these intruders is intercepted by two fighters from RAF Leuchars.

PART 3: COLD WAR

If you are scared to go to the brink, you are lost.

US Secretary of State John Foster Dulles

We shall bury you!

Nikita S. Khrushchev

16

BIG BANGS AND A LONG TELEGRAM

All this helps to explain why Truman and Attlee made common cause early in 1946 to resist Russian pressure for 'frontier adjustment' at the expense of Turkey, as though it were a vanquished enemy to be carved up by the victors. The UN Security Council was next used to condemn the continued presence in Iran of Soviet forces. It was a shot across Stalin's bows that proved Lord Palmerston's observation that the Russian bear would 'halt and frequently recoil when confronted by determined opposition'. Unwilling to risk open confrontation, Stalin reluctantly complied with the UN resolution, keeping a wary eye on the US Sixth Fleet, deployed in the eastern Mediterranean.

The big question being asked in London and Washington was what had happened to the Grand Alliance with the USSR? The answer came from the US chargé d'affaires in Moscow, in the absence of an American ambassador. With his fluent Russian, past service in the USSR and the Baltic republics as well as Germany and Switzerland, George Kennan[1] wanted the State Department to comprehend the realities of diplomatic relations with the Soviet Union. What he called his 'long telegram' – an 8,000-word cable dated 22 February 1946 to the State Department[2] – was a desperate plea for attention. As he was well aware, it could have been totally ignored in Washington, or resulted in his recall from Moscow in ignominy.

He made the point that Stalin's surly stand-off at the end of hostilities against the Reich was not caused by any action by the Western Powers, but a return to the traditional wariness of Russian autocrats, who were constrained by no democratic process. Concessions from the West, Kennan warned, would provoke no reciprocity in Russia, where the absolutist rule of the Tsars had been replaced by far more repressive government since the revolution. On the contrary, he argued, only the ultimate failure of the state-driven command economy might bring about a change in Russian foreign and domestic policy – and this was unlikely to happen so long as Stalin remained alive. In the meantime, the policy Kennan advocated for the West was to pursue a 'long-term, patient but firm and vigilant containment of Russian expansive [sic] tendencies'.[3]

Kennan knew his Russian history and understood that Stalin, although a Georgian, had assumed the mantle of Ivan the Terrible and Alexander Nevsky – and was determined to hold on to power by eliminating all external and internal challengers as ruthlessly as they had done.

Having already protested in Potsdam at the way Stalin was sealing off Eastern Europe from the West, Winston Churchill made a speech on 5 March 1946 at Fulton, Missouri, in which he contrasted the realities of life in the Soviet Union with the Anglo-Saxon tradition of civil freedoms epitomised in Magna Carta, the Bill of Rights, the principle of *habeas corpus*, trial by jury, English common law and the American Declaration of Independence. He went on to say:

> The people of any country have the right, and should have the power ... by free unfettered elections, with secret ballot, to choose or change the character or form of government under which they dwell; that freedom of speech and thought should reign; that courts of justice, independent of the executive, unbiased by any party, should administer laws which have received the broad assent of large majorities or are consecrated by time and custom.

Later in the speech, he said:

> A shadow has fallen upon the scenes so lately lit by the Allied victory. Nobody knows what Soviet Russia and its Communist International organization intends to do in the immediate future, or what are the limits, if any, to their expansive and proselytizing tendencies. I have a strong admiration and regard for the valiant Russian people and for my wartime comrade, Marshal Stalin. There is deep sympathy and goodwill in Britain – and, I doubt not, here also – towards the peoples of all the Russias and a resolve to persevere through many differences and rebuffs in establishing lasting friendships. We understand the Russians need to be secure on her [sic] western frontiers by the removal of all possibility of German aggression. We welcome Russia to her rightful place among the leading nations of the world. We welcome her flag upon the seas. Above all, we welcome – or should welcome – constant, frequent and growing contacts between the Russian people and our own people on both sides of the Atlantic.

> It is my duty however – for I am sure you would wish me to state the facts as I see them to you – to place before you certain facts about the present position in Europe. <u>From Stettin in the Baltic to Trieste in the Adriatic an iron curtain has descended across the Continent</u>.[4] Behind that line lie all the capitals of the ancient states of Central and Eastern Europe. Warsaw, Berlin, Prague, Vienna, Budapest, Belgrade, Bucharest and Sofia, all these famous cities and the populations around them lie in what I must call the Soviet sphere, and all are subject in one form or another, not only to Soviet influence but to a very high and, in some cases, increasing measure of control from Moscow.[5]

Although the metaphor of an iron curtain dated from the nineteenth century and had been used by Churchill already in a cable to President Truman dated 10 May 1945, such was the oratorical skill of Britain's wartime prime minister that the expression was thought by many to be his own creation made on the spur of the moment. It summed up graphically the fate of the Eastern European countries that had fallen 'into the Soviet sphere'.

Russia's Central Asian and Caucasian possessions had historically enjoyed few links with the West, but the Baltic states, Czechoslovakia, Hungary and Poland, had been part of Europe geographically, politically and culturally – as had been Bulgaria, Romania and Yugoslavia. Now, they were like a fast vanishing mirage: geographically of the Continent but politically distant as the puppet governments schooled in Moscow locked their citizens into a society where freedom of expression was a dangerous luxury and contact with the West liable to bring down severe sanctions.

If Winston Churchill gave currency to the expression 'Iron Curtain', the half-century stand-off between the Soviet bloc and the Western democracies was first referred to in public as 'the Cold War' by the American financier and presidential adviser Bernard Baruch during a US congressional debate on 16 April 1947. The influential political commentator Walter Lippmann picked up the phrase and used it as the title of a book. By September it was in use worldwide because of its increasing aptness to describe the international tension between the two power blocs, in which the temperature was kept below flashpoint by the terrible destructive power of nuclear weapons, ensuring that this new kind of war was waged on political, economic, and propaganda fronts by the major 'belligerents' and turned hot only on the periphery of their spheres of influence.

At the time the expression was coined, only the US had nuclear weapons. But these were in insufficient number for an effective pre-emptive strike against an enemy whose largely undemobilised conventional forces far outnumbered those of the West, giving it the advantage in a large-scale counter-attack, where nuclear weapons could not be used without killing unacceptable numbers of pro-Western civilians.

In terms of domestic politics, how quickly could public opinion have been weaned from wartime images of Roosevelt's smiling friend Uncle Joe to see him as the tyrant that he was, and 'our gallant Russian allies' as an implacable enemy against which a cataclysmic war was to be waged? In any case, the gradual process of Sovietisation even in Poland – and with Czechoslovakia being nominally a democratic republic until February 1948 and Hungary having the trappings of democracy until the elections of May 1949 – made it difficult to know when and where to draw a line in the sand.

The technique used by the Moscow-trained puppet leaders was the same everywhere. As recounted by Wolfgang Leonard, one of Ulbricht's team of eleven returnees to Eastern Germany, they were told by him not to appoint communists as head of any public authority except the police. The public was deliberately misled by the selection of respectable, unambitious bourgeois figureheads, who could be controlled behind the scenes by their deputies, all of whom were communists. Thus, there was an appearance of democracy in local and national governments, but control lay firmly with the party.[6]

The West's response to the progressive Sovietisation of Eastern Europe was the North Atlantic Treaty Organisation (NATO), which first assembled on 4 April 1949. The member states were Belgium, Canada, Denmark, France, Iceland, Italy, Luxembourg, The Netherlands, Norway, Portugal, the United Kingdom, and the United States – with power lying at the end of the alphabet, since only the US and United Kingdom would have the nuclear weapons that stopped the Cold War turning hot until France developed its own nuclear weapon in 1966. Later signatories were Greece, Turkey, West Germany and Spain.

When it became known in Washington and London that Stalin's A-bomb, midwifed by Beria, had been born on 29 August 1949 – under the poetic code-name *pervaya molniya* or 'first lightning' in the USSR, though dubbed more prosaically *Joe One* in the West – a secret debate took place within the US Atomic Energy Authority, where many nuclear physicists opposed the development of what was technically the next step: from fusion bombs to fission bombs theoretically capable of a thousand times more destruction to life and property. Their belated humanitarian concerns that the latter would be weapons of genocidal potential which should never be produced were overridden by the US joint chiefs of staff and other politico-military pressure groups in Washington. On 31 January 1950, advised by the Pentagon that the US stockpile of 200 A-bombs was still insufficient to guarantee victory if it came to a hot war with the USSR, Truman decided to step up production of nuclear weapons and announced that America was building 'a super-bomb', i.e. an H-bomb.

With 10 per cent of the federal budget devoted to the Economic Recovery Programme to kick-start the war-ravaged economies of Western Europe, the last thing Truman wanted was to have to build up conventional military strength to face the Soviet threat. Such a move could have been fatal in domestic American politics. So, the H-bomb seemed the better option for keeping the balance of power in favour of the West.

A race was now on between America and the USSR to pro-duce a workable H-bomb before the other side. In the West, public debate mirrored the private doubts of the scientists con-cerned. Influential public figures and media pundits argued that it was immoral to produce weapons causing radioactive fall-out that could wipe out the whole human race. The proponents of weapons development retorted that the dissenters were, know-ingly or not, 'batting for the other side'. Certainly Moscow mobilised all its agents of influence through the Cominform to sow doubt and distrust of the American government's decision in the US and among its allies, and to exploit the natural disquiet in any rational mind about weapons of this magnitude. High on the list of targets of this smear campaign was NATO, whose order of battle in Europe posed no offensive threat to the USSR. The US military presence in European countries was targeted by pro-Moscow politicians, and thousands of activists painted and chalked the slogan *US Go Home!* on walls from Holy Loch in Scotland to Naples in the south of Italy. No such public debate or protest occurred in the Soviet Union, where the teams of nuclear scientists working in the closed city of Sarov, which was barred to visitors and shown on no maps, knew better than to disobey instructions from the Kremlin that they should move directly into fusion research, full speed ahead.

Overcoming the considerable technical problems involved in fusion bomb technology – which essentially required a con-tained A-bomb explosion to produce the conditions necessary to explode an H-bomb – the first American fusion bomb was tested successfully at Eniwetok Atoll in November 1952. Such was the secrecy surrounding Soviet research that the explosion of the first Soviet H-bomb, of inferior yield, in August 1953 caused world-wide amazement at the speed with which the technology gap between the two sides had narrowed. On 22 November 1955, the Soviet Union successfully tested a thermonuclear bomb comparable with American weapons at the Semipalatinsk[7] test site in Kazakhstan.

Then an extraordinary thing happened. Andrei D. Sakharov, the nuclear physicist considered to be the father of the Soviet H-bomb, had been rewarded for his work with membership of the elite *nomenklatura* and the Soviet Academy of Sciences, but began to voice his moral misgivings about the consequences of atmospheric testing of thermonuclear devices – at first privately with Khrushchev and other leaders and then in public. His writings on arms reduction and the increasing repression of Soviet dissidents circulated inside the USSR as *samizdat*, or self-publishing. Since CPSU decided what could, and what could not, be published officially, individuals typed a few copies of a forbidden text or book, which were then in turn copied by others in the chain, and so on at considerable risk.

Published eventually in the West, Sakharov's writings earned him a Nobel Peace Prize. Sadly, the consequences mirrored those set off by Pasternak's *Doctor Zhivago* and Solzhenitsyn's *A Day in the Life of Ivan Denisovich*. Sakharov was stripped of all his honours and privileges in the USSR and eventually exiled to the closed city of Gorky,[8] with his wife, human rights activist Yelena Bonner, likewise convicted of 'anti-Soviet activities'.

17

LIVING ON THE FAR SIDE OF THE MOON

The all-pervading repression of Stalinist rule was astutely observed by America's first post-war ambassador in Moscow. In the early hours of 28 March 1946 a four-engined C-54 with US markings took off from Tempelhof airport in the American sector of Four-Power Berlin and headed north-east. Its passengers were diplomats, led by Walter Bedell Smith. The previous day, he had stood beside General Lucius Clay and Ambassador Robert Murphy on a reviewing stand watching a march-past of the Allied garrisons in the divided city. In his diary, he recorded feeling chilled, not from the cool spring air, but from the evidence of his eyes that the Soviet forces were still on a war footing, whereas the US:

> ... had demobilised in record time ... the most efficient and most powerful armed forces ever assembled. This was, of course, the result of the 'Bring the boys home' campaign which, launched just before a Congressional election year, had reached such intensity, inside as well as outside the Army, that no official could withstand it. It seemed to me that we had reduced our defence force to a greater extent than was justified by world conditions.[1]

Flying time from Hitler's former capital to Stalin's was, even in those piston-engined days, only five and a half hours. As the C-54 flew into the dawn, the American passengers saw unrolling below them endless plains and forests lacking in hardtop roads or other means of modern communication, with few cities or even villages of any appreciable size. Having a soldier's eye for landscape, Bedell Smith noted the lack of physical barriers in the land over which he was flying. Whilst understanding that the government to which he was accredited felt it necessary to construct a wall of buffer states around its borders, he was worried at the:

> ... alarming signs that the pan-Slav imperialism, so disturbingly enshrined by enthusiastic Russian writers, seemed even at this time to be reasserting itself in spite of Lenin's repeated denial of plans to conquer other nations, because, as he said, 'We Russians have never been able to make anything but serfs of conquered people.[2]

Bedell Smith reflected that Lenin's protestations of non-interference in the affairs of other states were a pack of lies because, '... the Soviet Union had violated one agreement after another in the dynamic expansion (both during and after [Lenin's] lifetime) which was extending the influence of the Kremlin across great areas of Europe and Asia.'[3]

In the twentieth century alone, the countryside below the C-54 had twice been laid waste by German armies, but, '... four times since the eighteenth century, Russian armies had stood at the Elbe. They took Potsdam from Frederick the Great and played a major part in the capture of Paris from Napoleon.'[4]

These were sobering thoughts for an ambassador at the start of his mission to the most powerful state in post-war Europe.

The C-54's hold was crammed with everything from fur coats for men and women down to altar candles for the single Catholic church in Moscow, by way of disposable sanitary towels and lipstick, chewing gum and whisky – all of which were unobtainable in the USSR even by diplomats in expensive hard-currency *valyuta* stores barred to most Russian citizens.[5] In Moscow, fresh eggs were so difficult to obtain, and so expensive, that one of the new ambassador's first acts was to buy some laying hens and keep them in a chicken run in the embassy garden. Goering's dictum that guns were better than butter still held good east of the Elbe, for the same chilling reason: this was a country not recovering from a war, but preparing for one.

To present his letters of credence in the Kremlin, Bedell Smith had to don top hat and morning dress in the diplomatic ritual that held good even in Soviet Russia. His reception in the Kremlin was cool. He noted Stalin's withered arm, uneven gait, under-average height, badly pockmarked face, bad teeth and bad breath – and the yellowed eyes. Accounting to some extent for his surliness and mood-swings, Stalin also had irritable bowel syndrome and a right lung weakened by tuberculosis contracted in Tsarist prisons.

Meeting Stalin was a privilege reserved for very few. Unlike Lenin, a demagogue who enjoyed haranguing live audiences, the paranoid *vozhd* had not risked walking the streets of Moscow since 1931, but spent his days and nights in the Kremlin or one of the ultra-secure *dachi* outside Moscow, commuting between them in an armed convoy that sped through streets emptied of other traffic and lined with armed police and soldiers. Ruling a one-party state, he felt neither need to contact his subjects nor interest in their living conditions. More alarmingly, his only knowledge of contemporary society outside the USSR came from viewing English and American films in his private cinema, commentated for him by a nervous employee of Sovexportfilm, the state film company. So far out of touch with reality was he that, when President Roosevelt's personal representative Harry Hopkins had apologised in 1941 for some delays in delivery of Lend-Lease supplies caused by striking factory workers, Stalin said, 'Strikes? Don't you have police?'[6]

Bedell Smith was aware that the man he met in the Kremlin had killed millions and personally pursued Trotsky to the very minute when Mercader buried the ice-pick in his brain – an act that was perfectly legal under Soviet law, which deemed an outlaw any citizen who refused to return to the USSR. A decree of the Central Executive Committee dated 21 November 1929 was crystal-clear: 'Outlawing involves the ... shooting of the outlaw within twenty-four hours after identifying him.'[7]

The Russian language was one barrier for the newly arrived ambassador. To complicate communication further, it was doubly encoded with the jargon produced by every totalitarian state. 'Peace-loving people' meant communist sympathisers and spies in the West. The USSR purported to be governed by 'the dictatorship of the proletariat', but what did this mean? Like most dialectic, it meant the opposite of what it seemed to say. In 1934, Stalin had written, 'Our Party does not share, and must not share the guidance of the state with any other party. That is what we mean by the dictatorship of the proletariat.'[8]

Another word in the Marxist-Leninist lexicon that confused Westerners was 'co-existence'. Stalin was fond of disarming foreign statesmen and journalists by saying that capitalism and communism could co-exist peaceably. Yet, as Bedell Smith noted in his diary, '...in his writings and speeches to the leaders of the Communist Party [Stalin] has repeatedly reaffirmed Lenin's basic theory that a future struggle is *inevitable* between the Soviet Union and the capitalist world which encircles it'.[9]

At the party congress in 1919, Lenin had proclaimed, 'The existence of the Soviet Republic side by side with imperialist states for a long time is *unthinkable*. One or the other must triumph in the end. Before that end supervenes, a series of frightful collisions between the Soviet Republic and the bourgeois states will be inevitable.'

In a 1920 speech to Moscow party members, he had told them, 'As soon as we are strong enough to defeat capitalism as a whole, we shall take it by the scruff of the neck.' For anyone hoping that circumstances, including the deaths of over 25 million Soviet citizens during the Second World War, might have modified this programme, Lenin's standing instructions to the 1918 congress were clear, 'In order not to lose direction during periods of retirement, retreat or temporary defeat, or when the enemy throws us back, the important and only theoretically correct thing is not to cast out the old basic programme.'[10]

The sense of the words had a familiar ring to Bedell Smith, echoing as they did Lord Palmerston's observations on Tsarist Realpolitik. Once the new ambassador had presented his letters of credence, life in post-war Moscow was like being on the far side of the moon. There was no contact with the population. Uniformed and armed guards of the *Ministerstvo Vnutrennikh Dyel* – the Ministry of the Interior, abbreviated to MVD – surrounded the embassy day and night, with relays of mobile plain clothes officers following every westerner at all times. In a despatch dated 27 January 1853 – sixty years before the October Revolution, Neill Brown wrote:

> Nothing is more striking to an American, on his first arrival here, than the rigor of the police. It would seem that the capital was in a state of siege … One of the most disagreeable features [an American] has to encounter is the secrecy with which everything is done. He can rarely obtain accurate information … and he may rely upon it that his own movements are closely observed by eyes that he never sees.

Nothing had changed in ninety years, as Bedell Smith and his small staff swiftly found. Xenophobia is paranoia writ large, and both were characteristics of Russian society unchanged by the revolution. Among information impossible for westerners to obtain were a street plan of Moscow and a telephone directory, both of which were considered classified information. Soviet citizens could ask for telephone numbers at special kiosks, where their identities and addresses were noted down, so that few availed themselves of the facility. Bedell Smith had brought his own Marine driver with him, but the local employees of the Embassy were all screened by the MVD and required to report everything they witnessed or overheard, with their families as hostages for their satisfactory performance in this respect.

The duties Bedell Smith was taking up were extremely onerous, with the rift between the USSR and its former allies opening wider by the day. During the visit to Moscow of Secretary of State Cordell Hull in October 1943, it had already been apparent that Roosevelt's unilateral decision to accept only unconditional surrender of all German forces meant that they would have to fight on to the bitter end, leaving Germany industrially ruined and devoid of the infrastructure of national and local government. At the Yalta conference in February 1944, it was agreed that Russia would occupy the eastern Länder of Germany; the western Länder being shared between Britain, the US and France. Since Berlin lay inside the Russian zone of occupation, access for the Western Allies to their sectors of the former German capital was guaranteed by Stalin. In an exchange of cables between him and President Truman in June 1945, the details were ironed out. US forces which had driven deep into Saxony and Thuringia withdrew, harassed and obstructed at every turn by the Soviet forces to whom they were ceding this conquered territory.[11] Similarly, Western forces arriving in their allotted sectors of Berlin were obstructed in every possible way by the Soviet administration that had been there for several weeks.

At Allied Control council meetings of representatives from all four occupying powers, Soviet plans for the occupation of Germany swiftly proved very different from those of the Western Allies. Trade between Russian- and Allied-occupied zones plummetted. Foreign trade was non-existent, banking services nearly so, road and rail communications destroyed. An Anglo-American subsidy of a half-billion dollars a year protected people in the western zones from starvation and epidemics. When agreed reparations from the Soviet zone did not arrive, the West stopped its flow of reparations eastwards.

The meeting of the Big Four foreign ministers held in Paris April–July 1946 not only failed to find a solution, but had to listen to Molotov demanding a share in the occupation of the Ruhr industrial area and the establishment of a single, centralised German state. These unacceptable demands were not his or even Stalin's, having been enunciated *in 1850* by Karl Marx:

> The democrats will either work directly for a federative republic or … strive to cripple the central government by giving the greatest possible autonomy and independence to the municipalities and provinces. The workers [i.e. communist activists]

must strive against this plan; not only for a German republic one and indivisible, but after it for a most decided centralisation of power in the hands of the [central] government. In a country like Germany, it is not to be tolerated under any circumstances that every village, every town, every province should put a new obstacle in the path of revolutionary activity, which can emanate in full strength only from the centre.[12]

Translated into normal language, Molotov was seeking to re-impose in Germany the rigid centralised government that Hitler had ruthlessly manipulated, so that it could be infiltrated, undermined and eventually controlled as rigidly as he had. Far from wishing to put the conquered nation back on its feet, Stalin's insistence on 10 billion dollars' worth of reparations was intended to impede economic reconstruction of Germany so that unemployment, misery and hunger would make the population more susceptible to political manipulation. As to what happened to most of the industrial plant transported eastwards, foreign observers found much of it rusting in railway sidings years later, despite protests from the GDR government that it made more sense to leave factories intact, producing goods for reparations.[13]

The three Western foreign ministers stood firm: their mandate for a federal government with considerable devolution of power to the individual Länder, including regional broadcasting organisations and no nationwide press, was expressly designed to prevent another totalitarian regime coming to power in Germany. In the face of these irreconcilable differences, in July 1946 Washington proposed economic union of the US zone with that of any other occupying power. By the end of the year, London had taken up the offer, creating a quasi-state named Bizonia. Thus, the Western Allies were already contributing to the renaissance of Western Germany.

In contrast, Poland had been written off. Symbolically, in the London Victory Parade on 8 June 1946, not a single Pole had been seen, although those who had worn RAF uniform were invited. They refused to march as a gesture of solidarity with their compatriots who had fought in the British Army and were forbidden to participate in case it upset Stalin. The shameful ruling tarnished the day. No longer prime minister, Churchill told Parliament how deeply he regretted the prohibition on the Poles' participation, lamenting the situation in Poland, where the Lublin government dared not have free elections in the presence of international observers. Many of General Anders' men who decided to return home after this last betrayal by Britain were arrested on setting foot in their homeland and eventually released with a black mark against them for life that guaranteed they would have only menial jobs in Bierut's communist state.

Those early post-war winters were grim even in the Labour Party's 'austerity Britain'. Grimmer still was the winter of 1946 for Bedell Smith, his staff and their families at the US Embassy in Moscow. Like Lenin and Molotov, a descendant of Russian nobility, CPSU Secretary and cultural boss Andrei A. Zhdanov was an attractive, outgoing 56-year-old who adored playing the piano for Stalin. Made responsible for implementing the Tseka's campaign against writers, musicians, architects, civil engineers and scientists all over the Soviet Union, he imposed a cultural repression labelled *Zhdanovshchina*. Under this programme, all vestiges of pro-Westernism or cosmopolitanism in Soviet life were to be ferreted out and their authors punished. Literary critics were denounced for daring to suggest that Russian authors had been influenced by Rousseau, Molière, Byron or Charles Dickens. Since Zhdanov aimed to eradicate every trace of 'servility to the West', all Western technology and scientific theories were claimed to be of Russian origin, from helicopters to the origin of species.

Despite *intelligentsia* being originally a Russian word, the intelligentsia in Russia were always suspect because it was they who had heard the echoes of the Renaissance, the Reformation and the American and French revolutions, and introduced dangerous new ideas into this vast land, isolated from Europe by geography and autocratic rulers. Less than a century had elapsed since those echoes reflected the wave of civil unrest during 1848 in France, Italy and Austro-Hungary that filtered through the Ice Curtain and incited Alexander II and his son Alexander III to despatch many intellectuals to years in Siberian exile.

Only for one decade, following the October 1917 revolution, had artistic life in Russia enjoyed that cross-fertilisation with other countries considered normal in the West. As early as 1929, with Stalin firmly in power, the pressure was on for *all* art and creativity to conform to the doctrine of Socialist-Realism – in other words, to reflect an exclusively Marxist view of life and the world, as interpreted by the party. Like many self-taught people, Stalin was an avid reader and considered himself a discerning critic, sending handwritten notes to authors, composers and playwrights with advice they could not reject. On 26 October 1932 he had called a meeting of the fifty most influential writers, including his favourite, Maxim Gorky. They were informed by him without equivocation, 'The artist ought to show life truthfully. And if he shows our life truthfully, he cannot fail to show it moving towards socialism. This is, and will be, Socialist-Realism.'[14]

If Stalin was the prophet of Socialist-Realism, Zhdanov was its high priest. The new American arrivals were amazed when the famous poetess Anna Akhmatova was expelled from the Union of Soviet Writers. She was denounced in August 1946 by Zhdanov for 'eroticism, mysticism, and political indifference' because she did not toe the party line. Her poetry designated 'alien to the Soviet people', she was publicly labelled by Zhdanov 'a harlot-nun'. Since the only publishers in the Soviet Union were the state publishing houses, her work was no longer published and she was denied entrance to public libraries. Yet Akhmatova was comparatively lucky because other writers labelled 'cosmopolitan' for having once inferred foreign influences in Russian art or literature found themselves in labour camps. The undoubtedly cosmopolitan Sergei Prokofiev was censured by the party for 'formalism' in his music. Shostakovich, once Stalin's favourite composer, was made to confess, 'I know that the Party is right and that I must search for and find creative paths which lead me to Soviet-Realistic popular art.'[15] Rather difficult, when one is writing for symphony orchestras.

One author who suffered similarly in Britain was George Orwell. His experiences with the International Brigades in Spain had given him an understanding of Stalin's betrayal of the revolution. The result was his timeless political satire *Animal Farm*. Completed in 1944, it was not published in Britain for two years because the Ministry of Information warned his publisher not to handle a book that might offend Stalin, who was portrayed as the ruling pig, called Napoleon.

Living in their apartments inside the medieval fortress of the Kremlin and emerging only to visit the closed world of their closely grouped *dachi*, reading only the approved party organs *Pravda* and *Izvestia* and books that slavishly conformed to the Socialist-Realist line, it is no wonder that Russia's leaders saw the world through the distorting mirror of their own delusions.

These were the people with whom Bedell Smith and British ambassador Sir Maurice Peterson had to go through the motions of *friendly* diplomatic relations.

18

A DAUGHTER BACK FROM THE DEAD

In the first British post-war general election of July 1945, the massive swing away from Churchill and the Conservative Party in favour of Labour, led by Churchill's wartime deputy Clement Attlee, won a stunning 393 seats in the House of Commons, against the 213 Conservative seats. Some commentators said this reflected how all the voters still in uniform were fed up with being ordered about for the last six years and regarded the Conservatives as 'the party of the bosses'. More sophisticated analysis attributed Labour's victory to its manifesto promising full employment, a cradle-to-grave welfare state and free medical services – which sounded like paradise to those who had known unemployment and poverty in the 1920s and '30s.

However, Stalin's gleeful prophecy to Molotov in 1939 that the impending major European war would provide the social chaos ideal for communist coups d'état proved wrong. With less than 60,000 members compared to the 800,000-strong French Communist Party and the Italian Communist Party with 1.7 million members, the CPGB received only 103,000 votes, but won two seats in Parliament. Gallagher was re-elected and Phil Piratin won the constituency of Mile End in east London, with Harry Pollitt failing to take Rhondda East.

And that was as far to the Left as things went in Britain because veteran Labour supporters and MPs despised the CPGB leadership for the way it had toed Stalin's *Class Against Class* line that all other socialist parties were enemies because they split the Left vote. Moscow's *ukase* now backfired. After Attlee became Britain's uninspiring but clear-headed prime minister on 26 July 1945, Labour stalwarts like Herbert Morrison, Ernest Bevin, Stafford Cripps, Hugh Gaitskell, Emanuel Shinwell, Aneurin Bevan and his wife Jennie Lee blocked every attempt by Pollitt, Dutt and Co. to gain a share of political power. In other countries also, Stalin's prophecy that the war would result in communist revolutions proved false.

In 1944, Churchill had attempted some horse-trading with Stalin, consigning Romania to the Soviet sphere in return for British predominance in Greece. Whether for this reason or not, the Kremlin did not order the well-armed Greek communist resistance movement EAM/ELAS to grab power in the wake of the German withdrawal. The inevitable confrontation was postponed until December 1944, when fierce fighting broke out between ELAS and a small British expeditionary force that had accompanied the Greek government on its return from exile in October. Churchill persuaded the Greek monarch George II not to return until after a plebiscite, in which the overwhelming majority voted to keep the royal family. In protest, the communists refused to participate in a general election held in March 1946, going underground instead and launching a full-scale guerrilla war, with atrocities on both sides.

By December 1947 EAM/ELAS, with covert arms shipments from the new communist regimes in Greece's northern neighbours Albania, Yugoslavia and Bulgaria, established a provisional government that controlled the north of the country. The financial burden of containing the conflict being too great for Attlee's war-bankrupted Britain, fumbling its way back to a peacetime economy of sorts, on 12 March 1947 President Truman announced a $400 million programme of military and economic assistance to Turkey and Greece, to prevent pro-Moscow guerrillas taking over these countries. The Greek Civil War nevertheless lasted until 1949, leaving a legacy of bitterness.

A strong supporter of what became known as the Truman Doctrine was his new Secretary of State George C. Marshall, who had been US Army chief of staff during the Second World War. He travelled to Moscow in April 1947 to discover Stalin's future intentions and found the *vozhd* typically unforthcoming. Fortunately Kennan's 'long telegram' to Washington had identified the problems of dealing with the Soviet leadership. Instead of being reprimanded for lecturing his superiors in the State Department, Kennan's acumen and courage were rewarded when Marshall recalled him to the US as chief planner of the European Recovery Programme (ERP), popularly known as the Marshall Plan.

This was a far-sighted attempt to revitalise the economies of the war-torn European states and curtail the conditions favourable to seizure of power by national communist parties: high unemployment, rationing of most consumer goods including food and shortage of housing after all the destruction of property during the war. In the case of western Germany a clear priority was to keep what remained of Hitler's military-industrial complex in the western zones from falling into the hands of the new enemy in Moscow.[1]

Initially the ERP was open to all European countries, but Stalin refused to let the captive populations of his satellites receive any help from the US. To undermine the plan's positive effects, in September 1947 he ordered the Comintern reborn as the Information Office of Communist and Workers' Parties, shortened to Cominform. Headquartered initially in Belgrade to feed the pretence that it was not a tool of Moscow, that sounded harmless enough, but its purpose was to control the foreign parties as the Comintern had formerly done, to infiltrate trade unions and influence public opinion in the democracies, to set up 'friendship societies' which would lobby for Russia and incite hostility towards the US under the banner of a so-called world peace initiative, later symbolised by Picasso's white dove. But there was nothing dove-like about the nationwide strikes in 1947 by communist-controlled trade unions in France and Italy in the attempt to undermine the ERP.

As veteran US diplomat Charles Bohlen remarked, the display of unity among the Allies during the Second World War had been a hollow myth. 'Reality was a complete disunity, with the Soviet

Union and the satellite [countries] on the one side and the rest of the world on the other. There are, in short, two worlds, instead of one.'[2]

In Paris, couturier Christian Dior created the New Look and gave European women back their feminine silhouette after the years of wearing trousers and boiler suits on farms and in the factories and shipyards. In London, Bill Rust, once again editor of the *Daily Worker*, created a new look for the paper, less grimly *Pravda*-like and more market-oriented – although Dutt still had only to pick up the phone for a story to be run, or not run, to be head-lined on the front page or relegated to an inside page.

The paper's headquarters were in a purpose-built office block in Farringdon Road, for which rising circulation was not the only source of income. Some of the staff, who were using a mythi-cal job as cover for their real activities, had their salaries paid by Soviet-front organisations and all the journalists travelled in expenses-paid luxury on assignments east of the Iron Curtain. Most importantly, half the print-run was paid for by Moscow twelve months in advance and flown daily to Eastern Europe. This added up to millions of copies, a few of which were read by the author while banged up in Cell No. 20 of the Lindenstrasse prison in Potsdam. As to the rest, it is anyone's guess where they ended up, the USSR being so chronically short of toilet paper that the Red Army issued none to its men.[3]

Although looking like a benign latter-day Pickwick, editor Rust rarely smiled. Cold as ice, he remained a devoted Stalinist to his death in 1949, never talking about the experiences of a daughter from his first marriage named Rosa after the German communist heroine Rosa Luxemburg. When her parents returned separately to Britain in 1937 – Bill Rust with his new Russian wife Tamara Kravets – Rosa was kept as a hostage for her father's continued loyalty. A measure of his importance was her gilded cage: she was a boarder at the exclusive school in Ivanovo-Vosnesensk where children of top foreign communists like Tito and Dimitrov were educated in conditions of great privilege.

On her fifteenth birthday, Rosa had to leave the school and was sent to a hostel for immigrants near the Lux Hotel in Moscow, from where she was evacuated to the east as the German forces approached the city, and set to work 12-hour shifts in a canning factory. Quite unaware that this was in the Volga German Republic, she fell victim at the age of 16 to Stalin's obsession that *everyone* in the republic was a potential traitor. The Volga Germans had already suffered terribly in Stalin's ethnic purges of 1937.[4] Rounded up with her neighbours, Rosa endured the weeks-long journey in cattle trucks to exile in Kazakhstan. Thousands died on the way to a land where the only shelter against the bitter winter of the steppes was in lice-infested semi-dugout sod huts, shunned by the natives and exploited as expendable labour by local party officials. Working on starvation rations, pushing steel trucks of ore along rails in a copper mine, Rosa fell seriously ill. In desperation she wrote to an old school-friend at Invanovo-Vosnesensk, who somehow forwarded the letter to Dimitrov.[5]

In his capacity as head of the Comintern, he arranged travel papers for her in the spring of 1943, it being necessary to have what amounted to a military leave pass before 'deserting' one's assigned place of residence in the USSR. As late as October 1953, the Passport Statute made it an offence for Soviet citizens to leave their place of residence for more than thirty days, and even this required a permit.

Rosa's journey on grossly overcrowded trains where soldiers had priority involved waiting weeks in several places for a connection. Her last stage was a seventeen-day nightmare with passengers taking turns to lie on the floor to sleep for a few hours. Back in Moscow, Rosa met *Daily Worker* correspondent John Gibbons, who informed her that Bill Rust had been pestered by his ex-wife for years to trace their daughter. Advised by Gibbons, Rust cabled back for Rosa to choose between staying in Russia or going to Britain. She opted to return to the land of her birth, although she no longer spoke English. Still very ill, she landed from a Soviet vessel at the Scottish port of Leith and was discreetly whisked to London incommunicado by Foreign Office officials who did not want her telling journalists of the horrific conditions she had endured in the USSR, then Britain's wartime ally.

Nor did her father want to know, despite the evidence of his eyes and ears. As a contemporary of his on the *Daily Worker* said, 'If anyone had described in our office one tenth of what Rosa lived through, Bill Rust would have denounced [this as] anti-Soviet lies and slanders.'[6] He was typical of hard-line western communists, who clung to each twist and turn of the party line, ignoring all evidence of conditions behind the Iron Curtain.

Inside the USSR it did not matter what anyone *thought*, so long as unwise thoughts were not voiced. In 1947, Bedell Smith copied from issue No. 4 of the Moscow magazine *Bolshevik*, 'In creating public opinion, the decisive role is played by the Communist Party and the Soviet state which, through various media, formulates public opinion and educates the workers in a spirit of Socialist awareness.'

In other words, you think as we tell you. Bedell Smith was also shocked to read that *krugovaya poruka* was still the law. Article 58-I-c of the Soviet Criminal Code enacted on 20 July 1934 had never been repealed. 'In the event of escape or flight across the border of military service personnel, the adult members of his family … are to be punished by deprivation of liberty for a term of five to ten years and the confiscation of all their property.' The remainder of the traitor's family, who were residing with him or were dependent on him at the time the crime was committed, were subject to deprivation of voting rights and exile to remote regions of Siberia for five years.

Desertion of serving military personnel is treated seriously in most countries, but in the USSR this law applied to the family of *any* adult who had ever served in the military, since reservist status was lifelong.

At the time Bedell Smith was writing, the only democratic country in Eastern Europe was Czechoslovakia, tottering towards its own inevitable communist takeover, sandwiched between Soviet-occupied Poland, Hungary, Ukraine, Romania and East Germany. With Moscow forbidding the Czechoslovakians from participating in the Marshall Plan and the country's economy foundering, puppet premier Klement Gottwald set out to gain power with an appearance of legitimacy. After concerted demonstrations in the main cities by armed bands of workers, supported by a police force hand-picked by the communist minister of the interior, a new government was formed on 25 February 1948, in which Gottwald's supporters held the key posts, with only a token representation of other parties.

As Stalinist repression extinguished the last embers of democracy in Eastern Europe and the borders of Czechoslovakia were closed, non-communist politicians fled rather than face imprisonment – as did thousands of business people and intellectuals, some by crashing cars through barriers or shooting their way to freedom. One British intelligence officer known to the author spent anxious days and nights on the Czech-Austrian border waiting for a colleague to return from a last-minute mission behind the extended Iron Curtain before accepting that he was dead. Stalin's satisfaction that he had thus plugged a serious gap in Russia's western line of

Russian expansion post-1945: the Soviet satellites

defence was short-lived. If anything had been needed to bring the US Congress solidly behind Truman and the Marshall Plan programme, the Czech coup d'état was it.

Just when Stalin was flattering himself that nothing could go wrong with his plans for Eastern Europe, Russia's foothold in the Balkans slipped out of control. Tito's trusted supporter Milovan Djilas had already complained to Stalin during a visit to Moscow in the winter of 1944 about looting and rapes by the Red Army during the liberation of Yugoslavia. In the spring of 1948, Stalin launched a campaign to purge the leadership of the Communist Party of Yugoslavia (CPY) but was unable to counter Tito's iron-fisted control over party, secret police and army. As with Trotsky, the remedy seemed to Stalin to lie in an assassination. Discovered in his writing desk at the Kuntsevo dacha after his death was a note from Tito dating from this time. It read, 'Stalin: Stop sending people to kill me. We've already captured five of them, one with a bomb and another with a rifle. If you don't stop sending killers, I'll send one to Moscow, and I won't have to send a second.'[7]

The rift between Moscow and Belgrade produced the bizarre situation of the country in which the Cominform had its headquarters being expelled on Moscow's orders from the organisation, which then removed itself to pro-Moscow Bucharest in Romania. Tito pragmatically turned to the West for help. Paradoxically remaining a communist police state, Yugoslavia began receiving economic aid under the Marshall Plan. The country was thus spared Stalin's maniacal purges of the next five years which saw millions of loyal Soviet citizens imprisoned, exiled or executed. Tito conducted his own purges of internal opponents, including Djilas, but on a smaller scale.[8]

Because the lack of a strong currency was an important factor in the economic stagnation of Germany, in June 1948 the adhesion of the French zone of Germany to the British/US Bizonia produced Trizonia, in which on 18 June the new Deutsche Mark became the official currency. This economic bloc with its own currency was bitterly opposed by Moscow, which wanted a weak German economy. After a four-power meeting of economic advisers in Berlin on 22 June ended in vociferous disagreement, the Soviet authorities immediately announced a new currency for their zone and all

sectors of Berlin. This was totally unacceptable to the three western commandants, who announced next day that the Deutsche
Mark was now the legal tender in their sectors of the divided city.

Stalin had expected post-war Germany to be the scene of a
second great communist revolution. After all, Karl Marx had
prophesied that *the* revolution would happen there – which,
given the massive communist vote in the last free election before
Hitler came to power, seemed a reasonable expectation. What
Bedell Smith called 'the dream of a happy union between Soviet
resources and manpower and German technical skill and administrative ability' had long been an obsession of the Politburo.

In an attempt to catch up with Western Europe, in January
1949 Moscow set up Comecon, an organisation designed to
speed up the economic development of the Soviet bloc. Its original members were the USSR, Bulgaria, Czechoslovakia, Hungary,
Poland and Albania, with the GDR joining in September 1950.
The economic potential of Comecon was hampered by the severe
difficulty imposed by the command economies of the member
countries arbitrarily deciding prices without reference to the real
market value of goods and services. This confined intra-Come-
con trading mainly to barter. However, Comecon did reorganise
Eastern Europe's railroad and electricity grids and laid the foun-
dations for Soviet power exports in the so-called 'Friendship'
pipeline bringing oil from the Volga to Eastern Europe.

It does not take long looking at a map to see why Khrushchev
would later remark: 'Berlin is the testicles of the West. Every time
I want to make the West scream, I squeeze on Berlin.' Completely
surrounded by the Soviet zone, the Western sectors of the city lay
more than 100 miles inside Russian-controlled territory. In revenge
for the new Western currency, on 24 June 1948 Stalin ordered
a desperate move to force the Allies out of Berlin. A complete
blockade was imposed on all surface traffic between Western
Germany and Berlin: trucks and other vehicles were turned back
at the interzonal checkpoints; barges were halted on canals and
rivers. Power supplies to Berlin from Eastern Germany were cut
off. From Moscow, it seemed a move that had to win, unless the
West wanted 2,240,000 Berliners in the three Western sectors of
the divided city to starve to death. An unexpected protest came

from the GDR leadership. At a meeting with the Soviet authorities on 28 June the East Germans protested that the blockade would put out of action their sugar refineries, steel mills and fishing fleets – all dependent on Western spare parts or raw materials.[9]

In the Control Commission, the Western representatives passed Notes to their Soviet opposite numbers, while General Clay and a considerable number of other Western commanders wanted 'to show the Russkies' by driving an armoured column along the Autobahn from Helmstedt to Berlin, blasting any opposition out of the way. As to where that would have led, given that the Soviet high command was waiting for such a move, the most likely answer is to a third world war. The conventional armed forces of the West, though, were largely demobilised. By mid-July, Soviet forces in Germany had increased to forty divisions, against eight Allied divisions. Three groups of US strategic bombers arrived in Britain as tension mounted: if it came to a shooting war, the only way to offset the enormous numerical superiority of Soviet and satellite ground and air forces would be to resort to nuclear weapons, which Russia did not possess at the time.

Reason won the day. After a British feasibility study suggested circumnavigating the blockade by supplying the Western sectors by air along the agreed flight corridors, General Clay informed West Berlin's mayor-elect Ernst Reuter and his aide Willy Brandt of the plan. They assured him that Berliners would rather tighten their belts than live through another war. By chance, General Albert Wedemeyer, US Army Chief of Plans and Operations, was in Europe on an inspection tour. Having commanded the American China-Burma-India theatre in the Second World War, Wedemeyer had first-hand experience of the American airlift from India 'over the Hump' of the Himalayas to the nationalist forces fighting the Japanese in China. His considered opinion was that an airlift to Berlin could work, bringing to the beleaguered city everything from aspirins and penicillin to coal and cement. Effective immediately, aircraft de-mothballed in many countries flew into Tempelhof, Tegel and Gatow airfields 24/7. On the return leg, some aircraft carried exports from West Berlin factories. The city came back to life.

Three times in August 1948, Bedell Smith met Stalin for what he termed 'poker games' in the Kremlin. Speaking also for Great

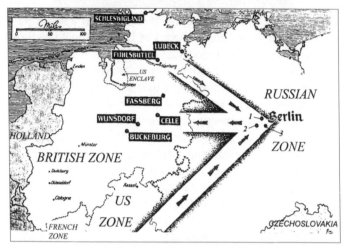

Contemporary map of Allied air corridors used in airlift. Airfields in Berlin:
1. Tegel (French sector) 2. Gatow (British sector) 3. Tempelhof (US sector)

Britain and France, the US ambassador stated their joint intention to stand firm on the agreed rights of access to Berlin. Stalin
and Molotov played a game, each modifying what the other had
said. Molotov moved goalposts and became increasingly truculent and difficult. When he handed Bedell Smith his final Note
after Stalin had departed on holiday at the Black Sea, it contradicted most of what little had been agreed.[10]

That winter, West Berliners huddled near their stoves, for which
there was precious little fuel, but somehow the city survived. As
Reuter and Brandt had predicted, the population's morale was
strengthened by this show of Western determination not to leave
them to Stalin's mercy, which they had already experienced briefly.
In the airlift, some planes crashed and pilots died, some civilians
were killed on the ground, but the city lived on. Only once was
there direct confrontation: on 5 April 1949 a Soviet Yak-3 pilot
misjudged his distance while harassing a BEA Vickers Viscount
and crashed into it, killing ten civilian passengers and the crew.
The airlift continued until 12 May, when the Russians backed
down after eleven months, having failed to achieve anything. The
barriers were opened on the Hanover-Berlin Autobahn and surface traffic again flowed into Berlin, albeit sluggishly at first, so

that General Clay's miraculous airlift continued at a slower pace until 30 September. For a total cost of $224 million it had delivered just over one ton of food, fuel, machinery, and other supplies per inhabitant of the Western sectors – a total of 2,323,738 tons.

There is a school of thought that espionage serves both sides. In May 1949 a Soviet mole inside MI6 landed the job of liaison officer in Washington with American intelligence. In this capacity, Kim Philby was allowed to visit Arlington Hall and read some of the Venona transcripts. Fellow Cambridge spies Donald Maclean and Guy Burgess were in key Foreign Office posts, feeding top-grade intelligence back to their Soviet case officers. It may be that their reports of Western determination to stand firm over Berlin played a part in Stalin's decision to end the blockade.

Or, it may have had something to do with the formidable baby shortly to be delivered by midwife Beria. The explosion of the first Soviet nuclear bomb on 29 August 1949 came several years before the Pentagon had expected it, thanks to Soviet spies like Julius and Ethel Rosenberg and traitors like naturalised Briton Klaus Fuchs and US diplomat Alger Hiss, who stole Western secrets and material to pass on to their GRU or KGB handlers. At 6 p.m. local time that day, in a bunker deep in a remote area of Kazakhstan closed off from the world by several cordons of NKVD troops, Beria witnessed the explosion. Like everything else in the USSR, the news was kept under wraps until Washington announced the Soviet test after US military aircraft had taken samples of airborne radioactivity.

President Truman's administration was confronted with the problem of adjusting its on-the-ground military presence in Europe now that it no longer had a monopoly on nuclear weapons. But Stalin also had his headaches. On 1 October 1949 Mao Tse-Tung, victorious at last in the long struggle with Chiang Kai Chek's Nationalist Army, proclaimed the existence of the People's Republic of China, appointing himself its first chairman. Two thousand years earlier, Virgil put into the mouth of the priest Laocoon the line, *Timeo danaos et dona ferentes* – I fear the Greeks even when they bring gifts – in that case a large wooden horse. On 16 December Mao arrived in Moscow bearing gifts that were coolly received.

At this time, the Gulag contained over 2.5 million Soviet citizens – more than ever before. Against so many ruined lives, what did a few more matter? In the hope of disarming his visitor into signing a Sino-Soviet treaty legitimising Soviet territorial claims along 3,000 miles of shared border, Stalin betrayed to Mao several Soviet agents inside the Chinese government. Mao wanted more than this – at least a treaty of mutual assistance accompanied by economic aid – and was nobody's patsy. The visit dragged on for two months, during which Molotov dutifully shuttled back and forth between the Kremlin and the dacha outside Moscow in which Mao was installed under surveillance.

Mistrusting all Jews because they had relatives in other countries, Stalin had made Molotov divorce his beautiful and adored Jewish wife Polina. At the Politburo meeting where her membership of the party was revoked, her husband had the courage to abstain, but then wrote a grovelling letter to Stalin, in which he voted belatedly for her expulsion and apologised for the political error of putting loyalty to wife above that to the party. Accused of espionage and 'internationalism' among other crimes, Polina was arrested and interrogated with more than 100 other Jews, possibly because of her close friendship with Stalin's second wife, who may have confided to her the reasons for her suicide.

To worry Molotov, Stalin at first pretended he had no idea where she was and allowed no one else to tell him. Finally putting his loyal foreign minister out of this temporary misery and into a longer one, he read to him the false confessions of men alleging that she had had group sex with them. Polina was jailed for a year, then exiled to Kazakhstan for five years, with Beria of all people – who had not been personally involved in the case – occasionally whispering to Molotov that she was still alive.[11]

Invited to the lavish celebrations of Stalin's 70th birthday, Mao sulked. Two months after his arrival, on 14 February 1950, having demonstrated that he was no vassal of Tsar Josef, he let his deputy Chou En-Lai sign a thirty-year mutual defence treaty that gave nothing much away on either side. Seen from London and Washington, however, it looked as though the two communist giants had concluded a marriage compact.

19

THE PROXY WAR THAT COST 4 MILLION LIVES

After both the Comintern initiative and a global war failed to produce communist coups d'état throughout Western Europe, Stalin decided that it would be more effective to attack the European colonial powers through the 'soft under-belly' of their overseas possessions, where the native peoples' desire for independence could be manipulated by Moscow's agents. The aim was to deprive the colonial powers of their sources of cheap raw materials and also deny them the huge markets in their colonies for their expensive manufactured goods, causing lay-offs and strikes in the manufacturing areas and putting stress on the whole fabric of the mother country's market-driven economy. A bonus was that post-independence chaos and lack of a trained native administration in the former colonies would make these ripe for pro-Moscow takeovers after the imperial troops had been withdrawn.

Spain had lost most of its once-huge empire long since. Portugal still had some colonies, which would be major targets for the Kremlin. Germany had been divested of its empire after the First World War. However, the Belgian Congo, rich in gold, diamonds, copper, tin, cobalt and zinc, was also an important source of uranium for the United States' nuclear weapons, and became an irresistible target. Epitomising nineteenth-century paternalism, the mines and plantations were worked by African indentured labourers, with public works constructed by forced labour, making the vast territory ripe for revolt. Despite this potential the 1978 Cuban-led invasion of Zaire from the breakaway Katanga province did not realise Moscow's dream.

Tens of thousands of African students attended Moscow's Lumumba University, but Africa – while a sparring ground for Russian, American and other intelligence agencies – proved infertile soil for implanting pro-Moscow totalitarian regimes, largely due to ethnic and tribal frictions. Once gaining power under whatever banner, African dictators tended to become despots, accepting aid from all sources but giving no loyalty in return. One West African businessman, asked by the author why he had sent a son to study in Moscow, replied, 'So he wouldn't become a communist. If I'd sent him to Harvard or Cambridge, he probably would have done.'

The Dutch East Indies, liberated from the Japanese by British forces, was a major supplier of rubber, coffee, cocoa and other commodities, and possessed substantial oil and natural gas reserves, the loss of which would reduce Holland's prosperity significantly. On the morning of 17 August 1945, when news of the Japanese surrender had been confirmed, the veteran anti-Dutch activist Ahmed Sukarno proclaimed his country the Republic of Indonesia. A series of nationalist uprisings convinced the British troops taking the surrender of Japanese forces in the territory that this was no flash in the pan. Dutch colonial administrators returned, hoping to reassert control, but were eventually forced to negotiate with Sukarno's prime minister Sutan Sjahrir. The failure of these talks led in 1947 to what was euphemistically termed 'a police action' mounted from Holland against the new republic, which invoked United Nations intervention. Although the struggle with the Dutch continued in parts of the territory until 1949, it was impossible for Holland to regain possession of the many islands which made up the former Dutch East Indies without provoking worldwide protests at the use of force.

Among Sukarno's political opponents was the Indonesian Communist Party that, despite support from Moscow, never threatened the political momentum of the nationalist movement because the speed with which Sukarno acted had cut the ground from under the feet of the communists. Moscow's frustration was still evident many years later when Sukarno made a state visit to Moscow in the early '60s and was involved in a KGB honey-trap with several 'air hostesses'. Shown the intended blackmail film next day, Sukarno laughed at threats of exposure, saying that his people would be very proud to see their middle-aged president having sex with so many pretty girls simultaneously.

At the end of the Second World War Britain and France still possessed their far-flung empires. Every British schoolchild used to gaze at maps of the world in wonderment that so much of the planet's land mass was pink, i.e. 'ours'. Similarly, French children felt proud that so much of Africa and Asia constituted *la francophonie*. It was calculated inside the Kremlin that deprivation of these immense and rich possessions would disintegrate the infrastructure of the two major European post-war powers.

In London, the Labour government's commitment to the transformation of the British Empire into a Commonwealth of Nations saw independence granted to India in 1947 after Mahatma Ghandi succeeded in achieving the Russian aim in the Great Game – prising the jewel in the British crown from its mounting. To Moscow's dismay, the ensuing social chaos, massive emigrations by Muslims to Pakistani areas in the north-west and north-east of the sub-continent and by Hindus from those areas into India itself, accompanied by appalling massacres, failed to bring the Indian Communist Party to power.

Malaya was an important source of tin and rubber for Britain. After becoming the Federation of Malaya in 1948, this British colony seemed to present a better chance of pro-Moscow takeover because the Communist Party of Malaya (CPM) had been the main resistance organisation against the Japanese occupation. Predominantly Chinese, its members had the organisation, experience, discipline and weapons to grab power from the politically less active Malays and other ethnic groups.

On Moscow's instructions, the CPM returned to the jungles, emerging in small gangs to murder British mine and planta- tion managers and their families, terrorise their workers, slash rubber trees and sabotage mines.

After the British government declared a state of emergency on 18 June 1948, troops under General Sir Gerald Templer initiated 'search and destroy' operations against the guerrilla strongholds. Forcible resettlement of the rural Chinese population into forti- fied 'new villages' denied the rebels their main source of food and manpower. A gradual programme of social and economic reform, the granting of citizenship to many Chinese residents, local elections and devolution of some administrative power to village councils reduced support for the insurgents, but the emer- gency did not end until 1960. Long before then, the Cold War developed a hot spot on the periphery of the two power blocs in another Asian country that few Westerners had even heard of.

Stalin had agreed at Yalta that Korea, a Japanese colony since 1910, should be given independence post-war since it had never declared war on the Allies. Soviet troops arrived in the north of the peninsula on 8 August 1945 and proceeded to take the surrender of Japanese forces north of latitude 38° N – a conveni- ent demarcation line that divided the peninsula in half. In the south, American troops landed on the same day and received the formal surrender of Japanese forces in their half of the coun- try on 9 August. With Soviet troops already sealing off the 38th parallel, there were now two zones of occupation in anticipation of nationwide elections to elect a Korean government as swiftly as practicable.

That, at least, was the Western understanding until Stalin's protégé Kim Il-Sung imposed an ultra-hardline communist government on the northern half of the country, appointing himself first premier of the new Democratic People's Republic of Korea in 1948. In 1948 and 1949 US forces withdrew from the southern half of the country, now called Republic of Korea (ROK), leaving it governed by the elected but corrupt Singman Rhee administration.

There were thus two governments in Korea, each threatening to unify the country by invading the other half.

Having served in the Red Army during the Second World War, Kim asked Stalin for military aid to carry out his plan. After losing the Berlin blockade gamble, Stalin was wary of testing Western resolve again so soon, until Kim assured him that victory would be won in three days of combat, giving no time for the West to intervene. The prospect of a pro-Moscow government of all Korea threatening Russia's old enemy Japan, a country on its knees industrially and politically after its recent defeat, was too attractive to turn down. There was also the recent statement by US Secretary of State Dean Acheson that the American 'defensive perimeter' did not extend to Korea because the Truman administration did not wish to become embroiled in a war on the Asian mainland which could easily spread.[1] Playing it both ways, Stalin promised Kim no troops, but a supply of Red Army surplus materiel to be delivered across the 12-mile-long Soviet-North Korean border south of Vladivostok. He also told Kim to discuss his invasion plan with Mao in Beijing. Communist China was not a member of the United Nations and therefore risked no sanctions in supporting Kim's large, but poorly equipped, conscript army.

Before dawn on 25 June 1950 long columns of the North Korean People's Army (KPA) crossed the 38th parallel, mostly on foot. Singman Rhee immediately appealed to Washington for help. The USSR was fortuitously boycotting the UN Security Council in protest at the non-admission of communist China, so Truman was able to obtain immediate UN condemnation of the invasion, with the Security Council calling upon UN members to give South Korea all assistance necessary to restore peace. On 27 June Truman issued the order for US air and naval forces based in Japan to support the ROK troops, which were giving ground so fast that the KPA entered the devastated southern capital Seoul next day.

On 30 June Truman stepped up the intervention by ordering into Korea three divisions of US forces then occupying Japan. Reinforcing the very fluid front in support of the retreating ROK soldiers though proved extremely difficult. The KPA continued to advance until the ROK/UN retreat ended in early August along the perimeter of a beachhead based on the port of Pusan in the south-east tip of the country. On 15 September the commanding general of the US Army's Far East Command, General Douglas MacArthur, executed a brilliant amphibious counter-attack that took the KPA in the flank at Seoul's main port of Inchon. Fighting their way back up the peninsula, by 1 October UN forces drawn from sixteen member states including Britain reached the 38th parallel. With UN General Assembly approval, MacArthur then pursued the KPA northwards, and had his forces nearly to the Chinese border by 26 October.

When appointed to supervise the demilitarisation of Japan after the surrender and revitalise the economy, imposing a liberal constitution in place of the previous quasi-medieval system, MacArthur became a total autocrat. So accustomed was he to enjoying unquestioned authority as the overlord of Japan that he now fell victim to his own wishful thinking in assessing the military-political realities in Korea.

Kim's desperate pleas to Beijing elicited massive reinforcements from the Chinese army because Mao wanted to keep a communist North Korea as a buffer between China and Western military presence in Asia. As the cruel winter struck, human waves of bugle-blowing Chinese troops – many unarmed but drilled to grab rifle and ammunition in combat from the nearest dead comrade – overwhelmed the most exposed UN positions, at times outnumbering them 10:1. Stalin certainly did not want UN forces reaching the Soviet-North Korean border, and ordered Second World War Soviet fighter aces to fly tactical support missions against UN ground and air forces, using the latest swept-wing MiG-15 jet fighters repainted in Chinese colours in order to be plausibly deniable.

The MiG-15s outclassed all the United Nations piston-engined and jet fighters in Korea until the arrival in theatre of swept-wing US F-86 Sabres, which outmatched the Soviet aircraft. Aware from close passes in combat that they were up against white Caucasian pilots, US aircrew were ordered not to talk about the only time that American and Russian servicemen confronted each other in combat during the Cold War.

Many downed US aircrew failed to return home after the cessation of hostilities, having been transported into the USSR with their damaged aircraft for experimental research. Other POWs returned after being subjected to *xi nao* or, literally, 'brain wash', and worked undercover for their former captors, the most famous case being that of British consular official George Blake, captured in Seoul. After repatriation, he worked for MI6 in Berlin and the Middle East, and admitted on his arrest in April 1961 to having betrayed at least forty-two British agents to the KGB and copied to his Soviet case officer every important document in his possession since 1953.

On 11 April 1951, President Truman sacked MacArthur because of his insubordination and intention to widen the conflict by bombing assembly areas within Red China. The combined communist forces pushed the UN back to the 38th parallel and continued pushing until nearly half South Korea had been re-occupied at enormous cost in lives. After the UN/ROK forces battled their way northwards across the 38th parallel again, in autumn 1952 both Mao and Kim wanted out, but Stalin refused permission, saying that they had 'nothing to lose but men'.

On both sides of the Iron Curtain there was relief that this protracted war could be fought without the American command resorting to use of nuclear weapons. Truman's restraint, however, was not for idealistic reasons. In the first two years of the Korean War, it was impossible for even the most hawkish denizen of the Pentagon to know how effective a nuclear bomb, designed to destroy a densely populated city on reasonably flat ground, would be if dropped on dispersed columns of PVA soldiers advancing along the valleys of very mountainous terrain on foot, carrying their own supplies. By January 1953, when wartime commander-in-chief General Dwight D. Eisenhower became the 34th president of the US, tactical, or battlefield, nuclear weapons were already being tested.

One theory why he was able to short-circuit the prevarications of the North Korean negotiators is that Pyongyang and Moscow were informed of this and of Eisenhower's intention, unless an armistice were swiftly signed, for the UN command to abandon its self-imposed limited war strategy and use *all* available weaponry in North Korea, plus air strikes north of the Yalu River.[2] However, a significant factor in the Korean armistice was the replacement of Kim's patron Josef Stalin, who died on 5 March 1953, by the uneasy *troika* of Khrushchev, Malenkov and Beria. The 'three-day war' that had dragged on for three years was brought to an official end on 27 July, by which time the conflict had cost an estimated 4 million Korean, Chinese and UN casualties, including civilians. Two-fifths of Korea's industry had been destroyed and one home in three devastated.

In the Kremlin, Nikita Khrushchev had NKVD chief Laventi Beria executed as a capitalist spy. In a replay of the succession to Lenin, he then outmanoeuvred rival Georgi Malenkov, considered by many as Stalin's heir apparent: Malenkov was demoted to manage a remote hydroelectric power station in Kazakhstan. For the time being the unchallenged master of the USSR, Khrushchev then continued the programme of armed struggle with the West, targeting French Indo-China..

20

THE DEADLY GAME OF DOMINOES

The contiguous Indo-China colonies were Vietnam, fronting onto the South China Sea, Cambodia on the Gulf of Thailand and land-locked Laos. A 'protectorate', i.e. effectively a French colony since 1862, Vietnam was, like Korea before the war sucked in so many thousand American, British and Commonwealth troops, another 'far-away country of whose people we know nothing', to misquote British Prime Minister Neville Chamberlain on another occasion.

Stretching more than 1,000 miles north to south, Vietnam is in places less than 25 miles wide, sharing common borders with Thailand and China as well as Cambodia and Laos. Its extensive coal and other mineral resources were important to France, as were the extensive rubber plantations exploited mainly by the Michelin company, a major employer in metropolitan France. Since the only forces fighting the Japanese during the Second World War occupation were the Viet Minh guerrillas commanded by ex-Comintern agent Ho Chi Minh and his military counterpart Vo Nguyen Giap, they saw no reason to welcome back their former French overlords after the Japanese surrender. Accordingly, on 2 September 1945, Ho Chi Minh proclaimed

Vietnam's independence with Moscow's backing. French ground, naval and air forces, plus Foreign Legion and colonial troops, were deployed in increasing numbers to re-impose colonial rule. From 1946 to 1954 Ho Chi Minh and Giap successfully used guerrilla tactics to soak up more and more manpower from France, its African colonies and locally recruited troops.

In March 1949, the so-called Elysée Agreement granted 'independence within the French Union' to Vietnam, Cambodia and Laos. In practice, little changed for the native populations. A US National Security Council (NSC) policy paper of 1949 stated:

> The USSR is now an Asiatic power of the first magnitude with expanding influence and interest extending throughout continental Asia and into the Pacific. Since the defeat of Japan, the Soviet Union has been able to consolidate its strategic position until the base of Soviet power in Asia comprises not only the Soviet Far East, but also China north of the Great Wall, Northern Korea, Sakahalin, and the Kuriles.[1]

Another NSC document of February 1950 stated, 'The presence of Chinese Communist troops along the border of Indo-China makes it possible for arms, materiel and troops to move freely from Communist China to the northern Tonkin area now controlled by Ho Chi Minh. There is already evidence of movement of arms.'

Later, when the possibility of supporting the French in Vietnam was being re-examined in Washington, an NSC report said, 'The Communist Chinese regime is already furnishing to the Viet Minh materiel, training, and technical assistance. Official French sources report that Chinese Communist troops are already present in Tonkin in some strength … Direct intervention by Chinese Communist troops may occur at any time.'[2]

With Truman inheriting Roosevelt's anti-colonial stance and the Pentagon wary of becoming entangled with Chinese communist forces, as had happened in Korea, American aid to the French war effort was limited to deliveries of materiel, although the State Department was aware that France's share of European Recovery Program funds was also being used indirectly to finance the conflict.[3] On the ground, the

French went it alone until their final defeat at Dien Bien Phu on 7 May 1954 when Giap's victorious troops took prisoner the surviving 11,721 men in the isolated camp – of whom, after deliberately protracted death marches through swamps and jungles, only 3,290 ever made it home. The defeat was due to massive miscalculation by the French command, which had failed to allow for the substantial quantities of materiel trucked in from China – including heavy artillery dismantled and manhandled by labourers through 400 miles of jungles and swamps and across mountain ranges that the French had considered impassable.

The peace agreements signed at Geneva on 21 July 1954 provided for a demilitarised zone at the 17th parallel, separating Ho Chi Minh's Communist Republic of North Vietnam from the pro-Western Republic of South Vietnam. Progressive infiltration of North Vietnamese Army (NVA) cadres and terrorist attacks by the guerrilla Viet Cong forces in the south led to conventionally armed US forces being progressively introduced, first as advisers to the South Vietnamese troops combating them and then in combat formations.

Why did the United States intervene, after having refused direct support for France's efforts to regain control over Vietnam? Dwight D. Eisenhower replaced Truman in the White House on 20 January 1953. Once France had been defeated in Vietnam, he considered that fighting the communist enemy was no longer a question of supporting French colonial aims, but of 'saving the world for democracy', as the contemporary slogan had it.

Dominoes originated in China as an alternative to playing cards sometime in the tenth century. They were apparently introduced into Britain and Russia – where Nicholas II spent his last days playing with them – by the French during the Napoleonic wars. In addition to the several games of dominoes, they were also used for party tricks, being lined up on their ends in complicated patterns so that when the first was pushed over, it knocked down the next in line, and so on. It was this game with, rather than of, dominoes that President Eisenhower had in mind at his press conference on the day that the French garrison at Dien Bien Phu was overwhelmed.

When asked by a reporter what the strategic importance of Indo-China was, he replied that it was threefold: firstly, the natural resources like tin, tungsten and rubber; secondly, the possibility of millions of people becoming subject to 'a dictatorship that is inimical to the free world' in Asia, which had already 'lost some 450 million of its peoples to the Communist dictatorship'; thirdly, he cited the falling domino principle. The metaphor apparently originated with General Claire Chennault, commander of the US Army air forces in China during the Second World War. Chennault prophesied that allowing the communists to win China would be 'the first domino falling'. With the Korean War not lost by the United Nations and ROK forces, but not won either, it looked as though he had been right.

The problem in Washington was where to draw the line in the sand – or line of containment, to borrow George Kennan's expression. The Asian mainland had originally been outside the line. Now it was not. In 1950 a joint chiefs of staff memorandum to the US secretary of defence stated:

> South-east Asia is a vital segment in the line of containment of Communism stretching from Japan southward and around to the Indian Peninsula. The security of the three major non-Communist base areas in this quarter of the world – Japan, India, and Australia – depends in a large measure on the denial of Southeast Asia to the Communists. If Southeast Asia is lost, these three base areas will tend to be isolated from one another. The fall of Indo-China would undoubtedly lead to the fall of the other mainland states of Southeast Asia. The fall of Southeast Asia would result in the virtually complete denial to the United States of the Pacific littoral of Asia. Soviet control of all the major components of Asia's war potential might become a decisive factor affecting the balance of power between the United States and the USSR. A Soviet position of dominance over the Far East would also threaten the United States' position in Japan. The feasibility of retention by the United States of its offshore island bases could thus be jeopardized.[4]

Eisenhower was convinced that if America let the communists win South Vietnam, its fall would lead to them conquering or subverting country after country. Stop them in Vietnam and you halt the process; that was his argument.

Falling dominoes was a simple metaphor that anyone could understand, so the press liked it. But Ho Chi Minh's thinking was even simpler and far more chilling. Ignoring the immense military-industrial might of the United States, he said that all the Vietnamese people had to do eventually to win a war against the American invaders of his country was to maintain a birth-rate that exceeded its casualties.

By 1969, more than 500,000 US forces were stationed in Vietnam, both regulars and draftees, doing their best to ensure that North Vietnamese deaths exceeded births in a very dirty war, which rapidly took on some characteristics of the Korean conflict, with the USSR sending materiel by sea and China funnelling materiel and advisers into the north to train and support the NVA. These supplies, transported along the clandestine routes through neutral Laos and Cambodia known collectively as the Ho Chi Minh trail, provided weapons and ammunition to the Viet Cong guerrillas who lived among the civilian population of South Vietnam – to use Mao's simile, like fish swimming in water. The Viet Cong were impossible to eradicate by conventionally trained US ground forces, supported by naval and tactical air power. In addition, land- and carrier-based aircraft, plus B-52F Stratofortresses carrying twenty-seven 750lb bombs internally and twenty-four on external racks, conducted a series of Arclight bombing campaigns from bases as far away as Guam, pounding strategic targets in North Vietnam from altitudes of 30,000-plus feet.

With the cost in American money and lives eventually proving too high for Congress and public opinion to tolerate, a cease-fire agreement was signed on 17 January 1973, after which the American withdrawal commenced. It continued when fighting flared up again, ending with the reunification of the war-ravaged country as the Socialist Republic of Vietnam on 2 July 1976. So horrific were the casualty figures that the official Vietnamese estimate was not released until 1995: approximately 2 million civilians died, as did 1.1 million NVA and Viet Cong fighters. Official US figures are that 250,000 South Vietnamese soldiers died in the war, plus 63,000 American, South Korean, Thai, Australian and New Zealand soldiers.

The neighbouring state of Cambodia achieved independence from France in 1953 under Prince Norodom Sihanouk, who adopted a neutral position during the Vietnam War, allowing NVA and Viet Cong forces to use sanctuaries inside Cambodia and to run supplies and reinforcements through Cambodian territory along the Ho Chi Minh trail. After Sihanouk was deposed in a right-wing army coup in May 1970, US and South Vietnamese forces invaded Cambodia to destroy the communist bases there. The US conducted intensive bombing of Cambodia until 1973 in an effort to disrupt the activities of Vietnamese and native Khmer Rouge communist insurgents, but after protracted civil war, the Cambodian capital fell to the Khmer Rouge in April 1975.

Renaming the country Democratic Kampuchea and putting the calendar back to year zero, dictator Pol Pot initiated an insane programme of forced collectivisation and destruction of centres of population, killing one third of the population in the process. Around 2 million people died from forced labour, malnutrition and disease, while tens of thousands died in torture factories like the infamous S-21 prison in Phnom Penh. Although initially trained and supported by North Vietnam, Pol Pot's Khmer Rouge were by the end of 1977 in open warfare with the NVA.

In December 1978 a Vietnamese army crossed the border and took only two weeks to eliminate organised resistance, before installing a puppet regime of Cambodian communists and renaming the country the 'People's Republic of Kampuchea'.

The Geneva agreements of 1954 provided for Laos, the third country of French Indo-China, to remain ruled by its royal family with the exception of two 'regroupment zones' adjacent to the border with North Vietnam under the control of the communist Pathet Lao forces. It was a recipe for chaos. In July 1962 another Geneva conference declared the country neutral, to be governed by a tripartite coalition of Pathet Lao supported by NVA, the Right supported by Thailand and the US and neutrals led by Prince Souvanna Phouma. Two uneasy years later, the Vietnam War engulfed Laos, the American withdrawal from Indo-China finally tipping the balance in favour of the Pathet Lao, with right-wing politicians fleeing the country by mid-1975. In December of that year, the communist government abolished the monarchy and renamed the country the Lao People's Democratic Republic.

At this point Chennault's metaphor of the line of dominoes was proving very apt, although Moscow's aim of destabilising France had not been achieved. The indirect attack on France next targeted French North Africa – also comprising three countries: Morocco, Algeria and Tunisia. With coastlines on both the Mediterranean and the Atlantic, Morocco had been a French protectorate since 1912, and was governed nominally by the hereditary sultan, in effect by the French Resident-General. During the January 1943 Allied summit meeting in Casablanca, President Roosevelt actively encouraged the sultan to demand independence from France after the war. This interference infuriated both collaborationist French colonial officials and Free French leader Charles De Gaulle. Post-war, Moroccan domestic politics complicated the long process by which France relinquished control in 1957, with the sultan adopting the title of king.

At the eastern end of French North Africa, Tunisia had begun the nineteenth century as a province of the Ottoman Empire and was occupied from 1881 by French forces 'pacifying' Algeria. Tunisia thus became a French protectorate, with the Bey of Tunis remaining its monarch and appointing his own ministers although, as in Morocco, ultimate power was vested in the French Resident-General. In July 1954, just after the fall of Dien Bien Phu, French premier Pierre Mendès-France announced that Tunisia would be granted full independence, which was achieved in March 1956, with moderate socialist Habib Bourguiba as prime minister.

Algeria was different. It had not existed as a political entity before the French conquered a number of Ottoman enclaves and surrounding Arabic- and Berber-speaking tribal territories between 1830 and 1847 and gave the resultant vast territory a name. An influx of European settlers then created cities in the north and centre of Algeria, modernising agriculture, exploiting mineral resources and progressively driving the native people into marginal land. Even after the Second World War, education and healthcare for the Muslim population was rudimentary outside the towns, despite De Gaulle declaring in 1942 that France owed them a better deal for the loyalty they had shown in both world wars.

With both Tunisia and Morocco on their separate ways to independence in 1954, Moscow's attention was therefore focused on Algeria as the best lever to destabilise France. Although divided into three administrative *départements* and technically part of France, the country was ripe for revolt. A number of young Algerians representing various left-wing sympathies merged themselves into Le Front de Libération Nationale (FLN) – an independence movement whose leaders had all been educated in France. Some of them had subsequently had rather different schooling in Russia and/or Egypt, like Houari Boumoudienne, who returned from Cairo to form L'Armée de Libération Nationale (ALN), the armed wing of FLN. Under his leadership, training camps were set up safely in Tunisia and Morocco, from where men and weapons were smuggled into Algeria.

On the night of 31 October 1954, thirty synchronised terrorist attacks on police and military installations woke Europeans all over Algeria to the realisation that they were living in a war zone. Responsibility was claimed by ALN. With just 37,000 troops in Algeria, Paris played down the events of All Saints Day: they made only two columns in *Le Monde* and even less in *L'Express.* On 12 November Mendès-France stated categorically that, whereas FLN's demand for complete independence was unacceptable, reforms would be introduced to improve living and political conditions of Muslim Algerians. Yet the violence escalated. In April 1955 a state of emergency was declared which placed the Aurès Mountains under military law, with the army authorised to destroy villages and move the inhabitants into 'resettlement areas', as the British had done in Malaya.[5]

The next move of the ALN came on 20 August with attacks all over eastern Algeria that claimed the lives of seventy-one Europeans and fifty-two Muslim 'collaborators'. The repression, assisted by armed settlers' vigilante groups, was violent. There were so many corpses afterwards that nobody could seriously contradict the FLN claim of 12,000 Muslim deaths.[6] On 24 August the government in Paris began calling up thousands of reservists for what was turning into a full-scale war. Although most of the country's Muslim inhabitants were disenfranchised and had no particular reason to love their French overlords, it was necessary for the ALN to mount a secondary campaign of assassination and torture directed against mayors, doctors, teachers, policemen and even postmen to drive a wedge of terror between the European settlers and the Muslim population.

Obedient to instructions from Moscow, the PCF supported the FLN and many PCF members became directly involved – some as fundraisers, others as providers of false papers and as *porteurs de valises* transporting across the Mediterranean large amounts of cash, largely raised by compulsory subscriptions from the 350,000 Algerians living and working in France. These 'suitcase carriers' thought themselves less likely to be caught by the security services than Muslim Algerian activists. However, those who were caught, of both sexes, were subjected to torture, many disappearing afterwards without trace. One female *porteur de valises* known to the author had a PCF lover who actually went into the *bled*, or countryside, and fought in an ALN commando. Had he been caught, his would truly have been a 'fate worse than death'.[7]

For the next six years, France fought a full-scale war employing universal male conscription and the recall of reservists, sending more than a half million men across the Mediterranean. In a futile attempt to stem the tide of history, they used fighter aircraft, napalm, heliportered troops and radar-guided artillery against small bands of *fellaghin* armed with nothing heavier than Second World War MG42 machine guns. Twin barriers of electrified wire and minefields stretching for hundreds of miles on both eastern and western frontiers failed to prevent *les fells* returning from their training camps in Tunisia and Morocco to join the anti-colonialist struggle.

The determination of successive French governments to hold onto Algeria drew on several factors. The country was the only home of nearly a million predominantly French-speaking settlers whose families had come from France, Italy, Spain and the Levant over a span of 130 years. They were as 'Algerian' as

Muslim neighbours. If that was their emotional justification for chanting, *'Algérie Française'* in street demos, a financial reason for Paris denying the FLN's call for independence lay under the sands of the Sahara in the far south of the country, where substantial oil and natural gas reserves had been discovered. The Algerian Sahara was also the place where France planned to test its nuclear weapons.

The long, drawn-out struggle in Algeria, characterised by torture, rape and murder routinely practised by both sides, was destroying the Fourth Republic. The final straw broke its back on 13 May 1958 when the newly elected Prime Minister Pierre Pflimlin banned right-wing organisations that had been protesting in the streets of Paris, but was impotent to do anything about the settlers in Algeria who seized control of the city of Algiers and declared an emergency government backed by renegade army units. With combat-ready troops patrolling the streets of Paris, it looked in Washington as though the war in Algeria was about to trigger a civil war in France. Under a covert programme dubbed 'Gladio', US operatives had set up in a number of European states, including France, a network of 'stay-behinds' – agents trained to remain in place after a possible communist takeover. Each had a sub-network of right-wing contacts and was equipped with quantities of weapons and explosives cached at strategic points ready for use. The true aim behind 'Gladio' was to cause civil unrest on a scale that would be seen to justify American intervention to 'restore order', although the less cynical of the agents believed they had a glorious patriotic destiny ahead of them. In Washington, at this juncture, such were the fears that the PCF would exploit the situation to grab power that the National Security Council seriously debated activating the 'Gladio' network in France.

Pflimlin appealed by radio for the population to support the government, but it was the broadcast on 27 May by a retired general living in Colombey-les-deux-Eglises which saved the day. With an authority justified only by his belief in his own destiny, Charles De Gaulle boldly ordered the rebellious troops in Algeria to return to barracks immediately and obey their legitimate commanders. On 3 June, the National Assembly invested him with full powers for six months. The session ended with the President of the Assembly announcing that its next meeting would be held 'at an unknown date'. Thus, under the threat of armed intervention but with no civil war, the Fourth Republic committed suicide. Its passing came just in time, with several thousand paratroopers on Corsica and in North Africa at readiness to jump on Paris itself and mount a right-wing military coup. Having ordered them to stand down and with his political opponents reduced to impotent mutterings in the background, the 67-year-old general appealed to the nation to give him its support in a broadcast speech of brilliant simplicity: 'It was very dark yesterday,' De Gaulle said, 'but this evening there is some light. Frenchwomen, Frenchmen, help me!'

The army in Algeria obeyed De Gaulle. Flying there without wasting any time, he stood on the balcony of the Gouvernement Général building in Algiers on 4 June 1958, raised his long arms in a giant V-sign and declared to a crowd of 100,000 Europeans, *'Je vous ai compris! Je sais ce qui s'est passé ici.'* The phrases 'I have understood you', and, 'I know what has been going on here', were universally taken by his listeners to mean that he would support the war until the last ALN terrorist had surrendered or been killed. What he intended them to understand is a matter of conjecture.

Early in July, US Secretary of State John Foster Dulles visited France's new leader to brief him on Washington's world-view. De Gaulle pooh-poohed the idea that communism was the driving force of Russian politics and told Dulles that the export model of Marxism was simply the tool with which Stalin had gained Eastern Europe as a buffer zone at relatively little cost to Russia – and which Nikita Khrushchev was now using in the hope of gaining the rest of the Continent.

On 4 September a huge rally was staged in Paris supporting De Gaulle's presidency. The PCF grouped its sympathisers for battle, but was denied access to the state-run radio channels, on which Gaullist sympathisers repeatedly exhorted the population to make the right choice. Few people needed to be told that voting NO would plunge the country back into a worse mess than before *le général* had re-entered politics. Like him or not, he was the only choice for anyone who wanted a stable society. If the price-tag was a more authoritarian form of government, a majority of the population was happy to pay it.

The European Algerians soon found that the new president was indeed going to end the war, not on their terms but in a way that might give France a good relationship with the country after swiftly granting it independence.

Desperate settlers staged a fresh uprising in January 1960 which fizzled out in nine days, but hard-line army officers and last-ditch settlers went underground to form the Organisation Armée Secrète (OAS) – a terrorist organisation to sabotage De Gaulle's negotiations with the FLN. There were thirty-seven attempts on his life by OAS action groups, but he did not waver. The initials OAS were scrawled on walls all over Algeria and France, but the writing on the wall which drove a million desperate European Algerians to flee the country was, *La valise ou le cercueil* – pack a suitcase or buy a coffin! They knew there was no place for them in a Muslim Algeria. After the exodus, a referendum held in July 1962 recorded 6 million votes in favour of independence. Only 16,000 lonely people voted against.

In Moscow, the mood was baffled anger at the way De Gaulle had again led his country out of imminent civil war and a possible communist takeover, as he had done in 1945 – and bafflement too that Algerian independence did not mean a communist Algeria. As Egyptian journalist Muhammad Heikal commented, no allowance had been made in the Kremlin for the burgeoning Arab nationalism that motivated the ALN and kept Egypt and Syria unaligned in the Cold War in spite of massive Soviet military aid and the financing of public works.[8]

Although happy to accept money, arms and other support from communist sources during the struggle for independence, the majority of the ALN leadership had no wish for their country to become a Soviet satellite. As in the aftermath of so many revolutions, the knives in Algiers were sharp and the pro-Moscow minority fell victim to the post-Independence purges. Thus France had lost, but the USSR had not won.

21

VOTING WITH THEIR FEET

While Stalin and his successors were seeking to undermine the Western European democracies in these ways, the captive millions behind the Iron Curtain were getting restive.

In March 1952, Stalin offered to merge the Soviet zone of Germany with the Western zones on condition that the reunited country remained a neutral state. The intention was to prevent the Federal German Republic, formed from the three Western zones in October 1949, from joining NATO. Since 1949, the Soviet zone had been calling itself the 'German Democratic Republic' (GDR). With the elected Parliament of the GDR merely a rubber stamp for decisions of the ruling Sozialistiche Einheitspartei Deutschlands (SED)[1], the real power lay with veteran communist functionary Walter Ulbricht. Although only deputy premier in the government, he was the boss of the SED and therefore the Politburo. A wannabe Stalin to the core, Ulbricht ignored all the lessons of the USSR's forced collectivisation in the '30s and imposed a command economy with state ownership of land and industry on the GDR with such harshness that living standards declined to below pre-war level, prompting massive emigration to the Bundesrepublik – West Germany.

True, the border between the two German republics was later sealed off by barbed wire, minefields and watch-towers, but it was relatively easy for GDR citizens to catch a train to East Berlin and take the S-Bahn overhead railway into the Western sectors, where they could demand asylum and resettlement. For those who were caught in East Berlin – because they were carrying too much luggage for a day-trip, or had been indiscreet or were betrayed – the penalty was months or years of interrogation by Stasi officers in remand prisons like the one in Potsdam where the author was incarcerated in 1959, followed by several years' imprisonment under penal regimes far more brutal than any in the West.

Most GDR citizens who did not try to flee adopted the Soviet logic: They pretend to pay us, so we pretend to work. A considerable minority actually worked for the organs of state security. The oppressively ubiquitous surveillance and the impotence of those caught in the Stasi's net are accurately depicted in the 2006 film by writer/director Florian Henckel von Donnersmark, *Das Leben der Anderen* – The Lives of Others.[2]

In Czechoslovakia surveillance was less obvious, yet Prague resounded with rumblings of discontent inside the party leadership itself. Rudolf Slánský had spent the war years in the USSR being groomed for his post-war role, playing a major part in the communist takeover of Czechoslovakia in February 1948, for which he was rewarded with the secretary-generalship of Komunistická Strana Československa (KSČ) and the post of vice premier, making him second in importance to President Klement Gottwald, of whom he was now a dangerous rival.

Expelled from the Politburo in September 1951, Slánský was arrested two months later. After twelve months' imprisonment and torture, he and thirteen other Czechoslovakian communist leaders confessed at a Soviet-style show trial in Prague to the charges of pursuing 'nationalistic' policies not approved by Moscow. Eleven other accused were Jews like Slánský and the prosecution alleged – pandering to Stalin's anti-Semitism – that they were Zionists spying for the West under cover of a Jewish charity. Slánský and ten others were executed in December 1952.[3]

In politics, as in humour, timing is all. Four months later, Stalin was dead and Lavrenti Beria, Malenkov and Molotov ruled the USSR. Given his previous record, Beria surprised Kremlin-watchers by forbidding further torture of prisoners in Lubyanka and Lefortovo prisons. He also halted the purges he had been conducting for the late *vozhd*, who lay embalmed beside Lenin in the mausoleum on Red Square. In addition, Beria devolved some autonomy on the non-Russian republics of the USSR and persuaded the Politburo to bring pressure on the Chinese and North Koreans to conclude the stalled Korean armistice negotiations at Panmunjon.

In the GDR, the SED Central Committee decided to tackle the economic problems caused by the crippling war reparations to the USSR and Ulbricht's industrialisation programme by introducing higher taxes, price rises and a 10 per cent increase of work norms without extra pay. At the beginning of June 1953, the Soviet government was so alarmed at MGB[4] reports of unrest in the GDR that Ulbricht was summoned to Moscow, where Malenkov warned him to ease up.

Too late. On 16 June, eighty building workers downed tools in protest on the Stalinallee – one of East Berlin's main thoroughfares. The event was reported gleefully on the American-financed radio stations RIAS Berlin[5] and Radio Free Europe, founded partly on the initiative of George Kennan to defeat Soviet censorship by beaming Western news across the Iron Curtain. Early the following morning, a half-million striking workers were in the streets.[6] In East Berlin, waving banners and chanted protests turned into demands for the government to resign. Protesters believed their safety was guaranteed by the presence of Western reporters and camera crews and the close proximity of US, British and French garrisons. Hundreds crossed into the Western sectors seeking assistance that was not forthcoming.

Ulbricht and other SED top brass spent 17 and 18 June cowering under Russian protection in the Red Army HQ at Berlin-Karlshorst, leaving 20,000 Soviet occupation forces with T-34 tanks and armoured personnel carriers, plus 8,000 riot police, to do the dirty work for them with water cannons, rifle butts and bullets. No official figures of casualties were ever released. According to a conservative West German report in 1966, deaths in the one-day uprising totalled 383, with a further 106 executed under martial law and 5,100 arrested, of which 1,200 were sentenced to a total of 6,000 years in hard-regime labour camps.

Bertolt Brecht, back in Berlin after being kicked out of the US, wrote a poem entitled *The Solution*:

> After the rising of 17 June
> the Secretary of the Writers Union
> had leaflets distributed in the Stalinallee,
> stating that the people
> had forfeited the confidence of the government
> and could win it back only by redoubled efforts.
> Would it not be easier
> in that case for the government
> to dissolve the people
> and elect another?

In a sense, that is what happened: 400,000 discontented GDR citizens fled that year to the West.[7] Curiously, the senior MGB officer in Berlin-Karlshorst commented, 'It was the reaction of people to the blunders of the country's leadership. Moreover, it was inadmissible to use tanks in such a situation.'[8]

A power struggle was going on in the Kremlin, where Beria's control of the state security apparatus caused Malenkov, Molotov and Khrushchev jointly to accuse him of being an 'imperialist agent and conducting criminal anti-Party and anti-State activities'. Immediately after his trial in December 1953, Beria was executed by firing squad, like so many of his own victims – actually because he was an unwanted witness to the crimes of the USSR's new leaders.

In an unguarded moment, Malenkov admitted publicly that 500,000 East Germans had fled westwards in the previous two years. In fact, by the end of 1956 over 1.5 million citizens of the GDR had fled west. Soviet diplomacy was not noted for subtle understatements, but the USSR ambassador in East Berlin commented, 'The presence in Berlin of an open and essentially uncontrolled border between the socialist and capitalist worlds unwittingly prompts the population to make a comparison between both parts of the city which unfortunately does not always turn out in favour of Democratic [East] Berlin.'[9]

A meeting in Berlin of the foreign ministers of France, Britain, the USSR and the USA in January 1954 discussed an Austrian peace treaty, which foundered on the refusal of the USSR delegation to forgo the strategic advantage of maintaining forces in Austria so long as Germany was not 'neutralized'. A year later, in February 1955, the Austrian government was invited to send a delegation to Moscow to discuss bilaterally the withdrawal of Soviet occupation troops on condition that Austria did not join NATO. On 15 May the four occupying powers signed the treaty re-establishing the Austrian republic in its pre-1938 frontiers as a 'sovereign, independent, and democratic state'. The price of the USSR's signature was high: $150 million to buy back the business enterprises taken over by the Soviets in Austria; $2 million for the confiscated assets of the First Danube Steamship Company; and 10 million metric tons of crude oil in return for restitution of the petroleum industry to Austrian ownership. To the Austrians, who knew what life was like for their Hungarian and Czech neighbours living on the wrong side of the Iron Curtain, the price seemed cheap.

At the 20th Congress of the CPSU in February 1956, Nikita Khrushchev made a speech behind closed doors cataloguing Stalin's crimes, but omitting his own murderous participation in them. Anticipating a parity of nuclear arsenals with the West, he rejected the thesis that wars were inevitable and stressed that peaceful co-existence was the aim until worldwide socialism was achieved by peaceful ends.[10] In a sense, he was setting the stage for Gorbachev thirty years later when he said that the only way for communism to succeed was to confront its failures and reform – in Russian, *perestroit'* – Soviet society. This was shattering news for the delegates, who had been taught that the party never made mistakes. It stunned his listeners – in one case, terminally. Polish CP leader Bolesław Bierut had a fatal heart attack on the spot.

After Bierut's funeral, the Polish Party took Khrushchev's speech so seriously that it started freeing political prisoners, dismissing Stalinist officials and reshuffling the party leadership to give it a more *Polish* face. Władisław Gomułka was released from prison, where he had been locked up for three years for disobeying Kremlin orders while secretary-general of the Central Committee. Khrushchev went ballistic. 'That's not what I meant,' he thundered after flying to Warsaw and threatening to order Soviet occupation forces onto the streets. However, the Poles talked him out of that.

The next challenge to Russian domination came in neighbouring Hungary, where Khrushchev deposed Mátyás Rákosi in July on the pretence that he was ill and urgently needed 'treatment in Moscow'. Everyone in Hungary knew what that meant. Inspired by the quiet revolution in Poland and irritated by Khrushchev's heavy-handedness, the Hungarians rose up against Moscow and their own communist leaders. On 23 October, peaceful demonstrations and demands for reform were rejected by the new Prime Minister Ernö Gerö – whose previous 'claim to fame' was during the Spanish Civil War, when he was one of the commissars accused of the murder of Andrés Nin and other leaders of the POUM faction. Gerö ordered the police to fire on the demonstrators. When some refused, this sparked a chain reaction. The Hungarian army distributed arms to demonstrators. Prudent party officials lay low. Officers of the AVH secret police who were careless enough to be caught by their erstwhile victims were gunned down in the streets. In the provinces, local councils sprang up, with peasants reoccupying their confiscated fields and political prisoners released from prisons and labour camps – among them Cardinal József Mindszenty, the Roman Catholic Primate of Hungary jailed for life in 1949 for resisting the communist takeover. Cheering crowds escorted him back to the primate's palace in Budapest.

On 25 October Imre Nagy, deposed as prime minister and expelled from the party in the spring of 1955 on Moscow's orders for the crime of being 'too Hungarian', was reinstated by popular demand as the only man to handle the crisis. After forming a coalition government of socialist parties to negotiate the withdrawal of Soviet occupation troops, on 1 November he announced Hungary's secession from the Warsaw Pact, which it had only joined the previous year, and requested the UN to recognise Hungary's neutral status, hoping this would lead to protection by the Western powers.

Timing was against him. France and Britain were embroiled in armed intervention in Egypt to recover the recently nationalised Suez Canal and Eisenhower was furious that his European allies dared to take such action without his approval. Seeking to legitimise its own armed intervention in Hungary, Moscow canvassed support from neighbouring Romania, Czechoslovakia and Yugoslavia. President Tito refused to leave his holiday island in the Adriatic, so Khrushchev and Malenkov made a nightmare journey to obtain his assent, partly in a light aircraft in bad weather and partly a small boat on storm-tossed seas. Nagy had received reassurances from Soviet Ambassador Yuri Andropov that the USSR would not interfere but, with Britain and France involved in the Suez crisis, Khrushchev judged that the US would not risk a global confrontation over Hungary. On 1 November he ordered Soviet occupation troops to 'restore order'.

On 4 November the five Soviet divisions already stationed in Hungary were reinforced by twelve more Warsaw Pact divisions, and the fate of the Hungarian uprising was a foregone conclusion with Budapest surrounded by 2,500 armoured vehicles plus artillery and multi-barrelled rocket launchers.[11] Eleven years after its 'liberation' by the Red Army, some parts of Budapest were again a battlefield; in others, life seemed normal and even telephones still worked. A BBC Hungarian Service translator calling a relative in Budapest for an update heard the trams running as usual in the background – and then the sound of heavy machine gun fire. When all was lost, Nagy advised Mindszenty to seek asylum in the US Embassy. A Marine corporal and a master sergeant were standing behind the grille at the entrance to the embassy with the air attaché, when the cardinal and an English-speaking Monsignor arrived and asked to enter the building. The corporal asked the attaché, 'What should I do, sir?' but received no reply. He then asked the master sergeant, who replied, 'Do your duty.' The corporal opened the door, his act justified a few minutes later when a telex arrived from Washington instructing the embassy to extend every courtesy should the cardinal request asylum. Mindszenty had to stay in the safety of the embassy for fifteen years. His 'brother in Christ', Canterbury's Reverend Dean Hewlett Johnson, condemned Britain for the Suez invasion, but said that 'politically, the situation is different in Hungary [where] the action of the Soviet Union was to prevent [a return] to fascism'.[12]

Nagy took refuge in the Yugoslav Embassy, which was swiftly surrounded by Soviet tanks. Minister of Defence Pál Maléter was invited to negotiate with the Soviet command, but was instead taken prisoner. In the early morning of the same day, János Kádár, who had been a member of Nagy's government until 1 November, broadcast a speech proclaiming a pro-Soviet government under the banner of the Hungarian Socialist Workers' Party with himself as prime minister. Retracting Nagy's secession from the Warsaw Pact, he promised however that once the 'counter-revolution' was suppressed and order restored, he would negotiate the withdrawal of the Soviet army of occupation. Some credibility was given to this and his promises of reforms because he had been imprisoned and tortured under the Stalinist regime of Máyás Rákosi, but armed confrontations between Hungarians and the Soviet troops continued.

Courage and rifles are no match for tanks, although Soviet losses totalled 1,250 wounded and more than 650 dead, against 17,500 wounded and 2,500 dead on the Hungarian side by the time the fighting ended in January 1957. The workers used the only other weapon they possessed and proclaimed a general strike. It was several months before daily life reverted to normality. Meantime, Nagy had been tricked out of the Yugoslav Embassy by the offer of a safe conduct signed by Kadár, but was forcibly abducted to Romania and eventually returned to Hungary for a trial in camera, his years of loyal service to Moscow as an agent of the NKVD[13] availing him nothing. He, Maléter and their associates endured an ignominious two-year captivity that ended with him being hanged in a Budapest prison on 16 June 1958. Lesser activists were deported to the Soviet Union, never to return. Before the borders were closed, 200,000 Hungarians voted with their feet and escaped to the West – an opportunity not missed by the AVH, which inserted a number of agents into the stream of refugees.

On 2 October 1957, Polish Foreign Minister Adam Rapacki presented to the General Assembly of the UN a plan for both German states and Poland to be made a nuclear-free zone. Soviet Defence Minister Rodion Malinovski was against the plan, but Khrushchev supported it because of its likely contribution to slowing the arms race – and was supported by the broadcasting over BBC Radio of George Kennan's 1957 Reith Lectures, in which Kennan argued that such a demilitarised zone could be the first step towards the withdrawal of all armed forces from Germany and Eastern Europe, with an obvious lessening of tension in the Continent. President Eisenhower was not convinced that disengagement would be that easy although he admitted to Secretary of State Dulles on 3 January 1958 that 'the idea, in the abstract, appeals to me'.[14]

At the NATO summit 16–19 December 1957, it was decided that nuclear warheads would be stockpiled on the territory of European member states, subject to their approval, and that the commander of NATO's European forces would have medium-range missiles at his disposal. The Bundesrepublik, Netherlands, Greece and Turkey all agreed to stock warheads, but only Italy and Turkey accepted medium-range missiles – a decision that was to bring the world to the brink of nuclear war.

Early in January 1958, Moscow proposed a summit of both NATO and Warsaw Pact states to discuss Rapacki's plan and hinted in Bonn that it might withdraw troops from Central Europe. The Polish government suggested that Czechoslovakia be brought into the 'nuclear-free zone', effectively pushing back the western-most Soviet rocket installations by 200 miles to the east. Heavy lobbying in all the Western European capitals supported these initiatives.

On 31 March 1958 France, Britain and the US agreed to a summit, partly because Eisenhower was coming to the end of his second term and saw clearly that the man with whom he would have to deal – if a deal could be made – was Khrushchev, who had survived an attempt by the Malenkov-Molotov 'anti-Party group' to bring him down in June 1957 and was now 'the man in the Kremlin'. Although the Bundesrepublik's Chancellor Adenauer was in favour of German reunification on the model of neutral Austria, he pushed through the Bundestag a resolution calling for the 'most modern weapons' to be supplied to the Bundeswehr if the disarmament negotiations failed. On 8 April the defence ministers of France, West Germany, and Italy signed an agreement for the joint production of nuclear weapons.[15]

Ulbricht was panicking, bombarding Khrushchev with suggestions for raising the international status of the GDR and forwarding wild rumours that US forces in West Berlin had sneaked nuclear weapons into the divided city. At the end of August, Khrushchev informed the Politburo that he would propose West Berlin be declared a free, demilitarised city to end the Western presence there, likening it to a pimple on the nose that must be squeezed out. Warned that the West would never stand for his plan to force the international community to recognise the GDR as one of two autonomous German states, neither having modern or nuclear weapons,[16] he retorted that the process could be achieved by stages. Would the Western Allies go to war if, for example, the first step was to make them show their travel papers on the Autobahn to GDR officials instead of Russian soldiers? Where was the line in the sand now?

In a public speech on 10 November he announced that the USSR was transferring its occupation rights to the GDR government and Gromyko informed the West German ambassador that talks could only continue if Adenauer renounced his demands for nuclear weapons and agreed to talk with the GDR leadership. In a feeble attempt to plug the GDR's population leak, Ulbricht announced to the faithful that by 1961 the standard of living in the GDR would begin to *overtake* that in the Bundesrepublik.[17]

No one believed that. By 1961 more than 2.5 million people had fled the GDR for a better life in the West, giving their abandoned homeland a rare statistic of which to be ashamed: since 1949 its population had declined from 19 million to 17 million. Ulbricht had long wanted to wall his citizens in physically, but Moscow refused to allow this. Even Hungary's János Kádár, who forced his reluctant population back into line after the 1956 rebellion, was against such an admission of the failure of communism.

In August 1961 Khrushchev finally agreed that, if the exodus of refugees was not to leave the GDR a land without doctors, teachers, lawyers and managers, a wall had to be built. The first barrier was erected on the night of 12–13 August. Originally of barbed wire and cinder blocks guarded by armed Volkspolizei and Nazionale Volksarmee (NVA) soldiers, it eventually consisted of electric fences and 15-ft-high concrete walls topped with barbed wire, extending for 28 miles through Berlin, splitting one side of a street from the other, separating lovers from each other, children from their playmates and parents from their children. A further 75 miles of watchtowers, machine guns and minefields around the city's western perimeter sealed the Western sectors off from the GDR. The barbarity caused scandalised horror in the free world, although President Kennedy remarked that 'wall' was better than 'war'.

On 26 October, it seemed that the one might lead to the other when Americans in civilian clothes were refused their right of access to East Berlin and returned with armed escorts, backed by ten US M-48 tanks and two M-113 APCs. Television viewers were glued to their sets as Soviet T-54/55 tanks at the Brandenburg Gate faced-off the US tanks, but neither Kennedy nor Khrushchev wanted this to go further. Two days later, the tanks were withdrawn and a compromise reached over access to East Berlin by US personnel.[18] The world relaxed. It was better for everyone except the GDR's captive millions that Berlin should not be the flashpoint that sparked a nuclear war.

The alternative would have been to revert to Stalin's original plan in 1945 and merge the GDR with the Bundesrepublik, using pan-German elections to select the first national government since the war. Had Khrushchev proposed this, it would have shown the world that a wind of change was truly blowing through the Kremlin corridors. It would also have saddled the Bundesrepublik, still struggling towards the *Wirtschaftswunder* of economic recovery, with 17 million new citizens of a lower standard of health, who lived in one of the most polluted areas in Europe, who had lost the habit of working, who lived in sub-standard accommodation, whose farms had been collectivised and neglected, and whose factories' machinery had been shipped east as reparations. What stuck in Khrushchev's gullet, however, was not just the impossible admission that communism was incompatible with a free society, but also the principal of losing this slender buffer zone less than 200 miles wide.

Braving attack dogs, tripwire-operated machine guns, minefields and searchlights, people still tried to escape the GDR: punk rockers wanting to play their illegal music; school kids expelled from every school in the country for 'anti-state activities' like telling a political joke; adults banned from any worthwhile job because of their *staatsfeindlich* – or dissident – attitude. If caught, they suffered penalties not only harsh, but sadistic. Pregnant women were allowed to give birth and keep their babies three months, after which they were imprisoned and the babies forcibly sent to state orphanages. One young mother, Jutta Gallus-Meck, was arrested at the border with daughters aged 4 and 6 and spent three years in jail, not knowing where they were.

After human rights pressure groups in the Bundesrepublik arranged the purchase of political prisoners from the GDR government – on the precedent of American grain shipments buying Soviet dissidents' freedom – payments totalling 3,436,900,755 DM or £1,000 million for the release of 33,755 prisoners became an important source of hard currency for Ulbricht's regime. Jutta Gallus-Meck was bought by the Bundesrepublik in a deal arranged by Wolfgang Vogel, an East Berlin lawyer. Once in the West, the anguished mother went each day for six months to Checkpoint Charlie holding up a large placard addressed to the Stasi boss, reading, 'Herr Mielke, please give me back my children.' After six years, they were reunited with the mother they could hardly remember.[19]

Taking a commission on each 'deal', Vogel became the richest self-made man in the GDR. After the fall of the Berlin Wall, justice briefly caught up with him in January 1996 when he was found guilty of perjury, blackmail and falsifying documents, given a two-year suspended sentence and fined DM 92,000 (£41,000) by a German court. A lawyer to the end, Vogel appealed, was acquitted and lived in style with his second wife in Bavaria until his death in August 2008.

22

KHRUSHCHEV'S SONOFABITCH

The Baltic, Balkan, Central and Eastern European states engulfed by the USSR during and after the Second World War were all contiguous with Soviet territory and therefore easily garrisoned by Soviet armed forces. Far more daring was Khrushchev's attempt to gain a foothold in the western hemisphere at the height of the Cold War in 1962.

As the Venona intercepts revealed, extensive clandestine radio traffic had been going on for thirty years between Moscow Centre and Soviet embassies and undercover agents in Latin America, in preparation for pro-Moscow coups d'état. From Mexico southwards to the Tierra del Fuego – especially in the banana republics of Honduras, El Salvador, Grenada, Nicaragua and Guatemala – there were all the prerequisites for revolution: political corruption, gross maldistribution of wealth, immorally low wages and brutal strike-breaking, poor or non-existent public education and health care, and landowning concentrated in the hands of a minute proportion of the population, often in league with US big business.

There were revolutions in one country or another almost every year, but none resulted in a secure foothold for the Soviet brand of communism until Marxist Salvador Allende Gossens was elected president of Chile in 1970. That lasted only three years, during which the US systematically undermined the economy of the country in various ways. In September 1973, the CIA-assisted counter-coup that brought Augusto Pinochet to power saw Allende dead during an attack on the presidential palace. The official version was that he committed suicide; his supporters continue to claim that he was killed by the attackers.

Although it was customary in Latin American revolutions for the deposed president and his cronies to depart into well-heeled exile, Allende's accession to power and the way it ended were within the area's political tradition.

What happened in 1962 was different, because it had the whole world staring into the abyss of nuclear holocaust for two weeks as Soviet and American naval vessels faced-off in the Caribbean.

In Russia, they call it *karibski krisis*; in Cuba it is called *la crisis de octubre*; the English-speaking world calls it the Cuban Missile Crisis. In whatever language, it was the hottest moment of the Cold War, triggered by the American deployment in northern Italy and Turkey of sixty Jupiter and Thor medium-range ballistic missiles (MRBMs). With ranges up to 1,500 miles, these could deliver thermonuclear warheads on military facilities and cities in the Soviet Union, including Moscow. Nikita Khrushchev's attempt to obtain a military base in America's backyard was – seen from Moscow – a not unreasonable retaliation.

He failed, however, to take into account American belief in the Manifest Destiny – an ethos as persistent as Neill Brown's strange superstition, and in which Brown had played his part, perhaps unconscious of the similarity. The grandly titled Seminole Wars, in which he served with distinction, were a combination of land-grab and ethnic cleansing. The Seminole Indians of Florida were driven off their traditional hunting grounds into a reservation north of Lake Okeechobee. When white Europeans coveting this land in turn invoked the Indian Removal Act to push them westwards, they refused to go. General Andrew Jackson commanded the operations that slaughtered the Indians and burned their villages. How many died, no one knows. Since the Seminoles managed to kill 2,000 of Jackson's soldiers, the number of Indian warriors, defenceless women and children killed must have been far higher.[1]

If the Manifest Destiny was the 'justification' for white Anglo-Saxon Protestant Europeans to exterminate the animistic Native American peoples and take their land, its foreign affairs counterpart was the Monroe Doctrine, enunciated by US President James Monroe in 1823. In part, the text ran:

> We owe it ... to the amicable relations existing between the United States and those [European] powers to declare that we should consider any attempt on their part to extend their system to any portion of this hemisphere as dangerous to our peace and safety.

In plain language, Monroe decreed that any attempt by a European power to interfere in the internal affairs of *any* nation in the western hemisphere would be construed as a hostile act against the United States, justifying armed intervention by US forces.

In addition to the nineteenth-century gunboat diplomacy indulged in by all the colonial powers – typically small-scale police actions to protect their citizens' lives and property during local unrest or revolution – the US also embarked on a number of armed interventions with more far-reaching intent.[2] In 1846, after the American government annexed the Republic of Texas and claimed that US territory continued south to the Rio Grande, President Polk despatched American troops to occupy the disputed territory. Skirmishes there with Mexican forces enabled Polk to claim that American blood had been spilled 'on American territory' and so declare war against Mexico. Under the peace treaty signed on 2 February 1848, the *yanquis* paid Mexico $15,000,000 for 525,000 square miles of territory – now the states of (northern) California, Nevada, New Mexico, Utah and Texas. The war proved a good investment for Washington.

Although the Monroe Doctrine acknowledged the right of European powers to keep existing western hemisphere colonies and dependencies, like Russian Alaska and British Canada, the desire of the United States to act as big brother to its predominantly Catholic, Spanish- and Portuguese-speaking neighbours did not end with the expansion into Mexico. When Spain was repressing the independence struggle in its colony of Cuba in 1898, US President Cleveland supported the insurgents with armed force while denying any US intention to annex the island. Under the peace treaty signed on 10 December 1898, Spain renounced all claim to Cuba, ceded Guam and Puerto Rico to the United States and transferred sovereignty over the Philippines to the US for $20 million. It was another good investment for the White House.

Seeing itself as the policeman of the western hemisphere, the United States intervened by force of arms in Cuba in 1906 and 1912; in Mexico, 1915–17; in Haiti, 1915–34; in the Dominican Republic, 1916–24; and in Nicaragua, 1926–33. The United States also occupied from 1903–79 the Panama Canal Zone, a 10-mile-wide area along the length of the canal from the Atlantic to the Pacific Ocean.

It seemed that the western hemisphere policeman was adopting a more twentieth-century role when President Franklin D. Roosevelt announced in his inaugural address on 4 March 1933 what he called his Good Neighbour Policy, in accordance with which, at the Montevideo Conference in December of that year, the United States claimed no right to intervene uninvited in the internal affairs of its neighbours.

In 1934 the US renounced its tutelage over Cuba, retaining only the Guantánamo base, and US Marines were at last withdrawn from Haiti – after which American domination of the hemisphere was more subtle: the United States was both the largest market for Latin American countries' exports and the source of huge loans. American agencies, licit and illicit, helped into power with arms and money the often corrupt political leaders who talked independence to the populace but happily accepted American money for their Swiss bank accounts. As Roosevelt reportedly said of the corrupt and murderous Dominican dictator Rafael Trujillo, 'He may be a sonofabitch, but he's our sonofabitch.'

The same thinking resurfaced in Guatemala 1953–54 after President Jacobo Arbenz Guzman's elected socialist government implemented a programme of land reform, distributing unfarmed but fertile land owned by big companies to landless local peasants. Since hundreds of thousands of these acres belonged to the United Fruit Company, UFC leaned on the US government. At the height of McCarthyism, the Eisenhower administration considered that the expropriations, admittedly compensated, looked suspiciously like Marxism. Approval was given to a CIA-engineered coup d'état that saw five successive *juntas* in the presidential palace in less than two weeks and led to four decades of military dictatorship and social unrest.

After all that and more, in 1959 it seemed that Khrushchev had finally got his own sonofabitch in the island of Cuba, lying only 100 miles south of Key West, Florida. Under the regime of dictator Fulgencio Batista 1952–59, the American Mafia controlled the gambling, drugs and prostitution activities that milked the *gringo* tourists on the island. In December 1956, Fidel Castro and eighty-one armed supporters returned from exile in Mexico to foment a revolution. All were killed or captured except Castro and ten others, who retreated into the Sierra Maestra to wage guerrilla warfare. With increasing public support for his avowed crusade to rid Cuba of Batista's corrupt regime, Castro eventually defeated the government forces, driving Batista into a luxurious exile on 1 January 1959.

Within six months Castro revealed his true colour: red. Once he began implementing Marxist policies as brutally as Stalin had in the 1930s, hundreds of thousands of Cubans fled to the United States and Washington broke off diplomatic relations. To show Cuba's truculent new dictator who was boss by bankrupting the island's economy, the US also stopped buying the sugar crop that was the main export. That was the cue for Khrushchev to buy up half the Cuban sugar crop at three times the world market price.[3] More alarming, so far as Washington was concerned, was his promise to defend the only communist government in the western hemisphere with Soviet arms in the event of an attack by the United States, and his agreement to supply conventional weapons to modernise Castro's armed forces.

To get rid of Castro, the CIA planned a deniable invasion of Cuba by Cuban émigrés and talked the inexperienced new President John F. Kennedy into approving the disastrous landing on Cuba's *Bahía de Cochinos* – the Bay of Pigs – on 17 April 1961. This fizzled out when the population failed to support the badly planned and inadequately supplied operation. After only two days' fighting, the 1,100 surviving invaders were all locked up in Castro's jails. Castro told Khrushchev that he feared the abortive invasion would be followed by landings in force by US troops. As a sovereign state, Cuba had the right to conclude alliances with whomever it chose, and to buy or be given whatever weaponry it wanted. The fact that a state is equipped to wage war not being a *casus belli*, Washington's reaction came in another covert CIA operation.

In a document dated 18 January 1962 it was officially labelled 'The Cuba Project' and approved by Kennedy. Code-named Operation Mongoose, its expressed aim was 'to help the Cubans overthrow the Communist regime from within Cuba and institute a new government with which the United States can live in peace'.[4] The scale of the operation was such that Mongoose was to mobilise nearly 4,000 of the agency's employees and agents, with uncounted Cuban émigrés on the payroll. Among the James Bond-ish sub-projects was one to introduce nerve gas chemicals into Castro's cigars.

In February 1962, Washington launched an economic embargo against Cuba. In July, Kennedy was told that the USSR had begun shipping to Cuba nuclear missiles comparable to the Jupiters and Thors, together with the engineers to construct the storage and launch sites, plus Soviet rocket forces personnel to operate the missiles. On 29 August, U-2 spy plane overflights showed extensive military installations being constructed by Soviet technicians on Cuba. By 14 October the presence of a ballistic missile on a launch site was reported.

That is the official version. As so often, the real story may be rather different. Operation Mongoose needed sources of HUMINT inside Cuba. With the former in-country eyes and ears of the CIA all behind bars and likely to stay there, a few days after the Bay of Pigs, invasion veteran US spymaster Allen Dulles asked a French denizen of Washington's intelligence community to make a trip to Havana and report on everything he saw and heard.

Philippe Thyraud was a former Gaullist *résistant* who still used his wartime cover name, De Vosjoli, but was referred to as 'Lamia' by his contacts inside the CIA. Officially, Lamia was a vice consul in charge of visa applications at the French Embassy in Washington, but his real job was to liase between the CIA and the Service de Documentation Extérieure et de Contre-Espionage (SDECE), which was then the main French intelligence and espionage service. From past activity in Cuba, he had a number of contacts there, including top army officers and Castro's sister Juanita. He was happy to oblige someone as important as Dulles, and his report – that of a trained intelligence officer – was considered very useful on his return to Washington.[5]

The CIA accordingly asked Lamia to set up a small, top-level spy network in Cuba – the payment for which was to be the passing to France of certain nuclear technology, officially embargoed under the MacMahon Act of August 1946. The deal was approved in Paris and the network was put in place, run by a cipher clerk at the French Embassy in Havana.[6] Lamia's James Bond scenario had not taken into account the cipher clerk's homosexual entanglements, in which the jealousy of a Cuban lover led to the clerk's betrayal to Castro's security service.[7] With him declared *persona non grata*, French ambassador Robert Du Gardier took over direct control in Havana. A man of many parts, he was not above welcoming incoming dissidents from Miami when they landed at midnight on remote beaches and hiding them on embassy premises, safe from Cuban security forces. Among his clandestine operations was personally assisting Juanita Castro to escape to Miami.[8]

On 18 August 1962, Du Gardier reported to Washington the arrival in Cuba of Soviet missiles, together with 4,000 technicians to construct launching facilities. He also confirmed that top Cuban army officers were having intensive Russian language lessons! The CIA-SDECE deal never made the headlines at the time because it suited both Washington and Paris to protect the in-country assets. Hence the pretence that all intelligence about Soviet missiles in Cuba came from American high-altitude reconnaissance photography.

By 29 August 1962, military construction and the presence of Soviet technicians on the island were indeed confirmed by high-altitude photo-reconnaissance. When this was reported in the American press, Kennedy played down the situation by claiming that the Soviet missiles in Cuba were for defensive purposes only. Early in October he received intelligence that a number of MiG-21 aircraft capable of delivering nuclear bomb-loads were also in Cuba. On 9 October, after photographs had been taken of Soviet freighters bound for Cuba with crated IL-28 bombers as deck cargo, Kennedy authorised a further U-2 reconnaissance mission over Cuba itself, which clearly revealed the presence of MRBMs with a radius of action close to 1,100 miles, plus teams of Soviet technicians constructing launch sites.

Two days later he was briefed by National Photographic Interpretation Centre (N-PIC) that Khrushchev had upped the stakes in the Cuban poker game from 'defensive' MRBMs to 'offensive' intermediate-range ballistic missiles (IRBMs) with a range of 2,200 miles. Such missiles could reach all the continental United States except the Pacific North-west, and had warheads twice as powerful as the MRBMs.[9] No such missiles had so far been sighted, but N-PIC was certain that two launch sites under construction were intended for IRBMs, and would be launch-capable in six to eight weeks. The overall plan was for twenty-four launch ramps for SS-4 MRBMs with 1-megaton warhead and range of 900 miles-plus and sixteen for SS-5 missiles with same size warhead but double the range. Support included 43,000 Soviet military, half of whom were combat troops to repel any invasion, with the others technical staff and engineers.[10] The first SS-3 MRBMs arrived in Cuba on the night of 8 September, with a second consignment on 16 September. The sites were protected by batteries of surface-to-air missiles.

On October 18, Kennedy met Soviet Foreign Minister Andrei Gromyko, who assured him that there were no offensive weapons in Cuba and that the USSR's involvement there was in land reform and defence. By 20 October 1962, Kennedy was looking in the Oval Office at pictures that N-PIC photo interpreters explained showed assembly areas and launch pads for sixteen ready-to-go SS4s. In addition, the French HUMINT feed reported an ongoing programme of construction of more launch pads for missiles, of which it estimated that only a dozen or so were already in Cuba.

It was at this point that Russian expansionism collided with the Monroe Doctrine. In more prosaic terms, Secretary of State Dean Rusk directly connected the Soviet move with the recent stationing of American missiles and nuclear-capable aircraft in Italy and Turkey. Rusk also highlighted the danger of the US isolating itself from its NATO allies by precipitate action – as the British and French had done in the Suez War of 1956.

This was the era of MAD – the acronym for 'mutually assured destruction' – the hypothesis that neither side in the US-USSR power struggle could afford a nuclear first strike, since this would result in such retaliation that both countries would become radioactive wastelands, together with much of the rest of the planet. A source of humour? One would not think so, yet the controversial film director Stanley Kubrick made a brilliant satirical comedy out of the situation. Released in 1964, *Dr Strangelove or: How I learned to stop worrying and love the Bomb* starred Peter Sellers in several roles and George C. Scott as the rabidly anti-communist Strategic Air Command (SAC) general intent on starting the Third World War.

The real SAC had an average of 180 aircraft in the air 24/7 with nuclear weapons on board, kept circling at their fail-safe points by mid-air refuelling as they awaited orders to destroy strategic targets all over the USSR. SAC's motto was 'Our profession is peace'. At one point in the Oval Office on 22 October, Kennedy interrupted the jargon-strewn conversation to ask what 'EDP' meant. Told that it stood for European Defence Plan, he was still baffled, until informed that it was a euphemism for nuclear war in Europe.[11]

To defuse the situation, Defence Secretary Robert McNamara considered that Italy would happily renounce the questionable kudos of hosting NATO nuclear bases, but that the Turks would be more bullish. Secretary of the Treasury Douglas Dillon injected a further note of realism by pointing out that the liquid-fuelled systems of the Jupiter missiles in Italy and Turkey were unreliable and obsolete; the missiles had only been stationed there as a political sop to their respective governments!

After considering alternatives ranging from an immediate seaborne invasion of Cuba, limited air strikes to take out the missile sites, or further diplomatic manoeuvres, Kennedy opted for a naval blockade to prevent further Soviet missiles reaching Cuban ports. The voice of reason once again, Rusk suggested calling it a quarantine because a blockade stops all shipments into an area, and is therefore considered an act of war, whereas a quarantine is selective – in this instance being restricted to stopping vessels carrying offensive weapons. Approval was obtained from the Organisation of American States for military action under the Rio Treaty – a western hemisphere forerunner of NATO which, incidentally, not only debarred the United States from invading Cuba, but theoretically should have called all the other signatories to Cuba's defence if the US or any other country did so.

Kennedy accordingly announced the quarantine on 22 October and warned that the US Navy would seize 'offensive weapons and associated materiel' which Soviet vessels might attempt to deliver to Cuba. During the next few days, a number of Soviet ships bound for Cuba altered course to avoid the quarantine zone while messages were exchanged between Kennedy and Khrushchev amidst mounting tension on both sides.

It was also on 22 October that Kennedy warned in his first public speech on the crisis, 'It shall be the policy of this nation to regard any nuclear missile launched from Cuba against any nation in the Western Hemisphere as an attack on the United States, requiring a full retaliatory response upon the Soviet Union.'

In the same speech he announced that the quarantine would see *all* ships bound for Cuba stopped by US warships and turned back if carrying offensive weapons. Some political capital was made out of his declaration that the quarantine would not deny food or medicines to Cuba, unlike the Soviet blockade of Berlin in 1948. More alarmingly, US armed forces were moved from the normal peacetime status of Defence Condition (DEFCON) 5 to DEFCON 3. On the night of October 23, for the first time in the long drawn-out Cold War, the joint chiefs of staff instructed SAC to go to DEFCON 2. DEFCON 1 was nuclear war. The message and its acknowledgements were deliberately transmitted uncoded for the benefit of Soviet monitors, to ensure the Kremlin got the message.

With SAC on DEFCON 2, the world was a single command short of nuclear war. Several hundred B-28 bombers were either in the air or on immediate readiness to take off and bomb military and civilian targets all over the USSR. SAC remained in this heightened state of readiness until 15 November. In addition, thousands of ground-warfare troops had been airlifted to bases in the southeast of the United States in readiness for an invasion of Cuba.

Kennedy issued Security Action Memorandum 199 on 25 October, authorising the loading of nuclear weapons onto NATO aircraft in Europe, which were tasked to execute the first air strikes on Warsaw Pact targets. On 27 October the CIA reported that all missiles in Cuba were ready for action. Just when it seemed that tension could mount no higher, the commander of a US warship dropped several depth charges near a Soviet submarine at the quarantine line, unaware that it was armed with one or more nuclear torpedoes, which its captain was empowered to launch if the submarine were 'hulled', or otherwise substantially damaged in action.

There was not at the time any 'hotline' over which American and Soviet leaders could talk. So, in the midst of all this tense military and political manoeuvring, Kennedy had to liase with Khrushchev partly through ambassadors, within the United Nations, and through various journalistic, intelligence and other back-channels. Meanwhile, in case worse came to worst, the State Department and US embassy staffs worldwide were working hard to build support for the Kennedy administration's position among NATO allies, the co-signatories of the Rio Treaty and the uncommitted nations, while Adlai Stevenson, American ambassador to the UN, was working day and night to expose the blatantly false arguments of Soviet delegate Valerian A. Zorin that there were no offensive Soviet weapons in Cuba. Kennedy also called emergency meetings of the Organisation of American States and United Nations Security Council to discuss the situation.

The crisis ended after two weeks on 28 October 1962 when Kennedy and Khrushchev reached an agreement to remove the missiles in Cuba in exchange for a US undertaking not to invade the island or allow others to do so. The removal of the missiles in Italy and Turkey was not made public by the Kennedy administration, but they were withdrawn shortly afterwards. After this apparent loss of face, Nikita Khrushchev survived another two years, but was never again allowed the same unfettered powers by his Politburo colleagues.

There is a postscript to this chapter. In 1970 Leonid Brezhnev tried to repeat Khrushchev's move into the US backyard by constructing a support base for Soviet ballistic-missile submarines in Cuba. Unknown to the public, President Nixon and Henry Kissinger faced down this initiative before it got off the ground and obtained reassurances that the base would not be constructed, nor would Soviet subs call at Cuba in the future.[12]

23

SPRING FORWARD,
FALL BACK

In the early 1960s the Czechoslovakian Communist Party (KSČ) was the largest outside the USSR, with pro-Moscow First Secretary Antonín Novotný appearing firmly in control when also re-elected president of the republic for a second term in 1964. However, the Soviet-style command economy imposed on the satellite countries was particularly inappropriate for Czechoslovakia, already a developed country when given its place on the map after the First World War. In consequence, the country was experiencing severe economic problems. Novotný's attempt to address these in his '1965 New Economic Model' increased the demands for political reform as well.

Although the de-Stalinisation of Czechoslovakian government had progressed more slowly than in other states of the Eastern Bloc, behind closed doors at Central Committee meetings Novotný was encountering increasing criticism, especially from nationalistic factions within the party of this country, where two nations speaking similar languages had been united by historical events outside their control – the Czechs in the industrialised west of the country and the Slovaks in the predominantly agricultural eastern region.

Since 1956 Czech and Slovak intellectuals, especially professional journalists and writers, had been defying the party's censorship, at first with clandestine *samizdat* publications and then more openly. In June 1967, a radical group within the Czech writers' union including Ludvík Vaculík and Milan Kundera dared to suggest in the union magazine *Literární Noviny* that literature should not have to endorse any party line. To show them who was boss, Novotný jailed journalist Jan Beneš, for 'anti-state propaganda', expelled three other leading writers from the party and dismissed another from the Central Committee, of which he was a candidate member. With editorial control of *Literární Noviny* now vested in the Ministry of Culture, this Stalinist repression led to an open rift at the October 1967 session of the KSČ Central Committee. Whether or not its members had read Milan Kundera's *Žert* – meaning, the joke – published that year in Czechoslovakia, hundreds of thousands of their citizens had done so, and were amazed and elated at its daring story of a young KSČ official travelling abroad who sends a joke postcard to his girlfriend. The message reads, 'Optimism is the opiate of the people! A healthy atmosphere stinks! Long live Trotsky!'

For this crime, he is expelled from university, declared an enemy of the state and sentenced to work in the mines. *The Joke* was a breath of freedom for its readers, but appalled Novotný and company. In the ČSK Central Committee he accused Alexander Dubček and other Slovak members of 'bourgeois nationalism' and requested Leonid Brezhnev as First Secretary of the CPSU to support him publicly against them. Brezhnev retorted, *'Eto vashe dyelo.'* 'That's your problem.'[1]

Dubček had impeccable credentials as a communist politician, having grown up in Soviet Kirgizstan with a conventional Soviet political education. At the November Central Committee meeting he rallied the reform elements in the KSČ and the Slovak nationalists behind him. With their backing, he replaced Novotný as first secretary on 5 January 1968, after which the stage was set for the radical reforms that together were called 'the Prague Spring'. The public was unaware of the political infighting because an article in the party newspaper *Rudé Právo* announced that Dubček's programme conformed with approved socialist goals.

Novotný resigned the presidency on 28 March, being replaced by 73-year-old veteran of Stalin's purges Ludvík Svoboda – whose surname happens to mean 'freedom'. On 8 April a new government announced a far-reaching political programme entitled *Czechoslovakia's Road to Socialism*. Dubbed 'Socialism with a human face', this included economic reforms and a liberalisation of Czechoslovakian politics accompanied by limits on the powers of the secret police. Even more shatteringly, the KSČ Central Committee boldly criticized the Soviet-style command economy that had damaged the country's industry and agriculture. For the first time since the communist takeover in 1948, a Czechoslovakian government proclaimed basic human rights and liberties. Victims of purges were rehabilitated. Key party and state officials were replaced. The press was given greater freedom. Travel restrictions were eased. Dubček also federalised the country into two separate republics, so that both Czechs and Slovaks could adopt measures inappropriate in the other half of the country.

An extraordinary document by 42-year-old journalist Ludvík Vaculík was published in *Literárni Noviny* and two important daily newspapers. Entitled *Dva Tisíce Slov* – 'Two Thousand Words to Workers, Farmers, Officials, Scientists, Artists, and Everybody' – and signed by many leading writers, intellectuals and academics, it began:

> The first threat to our national life was from the war. Then came other evil days and events that endangered the nation's moral well-being and character. Most people welcomed the socialist programme with high hopes, but [the party] fell into the hands of the wrong people. It would not have mattered so much that they lacked adequate experience in affairs of state, technical knowledge or education, if only they had had the common sense and decency to listen to the opinions of others and agree to being gradually replaced by more able people. The leaders' evil policies transformed a political party and an alliance of ideas into a political machine that attracted power-hungry individuals eager to wield authority. No one was allowed to criticise the

state or its economic organs. Parliamentarians forgot how to debate issues properly; the government forgot how to govern properly; managers forgot how to manage properly. Elections lost their significance.[2]

Without criticising communism, indeed writing as a communist, Vaculík traced the decline of his country from a state of law and order into a police state where, '... we could scarcely trust one another, honesty was a useless virtue and reward for merit unheard of. Personal relations were ruined, there was no more joy in work, and the nation entered a phase that endangered its spiritual well-being and its character.'[3]

Vaculík called the Party hierarchy a group of self-centred bureaucrats who foisted their theories on the population by pretending they represented 'the will of the workers'. He condemned the purges and destructive centralised planning. In praising the pro-democracy reforms enacted since the beginning of the year, he counselled vigilance: 'The summer holidays are approaching, a time when we naturally relax, but we can safely assume that our adversaries will not take a summer break. They will pressure everyone who is under any obligation to them and take steps to secure themselves a quiet Christmas.'[4]

Vaculík also foresaw that external enemies, in Moscow and the other satellite capitals, were monitoring developments in Czechoslovakia and might, 'interfere in our social evolution. Whatever superior forces may face us, all we can do is stand fast, behave honestly and make no dangerous moves [while showing] our new government that we will stand by it, with weapons if necessary, so that it may fulfil its mandate.'[5]

To publish such a manifesto openly and sign it was an amazingly courageous initiative in any Iron Curtain state. Although Dubček's government was progressive, who knew how long it would last?

Many people, especially the young, did not heed Vaculík's warnings. Western pop culture blossomed in the fun-starved republic. Miniskirts, jeans and transistor radios were seen on the streets of Prague and other cities – and condemned as decadent in the other Warsaw Pact capitals.

Most Czechoslovakians took no notice of their neighbours' disapproval because this was a heady period, with Dubček keeping open house for student leaders, workers' representatives and others, to make the point that he was listening to all sectors of the population, all ages and all shades of political opinion. Two of the students were due to travel to Holland to take part in a prearranged international debating contest for BBC Television. Meeting them at Schiphol airport, the author – then an assistant BBC television producer – was surprised to be told that they had come only to explain how things were evolving so fast in Prague that they could not be away for more than a few hours. After the senior BBC producer amended the motion of the debate to accommodate what was happening in their country, the students agreed to speak to the world before returning to Prague.

In what other European country did a premier ever genuinely invite people to drop into his office and chat about their priorities?

Rightly terrified that the Czechoslovakian liberalising 'disease' might infect other satellites, Leonid Brezhnev, who had replaced Khrushchev, summoned Dubček and the KSČ Central Committee to talks at Cierna nad Tisou, near the Slovak border with Ukraine, from 29 July to 2 August. The KSČ delegation was divided between reformers who supported Dubček and the old guard who did not. Brezhnev decided on compromise. If the KSČ delegates reaffirmed loyalty to the Warsaw Pact and Comecon, undertook to curb any 'anti-socialist' moves and not to permit a revival of the Social Democratic Party, he would agree in return to withdraw Soviet troops that had not left Czechoslovakia after the Warsaw Pact manoeuvres in June.

On 3 August, representatives of the USSR, GDR, Poland, Hungary and Bulgaria met the Czechoslovakian government in Bratislava and signed a joint declaration affirming their fidelity to Marxism-Leninism and 'proletarian internationalism'. The Soviet delegation, following the Brezhnev Doctrine, expressed its government's intention to intervene if any Warsaw Pact country introduced political pluralism. Soviet troops then left Czechoslovakia, but remained near the borders, while Brezhnev set up the next phase, code-named Operation Danube.

Two weeks later the Soviet Politburo passed a resolution to 'provide help to the Communist Party and people of Czechoslovakia through military force'. At the Warsaw Pact meeting on 18 August, Brezhnev announced the planned intervention and asked for 'fraternal solidarity', i.e. military participation, to which Bulgaria, the GDR, Hungary and Poland agreed. The date set for Operation Danube was 20 August.

British communist historian Monty Johnstone was in Prague, genuinely interested in Dubček's 'socialism with a human face'. That evening he dined with Jiři Pelikan, director of the national television chain, and chided him for even thinking that the Soviets would intervene directly. Pelikan knew better, but could not tell Johnstone that a warning of imminent invasion had been confidentially forwarded to Prague by the Czechoslovakian ambassador in Budapest

An hour before midnight, 200,000 Warsaw Pact troops with 2,000 tanks crossed the borders into Czechoslovakia, including contingents from the Soviet Union, the GDR, Bulgaria, Poland and Hungary. Simultaneously, a Soviet airborne division occupied Prague's international airport. The first flight to land brought 100 plainclothes agents, in preparation for an airlift in which giant Antonov-12 transport aircraft ferried in more Soviet troops with artillery and light tanks. Meanwhile, columns of tanks and motorized rifle troops headed from the borders toward the principal cities, meeting no resistance because Dubček did not want a repeat of the bloody Soviet incursion in Hungary twelve years before and had ordered the Czechoslovakian armed forces to remain in their barracks, which were swiftly sealed off by Soviet armour.

Conspicuously absent from the invasion forces that eventually peaked at 500,000 men was a Romanian contingent. President Ceausescu, one of the two most repressive heads of communist states, instead spoke out publicly *against* the intervention. Although Dubček's spokesman declared on the night of 20–21 August that the Warsaw Pact troops were crossing the borders without permission, Moscow claimed that several of the anti-Dubček old guard had written to Brezhnev asking him to 'lend support and assistance with all means at your disposal' to save the Czechoslovak Socialist Republic from the imminent danger of counter-revolution. When published unsigned in Soviet newspapers, this was widely taken to be a forgery because at the Fourteenth KSČ Party Congress, which was held in secret immediately after the invasion, no one admitted having signed such an invitation. Twenty years later, the letter resurfaced miraculously, complete with five signatures of anti-Dubček KSČ members.

A fluent Russian speaker, Monty Johnstone was awoken at 4.30 a.m. by the sound of tank engines outside his hotel room and went down into the street to tell the Russian tankers to go home and stay there. Since Russian language lessons were obligatory in school, the tanks were surrounded by Czechs haranguing the invaders, many from Central Asia and the Soviet Far East, with little idea of European geography,[6] whose officers

Poster home-made during Prague Spring. The legend reads: 'Socialism, yes. Occupation, no!!!'

had been told that Operation Danube was a gesture of fraternal support requested by the KSČ. That morning, the Soviet News Agency TASS issued photographs of Russian speakers arguing with the soldiers, claiming that these were scenes of welcome. Immediately, clandestine Czechoslovak broadcasting stations warned, 'Photographs are silent. Do not speak to the invaders.' The population obeyed, staying off the streets and denying the Warsaw Pact soldiers even food and water. Posters and graffiti on walls and pavements denounced the invasion and the Soviet leadership. Passive resistance went so far as to rename many towns and villages 'Dubček' or 'Svoboda'. With signposts uprooted or painted over, it was difficult for the invading troops without navigational equipment to find their way.

It was, as armed interventions go, comparatively bloodless: seventy-two civilians were killed, twenty-six seriously wounded and 436 less seriously so. In the morning of 21 August Dubček and his principal supporters were arrested and flown to Moscow. Anticipating their non-return, hard-liners asked Svoboda to create an interim government. Instead, he travelled to Moscow with Gustáv Husák to ensure that Dubček and his team were not imprisoned or shot. After days of severe psychological pressure, the Czechoslovak delegation caved in and signed a fifteen-point protocol, agreeing to the suppression of 'opposition groups', the restoration of censorship, dismissal of reformist officials and the 'temporary' presence of Soviet troops in Czechoslovakia – which continued until 1990. Svoboda's achievement was to ensure that the protocol did not stigmatise the situation in his country as counter-revolutionary. Thus, Dubček's group was allowed to return to Prague on 27 August, when he made an emotional radio appeal for all citizens to cooperate in the curtailment of his reforms, to avoid further bloodshed.

The unique blossoming of freedom in the Prague Spring and the betrayals that followed were food for many later works of art, the best-known being Milan Kundera's book *Nesnesitelná Lehkost Bytí – The Unbearable Lightness of Being* – which was banned in his own country until 1989, as was *The Joke* after the Soviet intervention. Belatedly, the Irish entry in the 2007 Eurovision Song Contest was entitled *They Can't Stop The*

Spring – a reference to a saying attributed to Dubček: 'They may crush the flowers, but they can't stop the Spring'.

Dubček remained first secretary of the KSČ until forced to resign in April 1969. Well before then, the promise of the Prague Spring had turned to ashes. In Autumn 1968, with the political clock put firmly back to Moscow time, the repression in Czechoslovakia was worse than anywhere else in Eastern Europe, except the GDR and Albania. Half a million members were expelled from the KSČ and many thousands lost their jobs. Unemployment being illegal in a socialist republic, a large proportion of the country's intellectuals spent the next two decades cleaning windows or acting as caretakers and market traders, while Dubček passed these years working in the Slovak forestry service.

Svoboda kept the presidency, but was growing rather old and forgetful, embarrassing colleagues by wandering from one office to another in Prague Castle asking where Dubček was, until forced to resign on grounds of health. Replacing him, Gustav Husák, who had also become first secretary of the KSČ, undid most of Dubček's reforms. His purges of 'unreliable' intellectuals severely hampered cultural and scientific work, since all jobs in these areas depended on party membership.

Most people in the country accepted the new regime, but discontent simmered among the intellectuals, many jailed by Husák's courts for 'criminal acts in pursuance of political objectives' – of which the most ridiculous example was the arrest of the rock band The Plastic People of the Universe in 1976, charged with 'crimes against the state' for holding a rock concert. Civil unrest peaked in January 1977, when a group of intellectuals including Václav Havel, Jan Patočka and Jiři Hajek signed Charter 77, a protest that threatened to inform the West about abuses of human rights. Many of the signatories were imprisoned but their efforts continued throughout the following decade.

Reaction to the Prague Spring in the West was largely bafflement. What action could be taken that would not risk escalation to nuclear confrontation? On the night of the invasion, Britain and the US called for a meeting of the UN Security Council, where the Czechoslovakian ambassador denounced the Warsaw

Pact intervention. The USSR ambassador replied that it was 'fraternal assistance' and used his veto to block a vote of censure. On 26 August a replacement Czechoslovakian ambassador withdrew his predecessor's protest.

The Prague Spring and its heavy-handed repression deepened pre-existing rifts in the Western communist parties, promoting Eurocommunism in preference to the Soviet model. Ignored by the CPGB since his denunciation of the invasion of Hungary in 1956, once back in London Johnstone found himself in demand to speak at party meetings again and was even asked by the YCL to write a pamphlet about the Czechoslovakian struggle. In desperation, the *Morning Star* – as the *Daily Worker* had been renamed – sent foreign editor Peter Fryer to Prague to dig out some pro-Soviet stories. There were none. Even worse, the CIA-subsidised Radio Free Europe picked up his despatches and used them. In revenge, Moscow cut its bulk purchase order from 12,000 copies per day to 9,000. After two years, the bulk purchases of the *Morning Star* increased again, together with all the perks for the staff.[7]

In 1987 Soviet leader Mikhail Gorbachev acknowledged that his policies of *glasnost i perestroika* – transparency and restructuring – which transformed the Soviet Union, owed much to Alexander Dubček's bravery and vision. Asked what was the difference that made Gorbachev's policies acceptable where Dubček's had not been, a USSR Foreign Ministry spokesman replied laconically, 'Nineteen years.'

24

ROLL TO YOUR RIFLE AND BLOW OUT YOUR BRAINS

Britain fought three wars in Afghanistan. The first (1839–42) demonstrated that it was possible to occupy part of the country temporarily, but impossible to pacify a tribal population riven by treachery and blood feuds, where the harsh terrain restricted military columns to the valleys in which they were easily ambushed by hill-dwelling tribesmen.

In October 1841, part of the first Kabul occupation force was ordered back to India. Constantly harassed by tribesmen, it fought its way to Gandamak, the commanding brigadier refusing to comply with orders to return to Kabul, where the reduced garrison was in trouble. By early November British officers had been murdered by rioting mobs and their Indian troops terrorised in their cantonments. Two months later a safe-conduct was obtained from the Emir of Kabul for the remaining British/Indian garrison to march to the Khyber Pass and thence back into India after leaving several British officers and their families behind as hostages. Dressed in red jackets and white trousers, 690 British and 3,800 sepoys made irresistible targets for the waiting tribesmen, who had no intention of respecting the safe-conduct. Hampering the mobility of the retreating column were

12,000 dependents including a small number of British wives and children riding camels and mules in the centre of a cavalry detachment.

All the field guns had been spiked and left behind in Kabul except for one horse-artillery battery and three mountain guns. Attacked from the moment it left camp by mounted tribesmen with swords and long-barrelled muskets, the strung-out, slow-moving column managed to make only 6 miles before nightfall. Without shelter of any kind, many died from exposure in the bitter winter weather. The column straggled through the 5-mile-long Khoord Kabul pass under attack from all sides, leaving behind 3,000 dead and wounded, traditionally mutilated before being killed. This inspired Rudyard Kipling to write:

> When you're wounded and left on Afghanistan's plains
> And the women come out to cut up what remains,
> Jest roll to your rifle and blow out your brains
> An' go to your Gawd like a soldier.

The Second Afghan War (1878–80) was triggered by Russia's advance into Central Asia, to counter which Prime Minister Benjamin Disraeli ordered the Indian Viceroy to 'secure' Afghanistan up to its northern border along the Amu Darya river and block Russia's southward expansion. The Viceroy sensibly resigned rather than take orders from distant politicians criminally ignorant of local conditions. His replacement, Lord Lytton, had to justify his new position by executing Disraeli's command, so he notified the Afghan ruler Sheer Ali that a British military mission was coming to Kabul. Permission was refused, to Lytton's fury.

In July 1878 Tsar Alexander II despatched an emissary to Kabul. After he was allowed to enter Afghanistan and a British envoy was insultingly turned back at the Khyber Pass in September, Lytton launched the Second Afghan War on 21 November 1878. A British/Indian force of 40,000 soldiers in three columns advanced into Afghanistan.

Emir Sheer Ali fled abroad, dying in exile the following year. By 26 May 1879 British forces occupied much of the country and

Sheer Ali's son Yaqub Khan signed the Treaty of Gandamak to end the war. Under the treaty, Yaqub was to receive an annual subsidy and Afghanistan's foreign relations were to be controlled by Britain. Tracts of the frontier area were ceded to Britain including the Khyber and Michni passes. Yaqub also agreed to the stationing of Sir Pierre Cavagnari as British Resident in Kabul.

Cavagnari imprudently installed himself in the town, where he was murdered with his guards and dependents shortly afterwards. To punish the perpetrators, Britain's most popular soldier, General Sir Frederick Roberts, led the Kabul Field Force deep into Afghanistan, occupying Kabul on 6 October. A further uprising in December was repressed. Yaqub Khan was forced to abdicate, with the British installing a cousin of his as emir. A series of uprisings were put down with heavy losses on both sides until the British departed nominally victorious, but having abandoned the idea of occupation, or keeping a political officer in Kabul.

In 1893 the British agreed a demarcation line with the ruling emir, known as the Durand Line, between Afghanistan proper and the adjacent tribal areas annexed into the Raj. In 1901 the impossibility of governing this turbulent frontier region as part of the province of Punjab was acknowledged by designating it 'the North-west Frontier Province' (NWF). In this area of some 40,000 sq. miles, British and Indian soldiers conducted punitive 'butcher and bolt' expeditions to subdue the tribesmen while political officers paid regular bribes to tribal leaders after each incursion.

Afghanistan remained neutral in the First World War despite pressure to support Muslim Turkey against the Christian Western Allies. King Habibullah nevertheless received money and armaments from the Central Powers after promising to attack British India. In exchange for an end to British control of Afghan foreign policy, he also made an offer to Britain to block any overland attack on India by the Central Powers. Habibullah was assassinated in February 1919, when power was grabbed by his third son Ammanullah Khan, who had all other contenders murdered. Seeking to unify the country against an unpopular external enemy, he moved part of his army across the Durand Line in defiance of a Raj exhausted by its contribution to the war in Europe.

On 6 May 1919, the Indian government declared this a *casus belli*. The initial conflict saw some local Afghan victories, largely aided by an anti-British uprising of Pathan tribesmen in the NWF. The British/Indian troops having machine guns, armoured cars, motor transport and aircraft, Ammanullah solicited and received from the new Soviet government a subsidy of 1 million roubles, plus small arms, ammunition and some aircraft, to even things up a little. When British planes bombed the royal palace, Ammanullah protested at the dual standard implicit in this act of a British government that had condemned the Zeppelin raids on London. The conflict lasted less than three months, with the armistice terms enshrined in the Rawalpindi Agreement, which conceded Ammanullah's demand that Afghanistan should henceforth control its own foreign relations, especially with its northern neighbours and Moscow.

Within the NWF, things changed so little that tribesmen attacked the fort of Razmak en masse as late as 1938. Four years later a young British sabultern named John Morris was posted to the Baluch Regiment of the Indian Army, serving there in the heart of tribal territory, surrounded by 2.5 million armed hostiles. He recorded that:

> … garrison life in the NWF revolved around Road Open Days [RODs] when the unmetalled military roadway that rose to 7,500 feet above sea level at the highest permanent fort in the British Empire was made safe for a convoy to pass. To travel along it otherwise risked death from Pathan ambushes or locals simply taking pot shots at any unprotected traffic.

> An ROD began with prophylactic fire from mortars and field guns making heights overlooking the road untenable by ambushers. RAF Hurricanes used rockets and cannons to clear the area while pickets were disposed on either side of the road to seize critical points, all having to retreat in sequence at the end of the day as per the drill manual marked 'Revised 1910'. They used different routes from the outbound journey to avoid being knifed by Pathans hiding in the scrub. Snipers lurked just outside the fort all night, killing the occasional

sentry. Our tents were half-dug-in, so that bullets coming over the wall passed through the canvas, but above the heads of sleeping soldiers.[1]

And this was well inside British territory, 25 miles from the Afghan border!

With a history of failed invasions that went back to Alexander the Great and earlier, Afghanistan thus seemed an unlikely place for Leonid Brezhnev's last attempt at expanding the USSR by force in December 1979. Despite Afghanistan's common borders with three Soviet Central Asian republics, the Soviet invasion had nothing to do with blocking a possible invasion route because neighbouring Iran and China already had common frontiers with the USSR. The accepted reason is that Brezhnev was trapped by his own doctrine, which required Soviet intervention to save a communist government at risk.

Since 1955 the Afghan government had received economic and military aid from the USSR worth many billions of dollars, while all Afghan officers went to the USSR for training, many returning as communists. In mid-1973 the monarchist regime was overthrown by the king's cousin Mohammed Daoud Khan, who imposed a one-party system run by what was known as the People's Democratic Party of Afghanistan (PDPA). Its attempted economic and social reforms were unsuccessful, partly due to resistance by traditionalists and friction within the PDPA between his Khalq – or masses – faction and the Parcham – or banner – faction led by Babrak Karmal, many of whose supporters fell victim to Daoud Khan's purges.

In June 1975, Islamic militants attempted to overthrow the government, but were defeated, many fleeing to Pakistan. In April 1977 Daoud Khan and his immediate family were assassinated by a group of Leftist army officers and replaced by pro-Moscow Nur Mohammed Taraki, who appointed himself President of the Revolutionary Council and Prime Minister of the Democratic Republic of Afghanistan.

Protest grew at the government's Marxist reforms – equal rights for women, closure of mosques, abolition of the *burqa* and the wearing of beards by men, introduction of land reform and the cancellation of peasants' crippling debts. Between April 1978 and the Soviet invasion in December 1979, an estimated 27,000 dissidents, religious and civil leaders were executed. According to KGB sources in-country, these included many pro-Moscow activists.

In February 1979, the US ambassador was kidnapped and killed by Islamic rebels despite attempts by Afghan security forces and Soviet advisers to free him. The following month, deputy prime minister Hafizullah Amin proclaimed himself prime minister, escalating the repression in a campaign so unpopular that half the 80,000-strong Afghan army deserted to the rebels. In desperation, Amin requested military assistance from Moscow to regain control of the country, but was told to mobilise the workers and students – advice that showed how little the Soviet leadership understood the medieval society of Afghanistan.[2] Only in June did the Soviet government send a detachment of tanks and armoured personnel carriers to guard government buildings and secure the most important airfields. In July an airborne battalion, disguised as technical advisers, arrived to serve as Taraki's bodyguard.

Moscow, however, stalled on further requests for military support until 14 September, when Kabul's Tajbeg Palace was stormed and Taraki suffocated to death. Declaring himself president, Amin attempted to improve relations with Pakistan and the United States while instigating a domestic campaign to eliminate the imams and professional classes.[3] KGB sources in Kabul warned Moscow that this would provoke a religious backlash that could bring down the government. That prompted intervention under the Brezhnev Doctrine in order to preserve the communist regime and prevent an Islamic take-over – which could have fomented disaffection in the neighbouring Soviet republics whose Islamic factions were growing stronger after six decades of Soviet atheism.

On 24 December 1979, Soviet airborne forces landed at several points. On Christmas Day they were in Kabul, where Amin moved his office into the Tajbeg Palace, believing this a safe location. According to Soviet sources he was fully informed of military movements, having requested assistance on 17 December.

On 27 December, 700 Osnaz and Spetsnaz special forces in Afghan uniforms isolated Kabul from the rest of the world and paralysed the Afghan army by disrupting both civilian and military communications. They also occupied important governmental and military buildings in Kabul, including their primary target, the Tajbeg Palace, during the assault on which Hafizullah Amin was killed and replaced by Babrak Karmal, who had spent some years safely out of the way as ambassador to Czechoslovakia. Two main columns of Red Army tanks, armoured personnel carriers and logistics transport then drove into Afghanistan under an umbrella of helicopters and fixed-wing aircraft. When the two columns met at Kandahar, it looked as though the invasion had been successful.

Mi-28 helicopter gunships strafed 'rebel' villages and laid waste crops. The latest MiG fighter-bombers obliterated villages, killing every inhabitant. Refugees fleeing to safety in Iran and Pakistan topped 2 million. Some observers, however, swiftly compared the Soviet use of hi-tech weaponry against guerrilla forces that melted away on contact with America's situation at the outset of the war in Vietnam. As more and more Soviet conscripts were sucked into the Afghan campaign, the resemblance became more obvious. It was swiftly apparent that the guerrillas, who called themselves *mujaheddin* – fighters in a holy war – were receiving massive quantities of American weapons through Pakistan in a covert CIA operation. Rockets fired from the hills regularly exploded inside Soviet bases. CIA-supplied American Stinger surface-to-air missiles brought down Soviet helicopter gunships. In the dirty war with no holds barred, Soviet deserters and soldiers captured alive were almost always tortured to death. It was *Roll to your rifle* all over again.

In the following decade, Karmal's puppet regime lost all credibility with the population. Armed resistance under various tribal and religious banners created more and more no-go areas for government forces. Despite the presence of 100,000-plus Soviet troops and the terror bombing of the mountain villages, resistance was strongest here because conventional forces could only control the cities and large towns, while the *mujaheddin* moved freely throughout the countryside.

To eliminate their support base, the bombing campaign depopulated rural areas, driving even more Afghans abroad. By 1982, 2.8 million Afghans were in Pakistan and 1.5 million in Iran – the total figure eventually escalating to a peak of 6 million or one-third of the population. Moscow's main asset was the traditional mistrust and treachery of the different tribes and warlords, which surprised many Muslim volunteers from abroad who came to fight alongside them expecting fraternal solidarity.

For the first time, there was a groundswell of protest inside the USSR at the casualties and expense of this unwinnable war, in which 620,000 men eventually served. Officially only 13,833 Soviet soldiers were killed and 49,985 wounded,[4] but Red Army medical care was notoriously poor and in the primitive living conditions of Afghanistan, 469,685 soldiers became unfit for combat. Conservative estimates indicate that about 2.5 million Afghani *mujaheddin* and civilians were wounded or killed during the Soviet intervention or the resultant famine and epidemics.

The gerontocracy in the Kremlin clung obstinately to Brezhnev's war throughout the brief reigns of his successors Andropov and Chernenko. With them both dying soon after taking office, it was left to Mikhail Gorbachev to end the war, but even he could not rapidly disengage. Then, in January 1988, an extraordinary thing happened. Three analysts at the Institute for the Study of USA and Canada – Russian acronym ISKAN – went public with their argument that the age-old Kremlin complex of being surrounded by enemies and treating virtually all foreign states as hostile was out-of-date. They announced that using it to justify ever-increasing defence expenditure caused serious domestic problems and colossal waste of resources. In the words of academician Nikolai Ryzhkov, 'This country is not simply a military-industrial complex, but a military-ideological complex.'[5] The conclusion was that the Soviet command economy benefited *only* the military-industrial complex, yet air defence forces that cost 15 per cent of the entire annual budget were ineffective – as demonstrated by the landing in May 1987 of a German light aircraft in Red Square after an unauthorised flight over more than 1,000 miles of Polish, Belorussian and Russian territory.[6]

Gorbachev was already aware that many military programmes – including chemical, bacterial and nuclear – were concealed from the Politburo and that the Soviet general staff habitually ignored its own and outside computer modelling which consistently demonstated the fallacies of its entrenched policies.[7] On 8 February 1988, he made a nationwide television speech that shattered the Soviet military by announcing the withdrawal from Afghanistan, to be completed by March 1989. On 15 February 1989, General Boris Gromov of the Soviet 40th Army was officially the last soldier to return across the ill-named Friendship Bridge near Termiz on the Afghan/Uzbekistan border. The event was staged for the benefit of the international news media, who were shuttled to the bridge in military helicopters. Gromov had actually been in Uzbekistan for days and only zipped back across the border into Afghanistan early that morning in time to be photographed jumping down from 'the last tank' to cross the bridge.

The real news story happened just before the media helicopters clattered in. The body of the last young conscript to die in Brezhnev's ill-starred war was carried across the bridge wrapped in a blanket by his comrades because body bags were among the many things the Red Army lacked. But nobody photographed that or talked about the deaths and the several hundred thousand men shipped home wounded or sick.

Although Gromov's stagey exit made the news in many countries, it did not fool the USSR-wide network of embittered veterans calling themselves *afgantsy*, and the thousands of women who had lost sons, fathers and partners in Brezhnev's pointless adventure. If any of them kept a sense of history in the midst of their personal grief, there might have been some solace in the thought that, just as the return of the beaten and humiliated survivors of General Kuropatkin's armies from the Russo-Japanese War in the spring of 1905 had foreshadowed the end of Tsarist Russia, so the little general smiling for the television and press cameras as he strode across the Friendship Bridge in February 1989 was heralding the end of the USSR while being fêted as 'the hero of Afghanistan'.

That, at least, was the accepted history until an interview was published in the French current affairs magazine *Le Nouvel*

Observateur. When asked a question about the memoirs of ex-CIA chief Robert Gates, President Carter's adviser Zbigniew Brzezinski said that Carter authorised the CIA on 3 July 1979 to begin destabilisation operations against the Afghan government under the code-name Operation Cyclone. According to the official version:

> CIA aid to the *mujaheddin* began ... after the Soviet army invaded Afghanistan ... but the reality, secretly guarded until now, is completely otherwise. Aid to the *mujaheddin* was part of a larger strategy to induce a Soviet military intervention. We didn't push the Russians to intervene, but we knowingly increased the probability that they would. That secret operation had the effect of drawing the Soviets into the Afghan trap. The day that the Soviets officially crossed the border, I wrote to President Carter, 'We now have the opportunity of giving to the Soviet Union its Vietnam War.'[8]

The CIA's first Afghanistan budget was a mere half-million dollars. From there, it jumped to $60 million, matched by the Saudis and with contributions from Britain. Thanks largely to a pushy congressman from Texas called Charlie Wilson, the no-longer-clandestine aid to the *mujaheddin* topped $250 million from the US and Saudi Arabia in 1985, plus $40 million that Wilson 'arranged' from the Department of Defense.[9] In the memoirs of Robert Gates, former director of the CIA, he wrote:

> All through 1985 we poured weapons into Afghanistan – heavy machine guns, SA-7s and the Oerlikon anti-aircraft guns, which began to produce increasing aircraft losses for the Soviets. [We] improved the logistics base [and laid] the basis for the extraordinary *mujaheddin* successes in 1986 and 1987, including supplying thousands of Chinese mules to transport weapons.[10]

25

AND ALL ERICH'S MEN ...

I n 1985, Gorbachev chose Boris Yeltsin to purge the corrupt Moscow party organisation and rewarded him for doing a good job with a non-voting seat on the Politburo. As first secretary of Moscow's CPSU committee and de facto mayor of the city, Yeltsin was a determined but tactless reformer, criticising the slow pace of change, the attitude of party conservatives, and even Gorbachev himself. He adored creating photo opportunities for Russian and Western media that showed him wearing hard hats on construction sites and looking dynamic. Whilst normal for Western politicians, this was condemned by his many enemies as evidence of a dangerous personality cult. For a complex of reasons, he was forced out of the Moscow party leadership in 1987 and from the Politburo in 1988.

Demoted to the post of a deputy minister for construction, where hard hats were acceptable, Yeltsin now staged a political comeback as *the* hands-on reformer. In March 1989, he returned to prominence after being massively elected on the strength of all those photo-calls to represent a Moscow constituency in the USSR Congress of People's Deputies – the Soviet parliament.

On 2 May of that year, the Hungarian government heeded Mikhail Gorbachev's edict that force could no longer hold together the house of cards which the Soviet Union had become, and decided to roll up the barbed wire and lift the mines along its border with Austria. On 27 June the Austrian and Hungarian foreign ministers together symbolically cut through the fence and 600-plus GDR citizens seized the moment to flee into the West. In July 1989, the Hungarian Supreme Court rehabilitated national hero Imre Nagy, hanged for presiding over the 1956 rebellion. Moscow could do nothing about it. Next door, in Poland, a similar challenge was issued to the Kremlin. On 4 June the first partially free elections in forty years saw Lech Walesa's Solidarność Party win 160 of the 161 seats allotted to non-Communist candidates. In the upper house, it held ninety-nine of the 100 seats.

On 19 August the 'Pan-European Picnic' organised by two Hungarian opposition parties was held at a crossing on the Austrian border advertised as being open for three hours. Hungarian frontier police refused to shoot or stop several hundred GDR refugees crossing into Austria. SED boss Erich Honecker told the world's press, '[They] distributed pamphlets right up to the Polish border, inviting East German holiday-makers to a picnic. When they came to the picnic, they were given presents, food and Deutschmarks, before being persuaded to go over to the West.'

On 10 September 1989, the Hungarian foreign minister was asked on television what the border guards would do if, say, 60,000 GDR citizens arrived at the Austrian border. He replied, 'They will allow them through … and I assume the Austrians will let them in.'[1] The border was formally open.[2]

All these and other events in Central Europe had less impact in the West than they might have done because they were overshadowed by the first stirrings of democracy in Beijing, where 3 and 4 June had seen huge anti-government demonstrations in Tienanmen Square put down by riot police and soldiers with the loss of hundreds of lives. The most memorable media image of the year was not gauntletted Hungarian border guards with wire cutters nor Polish politicians, but a solitary Chinese student in Tiananmen Square defying a line of tanks to drive over him.

In the twenty-one storey office block partly hidden in birch woods in south-western Moscow which KGB officers referred to as *les* or 'the forest', Leonid Shebarshin was the new director of the First Chief Directorate. His promotion came at a bewildering time. Shortly before General Gromov marched theatrically across the Friendship Bridge, a cable had been sent to every Soviet diplomatic post and KGB *rezidentura* announcing Gorbachev's new policy of non-interference in the affairs of the satellite states.[3]

To ensure they followed the new party line, Shebarshin summoned his subordinates to a conference, of which the mood was perhaps more frank than he and KGB Centre colleagues demoralised by the Afghan retreat had anticipated. The ghosts of Dzerzhinsky, Yezhov, and Beria must have turned in their uneasy graves on hearing Shebarshin's message that carrots and sticks were out because Russia could no longer afford carrots to dangle before its satellites and its big stick was broken. One after another, his subordinates painted the same picture: Poland had become Polish again after forty years of Russian occupation; the Hungarian government now looked for help to Vienna rather than Moscow. What US President Reagan memorably called 'the evil empire' was falling apart at the seams.

Even in Erich Honecker's GDR – the most pro-Moscow of all the Eastern European 'socialist republics' – Erich Mielke's repressive Stasi could no longer terrorise the population into sullen subservience. The author once remarked to his Stasi interrogator, 'I heard the bands in the May Day parades yesterday.' He was immediately rebuked: 'We do not have parades in the GDR, Mr Boyd. Parades are militaristic. What you heard were spontaneous demonstrations by the workers.'

If Lieutenant Becker was still alive in 1989, he would have seen the first truly spontaneous demonstrations in Leipzig since 1933. Several hundred courageous people marched through the streets on 4 September chanting, *'Nieder mit der Stasi!'* Down with the Stasi! A few weeks earlier, uttering a word against the organisation that held files on 6 million GDR citizens – one in every three men, women and children – would have been punished by years in prison. True, there were some arrests on 4 September but, far from discouraging further demonstrations, they had the effect of inciting more and more marchers in each succeeding week: 10,000 in early October, peaking at 300,000 in November. Desperate to plug the gap through Hungary, through which thousands were escaping to the West, 77-year-old Honecker put it out of bounds to his citizens. As a result, they headed into Czechoslovakia, where the West German Embassy in Prague was inundated by asylum-seekers.

On 7 October, the SED celebrated the fortieth anniversary of the foundation of the GDR. An uncharacteristically subdued Gorbachev sat on the rostrum watching the parades of uniformed communist youth organisations, some of whose members shouted, '*Gorby, hilf uns*!' There were 400,000-plus Soviet troops in the GDR, but when Honecker told him that the wall was there for keeps, so far as the ruling SED Party was concerned, Gorbachev said effectively, 'You're on your own, Erich.' The SED's pathetic response was to ban Soviet newspapers and magazines in case GDR citizens learned the dangerous news from Moscow.

The dam finally burst in mid-October 1989 when Honecker was forced by the SED Politburo to resign for being dangerously out of touch. Replaced by his hard-line deputy Egon Krenz, Honecker was stunned to be expelled from the SED and charged with abuse of power. Released a few months later, he sought asylum in Moscow, but was expelled to Germany in 1992 and imprisoned again on charges of murdering all the people killed by frontier guards on his orders. Benefitting from a clemency that he had never shown, he was liberated in 1993 with advanced liver cancer, fled to Chile, and lived his last months there with a daughter and her Chilean husband.

The other Erich – Mielke, the bureaucrat who had terrorised millions – was eventually prosecuted for the murder of two policemen back in the 1930s, but pardoned and even paid compensation for his time in prison, ending his days in a small subsidised apartment in Berlin near the Normannenstrasse HQ where he had enjoyed thirty-two years of untrammelled power.

By 4 November 1989, when a half-million protesters demonstrated at Berlin's Alexanderplatz, the GDR was imploding. The severe economic problems of the USSR meant no more subsidised exports, especially of oil, to the satellites. This was bad news for them all, but disastrous for the bankrupt GDR, a communist state paradoxically kept afloat only by Western loans – and which serviced the long-term loans by short-term borrowing, thus digging itself an ever-deeper grave.[4] In its last eighteen years, national debt increased tenfold, but debts to Western banks increased from 2 billion to 49 billion Deutschmarks.[5]

After 250,000 people had fled to the West through Poland, Czechoslovakia and Hungary, the SED Central Committee spokesman Günter Schabovski admitted publicly, 'They made it clear to the entire world that the GDR is not a civilised state, because they would not have fled, had it been so.' The Stasi itself reported 1.4 million people joining 210 public demonstrations against Honecker's remedy: the imposition of draconian travel restrictions that eventually stopped all ordinary citizens leaving the country for whatever destination.[6]

On 8 November the *New York Times* published a report headed 'East Germany's Cabinet Resigns'. It began, 'The entire East German Cabinet resigned today in testimony to the scale of the crisis that has seized the state under the pressure of mass demonstrations and mass flight.'

So unreal had the situation become that on the evening of 9 November Schabovski unwittingly cast himself as the angel of freedom at a televised news conference. He was supposed to announce new regulations coming into force next day that would allow GDR citizens to visit West Germany after obtaining exit visas, but his confused statement, resulting from inadequate briefing, was interpreted as meaning an *immediate* opening of the borders. Crowds gathered at crossing points in the wall, chanting demands to pass into West Berlin. Some border guards had seen Schabovski's televised press conference. Others had seen reports on West German television announcing the opening of the borders. All were confused, telephoning for instructions from superiors equally confused. The NVA and riot police were on standby with live ammunition, but no orders came for them to leave barracks.

Mielke was spending the night in the bedroom of his ample suite of offices in Stasi HQ, but took no steps to regain control of the situation, presumably realising that his time was up. In the absence of explicit orders to the contrary, border guards opened the barriers and allowed people they would have shot only hours before to cross the death strip and flood into West Berlin, where they celebrated their new-found freedom amid equally delirious West Berliners.

Sabine Ehrlich is the BStu[7] official who handed the author his Stasi file in 2008. Her memory of the night was still vivid:

I was living in East Berlin. My husband had been fired from a well-paid job for 'political unreliability'. He eventually found work as a cameraman in GDR Television and was working late that evening. My mother-in-law, whose apartment overlooked a crossing-point in the Wall, called to say, 'It's incredible. The Wall is open. People are just walking into the West.' I hurried across town and joined her at the window. Laughing and crying together, we watched the singing, dancing crowds surging through the gap in the Wall and West Berliners actually walking into East Berlin! It was cold, bitterly cold that night, but many people were not even wearing overcoats. If you've never been imprisoned in your own country, you can't understand what it meant to us. It was the most wonderful night of my life.[8]

Next day, a coup in Sofia toppled Bulgaria's top communist Todor Zhivkov. In the following weeks people from many countries travelled to Berlin for the simple pleasure of walking through what had been the most impenetrable section of the Iron Curtain. Many had been born since the Wall went up. Law student Sue Turner from Bristol said:

My spur-of-the-moment decision was a twenty-third birthday present to myself, stretching an already stressed credit card to the limit in those days before bargain airfares. *The Rough Guide* recommended a cheap hotel where no one spoke English. Because I spoke no German, I couldn't find the breakfast room in the morning and set out for the Wall by the overhead railway, grabbing a doughnut en route.

Getting off at the first stop in East Berlin, I became confused over which way to go. There were two streams of people. I realised later one was for Westerners and one for Easterners returning. I picked the wrong one and got a small taste of their lives as over-officious East German policemen shouted at them in a way which made clear that they were expected to be immediately obedient in a way I'd never seen people behave before.

Feeling out of my depth and wanting to get back to being *free*, I flashed my British passport and was shown to a different exit where no-one shouted at the passengers. The riotous wall-parties were over by then, but there were lots of people just wandering about – I suppose, because they were free to do so at last. To sample East German food, I queued up near the Brandenburg Gate at a hamburger stall. Poor quality meat and bread, it smelled bad and tasted worse. My God, it was cold – very cold for an English girl dressed in jeans with a not-well-insulated leather jacket. I'd never experienced that piercing, bitter East European wind before; it chilled me to my bones, but the locals didn't seem to notice. My souvenir of the birthday trip was a bit of crumbling Berlin Wall I kept for years – probably full of asbestos![9]

The bitter weather did not deter the politico-tourists, but the fortuitous political thaw in Berlin had not crossed the 'Friendship Border' into Czechoslovakia, where massive demonstrations on 16–20 January to mark the anniversary of Jan Palach's self-immolation in protest against the Soviet invasion of 1968 were broken up by riot police with water cannons, tear gas, attack dogs and batons. Hundreds were injured and 1,400 arrested.

This provided the catalyst that playwright Václav Havel and the other founders of Charter 77 had been waiting for. The following weekend, he summoned anti-communists of several factions to a meeting at the Magic Lantern Theatre and launched the Civic Forum movement. It was the first step in what became known as the Velvet Revolution with the police brutality sparking a nationwide protest movement of demonstrations and strikes. Within a month, the KSČ formed a coalition government with Civic Forum. Communist hard-liner Gustav Husák resigned the presidency on 10 December. On 28 December, the disgraced Alexander Dubček returned from the forests and was elected chairman of the Federal Assembly. Havel was elected interim president of the republic the following day by a parliament still predominantly communist – making him the country's first non-communist head of state since the bloody Soviet coup of 1948.

His close supporters, mostly intellectuals like himself, found themselves governing a country in crisis. One dilemma was what to do about the security apparatus – the internal Statní Bezpečnost and the foreign intelligence service První Sprava – which regarded their new political masters as dissident scum. Both organisations had worked closely with the KGB and its predecessors since 1948. Fortunately, Shebarshin's briefing meant his *rezident* in Prague advised them to go with the flow.

The end of that turbulent year also saw the toppling of the dictator of the most backward of all Moscow's satellites. In Romania, President Nicolae Ceauçescu and his wife Elena fled their network of luxurious palaces and bomb-proof bunkers, going on the run three days before Christmas as their army transferred its allegiance to the newly visible opposition. By Christmas Day, both Ceausescus were dead, riddled with bullets by an impromptu firing squad after a kangaroo court, where only she had the nerve to protest the lack of defence lawyers.

In the first weeks of 1990, Havel's government had to decide what to do with the Statní Bezpečnost files, in many of which they were the villains, spied on by 10,000 informers placed throughout federal and local government and in every factory and sports club. With commendable generosity, the new government ordered the files destroyed so that there could be no recriminations. The previous orientation of the security services was reversed, with MI6 officers from Britain invited to train a new generation of Czech intelligence officers and the CIA – known as the main enemy only months before – providing new communications equipment and training Havel's bodyguard. In return, all that was asked was the cover identities and whereabouts of KGB sleeper agents implanted in the West by První Sprava, but never activated. Getting rid of them proved less easy because many had become used to life in the West and acquired families in Britain or America, where they now felt more at home than back in the old country.

As Honecker had predicted, the opening of the Wall dealt a death-blow to the GDR. Instead of releasing the pressure for reform, it was followed by ever more insistent demonstrations. In mid-November, Egon Krenz was in turn replaced by moderate SED member Hans Modrow, who promised to arrange free elections at which other parties might present candidates. The first such election in March 1990 saw the rump of the SED defeated and the Christian Democratic Union in power with a mandate to speed up German reunification.

In July it was the turn of West Germany's Chancellor Helmut Kohl to dangle a carrot in front of Gorbachev, who dropped Russian objections to a unified Germany in return for a sizeable financial aid package to the Soviet Union. On 3 October 1990, Stalin's embalmed corpse should have turned in his grave outside the Kremlin walls[10] when the GDR ceased to exist after merging with the Bundesrepublik. All-German elections in December 1990 confirmed Kohl as Chancellor of the reunited nation. The cost of generous start-up cash payments to every citizen of the former GDR was concealed from the West German electorate, which was also not told that it would take fifteen years or more before the cost of modernising the eastern Länder was fully amortised. Germany was, however, once again a nation – albeit with a half-million Soviet troops stationed on its soil.

Repatriating them took four years. On 1 September 1994 the *New York Times* commented:

> The withdrawal of more than half a million Russian troops and dependents from Germany since 1991 is the biggest pullout ever by an army not defeated in battle. Along with soldiers and civilians of the former Soviet armed forces, Russia has removed more than 1,300 planes and helicopters, 3,600 artillery pieces, 4,200 tanks and 8,200 armored vehicles [and] 677,000 tons of ammunition, including an unknown number of nuclear-tipped tactical shells. The pullout has involved thousands of flights, trains, convoys and ship transports

across the Baltic. The withdrawal from Germany caps a five-year operation in which more than 700,000 Russian soldiers and 500,000 civilians have been brought home from Eastern Europe and from bases around the world.[11]

The future for the repatriated forces personnel was bleak, unemployment the only certainty ahead of them in the stagnant Russian economy.

26

THE END OF THE EVIL EMPIRE

As early as 1987 the CIA had warned President Reagan that Gorbachev's policy of using persuasion, rather than coercion, to keep the member states of the USSR in line had failed, with open disaffection in the non-Russian republics so widespread that military force was no longer an option. The State Department disagreed and held to its belief that each ethnic conflict was a local phenomenon. For once, the CIA was right.

What its director, Robert Gates, called the 'final act of the 70-year-old Soviet tragedy' began in a mountainous area of the Caucasus, of which few in the West had ever heard. Nagorno-Karabakh had, since ancient times, been on both a seismic fault-line and a racial one between Armenians and Azeris, with 90 per cent of the population Armenian, yearning since the revolution for formal attachment to the Armenian Soviet Republic.

Thinking that *perestroika* really meant restructuring, in the mid-1980s they applied for a frontier adjustment, which was refused. Epitomising the internecine hatreds of the area, by February 1988 the pressure reached bursting point, with riots in Yerevan and Nagorno-Karabakh targeting Azeris and mobs in the Azerbaijan capital Baku turning on Armenian residents.

Order was restored by MVD troops only after thousands of Armenians and Azeris had fled to safety across the borders.

With virtually no in-country assets, Western intelligence agencies learned of the latest developments through watching CNN. It rapidly became clear that Moscow had a shaky control in the cities, but elsewhere both sides were attacking isolated towns, cutting power lines and blowing up bridges. After the Armenian earthquake of December 1988 that caused 25,000 deaths, even international relief supplies were intercepted and looted.

With their common tradition of commercial and cultural links to the West, the three Baltic states had no such problems with each other and shared a deep resentment that the only 'justification' for their annexation into the USSR was Stalin's scandalous carve-up with Hitler in 1939. By June 1988, ethnic unrest in Lithuania was causing anti-Russian demonstrations and had led to the formation of a popular front of non-communist parties prioritising Lithuanian culture and language. Neighbouring Latvia followed suit in October. On 16 November, Estonia became the first country to declare its intended secession from the USSR. It was a bold move for a nation of 900,000 people, unwilling hosts to 400,000 Russians living within its borders.

By April 1989, the CIA was predicting that national independence movements could rapidly rend asunder the USSR.

Georgia shared borders with Armenia and Azerbaijan, and also had its own problems with the minority Abkhazians, who petitioned the CPSU Congress for permission to secede from Georgia. Permission refused, demonstrations in Tbilisi were put down by MVD troops using tear gas and clubbing some demonstrators to death with spades.[1]

In early August Latvia proclaimed its sovereignty. On 22 August the Lithuanian parliament pronounced its annexation by the USSR under the 1939 German-Soviet Pact *illegal*. Twenty-four hours later, television cameras brought the world the unique spectacle of a symbolic human chain of 2 million men, women and children demanding their freedom. It stretched 450 miles – all the way from Vilnius in Lithuania right through Latvia to Tallinn on the north coast of Estonia. Waves of unrest spread into Belorussia; Moldavia clamoured for reunion with Romania; Ukraine formed its own popular front to protect what was left of its native language, culture and environment. In September, the Georgian Supreme Soviet ruled that the country could ignore USSR laws that were against its interests. Azerbaijan and Armenia rewrote the statute books, discarding Soviet-era legislation.

In December 1989 the Lithuanian Supreme Soviet ended single-party government, its Communist Party declaring itself independent of the CPSU. On 11 January 1990 Gorbachev took courage in both hands and travelled to Vilnius in the hope of pressuring the Baltic states into submission by reminding them of their economic dependence on Russia, but the Balts were unmoved. MVD troops were sent into Azerbaijan and Armenia, followed by Red Army units, which had to fight their way into Baku. Just short of all-out war, another extraordinary thing happened: the Baltic states offered to mediate in the Caucasian conflict – and did.[2]

Gorbachev seemed not to realise the power of the genie he had let out of the lamp of *perestroika*. On 16 March he gave the Lithuanian government three days to come to heel. When no reply came, Soviet troops made a show of force in Vilnius. On 13 April he issued a final warning that the gas pipeline into Lithuania would be shut down. Late on 18 April the threat was carried out, but that did not stop Latvia declaring its sovereignty on 4 May, followed on 12 June by the Russian republic, with Uzbekistan following suit on 20 June, Moldavia on 23 June, Ukraine on 16 July and Belarus on 27 July.

All these republics now gave precedence to their own laws when in conflict with those of the USSR, leaving Gorbachev the president of a hollow sham – a supranational government whose member states had resigned from the club. However, like a dying mammoth, the USSR was still dangerous in its death throes. In early January 1991, Russian troops were in the Baltic states, Armenia, Georgia, Moldavia and Ukraine endeavouring to enforce conscription for military service in the USSR armed forces. In Vilnius, MVD OMON special-purpose detachments backed by tanks assaulted the city's television tower, occupied by protesters. Sixteen Lithuanians were killed and hundreds wounded. Later that month OMON troops stormed the MVD HQ in Riga, killing four Latvians and injuring ten.[3] Pleas for help from abroad went unanswered because Western media attention was focused on US-led coalition forces driving Saddam Hussein's troops out of Kuwait. Surprisingly, the repression caused widespread protests *inside Russia*, with journalists resigning from the Communist Party, criticism of the intervention voiced on radio and television and Politburo members marching in the streets.

The Supreme Soviet demanded a detailed report on the locally authorised operation,[4] but Soviet Defence Minister Dmitri Yazov reportedly ordered the commanding officer of the Soviet occupation forces in the GDR to form action groups of volunteers prepared to be airlifted back to Russia to suppress the groundswell of protest by force if necessary. The old parlour game of Russian gossip was played for real when Moscow's mayor Gavril Popov warned US ambassador Jack Matlock that a coup was brewing; Matlock informed Secretary of State James Baker, who told Aleksandr Bessmertnykh, briefly Gorbachev's foreign minister, and Matlock then went to the Kremlin to pass on the warning in person. Gorbachev ridiculed the idea,[5] having already been warned by Foreign Minister Edvard Shevardnadze, who resigned in December 1990, that sowing the wind meant reaping a whirlwind.

Elected president of the Russian parliament, Gorbachev's former protégé, the white-haired alcoholic Boris Yeltsin – remembered as the head of state who danced and drank himself to death, occasionally goosing women in front of television cameras – travelled to Tallinn to sign a mutual defence treaty with the Baltic states, after which Gorbachev withdrew his troops. On 9 February a referendum in Lithuania confirmed the people's desire for complete independence, with Latvia and Estonia following suit on 3 March. On 12 June Yeltsin was elected president of the Russian Federation with a mandate for economic reform. Collecting 57 per cent of the vote made him the first popularly elected president of the Russian republic, easily defeating Gorbachev's nominee, academician Nikolai Ryzhkov.

After the last Soviet troops withdrew from Czechoslovakia on 1 July, in Prague the Warsaw Pact disbanded itself. This was the last straw for the 'gang of eight' in Moscow which included Defence Minister Dmitri Yazov, KGB Chairman Vladimir Kryuchkov and other hard-liners determined to stop Gorbachev completely destroying the USSR. To give themselves standing, they formed the Gosudarstvenny Komityet po Chrezvychainomy Polozheniyu – or State Committee for the Extraordinary Situation – to prevent Gorbachev signing a treaty on 20 August that would have strengthened the republics at the expense of the USSR administration. CNN startled Western capitals by relaying a TASS announcement that the committee had decreed a six-month state of emergency,[6] yet over most of Russia the situation appeared normal.

In Moscow, most of the action was around the White House, home of the Supreme Soviet, surrounded by a huge and noisy crowd which erected makeshift barricades on the arrival of tanks and motorised infantry from the 2nd Tamanskaya Guards Division, an instant-readiness unit tasked with the defence of the capital. Five weeks after taking office, Yeltsin was at the height of his popularity. Racing to the White House with his habitual flair for theatrics, he clambered onto one of the tanks and rallied support for Gorbachev. The soldiers defied orders and revolved the tanks' turrets, so that their guns no longer threatened the parliament building and could even have been defending it. In Langley and Washington, intelligence officers watched these extraordinary events live on television, lamenting that the man in their White House now got his updates not from the CIA, but CNN.[7]

Kryuchkov had an armed snatch squad on standby to arrest Yeltsin, but this was impossible as long as he remained with his thousands of supporters behind the barricades. The coup became a farce on 18 August with Kryuchkov and Yazov commandeering an Aeroflot plane at Moscow-Vnukovo airport to fly to Gorbachev's holiday villa at Foros in the Crimea. Close behind came a second commandeered aircraft bearing Yeltsin's vice president Alexander Rutskoi. When Kryuchkov and Yazov arrived, they demanded Gorbachev's resignation, which he refused to give them. He and his family were then held prisoner, watching Kryuchkov announce on television that Gorbachev had been obliged to resign for reasons of health. That sounded ominous.

Rutskoi's party then arrived and arrested the coup leaders. The other hard-liners lost their nerve. Several committed suicide, one killing his wife first. Others fled. Fresh from Washington, the new US ambassador Robert Strauss could not be driven from the airport into Moscow in the embassy limousine because traffic was gridlocked with columns of tanks heading out of the city. For once, he was delighted to be stuck in traffic: it meant the coup was over.[8]

Gorbachev and his family were flown back to the capital with their erstwhile captors under armed guard at the rear of the air-craft. On landing in Moscow, Gorby smiled and waved tiredly for the world's cameras. Western media regarded Yeltsin's foiling of the coup as a victory for democracy, but being rescued by the secessionist president of Russia was an obvious humiliation for the last president of the USSR. At the bottom of the aircraft steps, Gorbachev refused to get into the armoured presidential Zil limousine with its driver and bodyguards from KGB Ninth Directorate, whose chief Yuri Plekhanov was now under arrest, together with Kryuchkov, Yazov and the other plotters. Ordering the bodyguards out of his way, Gorby seated himself in an ordinary Volga saloon, in which he was driven to the Kremlin in the customary cortège of flashing lights and wailing sirens without paying any tribute to Yeltsin, who had probably saved his life.

On 22 August Gorby cut his own throat politically at a press conference when he resigned as general secretary of the CPSU while Yeltsin was adroitly transferring to himself and the Russian Federation the remaining powers of the USSR. Latvia declared complete independence on 19 August, Ukraine on 24 August, followed by most of the other republics. By the end of September, as CIA Director Robert Gates remarked, 'Gorbachev was all that was left of the USSR.'[9]

In July, Yeltsin had publicly torn up his party membership card. On 6 November he issued a decree banning the Communist Party and making nonsense of the KGB's motto 'The Sword and the Shield of the Party'. The monolithic state security appara-tus was then dismembered, so that it could never again stage a coup d'état. First Chief Directorate, responsible for foreign intelligence, espionage and subversion, was re-born as Sluzhba

Vneshnei Razvedki Rossii (SVRR) – The Russian Service for External Intelligence. Second Chief Directorate, which had terrorised generations of USSR citizens and sent millions to the Gulag, became Federal'naya Sluzhba Bezopasnosti (FSB) – the Federal Security Service. The 250,000 KGB border troops[10] were placed under separate command, as were other directorates that corresponded to America's NSA and Britain's GCHQ. Taken together, all these changes meant that no one man would ever again enjoy the total power of Kryuchkov and his predecessors. Symbolically, the iconic bronze statue of 'Iron Felix' Dzerzhinsky outside the Lubyanka was removed to a scrapyard.

That autumn saw many functions of the USSR assumed by Yeltsin's administration in Moscow. On 7 December in Minsk, Belarus, he inaugurated Sodruzhestvo Nezavisemykh Gosudarstv – the Commonwealth of Independent States (CIS) with Stanislav Shushkevich of Belarus and Ukraine's President Leonid Kravchuk. On 17 December Gorby threw in the towel, announcing the imminent end of the USSR. On 21 December in Almaty, capital of Kazakhstan, Yelstin compromised with leaders of the Central Asian republics to prevent a Muslim breakaway commonwealth. On 24 December a federal Russian ambassador took over the USSR seat in the United Nations. Still protesting his belief in Marxism and the party he had destroyed, Gorbachev resigned the following day. The Soviet flag was lowered for the last time in the Kremlin, and President Reagan's 'evil empire' ceased to exist.

On that day, George Kennan's prediction in his 'long telegram' of February 1946 that the containment of Russian expansionism would eventually bring down the Soviet system seemed to be proven correct – far more quickly than most Kremlin-watchers would have dared suggest. The speed of the break-up left Western leaders gasping and their intelligence agencies frantically trying to discover who now controlled the former USSR's nuclear arsenal – reduced under the several strategic arms limitation treaties but widely distributed for strategic reasons in countries that were now independent states. The answer was Yeltsin, but subject to approval by the host nations.[11]

Boris Yeltsin embarked on a wide-ranging programme of reforms to convert Russia's stagnant command economy into a Western-style free market with multi-party elections. Interest rates were radically increased to restrict credit. To balance public spending and revenue, he imposed new taxes, cut government subsidies to industry and made radical cuts in the welfare system. Prices skyrocketed and the credit crunch crippled some industries, making consumer goods even more difficult to obtain. The standard of living for lower income groups worsened. Unemployment soared and savings were wiped out by inflation. Russia was on track for a 50 per cent drop in GDP.

Throughout 1992 Yeltsin was at loggerheads with the Congress of People's Deputies and the Supreme Soviet, whose speaker Ruslan Khasbulatov opposed the reforms while claiming to support Yeltsin's long-term goals. In December 1992 the Congress of People's Deputies refused to elect a young Yeltsin protégé as prime minister. On 20 March 1993, Yeltsin announced on national television that he was assuming special powers to push through his reforms. By August, the situation was summed up thus, 'The President issues decrees as though there were no Supreme Soviet and the Supreme Soviet suspends decrees as though there were no President.'[12] The best example of this was when Yeltsin suspended Vice President Alexander Rutskoi on 1 September. Two days later the Supreme Soviet refused to recognise the suspension and referred both parties to the Constitutional Court.

The sparring continued. On 21 September 1993, Yeltsin dissolved the Supreme Soviet and the Congress of People's Deputies. Since this act exceeded his constitutional powers, he tore up the constitution and called for new parliamentary elections, announcing on television his intention to rule by decree for the time being. This was the act of a new Tsar, but the Supreme Soviet rose to the occasion by declaring that his breaches of the constitution disqualified him for the presidency and proclaimed Rutskoi president, dismissing Yeltsin and the ministers of defence, security and interior.

On 23 September the Congress of People's Deputies convened. Although the 638 deputies present did not constitute a quorum, they voted to impeach Yeltsin anyway. His response was to cut off electricity and water supplies to the Moscow White

House. After clashes on 28 September between pro-Parliament demonstrators and Yeltsin's riot police, MVD troops sealed off the building with barricades and barbed wire, with 600 armed men reportedly inside the cordon.

The following days saw tens of thousands of demonstrators in the streets of Moscow and other major cities protesting their reduced standard of living, the widespread corruption and violent crime, the collapse of medical services and scarcity of food. After bloody clashes in many cities, the country was close to civil war. A former air force major-general, Rutskoi attempted to win over the army, but most troops stayed loyal to Yeltsin, who reversed his stance of August 1991 by ordering troops to force the recalcitrant deputies out of the White House.

At dawn on 4 October, ten tanks began shelling the upper floors of the parliament building with the dual aim of minimising casualties – most of the hundreds of people in the building were on the lower floors or in the basement – and scaring off the snipers there. Damage was considerable. By midday, security troops in full combat gear were using house-to-house combat techniques to clear the building floor by floor. Truces allowed people to leave the building. The full casualty figures were too embarrassing to publish. Government sources eventually admitted to between 149 and 187 killed and 437 wounded. Many of the dead and injured being removed by friends before any body count, unofficial sources ranged as high as ten times these figures, spread over all the confrontations. As this was the first street fighting in Moscow since 1917, Muscovites dubbed the extraordinary series of events 'the Second October Revolution'.

What Western leader would have been obeyed if ordering tanks to shell London's House of Commons, la Chambre des Députés in Paris, the Congress in Washington or the Bundestag in Berlin? And, if the order had been carried out, how could that Western leader have continued his or her political career?

It is a measure of how different Russia, after seven decades of Soviet rule, is from the European democracies that Yeltsin not only continued to exercise his presidential powers, but boldly curbed the powers of the trade unions and banned organisations, newspapers and political parties which opposed him.

He called on the numerous regional *soviety* that had disapproved his actions to disband themselves. Among his individual targets, the chairman of the Constitutional Court was forced to resign. Stalin would have approved.

Even after the financial crash of August 1998 when Russia defaulted on many of its debts and devalued the rouble, Yeltsin managed to keep his political balance. The central bank had been governed until 1994 by a man with zero knowledge of economics. As the commercial banks collapsed through incompetence and fraud, Russians in the new middle class saw their savings wiped out.[13] Clouds were on the political horizon as the Duma, flexing its post-Soviet muscles, gave unmistakeable signs that Yeltsin's erratic style of government and his corrupt 'family' had made him many enemies.

Yet, on the positive side, it did seem that at last the spectre of Russian expansionism had been well and truly laid, with all the republics of what Russians call *blizhneye zarubezhiye* – meaning, the near-abroad – revelling in their new-found independence.

THE MAKING OF THE PRESIDENT, RUSSIAN STYLE

So telegenic were all these events that few people in the West were aware that the newly appointed director of the FSB – Russia's retitled internal security organisation – was a man called Vladimir Putin.

Who is Vladimir Putin? The world asked.

The official answer was that he was born to Vladimir Spiridonovich Putin on 7 October 1952 in Leningrad/St Petersburg – the perfect place of birth for a Russian politician. However, Vladimir's wife Maria would have been 41 at the time – an unusual age in Russia for a woman to have her first child – and little evidence exists for young Vladimir's presence there before the age of eight. As near as one can get to the truth, he was born in 1950 to Vera Nikolayevna Putina in the Urals by a married lover called Platon Privalov. The child was raised by her parents for the first year while she completed her studies in Tashkent. Marrying a Georgian soldier named Osepashvili, Vera and her son went to live with him in Metehi, 40 miles from Georgia's capital Tbilisi, but Osepashvili disliked his stepson and gave him away to a childless ex-comrade. Managing to trace him, Vera took her son back to her parents, but the grandfather became ill and the unwanted boy was first sent to a boarding school, then given to a childless relative in Leningrad, who was Vladimir S. Putin.

When Vera Putina-Osepashvili tried to contact her long-lost son years later, she was told that he was already serving in the KGB and warned to keep away. Her few photographs of him were confiscated by secret service agents in January 2000, just before television reporters descended on her after an extremely suspicious plane crash killed several people investigating Putin's childhood for publication before the March elections. Without any documentary evidence, she was still convincing, but the footage was never aired because Russian voters would not have wanted a president of doubtful ethnic origin.[1]

If true, such a loveless early life might explain why Vladimir, nicknamed Volodya or Vova, was a lonely, silent, withdrawn boy, obsessed with physical fitness. After leaving school, he went to Leningrad University to read law in 1970 and entered the KGB at a low level in 1975. Ten years on, he was posted to Dresden in the GDR with the rank of major, earning money on the side by smuggling West German fashion catalogues back to Russia for dressmakers to copy the patterns. In the words of a colleague from this time, 'Volodya was polite, friendly, obliging and unobtrusive. [His motto was] why make things difficult for yourself by spitting against the wind?' Putin was always looking for a father figure. The same colleague recalled, 'He was capable of making anyone like him, but he was particularly successful with [men] who were old enough to be his father.'[2] So successful at this was Putin with his colonel that he received two promotions during the five-year stint in Dresden.

In January 1990, Putin and his wife Lyudmila returned to Leningrad. In the general chaos, armed forces and even KGB officers were not getting paid, but after three months Putin landed the job as KGB *rezident* in the rector's office of Leningrad University, snooping on Russian and foreign students and staff. His old tutor Anatoly Sobchak was now an up-and-coming politician and offered a job to his ex-student. As Putin tells it in his official biography:

I said, 'It would be a pleasure to work for you, but there is one thing that will probably make this transfer difficult. I must tell you that I'm a staff officer of the KGB.'

Sobchak started thinking. This was really a surprise for him. Finally, he said, 'So, who gives a f**k?'[3]

After Yeltsin, Sobchak was the highest-profile Russian democrat at the time, already elected to the Lensoviet, or city council of Leningrad, and aiming higher. Since the city was largely run by and for the convenience of the extensive KGB establishment there, he was happy to have Putin on his staff and Putin's superiors were delighted that he had so quickly hit it off with Sobchak. They told him there was no need to resign from the university in order to work for Sobchak, so now Putin had two jobs.[4]

An alternative explanation of this rapid success after a mediocre early career is that his duties in the rector's office included reading all the denunciations written by or about the academic staff. Leningrad politician Boris Vishnyevski said:

[There is a] possibility that Putin came across some denunciation signed by Sobchak, and what would have happened to Sobchak's unblemished image as the father of Russian democracy if this document had been published?[5]

Putin was now what was termed an 'active reserve officer' – still employed by the KGB but working ostensibly on the staff of Sobchak – who was soon elected head of Leningrad council. This embedding of active reserve officers in powerful companies and the entourages of important people was to become an increasingly potent leverage tool of the KGB. Sobchak could have been deposed by the other members of Lensoviet, so he was grateful when his obliging aide fixed his election to the newly created post of mayor in June 1990. In his customary deadpan style, Putin recalled, 'I managed to convince [many council members] that [his] mayoral position would be beneficial for the city.'[6]

After Leningrad was renamed St Petersburg in September, Putin's reward was to be appointed head of its International

Relations Committee (IRC), where he not only controlled economic relations but also coordinated the law enforcement agencies, the Justice Department and several other important city functions. At the end of 1991 Putin was made a joint deputy mayor. Shunning the limelight, he quietly consolidated his power, thanks to Sobchak's preference for leaving the mundane day-to-day business to his assiduous deputy, who had him sign blank sheets of headed paper, later filled in as he decided. Among the busy deputy mayor's activities was the registration of several thousand commercial enterprises and the facilitation of joint business ventures with multinational companies like Coca Cola and major banks. As co-founder of a number of elite clubs, Putin also met all the richest businessmen and gang bosses when the city was known as the crime capital of Russia, as reflected in television series and films like *Banditsky Peterburg*.

In 1992, Russia's economy was foundering, but the Leningrad IRC prospered by licensing companies – some foreign and not subject to Russian oversight and others owned by criminal interests, but all handpicked by Putin – to export commodities that were supposed to be paid for in food and medicine needed by the city. 'Unfortunately,' Putin later admitted, 'some of the companies … failed to fulfil their obligations to the city.'[7] With commission fees to IRC at up to 37 per cent totalling millions of dollars, these deals resulted in no return to the city's coffers. Profits not returned to Russia vanished into extra-territorial bank accounts. When investigated for allocating these licences without authority and because of enormous discrepancies between the prices on paper and in the commodity markets, Putin denied responsibility. The investigating commission's report criticised, '… failure to supply documents, discrepancies [stemming] from attempts to conceal the true state of affairs [and Putin's] special interest in forming contracts with and issuing licences to specific individuals and firms.'[8]

IRC also went into partnership with the organised crime syndicates that controlled gambling in St Petersburg, although Putin tells it like this: 'We created a municipal enterprise that did not own any casinos, but controlled 51 per cent of the shares of the city's gambling establishments.'[9] Licences were granted by a committee of Putin, Dmitri Medvedev – then a thrusting young lawyer who was head of the city's Treasury Department – and four others. Putin said that the proceeds were to have been used to finance urgent priorities like food and housing, but unfortunately [sic], 'The casinos' owners showed us nothing but losses … they were laughing at us.'[10]

Reading that, the most objective historian has to wonder how any criminals could so obviously cheat and 'laugh at' their partners, when those partners were effectively the St Petersburg FSB – the Federal'naya Sluzhba Bezopasnosti, or retitled Second Chief Directorate of the KGB, charged with internal security.

Medvedev was also the legal adviser to IRC, in which capacity he found a neat way round the legal inhibition on any government body involving itself in a joint-stock enterprise. From this point on, such companies mushroomed bewilderingly, many sharing the same addresses and passing money to each other so rapidly that it was impossible to know what profits had been made by whom. The St Petersburg public prosecutor's office did its best to investigate all this, but was always several moves behind the Putin-Medvedev machine.

In October 1993, when Russia underwent a political crisis and Yeltsin sent the tanks in to subdue the Russian parliament, there were more urgent and weighty matters than checking the profits from casinos. In any case, Putin shrugs off allegations of corruption by saying they were politically motivated. However, the casino set-up continued for five lucrative years, although he said in one interview, 'I would have finished off these casinos, if Sobchak had not lost the 1996 elections. I would have forced them all to work for the needs of society and to share their profits with the city. The money would have gone to retired people, teachers and doctors.'[11]

That sounds very commendable, but by now Putin was living in a house worth $500,000 – considerable riches at the time for a Russian local government officer. After it was burnt down, the construction company rebuilt it for free, even more luxuriously than before. Perhaps this was a charitable gesture to a civil servant out of a job after Sobchak failed to be re-elected? Putin's former rival as joint deputy mayor was now sitting in the mayor's seat, but when Volodya went to ask him for a job, the new mayor refused to see him, saying, 'I don't want to hear any more about that ass-hole [sic].'[12]

However, *Chekisty* always look after their own. To place him well out of reach of the investigation into IRC, Putin was moved to Moscow under the auspices of Yeltsin's chief of staff, fellow-Leningrader Anatoly Chubais. Putin's first job in the capital was as deputy head of the Presidential Property Management Department (PPMD), a body set up by Yeltsin to oversee state-owned real estate in seventy-eight other countries, worth $600 billion. In the ex-GDR, for example, the withdrawal of a half-million troops left entire towns built for them dilapidated but still saleable.

Yeltsin's 1990 election campaign had given high priority to resolving the legal status and powers of the non-Russian regions of the Russian Federation. On 31 March 1992 he and Ruslan Khasbulatov, chairman of the Supreme Soviet, signed a treaty of federation with eighty-six of the eighty-eight regions, most of which were granted a degree of autonomy. A new word was invented to replace *russkii*, meaning ethnically Russian; *rossiyanin* meant a citizen of the federation, from whatever ethnicity. In the spring of 1994, Tatarstan also signed after obtaining many concessions. That left only Russia's ancient enemies, the Chechens, out in the cold, because a coup in September 1991 had declared independence, and MVD troops, sent to oust the coup leaders two months later, had been forced to withdraw.

It was one thing to let go of the European satellite states, but Chechnya was considered by the men in the Kremlin to be an intrinsic part of Russia since its difficult conquest in 1859, after which Tolstoy's 1863 novel *The Cossacks* described the constant skirmishing along the River Terek. In a replay of Claire Chennault's domino theory, the argument in the Kremlin was that if the Muslim Chechens broke away completely, all the other non-Russian regions would secede from the CIS, especially the Muslim Central Asian republics.

Inside Chechnya, the situation deteriorated rapidly, the economy failing fast and non-Chechen residents fleeing what was effectively a civil war, in which Russian financial and military support for the opposition forces was embarrassingly revealed when twenty Russian regulars and fifty mercenaries hired by the FSB were taken prisoner. On 29 November 1994, Yeltsin ordered a ceasefire. When the breakaway government refused to negotiate, Russian Defence Minister Pavel Grachev assured Yeltsin that he could complete an almost bloodless takeover in less than a month. Given the go-ahead, on 11 December Russian forces launched a three-pronged ground attack on the Chechen capital Grozny, which halted prematurely after the commanding general resigned in protest, as did Afghan veteran General Gromov, who foresaw that the war would be 'another Afghanistan'.[13]

Another 800 officers and men refused to fight, eighty-three being court-martialled and the others discharged from the service.

Despite atrocity bombing of civilian targets, and thousands of reinforcements being sent in, on the Russian side there were officially 5,500 deaths, although many double that figure, while Chechnya claims that 160,000 independence fighters and civilians died or are 'missing' after attacks by Russian aircraft and tanks.[14] On the plains and in the cities, sheer force of arms could often win the day, given Russian superiority in numbers and equipment, but eventual widespread demoralisation of the invading troops and hostility to the war at home forced Yeltsin to order a withdrawal in August 1996.

Amazingly, despite failure of his war in Chechnya and of his free-enterprise reforms, Yeltsin staged another surprise comeback, being re-elected president of the Russian Republic in July 1996. By this time, Putin had managed to dispossess all other government departments that had claims on Russia's properties abroad. Building a body of 'grateful friends', he staffed the PPMD with former colleagues. One of them remarked, 'My work consisted of trying to bring some order into use of Russia's foreign possessions and of returning to the government what it had once owned and lost due to poor management. Sometimes, things came to light that made your hair stand on end.'

Putin's thinning hair is never out of place but one of the 'things that came to light' was the formation of companies to sell off the more valuable real estate. Since the properties could be transferred to parties in those countries with prices decided by the PPMD, which might or might not be the prices shown in contracts, the differences amounted to millions of dollars vanished into the pockets of those involved.[15] The game was fairly widespread at the time. After Putin's nominal boss Pavel Borodin issued a contract to a Swiss company to renovate the Grand Palace in the Kremlin for $492 million, Swiss investigators found that this sum included commissions of $62 million, of which $25 million went into the Swiss bank accounts of Borodin, his daughter and son-in-law.[16]

The economic hiccups in the transition from the command economy of the USSR to a compromise market economy were accompanied by a matching series of upheavals in Russian society generally, during which enormous fortunes were amassed. Aristotle used the term *oligarchia* to mean unjust rule by a few men of evil intent, whereas aristocracy was originally rule by the best individuals of a society. At the end of 1966, Alexander Solzhenitsyn wrote:

> Skilful members of the upper and middle echelons of the old Communist government, together with parvenus who have suddenly acquired wealth by devious means, have formed a stable and closed oligarchy of about 150–200 individuals, which decides the fate of the nation. [Driven] by a shared lust for power and money, they display no higher motives to serve the Fatherland and the people.[17]

In March 1997, Putin stepped up from the PPMD to the post of Yeltsin's deputy chief of staff and head of the government's Main Control Directorate, announcing his intention to prosecute abuses in regional government. Miraculously, during the fifteen months he spent in this job, despite a wealth of incriminating evidence against many of the eighty-nine regional governors, no one appears to have been prosecuted.

In July 1998, Putin was named head of the presidential commission charged with demarcating federal and regional authority in post-USSR Russia – still an area of conflicting laws. After only ten days in that job, he was promoted by Yeltsin to director of the FSB. This meteoric rise raised eyebrows within the organisation, where his subordinates all knew of his uninspiring KGB career and were unimpressed by his substantive service rank of lieutenant-colonel.

At the time, most FSB officers in St Petersburg and Moscow were also in the protection and security business to augment their inadequate salaries. Putin's first move was to sack 2,000 officers, including all those in the economic departments and the senior generals, moving into these key positions more old comrades from his Leningrad days, new to Moscow and therefore unswervingly loyal to him. It was a brilliant move, followed by an even better one when he re-appointed all the dismissed officers in six newly formed departments after a month in the wilderness to show them who was boss. Whatever enemies he made kept quiet after he agreed pay rises that gave parity with colleagues in the SVRR, formerly the elite KGB First Chief Directorate.

When the Swiss investigation of the Kremlin renovation scandal primed Russia's General Prosecutor Yuri Skuratov to bring charges against important people in Yeltsin's entourage, the mode chosen to neutralise him was pure old KGB-style entrapment. In a specially rented apartment, a videotape was made of 'a man resembling General Prosecutor Skuratov' having sex with two prostitutes. Skuratov fought back until the videotape was shown on television.

On 9 August 1999 Boris Yeltsin created a third deputy prime ministerial post and appointed Putin to it. On the same day, Prime Minister Sergei Stepashin was dismissed and Putin promoted to acting prime minister. His constitutional eligibility for this was the deputy premiership he had held *for a few hours*. True, he was Yeltsin's fifth prime minister in less than a year, but the president said on television, 'I have now decided to name a person who, in my opinion, can bring society together [and] ensure the continuation of reforms in Russia. This is the secretary of Russia's Security Council, the Director of the FSB, Vladimir Vladimirovich Putin.'[18]

In September 1999, Chechen Islamic terrorists were blamed for a series of terror bombings in Russia, which many people believed to be the work of special forces and FSB provocateurs after an incident in Ryazan, some 130 miles south-east of Moscow. Residents there surprised several men placing sacks of hexogen explosive with a timer set for 5.30 a.m. in the basement of an apartment block. Accosted, the perpetrators produced FSB identity cards and fled. After some confusion, the local authorities announced that the yellow granulated substance in the sacks was sugar and new FSB director Nikolai Patrushev claimed it was all an exercise to keep the local police on their toes.

Were the bombings carried out by Chechen terrorists or provocateurs? If by terrorists, why did the Kremlin seal all files relating to Ryazan for seventy-five years, and why did Duma deputies and journalists who pursued this trail die off like witnesses in Dallas after Kennedy was shot?[19]

The bombings were used by Prime Minister Vladimir Putin in October 1999 to declare the Chechen government of Aslan Maskhadov illegitimate. A new invasion 'to restore constitutional order' was announced. Eleven days later, Russian ground forces crossed the River Terek and advanced in two columns on Grozny. With memories of the previous invasion still fresh, more than a quarter of the population fled the artillery and air bombardments, seeking asylum abroad.

The winter siege of Grozny left the city totally devastated in a way that has not been seen in Europe since the end of the Second World War. If anyone wondered where the Chechen independence fighters and their Muslim allies from many countries had obtained the weapons with which they desperately defended their ruined country, the answer appears to be that they were 'left behind' after the previous invasion in return for multi-million dollar bribes paid to three of Yeltsin's close associates in the state armament company Rosvooruzhenie.[20] Nevertheless, within a few weeks, Russian forces occupied 80 per cent of Chechnya. On 6 December, Putin proudly announced that Grozny was to be bombed flat, together with any residents who chose to stay there. Even for a Russian premier, such language was harsh. The threat was modified shortly afterwards to apply only to 'terrorists and bandits' in Grozny.[21] How they were to be distinguished from the general population was not made clear.

On 31 December 1999, Boris Yeltsin announced his resignation and named Prime Minister Vladimir Putin acting president of the Russian Federation. The choice was not difficult. A communist successor would have put Yeltsin in jail for shelling the White House; a democrat would have done the same for starting the Chechen wars. Putin and his ex-KGB 'family' did not care about things like that. His first official act was to grant immunity from prosecution to Yeltsin for any illegal acts committed during his administration. As the year 2000 dawned, they could both congratulate themselves that things had turned out rather well, all things considered.

In the election held in March 2000, Putin was duly elected president with a lot of help from old friends, winning 52.9 per cent of votes. As to how they were counted – or, if for the wrong candidate, not counted – it would take another book to tell that story. Yet his clean-cut and athletic appearance and efficient, brisk, manner were preferred by the voters to boozing, bottom-pinching Boris.

Perhaps unaware of Tacitus' dictum 'they make a desert and call it peace', Putin claimed then that Chechnya had been 'pacified'. Yet, on 23 October 2002, Chechen women, whose menfolk had been killed by Russian forces, strapped explosives to themselves in a Moscow theatre, which was stormed by security troops using poison gas at a cost in lives of 129 hostages and thirty-nine of the Chechen women. On 1 September 2004, a group of armed Chechens demanding an end to the Second Chechen War took 777 children and over 300 adults hostage at a school in Beslan, in the North Ossetian region of the Russian Federation. On day three of the siege, Putin's anti-terrorist operation stormed the school using tanks, rockets and other heavy weapons. In the ensuing battle between the hostage-takers and Russian security forces at least 334 hostages were killed, including 186 children, with hundreds more wounded or reported missing.[22] What Western president could have talked his way out of that?

According to BBC News Online, the Second Chechen war did not end until 16 April 2009, by which time it was estimated that pollution by bombing of oil storage areas and chemical plants and the destruction of sewage systems had contaminated Chechnya's water resources to a depth of 650-plus feet with heavy metals and other poisons. As much as 40 per cent of the country was considered in a condition of 'ecological disaster' and another 40 per cent termed 'a zone of extreme environmental distress'. Is it coincidence that the two zones equal the area occupied by Russia in the second invasion?

In 2006 it was Georgia's turn to feel the knout. From March to May Russia imposed import restrictions on Georgian wine and spirits, vegetables, fruit and mineral water. On 8 July the only land crossing was closed, halting all exports to Russia. On 27 September, Georgian President Mikhail Saakashvili arrested four GRU officers accused of planning a pro-Moscow coup and paraded them before television cameras. Russia recalled its ambassador in Tbilisi and cut postal, phone and banking links, with Gazprom hiking the price for gas deliveries from $110 per thousand cubic metres to $230. Within Russia, anyone with a Georgian name became a target for police harrassment or deportation.[23]

In compliance with the Russian Constitution, after completing his second presidential term in May 2008, Putin stepped down from the presidency to become prime minister again, swapping jobs with Dmitri Medvedev. The dip in salary, moving from the president's office to that of the prime minister, would not worry Vladimir Putin. Among his acquisitions on the road to power are, according to one source, 37 per cent of oil-producing giant Surgutneftgaz worth $20 billion and 4.5 per cent of major gas producer Gazprom worth $13 billion, plus many other perks picked up along the way.[24] Western intelligence trackers say his personal fortune is 'only' $11 billion; a well-informed Swedish source puts it several times higher.[25] Every country has its share of political corruption, but such figures are difficult for Westerners to credit – which is why the ultra-staid and reliable *Economist* carried an article in its 27 November 2008 edition on the scale of corruption in Russia, estimated to siphon off $300 billion per year, or 20 per cent of Russia's GDP.

They make a classic good-cop-bad-cop pair: the unsmiling, hard-as-nails Putin and his smooth lawyer partner, Medvedev, relaxed and smiling for the cameras. Medvedev can afford to smile: for the lives or liberty of a few hundred uncoopera-tive bankers, over-confident business tycoons and inquisitive journalists, Putin and he have established what historian Yuri Felshtinsky calls 'Corporate Russia'. This is Russia run by *kontora* – 'the firm' – in which most of the money and power are, as Solzhenitsyn wrote, in the hands of a few hundred *siloviki* – men of power, many of them drawn from the former KGB[26] and happy to use threatening tactics internationally and violence and corruption at home to achieve their ends. Independent think-tank Transparency International considers Russia's widespread corruption to place it at an all-time low between Niger and Sierra Leone. In 2005, democracy watchdog Freedom House considered that Russia 'had experienced the largest decline in democratic standards among all former Communist states'.[27]

The other important element in *kontora* is made up of lawyers – many from Leningrad/St Petersburg like Medvedev. They have elaborated a strategy of acquiring shares in colossal investments 'downstream' in the gas-consuming countries, where their partner companies put up most of the cost and exert leverage on their governments to go along with Russian plans and ensure that Western stock exchanges freely trade shares in Russian companies whose assets have been acquired by threat and theft.

Putin's side of the *dvoika* is less subtle, still in the bully-boy stance of the old KGB. No Western politician protests too loudly about the routinely intercepted flights by Russian military aircraft over Germany or Britain, but when they overfly Georgia and Chechnya, which have virtually no anti-aircraft defences, they are far more menacing, especially if the aircraft are attack helicopters firing cannons and rockets at inhabited villages. When Latvians, Estonians and Lithuanians see Russian aircraft overflying their small countries end-to-end in minutes, their only defence is a single squadron of fighters borrowed from NATO, which is no deterrent to a serious incursion.

The governments in Tallinn, Vilnius and Riga remember how the Western democracies did nothing when Hitler 'protected German-speakers' by annexing the Sudetenland from Czechoslovakia in 1938, leading to the invasion of Poland and a war that killed millions. In April 2000, Putin categorised 'discrimination against Russian-speakers' in the near-abroad as 'a military threat facing Russia'. Massive Russian manoeuvres took place in 2007 on the borders of Latvia and Estonia, simulating a reconquest of those countries 'to protect the Russian-speaking minorities there'.[28]

Was this a threat or a warning? After the paralysing cyber-attack that punished Estonia for re-siting the Soviet war memorial in 2007, the Russian government youth newspaper *Konsomolskaya Pravda* published a clear answer under the heading 'The day of victory comes again – forward to Tallinn, soldiers defending [Russia]'. The verse below was doggerel, but the message was clear:

A short forced march and Tallinn falls.
They may say public opinion will be against it
now that Estonia is in NATO.
So what? Who in NATO cares?
So what if they call it an occupation?
They will grumble and grind their teeth,
saying freedom's flame is doused again,
but we will settle with those greedy swine
who would sell their father and mother for gas.
I am not scared to tell you, Estonians,
the EU will not be able to help you.[29]

Is that the bombast of a shrinking world power? The gas and oil reserves will not last forever and some demographers predict that poor health care and a very low birth-rate among ethnic Russians will bring their numbers below 100 million by 2050, against the rising birth-rate in the Islamic Central Asian republics and a population of over 1.3 *billion* in neighbouring China.

There is more to it than that. Flushed with their ill-gotten personal prosperity after seventy years of scant private wealth in Russia, its leaders believe that the near-abroad, in which 25 million ethnic Russians still live, is theirs by right and deeply resent Western intrusion into it by granting membership of the European Union and NATO to these countries. There is even a body of opinion in Western corridors of power that these countries should be written off, in order not to incite the bear to show his teeth.[30]

PART 4:
UPDATE FOR THE SECOND EDITION

28

THE POT AND
THE KETTLE

In the five years that have passed since the first edition went to press, what has happened in the Russian Federation and how, if at all, has its foreign policy changed?

One thing is certain: geopolitically, Russia is centre-stage. That sober magazine *The Economist* lavished one-third of its 2013 covers on images of the voracious Russian bear and/or a usually bare-chested Putin. Macho photographs of him are ubiquitous, hunting, fishing, sailing, horse riding and arriving at biker rallies astride a powerful machine. As foreseen earlier, Putin took back the presidency for a third term in 2012. In compliance with the rules of the election campaign, he declared his annual income, claiming it was equivalent to $113,000. This caused one of the other candidates to wonder how he had managed to indulge the old Russian obsession with wrist-watches by assembling a collection of luxury timepieces worth $700,000. In addition to twenty palatial residences – the US president has two, but the British royal family has many more – Putin's true personal wealth is estimated by various reliably informed sources at between 40 and 70 *billion* US dollars. With that many zeroes, the margin of error hardly matters.

The political party he founded in 2001, Yedinaya Rossiya – meaning One Russia[1] – gained 64 per cent of the votes in the 2007 Duma elections, which declined to 49.32 per cent in the 2011 elections, but it is still by far the largest party in the Russian Federation. In one phase of the swap-around between Putin and Medvedev, the latter became chairman of the party, for what that was worth.

The main event of 2010 was the long, hot summer breaking records that had stood for more than a century in Russia. Vast, uncontrollable wild fires ravaged the forests, creating smoke clouds visible from space. The drought was so disastrous for agriculture that exports of grain were forbidden. Prices inside Russia soared and the resultant shortage on the international market was blamed on the Russian government, which was somewhat unfair, since every good government looks after its own first.

At the twelfth One Russia party congress in 2011, then current president Medvedev sponsored Putin to replace him in the 2012 presidential election. To no one's surprise, then current prime minister Putin in turn proposed Medvedev to run for the premiership. The 10,000-plus members attending the congress approved overwhelmingly, but outside the party, many former supporters drifted away at this added proof that Putin was playing at being a new type of Tsar.

Although some 30 per cent of voters were still said to support One Russia, it was dubbed by its enemies *partiya zhulikov i vorov* – the party of crooks and thieves. In December 2011, Putin shrugged off the accusation, saying that corruption was not peculiar to his party, but just an inevitable side-effect of power – a remark that no Western leader would have dared to make, however true. He also promised that One Russia would stamp it out *after* his return to the presidency following the March 2012 elections. A growing number of opposition supporters showed what they thought of this communist-era double-talk by taking to the streets in Moscow – where 5,000 marched – and other major cities, during early December 2011, protesting at the official announcement that *only* 11.5 per cent of the 1,100 officially reported election frauds had been confirmed. Among the most blatant were the many cases of 'carousel voting', where One

Russia voters were bussed from one polling station to several others in order to cast multiple votes. Where buses were lacking, trucks were 'borrowed' from nearby army bases.

At least 300 demonstrators were arrested, some of them sentenced to terms of imprisonment for chanting, '*Doloi Putina*!' 'Down with Putin.' Among other slogans was, '*Rossiya bez Putina*!' 'Russia without Putin.' Armed MVD troops were called out to discourage further protests, a government spokesman having announced that 'unsanctioned' demonstrations had to be stopped by the forces of order. In an unlikely alliance, neither the Communist Party of the Russian Federation nor Orthodox Patriarch Kiril accepted the election results. In his subsequent Christmas broadcast, Kiril asked the government to pardon the demonstrators.

Observers from the Organisation for Security and Cooperation in Europe (OSCE) – to which the Russian Federation belongs – considered that the coming presidential elections were also slanted in favour of One Russia and Putin. US Secretary of State Hillary Clinton echoed this sentiment and Republican Senator John McCain trod on even more Russian toes by tweeting a warning for Putin to behave. In reply, Medvedev predictably retorted that the West had no business commenting on Russia's political system.

In its edition of 11 December 2011, *The Economist* printed its Moscow correspondent's report on a different kind of demo by young and professional people that had taken place the previous day, largely organised via Facebook's *Subbota na Bolotnoi Ploshchadi*, or Saturday-at-Bolotnaya-Square page. Moscow Council's choice of this place for the rally was ominous: it had traditionally been used for public executions of rebels, in particular Stenka Razin in 1671 and Yemelyan Pugachoff in 1775. Since 30,000 Facebook users had said they would attend, the Moscow city council approved the attendance of 30,000 people. The federation government then did its best to minimise attendance with anonymous spoof telephone calls to the independent media and, most bizarrely, a warning from chief public health official, Gennady Onishchenko, that so many protesters gathering together risked giving each other respiratory infections such as flu or the SARS coronavirus. The police also publicised a warning that they would be scanning the crowd for draft dodgers, who would be immediately arrested. School pupils and older students were ordered into the classrooms at the time scheduled for the demonstration for an obligatory examination or extra classes. Opposition Twitter posts were spammed by a government botnet. *Daily Telegraph* Moscow correspondent Andrew Osborn was not the only Western observer to note that the mobile phone network in the area seemed to have been switched off during the demo. *The Economist* report on the Bolotnaya Square protest read in part:

> Tens of thousands of middle-class Muscovites held a peaceful rally in the centre of Moscow, the biggest such event since the early 1990s. Astonishingly, there was not a single arrest. Indeed, some of the thousands of policemen and interior-ministry troops showed sympathy for the protestors.
>
> This was an uplifting display of both dignity and indignation. Citizens were riled not only about the electoral fraud, but at being treated as imbeciles by their leader, Vladimir Putin. There was anger at the Kremlin [and Putin and One Russia], but no aggression. The crowd contained not only liberals but also Communists, anarchists and some nationalists. But protestors were almost conspicuously polite towards each other. Some carried white flowers, which they tried to give to the police. They made jokes. '146% of Muscovites are for free elections' one sign read. Another said: 'I did not vote for these bastards. I voted for other bastards. I demand a recount.'[2]

The police later announced that an estimated 25,000 people took part, whereas the organisers claimed 50–60,000. Similar, but smaller, demos took place in cities from St Petersburg on the Baltic to Vladivostok in the Pacific Far East and some ninety other cities in between. Although Putin warned that any unrest would be ruthlessly suppressed, most of these events passed off peacefully, with the worst repression in Kazan, where 100 arrests of young people were made.

The crowd at Bolotnaya Square was addressed by media figures and liberal politicians, who claimed that nationwide arrests the previous week had reached four figures and demanded the release of all those detained. Another important demand was for the recognition of all opposition parties, not only those sanctioned by the Kremlin. Demonstrations on a lesser scale continued throughout the winter in many cities. During the campaign, Putin made only one major speech – to a claimed audience of 100,000 supporters, who cheered themselves hoarse when he uttered Molotov's Second World War slogan, '*Pobeda budyet za nami*!' 'Victory will be ours!' The Liberal Democratic candidate Vladimir Zhirinovsky chose as a more original slogan, '*Zhirinovskii, ili budyet khuzhe!*' '[Vote for] Zhirinovsky, or things will get worse.' He also demonstrated what his political label meant in Russia by calling famous pop star Alla Pugacheva, who supported another candidate, a prostitute. Just as Russian as he, she retorted, 'I thought you were a clever politician, but you're just a clown and a psycho!'

On 2 March 2012, retiring president Dmitri Medvedev made a speech on national television channels, inviting all citizens to vote in the presidential election to be held on 4 March, in which five candidates had been approved and ten rejected for various reasons, two of those being women. And One Russia gained a surprise supporter. Patriarch Kiril proclaimed his disapproval of pre-election protests on the grounds that they would coincide with the beginning of the Orthodox Lent. On the same day, reciprocating Putin's many public overtures towards the Orthodox Church, he openly endorsed him as the Church's approved candidate for president.

There were 108 million people eligible to vote in 95,000 polling stations. Officially, Vladimir Putin received 63.64 per cent of votes cast and, due to a change in the constitution, was the first president to be elected for a six-year term. OSCE observers assessed the election positively on balance, but said that the vote counting in one-third of polling stations left much to be desired. For his part, Putin shrugged off allegations of vote-fixing not by denying them, but by alleging that it made little difference to the outcome.

On 6 May 2012, the day before Putin's inauguration for his third term, fresh protests broke out in Moscow. In renewed scuffles, police arrested some 400 people. Official sources said that *only* eighty had been injured. With more protests the following day, another 120 were arrested in Moscow alone. To make sure the people got his message, Putin pushed through new legislation in June, banning unauthorised protests and imposing heavier penalties for participants in such events. Tsar Vladimir was back in the Kremlin, his feet firmly under the desk.

What did the rest of the world make of this? There is a metaphor from the time when cooking was done over open fires and soot gathered on cooking vessels. When two parties equally lacking in innocence were accusing each other, people used to say it was 'the pot calling the kettle black'. And so it was here. Russia's main Cold War enemy the United States was bloodily edging its way out of the second Iraq war, long years after international investigators had found no weapons of mass destruction or any evidence of a link between Saddam Hussein and al-Qaeda – the two most prominent 'justifications' advanced when President George W. Bush declared war. There was also increasing unease in Washington about Iran's nuclear intentions.

Independent commentator John Miller, a former senior NATO intelligence analyst writing in the Australian online magazine *National Observer*, was not alone in observing, '… it's quite fascinating that a country, with which the US was toe-to-toe under the threat of a nuclear exchange for the best part of three-quarters of a century, tends to be of little apparent concern [there] these days.'[3]

Hypocrisy will never go out of fashion among politicians but, as Miller's article, entitled 'The West's failure to understand Putin's Russia', pointed out, this lack of overt criticism was due to the United States' preoccupation with domestic issues, its War on Terror, the entanglement in an increasingly hostile Afghanistan and the political unrest spreading throughout the Middle East that was originally dubbed somewhat optimistically the Arab Spring.

It was also difficult for Western leaders to point the finger at Russia when protests against the enormous and increasing disparity of wealth in their own countries gained media attention with the Occupy Wall Street demo of September 2011 in New York. Three weeks later, this had spread to nearly 1,000 other cities in 82 countries. By mid-November the forces of law and order were breaking up the Occupy camps and arresting key figures; by the end of February 2012 most visible signs of Occupy had been removed. This, conveniently for Putin, covered the main period of protests in Russia.

Simplifying its slogan, Occupy inferred that 1 per cent of Americans owned 99 per cent of US wealth. Independent economists estimated the true figures showed that the richest 20 per cent of Americans owned 85 per cent of the country's wealth. Other methods of calculating wealth showed that the less wealthy 80 per cent of the population actually only owned something like 7 per cent of wealth. In addition, the corporate mega-rich used the forces of law and order to suppress popular demonstrations against, for example, bankers' manipulations that deprived people of their homes. The establishment – a euphemism for the richest stratum of capitalist society – also blatantly exploited modern technology in collaboration with government agencies to snoop on those who wanted reform.

In an earlier book,[4] the author mentioned how the American COMINT agency NSA monitors British government, military and civilian communications via an out-station in the embassy in Grosvenor Square, with *all* British telephone, telex and data transmissions being fed by dedicated landline from the telecoms tower at Hunter's Stones to the world's largest SIGINT facility at Menwith Hill in Yorkshire[5] and thence to the Kray super-computers in NSA's HQ in Fort Meade, Maryland. At Chicksands in Bedfordshire, US Air Force Security Service (USAFSS) similarly monitors and records civil and military transmissions of its NATO allies and other European countries, including Britain.

In 2013 the world learned from Edward Snowden, who had been working for Booz Allen Hamilton, an important contractor employed by the NSA, about Prism and other programmes known as SIGADs, which are covert 'data mining systems' that have been sweeping up just about everything happening on the Internet since 2007 by forcing and/or paying companies like Google, Microsoft, and Yahoo to disclose communications, the identities of those involved and their geographical locations. On 6 June 2013, the *Guardian* and the *Washington Post* carried the story, which Snowden had been preparing by downloading secret files for a year. They also mentioned NSA snooping on telephone conversations. The subsequent statements from President Obama and others in Washington that these programmes were used under legal control and therefore not intrusive rang rather hollow. Snowden made his first disclosures while in Hong Kong, then flew to Moscow for asylum, which was granted for one year, since he was liable to a long prison term if he returned to the US. A spate of global protests led to comments by those in power including British Prime Minister David Cameron and Foreign Minister William Hague assuring the public that everything was under control. As the satirical publication *Private Eye* says on these occasions, 'So that's all right, then.' So GCHQ in Britain and the Bundesnachrichtendienst could happily continue to share data with NSA.[6] According to Snowden, NSA had and has similar arrangements with many other SIGINT organisations, so arranged that national leaders could truthfully deny they personally knew anything about this collaboration.

Despite United States prosecutors charging Snowden on 14 June 2013 with espionage and theft of government property, the disclosures continued throughout the year, a significant proportion of his estimated 1.7 million downloaded documents being obtained and published in part by responsible journals in many countries. In December 2013 *Guardian* editor Alan Rusbridger told a Parliamentary committee, 'We have published, I think, twenty-six documents so far out of the 58,000 we've seen.' These 58,000 were just the files that directly referred to the UK. Protest organisations in many countries sprang up at this breach of what were considered normal civil liberties in a democratic country. In April 2014, Brazil became the first country to make spying on all its citizens illegal.

With Western media concentrating on all these domestic problems, apart from denizens of the intelligence community, no one seemed to be talking about the ever-increasing industrial espionage of SVR and the quiet beavering away of the GRU. This organisation was still executing its Cold War task of keeping up with Western military intentions although, from time to time, Western media exposed such incidents as the Russian mistress of a British MP with access to confidential material, or the group of ten deep-cover agents of SVR deported from the USA in 2011, after a long surveillance by the FBI. A major task of CIA analysts and their colleagues in London and Cheltenham was to attempt to work out exactly who was in charge of what in Moscow. Lending them a hand, Russian sociologist Dr Olga Kryshtanovskaya helpfully analysed the background of 1,016 siloviki or 'men of power', such as the super-rich, politicians, functionaries in the presidential administration, members of government, deputies of both houses of parliament and heads of regional government.

As reported by John Miller, she found that 26 per cent admitted a background of service in the KGB or its associated and successor agencies. The true figure, however, after allowing for unexplained gaps in their public résumés, alleged but unlikely career paths or service in organisations affiliated with the KGB or in the military[7] suggested that the true figure of ex-Chekisty in positions of power or wealth was a startling 78 per cent. And as Putin has many times averred, 'There is no such thing as a former Chekist'. Being an ex-KGB active service officer and having served as a reserve officer at the outset of his political career, he should know better than most. This makes for a very cosy and exclusive relationship between the men running the Russian Federation and the state organs of FSB (internal security) and SVR (external espionage).

Miller concludes that the political system now called Putinism is characterised by a slow and steady concentration of ultimate power into a few hands, especially in the power and energy sectors. Given that the Soviet Union's vast military has been much reduced and much of its Cold War materiel is rusting away, it is Russia's huge natural resources that are Putin's weapons to achieve leverage in Europe in the near future. But these are not so effective against the Muslim former Soviet republics like Kazakhstan, Kyrgyzstan, Tajikistan, Turkmenistan and Uzbekistan. In the Caucasus the same enemy lurks in Abkhazia, Chechnya, Dagestan and North Ossetia. And supplying arms to

Middle Eastern countries, which is an important source of for-eign exchange for Russia, brings the risk of those arms eventually being used against Russian soldiers. One of the arms buyers was Assad's Syria and here Putin did the world a favour by defusing a planned US-France operation to use air strikes against Assad's chemical weapons stocks after the Al-Ghouta sarin attack on 21 August 2013, for which responsibility is disputed. Leaving aside how one attacks such a target without releasing any of the toxic gases, this was part of Washington's intention of usurp-ing Assad's government in the vague hope of replacing it with a 'democratic' regime – something that has not happened in any other Arab country. The outcome of the Putin-Obama strong-arm contest was an international initiative to *remove* all the Syrian government's chemical weapons which could have been used against anti-government forces.

It is in Syria that a new relationship between Russia and the USA was first tested. Washington appeared on the point of ignoring the lessons of its previous intrusions into the Middle East quagmire by supporting the Syrian rebels to bring down the government – as though this would lead automatically to the installation of a democratic successor. No official in Washington seems to have objected on the grounds that many of the 'rebels' are neither Syrian nor rebels, but foreign jihadists who include members of al-Qaeda and its affiliated factions fighting an inter-necine war to crush the Alawite sect to which Assad belongs. Most Americans would not wish to see their tax money spent on arming and equipping these people, who would be regarded as terrorists in the US.

29

AFTER UKRAINE, THE DELUGE?

Russia also has its problem with Muslims, especially the near neighbours in Chechnya, Dagestan and other Caucasian states. To Doku Umarov, leader of the Caucasian Emirate – an umbrella organisation for all the autonomous extremist groups – it seemed like a gift from Allah when Russia's bid to host the 2014 Winter Games was accepted by the International Olympics Committee. To be held in and near Sochi, the event would make a wonderful target for terrorist attacks. The city had become rich Russians' winter capital after Khrushchev gave the Crimea to Ukraine in 1954. With its mild climate on the Black Sea Riviera, but with snow-covered mountains within easy reach, it was an ideal location, except for its proximity to the border with Georgia, 2.5 miles to the south, and to the Caucasian Muslim republics.

With several thousand migrant workers employed on the multiple sites at Sochi, the suicide bombers started work in Autumn 2013. On 21 October, Naida Asiyalova, a 30-year-old woman from Dagestan, blew up herself and a bus full of people in the city of Volgograd, 400 miles north of Sochi. Her device was an explosive belt containing half a kilogram of TNT.

Seven other passengers were killed and at least thirty-six others injured. Because so many drivers there use car cams to prove their innocence in the frequent accidents on the roads of Russia, the explosion was recorded by a car following the bus. On 16 November, Russian security forces tracked down Asiyalova's husband, killing him and four other terrorists of his group.

In early December, a presidential decree shut down the news agency RIA Novosti, which had gained international respect for its balanced treatment of the anti-Putin demos. Although no official reason was given, it was assumed that Putin wanted a more controllable news agency reporting what went on in Russia.

On 27 December a car bomb exploded in Pyatigorsk, only 170 miles east of Sochi, damaging a government building and causing some casualties. At 12.45 p.m. local time on 29 December – with only six weeks to go before the opening of the Olympics – security cameras caught the fireball blowing out the windows of Volgograd's main train station as another female suicide bomber detonated her device just before she would have set off the metal detector at the main entrance. She killed several travellers and maimed many more. At the time, the station was packed with family groups travelling to celebrate the New Year with relatives. On the following day, a trolley bus was blown up in the same city, bringing the total of dead that week to thirty-four, with scores more injured and shocked. Both NATO and White House spokesmen expressed sympathy and horror.

Thousands of local residents had been forcibly resettled from the Sochi area, their home and land compulsorily purchased for stadia and the outlying sites, plus the road and rail links giving access to the sites, an extension of the airport, an entirely new sewage treatment facility and a cutting edge television, Internet and cell phone infrastructure. After the bombings, security was stepped up to a level not seen in Russia since the end of the USSR. Far from complaining, people living near Sochi said it made them feel secure.

The original global budget for the games had been $12 billion, but expenditure climbed eventually to over $51 billion, making this the most expensive Olympics ever. However, in a typically Putinesque solution to this budget overrun, Tsar

Vladimir 'invited' a number of oligarchs to do him a personal favour and pay for this stadium or that development project. They, of course, were delighted to comply out of the profits they had amassed from exploitation of what had formerly been state property. Even so, the pre-Olympic period was marred by many allegations of corruption between contractors and officials awarding the contracts. There were also concerns that gay and lesbian athletes and visitors to the Games might be harassed under Russia's recent anti-gay legislation.

To win some hearts and minds, Putin announced an amnesty for those convicted of non-violent crimes and the convicted mothers of young children – the latter category including two members of the punk feminist band Pussy Riot still detained in separate hard-regime jails for desecrating Moscow's Cathedral of Christ the Saviour on 21 February 2012. Although their 'performance' was halted by cathedral officials, it had already been videoed and was uploaded to the Internet that evening entitled *Punk Prayer – Mother of God, chase Putin away!* The women taking part said that the event showed what they thought about Patriarch Kiril's endorsement of Putin's election campaign. Two members of the group fled Russia, but the other three who had taken part were arrested and charged with 'hooliganism motivated by religious hatred' on 16 March. Held in custody into 17 August, they were sentenced to two years' imprisonment. Outside Russia, pop icons protested, but Putin reflected what most Russian thought when he shrugged, 'They got what they deserved.'

In the December clemency, Putin also pardoned the former owner of the Yukos oil company, the oligarch Mikhail Khodorkovskii, who looked remarkably fit and well-fed after being released on 20 December, having served ten years for tax evasion, theft and fraud. Cynics assumed that Khodorkovskii, formerly Russia's richest man, with his own political ambitions, had bought his Get-Out-Of-Jail card in some undisclosed deal with the Kremlin. Exceptionally lucid when interviewed by the media after flying into Berlin a few hours later, Khodorkovskii said he had no intention of returning to Russia, despite having been informed that he faced no further prosecution back home.

Although independent of Russian hegemony since August 1991, Ukraine was known as 'Little Russia' in the nineteenth century, in the same way that Belarus is literally 'White Russia'. The name Ukraine comes from the Slavic root *krai*, meaning in this sense a borderland or march. Like most such territories, its history is of repeated war with neighbours, most importantly Belarus, Moldova, Hungary, Russia, Romania and Poland, but also the Ottoman Empire; even Sweden was in this game for a while. Historically – and this is important for understanding the troubles there beginning in 2012 – the stretch of land making up the modern state of Ukraine was inhabited predominantly in the east by the Don Cossacks and in the west by the Zaporozhian Cossaks, or Cossacks 'beyond the rapids'. There were a number of other Cossack hosts in the Caucasus and the generic term 'Cossack' was taken as meaning a free person who did not fit into feudal Russian society. Notwithstanding this, many thousands of Cossacks did serve as mercenary cavalry in the Imperial Russian armies, were used to restore civil order at times and fought on both sides in the Civil War.

In the eighteenth and nineteenth centuries, more Russian speakers found their way south into this territory. By the beginning of the twentieth century, Russians formed the largest single ethnic group in the main cities, ranging from 54 per cent in Kiev to over 60 per cent in Sevastopol and Yalta on the Crimean peninsula, where, as already related, many residents never heard the Ukrainian language spoken. To complicate the political geography, when Stalin forcibly exiled the Turkic Crimean Tatars to Central Asia in 1944, he repopulated their homeland with more Russians than Ukrainians. In 1954, after his death, the Supreme Soviet of the USSR transferred the peninsula to the Ukrainian SSR which, of course, was a member state of the USSR at the time. This had the effect of increasing the Russian population of Ukraine by nearly 1 million people. However, in 1997 a treaty between the Russian Federation and Ukraine recognised Ukraine's sovereignty over the Crimea. A process of increasing 'Ukrainianisation' saw Russian-language schools being closed and pupils forced to take lessons in Ukrainian, which was declared the republic's sole official language. Russian cultural and religious institutions were also vandalised repeatedly, including during the 2004 Orange Revolution – which was not a revolution but a nationwide protest over the economic situation and corruption in the presidential elections that year, of which the second round saw the presidency awarded to Viktor Yanukovych, who shared with Josef Stalin a childhood as a barefoot street urchin and who had two convictions for assault in his early adult life. Of mixed Russian, Polish and Belarusian origins, Yanukovych came from the predominantly Russian-speaking east of the country and enjoyed most support in the Russophone south and east of Ukraine.

In 2013, Yanukovych defied the Ukrainian Parliament by refusing the IMF's demand that 'the Greek solution' of austerity and devaluation be applied to Ukraine's ailing economy. As unrest in the streets grew, the US Assistant Secretary of State Victoria Nuland was one of many foreigners to fly into Kiev and support the protesters, handing out cookies to those near her in Maidan Nezalezhnosti or Independence Square. The main motivation of the crowds in the streets and squares of Kiev for the initially peaceful demonstrations was their expressed desire for membership of the European Union, which they believed would make them more prosperous. They were unaware that it would most probably have seen their country joining Greece, Spain and Portugal as another exploited 'third class' member of the Union, while their assets and natural resources were plundered by Western institutions.

With the protests against Yanukovych gaining force amid increasing violence, on the night of 21–22 February – as shown on a video released on Youtube – a man, a woman, their luggage and a small dog were taken on board a helicopter at what appeared to be a military airfield outside Kiev. This was apparently the departure of Yanukovych for Kharkiv, one of his power bases in eastern Ukraine. The crucial later stage of his journey was by boat from the Crimean port of Simferopol to a Russian Black Sea port after a private aircraft in which he was planning to fly to Russia from Donetsk was refused permission to take off by border police.

On 22 February – the same day that President Yanukovych was impeached by the Ukrainian Parliament – Associated Press reported that the parliament also voted to release from a prison hospital in Kharkiv Yanukovych's political enemy, 53-year-old exprime minister Yulia Tymoshenko. She had been sentenced to seven years' imprisonment in 2011, accused of abuse of power in fixing the nation's gas deal with Putin at an unjustifiably high price. Her first public appearance, seated in a wheelchair, was in Maidan Nezalezhnosti, dubbed by the Western media 'Euromaidan', where she called the people who had died in the demostrations heroic for 'ridding Ukraine of a cancer'.

As the demonstrations grew less and less 'peaceful', EU foreign policy chief Catherine Ashton and US VIPs went to Kiev to congratulate the regime-changers who had driven out their elected president. These visitors closed their eyes to the Pravii Sektor, an informal association of right-wing and neo-fascist groups[1] which had seized arms and ammunition from an Interior Ministry arsenal,[2] and whose tactics grew more excessive day by day until policemen and soldiers were being set on fire with Molotov cocktails and anonymous snipers were shooting dead demonstrators and uninvolved passers-by in the streets. Although Estonian Foreign Minister Urmas Paet informed Ashton that provocateurs were behind the killings in Independence Square, she continued to support the regime-changers. US Secretary of State John Kerry also encouraged them from afar.

According to the *Washington Post* of 6 March, ex-Secretary of State Hillary Clinton refused to retract her comparison of Putin with Hitler in 1938. Vice President Joe Biden flew to Kiev to give the interim prime minister, banker Arseny Yatsenyuk, his blessing as the man likeliest to obey IMF instructions. CIA Director John Brennan paid a publicised 'secret visit' to Kiev, where a clandestine hard core of CIA officers was installed – apparently for psy-ops actions to further stir the muddy waters of Ukrainian politics. Although the EU and US seemed to be on the same side at the negotiating table, in a hacked phone conversation with American ambassador to Ukraine Geoffrey Pyatt, Victoria Nuland expressed the desire to 'fuck the EU' [sic][3] because Europe had reasons, like the oil on which it depends, to tread gently in imposing trade and other sanctions against Russia, while the Obama administration, safely in Washington, wanted to look bullish. What are the 'sanctions' so far? Travel restrictions on a small number of Russian VIPs and a discussion about embargoing certain exports from the US to Russia.

As political commentator George Friedman wrote on 29 April:

> The US sanctions strategy is therefore not designed to change Russian policies; it is designed to make it look like the United States is trying to change Russian policy. And it is aimed at those in Congress who have made this a major issue and those parts of the State Department that want to orientate US national security policy around the issue of human rights. Both can be told that something is being done – when in fact nothing can be done. In a world clamouring for action, prudent leaders sometimes prefer the appearance of doing something to actually doing something.[4]

Those parts of the State Department? On a number of occasions, Nuland referred to the 5 billion dollars the US had 'invested' in Ukraine since its independence from Moscow to procure its transition to what Capitol Hill would regard as democracy.

At meetings in Geneva in February and March, between US, EU, Russian and Ukrainian negotiators, Kerry faced Sergei Lavrov, Russia's unexcitable foreign minister. Interviewed later about the Geneva accords by Sophie Shevardnadze, granddaughter of former Soviet foreign minister and ex-president of Georgia Eduard Shevardnadze, on the satellite TV channel Russia Today, Lavrov made the point that for Russian politicians publicly to support anti-American movements in, say, Canada, Mexico or Central America would be construed as a very hostile act in Washington, just as EU and US intrusion in Ukraine is interpreted as hostile by his government. Some moves towards de-escalation were agreed on paper in the negotiations, but each side then accused the other of failing to stand by its undertakings. Two conditions were the evacuation of government and other premises in Kiev forcibly occupied by 'protestors', and the disarming of those extremists. In apparent conformity, Pravii Sektor handed over some weapons, but kept others.[5] The interim Kiev administration got round the impossibility of dislodging the armed squatters in its offices by leasing the buildings to them, so they were not squatters, but legitimately there. The Ukrainian and Western negotiators argued that Moscow was controlling the Russian-speakers in eastern Ukraine and should disarm them; Lavrov denied they were under Kremlin control.

The Westerners argued that Russian military manoeuvres near the eastern border of Ukraine constituted a deliberate threat to stability in Ukraine. Lavrov replied that they were taking place on Russian soil and were nobody else's business. It seemed not to occur to anyone that American boots on the ground in Poland and the Baltic republics – although few in number – were hardly likely to cool things down.

In April 2014, British journalist James Delingpole travelled to Vienna to interview Ukrainian oligarch Dmitry Firtash, guarded by several circles of associates and 'a Rosa Kleb-like minder' while 'under effective house arrest, awaiting extradition on corruption charges to the US, with his bail set at a whopping 125 million euros'.[6] From humble beginnings, Firtash made his pile by trading Ukrainian food for Central Asian gas in the chaos after the collapse of the USSR. Now a major player in Central and Eastern European chemical and energy industries, he employs 100,000 people in several countries with an annual turnover, in 2012, of 6 billion US dollars. So, how does he differ from other Eastern European oligarchs? According to Delingpole, Firtash educates his children in Ukraine – not at Eton and Harrow – and invests his money in Ukraine. In 2006 he negotiated a deal whereby Ukraine could keep its energy costs down by importing some gas from Turkmenistan without angering Russian gas giant Gazprom, but his deal was undone by Tymoshenko – as a result of which Ukraine now owes Gazprom US $2.2 billion.[7] According to Delingpole, Firtash may have the expertise, personal wealth and political leverage 'to steer his troubled country towards stability and prosperity'. However, he cannot do that from inside an American jail cell, so why does Washington want to lock him up?

The month after Delingpole's article in The Spectator, anti-Russian Petro Poroshenko was elected president of Ukraine, having collected 56 per cent of the votes in an election where many Russian-speakers were denied the chance to vote. One factor in his rise to power was his own Channel Five television network. Another was his personal wealth, equivalent to several billion dollars – some of it amassed from his manufacture of chocolate. This earned him the cuddly nickname of 'the Willy Wonka president', which does not sit well on the man who has unleashed an all-out ground and air war on the Russian-speaking civilians in the east of the country.

It has been said that one cannot write history less than fifty years after the events. However, there are some comments to be made at the time of going to press.

In a belated echo of Neville Chamberlain's talk in 1938 of 'a quarrel between people in a faraway country of whom we know nothing', the civil war in Ukraine seems to have attracted little attention in Western Europe until Malaysian Airlines flight MH17 crashed on 17 July causing the deaths of 240 Western European passengers. The International Civil Aviation Organisation had apparently left it to individual airlines to decide whether or not to over-fly Eastern Ukraine on that day, although it was known to be a zone of no-holds-barred warfare in which a number of Ukrainian government helicopters and fixed-wing aircraft had been shot down while on combat missions against civilian targets in Russophone East Ukraine. In addition, it was known for at least five weeks before the crash that Ukrainian government warplanes were flying in the radar shadow of civilian airliners to screen their approach from ground-based radar, which would otherwise have warned the separatists of their potentially lethal approach. There was nothing new about the tactic – an old trick from the Cold War. To remind those with short memories, a televised interview with a female militia soldier in Slovyansk, talking about this, was posted to YouTube on 18 June.

Even if it was, as Western media widely reported, a Russian 'Buk' missile that caused the crash, since all Ukrainian military hardware is of Russian origin – and that includes Buk missile batteries – this does not prove who launched it. Russian satellite photographs show that there were three or four Buk batteries in government-held territory very close to the front lines in the days leading up to the crash, all of which were removed shortly afterwards. Since the separatists had no aircraft, why did Kiev place these batteries there? On 17 July there were nine associated Kupol-Mi 9518 target-acquisition radars active in the area – double and treble the number on other days.

With most Western media reporting Obama's accusations that Moscow was guilty of shooting down MH17, the Russian Defence Ministry gave a televised press conference on 21 July showing radar plots of several civil airliners passing along the corridors above Eastern Ukraine just before the crash. Flight MH17, however, was instructed by Ukrainian ATC to deviate from the safe corridor shortly before the incident. An 'unidentified aerial object' – a euphemism for a Ukrainian SU-25 fighter with no transponder transmitting its serial number – was plotted climbing fast at a distance of 3–4km from MH17 and remained in position until it had crashed. Armament of an SU-25 includes R60 air-to-air missiles, easily within kill range at that distance once locked onto an airliner. The Russian press conference could, of course, be disinformation, but the point was made during it that an American satellite of a type used to detect missile launches was 'coincidentally' passing over the crash site at the crucial time, yet Washington has not revealed any evidence to support its allegation that pro-Russian forces launched a 'Buk' and caused the crash. Even the CIA's new office in Kiev stayed mute.

On 29 July the respected Canadian broadcaster CBC World Television broadcast an interview by reporter Susan Ormiston, speaking in Donetsk with one of the two Organisation for Security and Cooperation in Europe (OSCE) observers who reached the crash site first. Michael Bociurkiw is a Canadian of Ukrainian origin, speaking both Ukrainian and Russian. His ability to converse with locals at the crash site got him in there ahead of other OSCE colleagues. He told Ormiston about examining and photographing a fuselage panel from the flight deck pierced by multiple holes he attributed to 'machine-gun fire'. Was this the Su-25's pilot's way of destroying the controls, killing the pilots before they could indicate the fighter's approach on the black box flight recorder and causing an abrupt depressurisation? Or were the holes made by the close-proximity explosion of a missile warhead?

In addition to deviating from the normal flight corridor, MH17 abruptly reduced speed to 200km. just before disappearing from the radar screens. Compounding the mystery, several telephone messages from a Spanish-origin air-traffic controller apparently present in the Kiev tower on 17 July spoke of 'outsiders from the Ministry of Defence' aggressively taking over the tower on that day, for purposes unknown. He was apparently warned by friendly foreigners to leave Ukraine swiftly after making his calls, and did so. That could, of course, be a hoax.

Whichever explanation turns out to be correct, the tragedy revealed a very one-sided view of the conflict held by many Westerners, unquestioningly believing the Obama-White House version of events: Putin is a bad man, therefore, he killed all the people on MH17.

When the USSR imploded in 1989, 8.3 million Russians were left living within the boundaries of Ukraine, most of them unable to speak the official language of the country that overnight became an independent state. With President Petro Poroshenko's anti-Russian regime in power in Kiev, Moscow has as much sympathy for their predicament as one would hope a British government would have for 8 million Britons in a similar situation. It has apparently supplied the separatists with defensive weaponry, including MANPADs (man-portable air-defence systems) to shoot down low-altitude attacking fighter-bombers and helicopters. None of these missiles could reach a civil airliner at a height of 30,000ft. Volunteer irregulars with light weapons can also pass into Eastern Ukraine, to reinforce local militias fighting off attacks by the government in Kiev.

So, which of the conflicting explanations of the crash of MH17 is correct? With time running out for the separatists in East Ukraine as Kiev's forces close in on their last strongholds, there are rumours that he will shortly send armoured vehicles into Eastern Ukraine, to even up the odds there. If he does, is this a prelude to grabbing back formerly Russian territory, or is he trying to protect Russian civilians trapped on the wrong side of a recently established border, where a hostile government is deploying all the weapons of modern war against them?

Will it be fifty years before we know the truth about flight MH17, and the air and ground offensive that the government in Kiev is conducting against its own citizens in Eastern Ukraine?

ACKNOWLEDGEMENTS

Although the USSR is now history, for many people the trauma of the Cold War has not ended. Several Eastern Europeans who commented helpfully on sections of this book asked not to be identified because of family 'back home'. Even more surprising was the reaction of a retired American diplomat, who attacked the author for 'arguing [sic] that Ukraine and the other countries of what Russian call "the near-abroad" should enjoy independence'. He seemed to think the West ought to write them off in order to mollify Moscow. A former CIA officer considered the book anti-American, presumably for mentions of the Manifest Destiny and the Monroe Doctrine. Intentionally or not, they all helped, for surely some Russians will find this history of their nation hostile; if Americans also do, perhaps the historian's aim of objectivity has been achieved. My favourite translator, Miguel Mata, was helpful as always, and Richard Boyd unearthed some very relevant material.

Among those who have helped and can be named are Nikolai I. Kravchenko, Dmitri Makarov and Maître Mandre-Methuselem – instructors at that extraordinary institution The Joint Services School for Linguists (JSSL) at Crail in Fifeshire who first fired the author's interest in Russian history. In Berlin, Ingrid Manley fixed many things, Oberst A.D. Herter, last commander of the former RAF Gatow base, was a mine of information, and Sabine Ehrlich talked of her experiences when handing over the author's Stasi file at the Bundesbeauftragte für die Unterlagen des Staatssicherheitdienstes der ehemaligen Deutschen Demokratischen Republik. In Potsdam, Gabriele Schnell, Beauftragte für die Gedenkstätte Lindenstrasse 54/55, gave a warm welcome to a rather traumatised former prisoner and showed unlimited generosity in lending published and unpublished transcripts of her interviews with former prisoners of the NKVD and Stasi in the Lindenstrasse prison. In Washington, Alix Sundquist, surely one of the most inspiring diplomats ever to represent her country, was never too busy to help. There, too, researcher extraordinary Joan Goodbody dug up material on Neill S. Brown not accessible in Europe. In Paris, Hélène Auclair talked of the Algerian war. Jiři Studnička relived the Prague Spring from the Czech viewpoint and Dominika Minarovič found a Slovak source, whose anonymity is respected. The late John Morris – sometime second lieutenant with the Baluch Regiment – recalled his service on the North-west Frontier and permitted use of his unpublished memoirs. Sometime Royal Navy coder and Russian linguist Gareth Mulloy loaned material on JSSL. Hedvig Primärii described what it was like for Estonians targeted by Putin's cyber-attack. Marge Ben-Tovim gave permission to use the unpublished memoirs of her mother, former Comintern agent Frieda Truhar. Chris 'Biggles' Turner once again helped with matters aviational and financial, as did Major Len Chaganis with matters military.

Lastly, I thank 'Dmitri' and 'Sofia', for our little adventure in 2011.

GLOSSARY

Including titles of Soviet and Russian security services

1917–22	**Cheka**	Chrezvychaynaya Kommissiya po borbe s kontrrevolutsiey i sabotazhem (Special commission for combating counter-revolution and sabotage)
1922–23	**GPU/NKVD**	Gosudarstvennoye Politicheskeye Upravleniye (State political administration), part of Narodny Kommissariat Vnutrennikh Dyel (People's commissariat of internal affairs)
1923–34	**OGPU**	Obyedinyonnoye Gosudarstvennoye Politicheskiye Upravleniye (United state political administration)
1934–43	**GUGB/NKVD**	Glavnoye Upravleniye Gosudarstvennoi Bezopasnosti (Main administration of state security), part of NKVD and briefly, in 1941, NKGB
1943–46	**NKGB**	Narodny Komissariat Gosudarstvennoi Bezopasnosti (People's commissariat of state security)
1946–53	**MGB**	Ministerstvo Gosudarstvennoi Bezopasnosti (Ministry of state security)
1953–54	**MVD**	Ministerstvo Vnutrennikh Dyel (Ministry of internal affairs)
1954–91	**KGB**	Komityet Gosudarstvennoi Bezopasnosti (Committee of state security)
1991–93	**MB**	Ministerstvo Bezopasnosti (Ministry of security)
1991–	**SVR**	Sluzhba Vneshnei Razvedki (Foreign intelligence service)
1992–	**FSB**	Federal'naya Sluzhba Bezopasnosti (Federal security service)

ALN	Armée de Libération Nationale, the armed wing of FLN (q.v.)
Atlantic Charter	the joint declaration by Churchill and Roosevelt, signed on 14 August 1941, which became the foundation stone of the post-war United Nations Organisation
AVO / AVH	Hungarian secret police
Bizonia	the economic union of the British and American zones of occupied Germany
blizhneye zarubezhiye	Russian for 'the near-abroad', i.e. the neighbouring states considered by Moscow to be a vital buffer zone
Bolshevik	the name chosen by Russia's most extreme socialist revolutionary party, literally a claim to be 'the majority'
Brest-Litovsk Treaty	the agreement(s) signed there to end First World War hostilities between Russia / Ukraine and the Central Powers
Brezhnev Doctrine	doctrine 'justifying' armed Soviet / Warsaw pact intervention in any breakaway communist state
BStU	abbreviation for 'Bundesbeauftragte für die Unterlagen des Staatssicherheitsministeriums der ehemaligen Deutschen Demokratischen Republik' (Stasi archives office)
CIA	Central Intelligence Agency, the principal external intelligence agency of the US
Central Powers	First World War coalition of German, Austro-Hungarian and Turkish empires
Cheka	the Bolshevik secret police formed on 20 December 1917
chekist, pl. *chekisty*	officer of Soviet / Russian state security services
chernozem	literally, 'black soil'; the fertile, grain-growing Ukrainian plain
CIS	English initials of Sodruzhestvo Nezavisemikh Gosudarstv, the Commonwealth of Independent States.
Class against Class	Comintern-imposed party line rejecting all other Left parties
Comecon	Soviet-controlled organisation to promote trade between Eastern bloc countries
Cominform	successor of Comintern (q.v.)
Comintern	abbreviation of 'Communist International', the organisation controlling foreign communist parties, transporting clandestine subsidies to them and promoting subversion of the democracies, also used for espionage
Cossacks	originally free nomadic peoples dwelling north of Black and Caspian seas in modern Poland, Ukraine and Russia; mounted troops drawn from those peoples used to suppress disorder in Tsarist Russia
CPGB	Communist Party of Great Britain.
CPM	Communist Party of Malaya.
CPSU	Communist Party of the Soviet Union.
dacha, pl. *dachi*	Russian for 'country cottage or villa'.
DEFCON	acronym for 'defence condition', i.e. war-readiness
democratic centralism	a euphemism for Moscow's control of the foreign parties through the Comintern

Democratic People's
Republic of Korea   North Korea
Duma   Russian parliament.
Dvoika   Russian for 'two', i.e. a pair
EAM/ELAS   Ethnikón Apeleftherotikón Métopon-ethnikós Laïkós
    Apeleftherotikós Strátos, Greek for National Liberation
    Front-National Popular Liberation Army
Entente   French for 'an understanding' or 'agreement'
ERP   European Recovery Programme, otherwise known as the
    Marshall Plan
la francophonie   the community of countries where French is the first or
    second language
GDP   gross domestic product
GDR   German Democratic Republic, formerly the Soviet-occupied
    zone of Germany
Front de Libération Nationale (FLN) – National Liberation Front of Algeria
Gensek   general secretary of a communist organisation or party
glasnost   Russian for 'openness'
GRU   Glavnoye Razvedyvatel'noye Upravlenie (Soviet military
    intelligence)
Gulag   acronym of Glavnoye Upravlenie ispravitelno-trudovykh
    Lagerei, the main administration of 'corrective labour' camps
holodomor   the famine, especially in Ukraine, resulting from collectivi-
    sation
HUMINT   acronym of 'human intelligence', i.e. agents on the ground
    in a hostile state
ICBM   intercontinental ballistic missile
IM   an usually unpaid informant of Stasi
IRBM   intermediate-range ballistic missile
IRC   International Relations Committee (interface between St
    Petersburg administration and foreign companies)
ISCOT   British code-breaking operation (etymology unknown)
Iskra   Russian for 'spark'; name of Lenin's Bolshevik schism, also
    of its publication
Khozyaïn   Russian for 'boss'
Kipchaks   a nomadic people of Asiatic origin
KPA   North Korean 'People's Army'
KPD   Kommunistiche Partei Deutschlands (German Communist
    Party)
Kremlin   Russian for 'fortress' or 'citadel'
krugovaya poruka   literally, 'collective guarantee', but used under Soviet penal
    code to mean 'collective guilt'
KSČ   Komunistická Strana Československa, the Czechoslvakian
    Communist Party
kulak   successful peasant, especially under NEP
Land, pl. *Länder*   German for 'province'
Lux, or Hotel Lux   the principal accommodation for Comintern workers in
    Moscow

MAD	acronym of 'mutually assured destruction' – the theory that neither side would survive a full nuclear war
magistral'	main line railway
Manchukuo	Japanese-occupied Manchuria
Marxism-Leninism	the political theories of Marx amended by Lenin and his successors
Menshevik	a socialist party opposing the Bolsheviks at the time of the Revolution.
MRBM	medium-range ballistic missile
MVD	Ministerstvo Vnutrennikh Dyel, Soviet Ministry of the Interior
Narodnik	a believer in peasants' 'wisdom of the soil'
NATO	North Atlantic Treaty Organisation
NEP	New Economic Policy, Lenin's attempt to kick-start the economy by incentives after the disastrous period of 'war communism'
Nomenklatura	literally, 'the people with names', i.e. those whom Stalin's paranoia allowed to be appointed to important positions because he already knew their names
N-PIC	National Photographic Interpretation Centre
NSC	US National Security Council
NWF	North-west Frontier of British India
NVA	Nazionale Volksarmee, the 'national people's army' of the GDR
NVA	North Vietnamese Army
Okhrana	acronym for the Tsarist secret police
OMON	black beret riot police of the MVD (q.v.)
Oprichniki	originally, Ivan the Terrible's bodyguard
OAS	Organisation Armée Secrète, the European terrorist organisation in French Algeria
PCF	Parti Communiste Français
PDPA	People's Democratic Party of Afghanistan
Pechenegs	a nomadic people of Asiatic origin
Perestroika	Russian for 're-structuring'
Politburo	literally, 'political office'; the small committee holding ultimate power in a communist state
PPMD	Presidential Property Management Department, responsible for selling off Russian state property abroad
Protocols of the Learned Elders of Zion	a Tsarist police hoax allegedly proving a worldwide Jewish conspiracy
POUM	Partido Obrero de Unificación Marxista, the Spanish Marxist party whose members were murdered by Soviet agents during civil war
První Sprava	communist Czechoslovakian external intelligence agency
Quai d'Orsay	French Foreign Ministry
RCMP	Royal Canadian Mounted Police
ROK	Republic of Korea, i.e. South Korea
rezident	senior officer of Soviet intelligence abroad

Rezidentura	the secure office of a *rezident*
Rio Treaty	mutual defence treaty of western hemisphere
SA-7	a type of US surface-to-air missile.
Samizdat	Russian acronym from *sam*, meaning 'self' and *izdat* meaning 'to publish', i.e. making illicit copies of banned material in the USSR
SB	Statní Bezpečnost, the communist Czechoslovakian interior state security organisation
SDECE	Service de Documentation Extérieure et de Contre-Espionage, the principal French external intelligence service
Securitate	Romanian state security organisation
siloviki	Russian for 'men of power', i.e. the oligarchs
SAC	Strategic Air Command, the US nuclear strike force
Shmersh	acronym for *smert' spionam*, meaning 'death to spies'; Soviet assassination
soviet	Russian for 'council'
SED	Sozialistische Einheitspartei Deutschlands, the communist front 'Socialist Unity Party' in GDR (q.v.)
Stasi	acronym of Staatssicheitsministerium, the State Security Ministry of GDR
streltsy	'the archers', a military corps of sixteenth and seventeenth centuries
TASS	Telegrafnoye Agentstvo Sovietskovo Soyuza, Soviet news agency
Trizonia	the evolution of Bizonia (q.v.) after the French zone joined
Tseka	acronym for *tsentralny komityet*, meaning 'Central Committee'
UB	Polish state security organisation
UN	United Nations
USSR	Union of Soviet Socialist Republics, the post-revolutionary Russian empire
valyuta	Russian for 'hard currency'; the stores where only Westerners and privileged Soviet citizens could buy goods not available elsewhere in the USSR
Varangians	early medieval people of mixed Viking and Russian blood
Venona	code-name for a US code-breaking operation
VC	Viet Cong, the pro-communist guerrillas in South Vietnam during the American war
Viet Minh	communist guerrillas during Japanese occupation of Vietnam and during war with France to 1954
vozhd	Russian equivalent of 'der Führer'
war communism	universal state control imposed after the Revolution, abandoned for NEP (q.v.) after its disastrous failure
Warsaw Pact	Soviet-dominated counterpart of NATO
Zemsky sobor	a council of nobles
Zhdanovshchina	the cultural repression under Andrei Zhdanov

NOTES AND SOURCES

All translations are by the author unless otherwise attributed.

Russian words have been rendered phonetically, e.g. *pervovo* and not *pervogo* – except where a different Western spelling already exists, e.g. Soviet, Khrushchev, Gorbachev and not *soviet / sovyetskii*, Khrushchoff and Gorbachoff.

All illustrations are from the author's collection.

Every effort has been made to trace copyright owners. In the event of any infringement, please communicate with the author, care of the publishers.

INTRODUCTION

1. E. Lucas, *The New Cold War*, London, Bloomsbury 2008, p. 245. See also Z. Barany, *Democratic Breakdown and the Decline of the Russian Military*, Woodstock, Princeton University Press 2007, p. 54.

1 GENGHIS KHAN, UNCLE JOE AND VLAD THE GASMAN

1. K.E. Shewmaker, 'Neill S. Brown's Mission to Russia 1850–53' *Diplomacy and Statecraft* Vol 12/4 December 2001, p. 81.
2. J. Baylen, 'A Tennessee politician in Imperial Russia' *Tennessee Historical Quarterly* Vol 14/1955, p. 241.
3. A.F. Chew, *An Atlas of Russian History*, New Haven and London, Yale University Press, 1970, p. 82.
4. Shewmaker, p. 84.
5. Chew, p. 83.
6. Baylen, p. 232.

7. Shewmaker, p. 92.
8. *The Oxford Dictionary of English Etymology*, Oxford, Clarendon Press, 1966.
9. L. Rees, *Behind Closed Doors*, London, BBC Books 2008, p. 130.
10. Rees, pp. 198-9.
11. G.F. Kennan, *Memoirs 1925–1950*, New York, Pantheon, 1967, p. 523.
12. Acronym of Otdeleniye po Okhraneniyu Obshchestvennoi Bezopasnosti i Poryadka – the Department for Defence of Public Security and Order.
13. E. Gazur, *Alexander Orlov: the FBI's KGB General*, New York, Carrol and Graf, 2002, pp. 451–9.
14. Gazur, pp. 469–71.
15. Kennan, *Memoirs 1925–1950,* p. 523 (abbreviated by the author).
16. Quoted in W. Bedell Smith, *Moscow Mission*, London, Heinemann, 1950, p. 305.

3 A TIME OF GIANTS: PETER AND CATHERINE; ALEXIS AND NAPOLEON

1. M. Hughes, *Inside the Enigma*, London, The Hambeldon Press, 1997, p.4.
2. A. George and E. George, *St Petersburg, a History*, Thrupp, Sutton, 2006, pp. 7–9.
3. J. Carmichael, *Russia, an illustrated history,* New York, Hippocrene Books, 1991, pp. 81–2.
4. German name, Memel.

5 LIES, SPIES AND BLOOD IN THE STREETS

1. By 1913 the total cost had risen to 1.455 *billion* roubles, making it the most costly enterprise of any kind in Russia until the country was crippled by its military budget for the First World War. As a bank employee in the 1950s, the author recalls seeing bundles of bonds in pre-revolutionary script kept in safe custody boxes by investors still vainly hoping for a dividend, forty years after the Revolution.
2. A gauge inherited from the most common gauge of industrial wagon-ways.
3. To this was added in 1907 the Anglo-Russian Convention. In conjunction with the existing Franco-British Entente Cordiale, this produced the Triple Entente that confronted the Central Powers in the First World War.
4. The treaty, as amended, remained in force until after the First World War.
5. Bilingual in Russian and French, Cheminon epitomises the dashing French lover. He rescued two beautiful Russian sisters in St Petersburg by the skin of their teeth during the 1917 Revolution, brought them to Paris, married one and then the other when the first wife died.
6. General Hamilton noted in his scrapbook the shock he felt on seeing tall Caucasian prisoners guarded by short Asiatic soldiers.
7. The four Duma sessions were 10 May – 21 July 1906, 5 March – 16 June 1907, 14 November 1907 – 22 June 1912 and 28 November 1912 – 11 March 11 1917.

6 DEATH IN SARAJEVO, MONEY IN THE BANK

1. After trial in Sarajevo, Princip was sentenced to twenty years' imprisonment, the maximum legal penalty for a person less than 20 years' old at the time of his crime. He subsequently died of complications after amputation of an arm caused by tuberculosis in a hospital near his prison.
2. Also called 'the Black Hand'.
3. Not the result of a single treaty, the alliance was the product of the Franco-Russian alliance of 1894, the Anglo-French Entente Cordiale of 1904 and an agreement between Britain and Russia in 1907.
4. R. Bruce Lockhart, *Memoirs of a British Agent*, London, Putnam, 1934, p. 237.
5. Also spelt Braunstein.
6. Lockhart, pp. 226–7, abridged by the author.
7. Schlieffen had died in 1913. His successor, Helmuth von Moltke, watered the plan down, which is often seen as the reason for Germany's failure to take Paris and win a decisive victory.
8. G. Elliott & H. Shukman, *Secret Classooms*, London, St Ermin's Press/Little Brown, 2002, p. 173.
9. Z.A.B. Zeman, *Germany and the Russian Revolution*, London, Oxford University Press, 1958, p. 3.
10. Zeman, p. 6, text of Report 794 dated 30 September 1915 from the German minister in Berne to German chancellor Theobald von Bethmann-Hollweg.
11. Zeman, p. 24.
12. Carmichael, p. 193.
13. The Socialist Party of America declared the first National Woman's Day in 1909.
14. E.N. Burdzhalov, *Vtoraya Russkaya Revolutsia*, Moscow, Nauka, 1967, unattributed English translation on www.google.books, p. 147.
15. Hughes, pp. 102, 105.
16. Zeman, p. 26, text of telegram 371 from High Command to Foreign Ministry.
17. See http://reformed-theology.org/html/books/bolshevik_revolution/chapter_03.htm
18. M. Occleshaw, *Dances in Deep Shadows*, London, Constable & Robinson, 2006, p. 6.
19. Zeman, p. 35, text of telegram 603 from German minister in Berne to Foreign Ministry.
20. M. Pearson, *Inessa – Lenin's Mistress*, London, Duckworth, 2001, p. 87.
21. See http://reformed-theology.org/html/books/bolshevik_revolution/chapter_o3.htm
22. The correct Polish spelling is Dzierżyński.
23. Occleshaw, p. 41.
24. M. Hoffman, *War Diaries and other papers*, London, Secker, 1929, Vol II, p. 117.

7 THE RAINBOW OF DEATH

1. *Pravda*'s first issue was on 22 April 1912, but its circulation was small until the German subsidies arrived.
2. Occleshaw, p. 25.

3. Zeman, p. 75.
4. R. Service, *Stalin – a Memoir*, London, Pan, 2005, p. 154.
5. Service, p. 161.
6. See Zeman for texts of relevant memoranda and telegrams.
7. G.F. Kennan, *Memoirs,* New York, Bantam Books, 1967, pp. 562–3
8. It was renamed the All-Union Communist Party in 1925 and finally the Communist Party of the Soviet Union in 1952.
9. Zeman, p. 120. Other accounts of the agricultural situation bear out that only 30 per cent, or at most 50 per cent of the cultivable land was under the plough at this time.
10. In 1976 a team of Russian scientists located the remains but kept the discovery secret until the collapse of the Soviet Union. By 1994, DNA analysis had positively identified the remains as those of Nicholas, Alexandra, three of their daughters and four servants. The remains were given a state funeral on 17 July 1998, and reburied in the crypt of St Petersburg's Cathedral of St Peter and St Paul.
11. In April 1920 Denikin handed command to Wrangel and settled in France to write his five-volume memoirs. He immigrated to the United States in 1945 and died there two years later.
12. Carmichael, pp. 204–5.
13. D. Rayfield, *Stalin and his Hangmen*, London, Penguin, 2005, p. 80.
14. Service, p. 175.

8 THE COMINTERN: WAR ON THE CHEAP

1. N. Pokrovskiy and S. Petrov, *Politburo i tserkov 1922–25*, Moscow, 1997, Vol. I, pp. 141–2.
2. Elliott & Shukman, p. 151.
3. F. Beckett, *Enemy Within: The Rise and Fall of the British Communist Party*, London, John Murray, 1998, p. 12.
4. Beckett, ibid, pp. 17, 18.
5. ibid, p. 13.
6. ibid, pp. 28–9.
7. ibid, pp. 27–9.

9 SECRET AGENTS IN SKIRTS

1. Unpublished memoirs of Frieda Truhar-Brewster.
2. ibid.
3. A neologism denoting the few hundred people in the USSR of whom Stalin had heard, and who could be appointed to key posts because he knew their names, his paranoia making him wary of any unknown.
4. Truhar-Brewster.
5. ibid.
6. B. Wasserstein, *Secret War in Shanghai*, London, Profile, 1998, p. 7.
7. Truhar-Brewster.

8. G. Schnell, ed. *Potsdamer Frauen*, Potsdam, Potsdamer Verlagsbuchhandlung, 1993, p. 104.
9. ibid, pp. 99–108.

10 FAMINE, PURGES AND BUNDLES OF USED NOTES

1. Beckett, *Enemy Within,* pp. 31–4
2. K. Macksey, *The Searchers*, London, Cassel, 2003, p. 61.
3. Beckett, *Enemy Within,* p. 61.
4. G. Dallas, *Poisoned Peace,* London, John Murray, 2005, p. 464.
5. Article in *Manchester Guardian*, 27 March 1933.
6. ibid.
7. Article in *Manchester Guardian,* 25 March 1933.
8. M.S. Colley, *Gareth Jones – a Manchukuo Incident*, pub. privately 2001, pp. xx, xxi.
9. ibid, p. xxi.
10. ibid, p. 26.
11. ibid, p. 31.
12. Rayfield, p. 211.
13. ibid, p. 184.
14. ibid, p. 185.
15. S. Sebag Montefiore, *Stalin, the Court of the Red Tsar*, London, Phoenix, 2004, pp. 86, 87, 92.
16. Obituary notice in *The Independent*, 31 May 2006.
17. Then the Fourth Chief Directorate of the Red Army High Command, later the GRU.
18. Gazur, pp. 51, 152.
19. J. Baker White, *The Soviet Spy System*, London, Falcon Press, 1948, p. 112.
20. Beckett, *Enemy Within,* pp. 50–1.
21. ibid, p. 52.
22. Orlov claimed to be a general, to make himself a more attractive asset to the FBI.
23. P. & A. Sudoplatov, *Special Tasks – The Memoirs of an Unwanted Witness, a Soviet Spymaster*, London, Little Brown, 1994, p. 46 and Gazur, pp. 82–101.
24. Gazur, pp. 102–11.
25. Beckett, *Enemy Within,* pp. 68, 73.
26. An acronym of *schmert' spionam*, meaning 'death to spies'.
27. Rayfield, pp. 261–2. More accurately translated as 'collective guarantee', the concept of *krugovaya poruka* was used in Tsarist Russia to collect from a community fines or taxes due from one of its members. As late as the mid-1980s, when a brilliant Jewish mathematician known to the author was eventually allowed to leave the USSR with his parents, his secondary school and university tutors were punished for his ingratitude to the state by being demoted, deprived of their comfortable apartments and relocated to less desirable parts of town.
28. Carmichael, pp. 218–9.
29. Beckett, *Enemy Within,* pp. 71–2.
30. Montefiore, p. 255.

31. ibid, pp. 233–4.
32. ibid, p. 277.

11 ONE MAN, ONE PISTOL, ONE MONTH = 6,287 MEN DEAD

1. Rayfield, p. 254–5
2. The text of the speech was unearthed in the Kremlin Special Archive in 1994 by T.S. Bushueva – see C. Pleshakov, *Stalin's Folly – The Secret History of the German Invasion of Russia, June 1941*, London, Weidenfeld & Nicolson, 2005, pp. 43–4.
3. Beckett, *Enemy Within,* p. 91.
4. Truhar-Brewster
5. J.T. Gross, *Revolution from Abroad – Documents from the Hoover Institution for War, Revolution and Peace*, Princeton, Princeton University Press, 2002, pp. 268–9.
6. ibid, pp. 22–48.
7. ibid, pp. 155, 158.
8. ibid, pp. xiv, xv, 146.
9. Rees, p. 47.
10. ibid, pp. 48–9.
11. ibid, pp. 49–50, abbreviated by the author.
12. ibid, pp. 50–1.
13. ibid, p.33.
14. Pleshakov, pp. 43–4.
15. Gross, p. 350.
16. Service, p. 303.
17. Rees, p. 57.
18. Montefiore, p. 342.
19. Sudoplatov, p. 3.

12 THE POLITBURO TAKES A SHORT RIDE

1. C. Bellamy, *Absolute War: Soviet Russia in the Second World War*, London, Macmillan, 2007, p. 97.
2. Pleshakov, pp.1, 2, 62–8.
3. ibid, p. 83.
4. Officially, Chairman of the Council of People's Commissars. This was his first official government post since 1923, but he also remained First Secretary of the CPSU.
5. Gross, pp. 179, 181.
6. A. Mikoyan, *Tak i bylo,* Moscow, Vagrus, no date, p. 390–2.
7. An alternative explanation of Stalin's inactivity at this crucial time is that he was acting a part and testing their loyalty and obedience. However, given his nervous breakdown when the Finnish invasion did not at first succeed, and also that the situation this time was a thousand times more serious, that is unlikely.

Voznesensky eventually paid the price for his daring – and for being too successful in keeping Leningrad going during the siege – by being arrested and dying of hypothermia in transit between prisons after the war.

8. Mikhail Gorbachev, who had access to the records, estimated the loss as being approximately 27 million lives.
9. Montefiore, p. 401.
10. Q. Reynolds, *By Quentin Reynolds*, New York, Pyramid, 1964, pp. 241–4, abridged by the author.
11. ibid, pp. 244–5, abridged by the author.
12. Rees, pp. 110–11.

13 MY ENEMY'S ENEMY IS ALSO MY ENEMY

1. Montefiore, p. 417.
2. Rees, pp. 151–2.
3. Macksey, p. 171.
4. Personal communication with the author by a former Y station monitor.
5. The intercept programme had earlier code names JADE, BRIDE and DRUG. Some 3,000 decoded messages can now be consulted on http://nsa.gov/venona/
6. Rayfield, p. 391.
7. ibid.
8. T. Hickman, *Churchill's Bodyguard*, London, Headline, 2005, pp. 167–74.
9. F. Kersaudy, *De Gaulle et Roosevelt: Le Duel au Sommet*, Paris, Perrin, 2004, p. 352–3 quoting FRUS 1943 Teheran Conference USGPO Wash, 1961, pp. 484-5 11/28/43
10. J.L. Gaddis, *The United States and the Origins of the Cold War*, New York, Columbia University Press, 1972, p. 41.
11. Rees, pp. 236–9.
12. Montefiore, pp. 480–1.
13. Montefiore, p. 481.
14. Rayfield, p. 393.

14 POOR POLAND!

1. Rees, p. 254, quoting J.O. Pohl, *The Deportation and Fate of the Crimean Tatars*, [sic] – paper presented at Columbia University Convention, April 2000.
2. Polish name, Lwów
3. W. S. Churchill, *The Second World War*, London, Penguin Classics, 2005, Vol 4, p. 118.
4. Rees, pp. 294–5.
5. Personal communication to the author.
6. Personal communication to the author.
7. Rees, pp. 299–301.
8. ibid, p. 345.
9. W. Anders, *An Army in Exile*, London, Macmillan, 1981, p. 256.

10. Dallas, p. 422.
11. Rees, p. 354.

15 A VERY DIFFERENT KIND OF WARFARE

1. Rees, pp. 129, 132.
2. Details taken from official guide to Hohenschönhausen prison, now a memorial with guided tours visited annually by 200,000 people including school groups.
3. G. Schnell, interview with H. Paulmann in *Potsdamer Bulletin Nr. 36/37* Zentrum für Zeithistorische Forschung Potsdam e.V, Potsdam 2006, pp. 56–73.
4. ibid.
5. ibid.
6. Montefiore, p. 513.
7. ibid, p. 524.
8. ibid, p. 524.
9. T. Toranska, *Them: Stalin's Polish Puppets*, London, CollinsHarvill 1987, p. 146.
10. Baker White, pp. 13–133.
11. A. Knight, *How the Cold War Began*, Toronto, McClelland & Stewart 2005, p. 101.
12. ibid, p. 187.

16 BIG BANGS AND A LONG TELEGRAM

1. After leaving the diplomatic service in 1950, he was a respected political commentator and historian, who served as US ambassador to USSR and Yugoslavia.
2. G.F. Kennan, *Memoirs 1925 – 1950*, pp. 547–59
3. Quoted in J.L. Gaddis *The Cold War* London, Penguin, 2005, p. 29.
4. Author's italics.
5. For the full text of the speech, see http://www.historyguide.org/europe/churchill.html
6. G. Clare, *Berlin Days – 1946-47*, London, Macmillan, 1989, pp. 31–2.
7. Since renamed Semey.
8. Now again called Nizhny Novgorod.

17 LIVING ON THE FAR SIDE OF THE MOON

1. Bedell Smith, pp. 23–4.
2. ibid, pp. 25–6.
3. ibid, p. 35.
4. ibid, p. 25.
5. These were run by the Torgsin organisation, set up in 1929, after the Soviet government banned food parcels from the West.
6. Bedell Smith, p. 112.
7. ibid, pp. 113–4
8. J.V. Stalin, *The October Revolution*, New York, International Publishers 1934, p. 141.

9. Bedell Smith, p. 44 (author's italics).
10. ibid, p. 49.
11. ibid, pp. 225–6
12. ibid, pp. 226–7 (abridged by the author).
13. D.E. Murphy, S.A. Kondrashev & G. Bailey, *Battleground Berlin*, New Haven & London, Yale University Press, 1997, pp. 492–3.
14. Montefiore, p. 96.
15. Bedell Smith, pp. 277–91, abridged by the author.

18 A DAUGHTER BACK FROM THE DEAD

1. Gaddis, p. 101.
2. ibid, p. 83.
3. Fortuitously, MI6 discovered a repugnant but useful source of intelligence in the pages torn from outdated code books and used for this purpose during manoeuvres in the satellite states.
4. Service, p. 351.
5. F. Beckett, *Stalin's British Victims*, Thrupp, Sutton, 2004, pp. 99–110.
6. Beckett, *Enemy Within*, pp. 126–7.
7. Service, p. 592.
8. Gaddis, p. 100.
9. Murphy, Kondrashev & Bailey, p. 58.
10. Bedell Smith, pp. 230–44.
11. Montefiore, pp. 602–4.

19 THE PROXY WAR THAT COST 4 MILLION LIVES

1. Gaddis, pp. 41–2.
2. D. Stone, *Wars of the Cold War*, London, Brassey's, 2004, p. 120.

20 THE DEADLY GAME OF DOMINOES

1. *The Pentagon Papers, Gravel Edition*, Boston, Beacon Press, 1971, Vol 1, pp. 179–214, abridged by the author.
2. ibid, abridged.
3. ibid.
4. ibid, abridged.
5. S. Stora, *Histoire de la Guerre d'Algérie* Paris, Editions La Découverte, 2004, p. 15.
6. ibid, p. 18.
7. Personal communication with the author.
8. J. Steele, *World Power – Soviet Foreign Policy under Brezhnev and Andropov*, London, Michael Joseph, 1983, p. 179.

21 VOTING WITH THEIR FEET

1. Formed by the post-war fusion of the Communist and Social Democratic parties in East Germany.
2. Released April 2007 in the United Kingdom, the film traces the consequence of a Stasi officer becoming illicitly involved in the lives of the people on whom he is snooping.
3. The blatantly false charges were later such an embarrassment for the KSČ that his name was cleared and his party membership restored posthumously in 1968.
4. Following Stalin's death in March 1953, the MGB was merged with Ministry of Internal Affairs (MVD) under Beria. In 1954 the KGB assumed its role as the 'sword and shield of the Party'.
5. Acronym of 'Rundfunk im Amerikanischen Sektor'.
6. Stasi figures quoted in F. Taylor, *The Berlin Wall*, London, Bloomsbury, 2007, p. 129.
7. ibid, p. 149.
8. Murphy, Kondrashev & Bailey, p. 163.
9. H.M. Harrison, *Driving the Soviets Up The Wall*, Princeton, Princeton University Press, 2003, pp. 72, 99–100.
10. W. Loth, *Overcoming the Cold War*, Basingstoke and New York, Palgrave, 2002, p. 35.
11. Stone, p. 73.
12. L.S. Wittner, *Resisting the Bomb*, Stanford, Stanford University Press, 1997, p. 89.
13. Sudoplatov, p. 367.
14. Loth pp. 44–5.
15. ibid, pp. 46–7.
16. ibid, p. 48.
17. D. Reynolds, *One World Divisible: A Global History since 1945*, New York, Norton, 2000, p. 134.
18. Stone, p. 78.
19. Interview recorded in Programme 1 of BBC TV series *The Lost World of Communism*, transmitted March 2009.

22 KHRUSHCHEV'S SONOFABITCH

1. See under 'Seminole Wars' in *Encyclopaedia Britannica Ultimate Reference Suite*, Chicago, Encyclopaedia Britannica, 2009.
2. A comprehensive list may be found on http://en.wikipedia.org/wiki/List_of_United_States_military_history_events
3. Steele, p. 312.
4. Program Review by General Lansdale, Chief of Operations, Operation Mongoose. Source: Department of State, Central Files, 737.00/1-2062 and see U.S., Department of State, 'Foreign Relations of the United States 1961-1963', Vol X Cuba, 1961-1962 Washington, D.C.
5. V. Jauvert, *L'Amérique contre De Gaulle* Paris, Seuil, 2000, pp. 64–5.
6. ibid, p. 66.

7. ibid, p. 68.
8. ibid, pp. 69-70.
9. E.R. May & P.D. Zelikow, ed. *The Kennedy Tapes*, New York and London, Norton, 2001, p. 76.
10. Loth, p. 69.
11. May & Zelikow, p. 150.
12. R.M. Gates, *From the Shadows*, New York, Simon & Schuster, 1996, p. 40.

23 SPRING FORWARD, FALL BACK

1. Steele, p. 97.
2. J. Navratil, *The Prague Spring 1968*, Budapest, Central European Press, 1998, pp. 177–81, abridged by the author.
3. ibid, abridged.
4. ibid.
5. ibid.
6. One of the author's fellow-linguists at RAF Gatow approached a sentry at the Soviet War Memorial in West Berlin and asked him in Russian how he liked being stationed in Berlin. The Red Army man replied, 'Berlin? What's that?'
7. Beckett, *Enemy Within*, pp. 164–5.

24 ROLL TO YOUR RIFLE AND BLOW OUT YOUR BRAINS

1. J. Morris, *The Mountains of War* (unpublished MS loaned to the author).
2. W.E. Odom, *The Collapse of the Soviet Military*, London, Yale University Press, 1998, pp. 83, 103.
3. Stone, p. 253.
4. Barany, p. 71.
5. Odom, p. 223.
6. ibid, pp. 152–7.
7. ibid, pp. 143, 166–7.
8. Interview in *Le Nouvel Observateur* edition of 15–21 January 1998, tr. W. Blum, abridged by the author. See also Gates, pp. 146–7.
9. Gates, p. 321.
10. ibid, p. 349, abridged by the author.

25 AND ALL ERICH'S MEN …

1. Taylor, p. 602.
2. Gates, p. 467.
3. Bearden and Risen, pp. 379–82.
4. Taylor, pp. 606–7.
5. ibid, pp. 615–6.
6. Bearden and Risen, p. 395.

7. Abbreviation of 'Die Bundesbeauftragte für die Unterlagen des Staatssicherheitsministeriums der ehemaligen Deutschen Demokratischen Republik'.
8. Personal communication with the author.
9. Personal communication with the author.
10. It was removed from the Lenin mausoleum in October 1961 as being 'inappropriate' after Khrushchev's denunciation.
11. Extract abridged by the author.

26 THE END OF THE EVIL EMPIRE

1. Odom, p. 253.
2. Gates, pp. 509–12.
3. Odom, pp. 268–9.
4. Bearden and Risen, pp. 482-3.
5. M.R. Beschloss & S.Talbott, *At the Highest Levels*, London, Little Brown 1993, pp. 398–9.
6. ibid, p. 422.
7. Bearden and Risen, p. 518.
8. Beschloss & Talbott, pp. 435–6.
9. Gates, pp. 524–5.
10. Odom, p. 33.
11. Odom, pp. 369–70, 394.
12. Article in *Izvestiya*, 13 August 1993.
13. Lucas, pp. 43, 54.

27 THE MAKING OF THE PRESIDENT, RUSSIAN STYLE

1. Y. Felshtinsky & V. Pribylovsky, *The Age of Assassins – The Rise and Rise of Vladimir Putin*, London, Gibson Square, 2008, pp. 116–120.
2. KGB Lt Col V. Gortanov, quoted ibid, p. 46.
3. N. Gevorkian, A. Kolesnikov & N. Timakova, *Ot Pervovo Litsa*, Moscow, Vagrius, 2000, p. 43, abridged by the author.
4. ibid, p. 79.
5. Felshtinsky & Pribylovsky, p. 50.
6. Gevorkian et al, pp. 104–5.
7. ibid, pp. 89–90.
8. Felshtinsky & Pribylovsky, pp. 57–62.
9. Gevorkian et al, pp. 93–4.
10. Felshtinsky & Pribylovsky, p. 64.
11. ibid, p. 68.
12. ibid, p. 77.
13. C. Gall & T. de Wall, *Chechnya: Calamity in the Caucasus*, New York, New York University Press, 1998, pp. 177–181.

14. Barany, p. 75.
15. Felshtinsky & Pribylovsky, pp. 82–3.
16. ibid, pp. 84, 94.
17. A. Solzhenitsyn, *K nyneshnemu sostoyanii Rossii* in *Oschaya Gazeta, No 47/175*, 28 November to 4 December 1996, quoted in Felshtinsky & Pribylovsky, p. 78, abridged by the author.
18. Quoted in Felshtinsky & Pribylovsky, pp. 101–2, abridged by the author.
19. Lucas, p. 36.
20. Felshtinsky & Pribylovsky, p. 36.
21. ibid, pp. 108–9.
22. Lucas, p. 68.
23. ibid, pp. 185–6.
24. Felshtinsky & Pribylovsky, p. 300.
25. Lucas, p. 297.
26. ibid, p. 27.
27. Barany, p. 172.
28. Lucas, p. 189–92.
29. Abridged by the author. See unabridged in Russian on www.kp.ru/daily/23896.3/66766 dated 3 May 2007.
30. Personal communication by a retired US Foreign Service officer who wishes to remain anonymous.

28 THE POT AND THE KETTLE

1. Sometimes rendered into English as United Russia.
2. *The Economist*, 11 December 2011 (abridged).
3. Article by John Miller in *National Observer No. 85, 2012*.
4. D. Boyd, *De Gaulle: The Man who Defied Six US Presidents*, The History Press, 2013, pp. 20–1.
5. Designated Field Station 83.
6. According to *Der Spiegel* current affairs magazine, NSA sweeps up about half a billion communications in Germany each month.
7. ibid.

29 AFTER UKRAINE, THE DELUGE?

1. *Die Welt*, 22 February 2014.
2. Article by A. Kramer in *New York Times*, 20 March 2014.
3. Although a sanitised version of the conversation also appeared, BBC News Europe 7 February 2014 included her most undiplomatic remark in full.
4. *The U.S. opts for Ineffective Sanctions on Russia*, *Stratfor*, 29 April 2014.
5. Article by A. Kramer in *New York Times*, 20 March 2014.
6. Article by J. Delingpole, *Can this man save Ukraine,* in *The Spectator* 19 April 2014.
7. ibid.

FURTHER READING
IN ENGLISH

Z. Barany, *Democratic Breakdown and the decline of the Russian Military Woodstock*, Princeton University Press, 2007.

F. Beckett, *Enemy Within: The Rise and Fall of the British Communist Party*, London, John Murray, 1998.

F. Beckett, *Stalin's British Victims*, Thrupp, Sutton, 2004.

C. Bellamy, *Absolute War: Soviet Russia in the Second World War*, London, Macmillan, 2007.

G. Dallas, *Poisoned Peace*, London, John Murray, 2005.

Y. Felshtinsky & V. Pribylovsky, *The Age of Assassins – The Rise and Rise of Vladimir Putin*, London, Gibson Square, 2008.

J.T. Gross, *Revolution from Abroad – Documents from the Hoover Institution for War, Revolution and Peace*, Princeton, Princeton University Press, 2002.

W. Loth, *Overcoming the Cold War*, Basingstoke and New York, Palgrave, 2002.

E. Lucas, *The New Cold War*, London, Bloomsbury, 2008.

M. Hughes, *Inside the Enigma*, London, The Hambeldon Press, 1997.

E.R May & P.D. Zelikow ed. *The Kennedy Tapes*, New York and London, Norton, 2001.

S. Sebag Montefiore, *Stalin, the Court of the Red Tsar*, London, Phoenix, 2004.

M. Occleshaw, *Dances in Deep Shadows*, London, Constable & Robinson, 2006.

W.E. Odom, *The Collapse of the Soviet Military*, London, Yale University Press, 1998.

C. Pleshakov, *Stalin's Folly – The Secret History of the German Invasion of Russia, June 1941*, London, Weidenfeld & Nicolson, 2005.

D. Rayfield, *Stalin and his Hangmen*, London, Penguin, 2005.

L. Rees, *Behind Closed Doors*, London, BBC Books, 2008.

R. Service, *Stalin – a Memoir*, London, Pan, 2005.

D. Stone, *Wars of the Cold War*, London, Brassey's, 2004.

F. Taylor, *The Berlin Wall*, London, Bloomsbury 2007.

Visit our website and discover thousands of other History Press books.

INDEX